Opium to Java

Asia East by South

A series published under the auspices of
the Southeast Asia Program, Cornell University

*Opium to Java: Revenue Farming and Chinese Enterprise in Colonial
Indonesia, 1860–1910,*
by James R. Rush

ALSO IN THE SERIES

An Age in Motion: Popular Radicalism in Java, 1912–1926,
by Takashi Shiraishi

OPIUM
TO JAVA

Revenue Farming and
Chinese Enterprise in
Colonial Indonesia,
1860–1910

James R. Rush

Cornell University Press

ITHACA AND LONDON

First published 1990 by Cornell University Press.

International Standard Book Number 0-8014-2218-3
Library of Congress Catalog Card Number 89-45974
Printed in the United States of America
Librarians: Library of Congress cataloging information appears on the last page of the book.

⊗ The paper used in this publication meets the minimum requirements of the American National Standard for Permanence of Paper for Printed Library Materials Z39.48–1984.

Contents

Maps

Illustrations

Acknowledgments

Research for this book began at Yale University, and I owe my first debt of gratitude to my mentors there. Harry J. Benda led me to examine Indonesia and provided inspiration for a study like this one. Unfortunately he died before the work really began. Subsequently Bernhard Dahm suggested "opium" and helped me to formulate the research; Anthony Reid launched me into the archives; Milton Osborne was on hand as I began writing; and Robin Winks saw the project through to its conclusion—providing crucial support and sound counsel (as always) and contributing to my understanding of things in Java his own rich insights into the larger colonial world. Each one helped to shape this work, and its good qualities owe much to their knowledge and advice.

Others at Yale who aided me then and later include the Southeast Asia curator at Sterling Memorial Library, Charles Bryant; the geographer Karl J. Pelzer; linguist Joseph Errington; and historians C. S. Gray and Onghokham. In fact, as a friend and colleague in the study of nineteenth-century Java, Onghokham has contributed enormously to the evolution of my work over the years. It was he who introduced me to a key figure in my search, when, one rainy day in the Netherlands—I had just arrived—he asked me, "By the way, have you ever heard of Charles TeMechelen?"

In the Netherlands I received generous assistance from the staff members at various archives, including the Ministerie van Binnenlandse Zaken and the Algemeen Rijksarchief in The Hague; the Hulpdepot of the Algemeen Rijksarchief in Schaarsbergen; and the Gemeente Archief in Leiden. At the Koninklijk Instituut voor Taal-,

viii
Acknowledgments

Land- en Volkenkunde in Leiden, whose facilities I used extensively, F.G.P. Jacquet unraveled for me the mysteries of the colonial
archive system. Go Gien Tjwan, J. Soegiarto, P. Creutzberg, Sudibbyo Sastrowardhoyo, Soemarsaid Moertono, Anthony Day, and
Heather Sutherland were among the others in Holland who helped
the work along at various stages. William O'Malley, Barbara Watson
Andaya, Akira Oki, and Jean Taylor Gelman were there at the same
time; we shared our discoveries in libraries and archives, and I
turned to them for practical advice and good company. Mevrouw
Koolemans Beijnen-Uljee, whose father was the Dutch resident of
Rembang, Java, from 1888 to 1892, talked about her childhood with
me. She was ninety-three years old when I met her, my only eyewitness.

My research in the Netherlands was funded by a Fulbright-Hays
Doctoral Dissertation Fellowship. Also, much of it could not have
been accomplished without the help and support of Jane Wiseman.

The work has also benefited from critical reading by many others.
Chief among these are Carl Trocki and John Butcher, historians
and fellow students of revenue farming in Southeast Asia. Also of
immense value was a critique by Will Gerritsen ("James Robert
Rush' *histoire intégrale* van de prive exploitatie van een negentiende
eeuws koloniale gouvernementsmonopolie"), which he presented to
the Catholic University of Nijmegen as his *Doctoraalscriptie* in 1982.
This book also profited from colloquia at Monash University, Australia National University, and Griffith University in 1982. I am
grateful to Glenn May for helping to arrange these meetings and to
the Australian-American Educational Foundation for funding my
visit to Australia. Special thanks go to Benedict O'Gorman Anderson for his encouraging support.

Among those who typed versions of the manuscript at one time or
another, and flawlessly, were Julie Lavorgna and Gwenda Smith.

Portions of the book draw on three articles of mine, previously
published: "Opium in Java: A Sinister Friend," *Journal of Asian
Studies*, 44 (May 1985), 549–60; "Social Control and Influence in
Nineteenth Century Indonesia: Opium Farms and the Chinese of
Java," *Indonesia*, no. 35 (April 1983), 53–64; and "Opium Farms in
Colonial Java, an Introduction," proceedings, *Conference on Modern
Indonesian History, July 18–19, 1975*, Center for Southeast Asian
Studies, University of Wisconsin–Madison.

J.R.R.

New Haven, Connecticut

Abbreviations

BKI	*Bijdragen tot de Taal-, Land- en Volkenkunde*, journal of the Royal Institute of Anthropology (Netherlands), Koninklijk Instituut voor Taal-, Land- en Volkenkunde
DBB	Directeur van Binnenlandsch Bestuur, director of internal administration, head of Colonial Service
DF	Directeur van Financien, director of Finance Department, Batavia
DJ	Directeur van Justitie, director of Justice Department, Batavia
DMD	Directeur van Middelen en Domeinen, director of Means and Estates, Batavia
ENI	*Encyclopaedie van Nederlandsche-Indie*, first edition, 1905
ENI (2d)	*Encyclopaedie van Nederlandsche-Indie*, second edition, 1917f., with supplements
Exh	*Exhibitum*, one of several classifications for files of documents in the Dutch Colonial Archives
f	A Dutch guilder or gulden, circa 1900 worth U.S. $0.40
GG	Governor general
HGvNI	Hoog Gerechtshof van Nederlandsch-Indië, Supreme Court of Netherlands India
HIOR	Hoofd inspecteur van het Opium Regie, chief inspector of the Opium Regie
IG	*Indische Gids*, Indies Digest
IT	*De Indische Tolk van het Nieuws van den Dag*, The Indies Interpreter of the Daily News
IWR	*Indisch Weekblad van het Recht*, Indies Law Weekly
JAS	*Journal of Asian Studies*
KITLV	Koninklijk Instituut voor Taal-, Land- en Volkenkunde, Royal Institute of Anthropology (Netherlands)
KVvNI	Koloniale Verslagen, annual colonial reports
MR	Mailrapport, bundle of documents mailed from Batavia to the minister of colonies in Holland; one of several classi-

	fications for files of documents in the Dutch Colonial Archives
MvK	Minister van kolonien, minister of colonies, The Hague
MvO	Memorie van overgave, a colonial official's transfer report, written for the benefit of his successor
NHM	Nederlandse Handel-Maatschappij, Dutch Trading Company
NNBW	*Nieuw Nederlandsch Biografisch Woordenboek*, New Netherlands Biographical Dictionary
RAvNI	Regeerings Almanak van Nederlandsch-Indië, Government Gazette for Netherlands India, annual
RvJ	Raad van Justitie, Council of Justice
RvNI	Raad van Indie, Indies Council, Batavia
SvD	Staat van dienst, service record of colonial official
SvNI	Staatsbladen van Nederlandsch-Indie, statutes and proclamations for Netherlands India, bound annually
TBB	*Tijdschrift voor het Binnenlandsch Bestuur*, Colonial Service Magazine
THHK	Tiong Hoa Hwe Koan [Chung-hua hui-kuan], Chinese cultural and reform association, founded 1900
TM	Charles TeMechelen
TMC	Charles TeMechelen Collection, KITLV
TNI	*Tijdschrift voor Nederlandsch-Indie*, Netherlands India Magazine
TNLNI	*Tijdschrift voor Nijverheid en Landbouw in Nederlandsch-Indie*, Magazine for Industry and Agriculture in Netherlands India
V	Verbaal, commonest classification for files of documents in Dutch Colonial Archives
VBG	*Verhandelingen Bataviaasch Genootschap*, Proceedings of the Batavia Society of Arts and Sciences
VIG	*Verhandelingen Indische Genootschap*, Proceedings of the Indies Society, Netherlands
VKG	Verbaal Kabinets Geheim, a secret Verbaal
VOC	Vereenigde Oost Indische Compagnie, Dutch East India Company
VR	Verslag Opium Regie, monthly reports of Dutch Opium Regie
VS	Verslag Sluikhandel, monthly reports on government antismuggling efforts during Regie period

Opium to Java

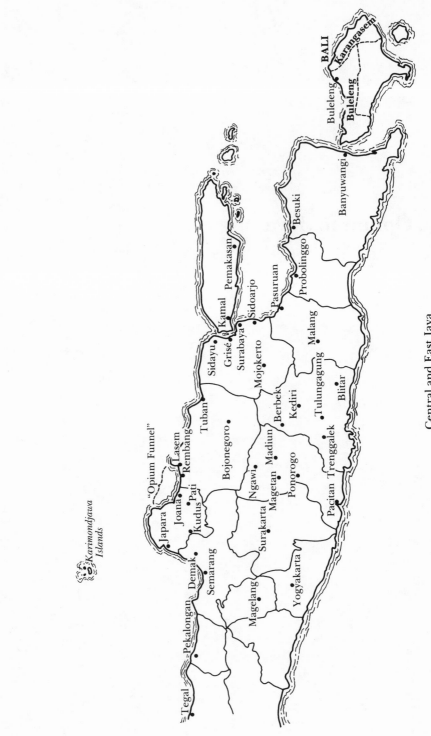

Central and East Java

Introduction

An opium farm was a monopoly concession for selling opium. Ordinarily such a monopoly was granted by a state to a concessionaire, or "farmer," for a limited period of time, and it applied to a strictly delineated territory—a city, a district, a province. On Java during the nineteenth century, Chinese merchants paid dearly for this privilege and thereby yielded great sums of revenue to the island's Dutch administration. For this and other reasons to be explored in this book the opium farm became a powerful institution there. Indeed, it was one of the distinctive institutions of colonial Java.

But in nineteenth-century Southeast Asia, opium farms were hardly unique to Java. Java was only one of many Dutch possessions in the Indonesian Archipelago where opium was sold under a government monopoly. Opium was imported into every other European colony in the region besides, and sold to the Asian subjects of Britain, France, and Spain through one sort of arrangement or another, commonly a revenue farm run by local Chinese like those on Java. Opium also provided an important source of income for the region's waning native states—in 1849, for instance, the sultan of Lingga, already under Dutch "protection," raised more than half his direct income through an opium farm—as well as for the one indigenous state that did not succumb eventually to advancing Europeans, the kingdom of Thailand.[1]

1. See Hong Lysa, *Thailand in the Nineteenth Century: Evolution of the Economy and Society* (Singapore, 1984); and "De toestand der residentie Rio in 1849," *TNI*, 15, 1 (1853), 415.

Introduction

Opium aside, revenue farming generally was among the commonest forms of taxation in the region. In one place or another,
Buddhist kings, Malay sultans, and colonial proconsuls leased to
Chinese revenue farmers the exclusive rights to buy up areca nuts
and jungle gums and vines; to collect taxes on land and on certain
animals and plants; to impose duties on goods in transit along
roadways and in seaports; to run markets, pawnshops, gambling
dens, and brothels; and to sell salt and spirits.[2] Dutch Java's lux-
uriant array of tax farms, which included many of these and then
some—for example, the right to harvest from limestone caves the
swallows' nests precious to Chinese traders and cooks—fit within a
regionwide pattern.

As European governance superseded native rule everywhere but
Thailand, Europe's men-on-the-spot were quick to assume control
over existing revenue farms and to set up new ones. Tax farms thus
helped to underwrite empire building and in some places paid a
huge proportion of the cost of colonial administration, as in British
Malaya and the Straits Settlements.[3] Similarly, in Thailand revenue
farms facilitated the concentration of royal power in Bangkok in the
late nineteenth and early twentieth centuries. During the same period opium revenues, collected partly from farms, made it possible
for the Dutch to pay for their massively expanding presence in the
Indonesian Archipelago without incurring an equally massive deficit.[4]

As the states of the region took on ever more definitive shapes,
however, the convenience of tapping Chinese-run revenue farms
for ready cash was eventually overtaken by a larger consideration.
This was the need to make the authority of central governments
thorough and comprehensive. Aided by new roads, railways,
bridges, and telegraph lines, and by steamships and modernized

2. John G. Butcher, "Revenue Farming and the Changing State in Southeast Asia:
A Preliminary Discussion," paper presented to the Conference on Revenue Farming
and Southeast Asian Transitions, Australian National University, 1988, pp. 4–5.
3. John G. Butcher, "The Demise of the Revenue Farm System in the Federated
Malay States," *Modern Asian Studies*, 17, 3 (1983), 388; and Carl A. Trocki, "Paying for
Free Trade: The Opium Farms of Singapore, 1820–1920," paper presented at the
Conference on the Historical Context of Opium Use, University of Pennsylvania,
1981.
4. See F. W. Diehl, "The Opium-Tax Farms in Java, 1813–1914," paper presented
to the Conference on Indonesian Economic History in the Dutch Colonial Period,
Australian National University, 1983, pp. 8–9. As Diehl shows, however, opium
revenues did not eliminate the deficit altogether.

ports, efforts to do so occurred simultaneously in Southeast Asia from the 1880s onward, accelerating at the century's turn. This process involved filling newly surveyed territories with swarms of colonial bureaucrats bearing grand plans and procedure manuals, and, at the same time, eliminating semiautonomous institutions like revenue farms. As *imperia in imperio* the farms were awkward within the increasingly centralized and bureaucratized states, all the more so because they were invariably bases of local Chinese influence and power. All Southeast Asia's major revenue farms were abolished within a brief span of thirty years. Befitting the times, opium farms were nearly everywhere replaced by new opium agencies run directly by central governments.[5] The Opium Regie of Netherlands India, inaugurated in 1894, was the second of these—based as it was, loosely, on an 1882 French scheme for Cochin China—but it was the first *full-fledged* exemplar of the trend and the model for others.

Clearly, Java's opium farms and their fate had parallels elsewhere. They were part of dynamic historic processes, many of them worldwide, which affected all Southeast Asia.

In important ways, however, the Java opium farm was unique. To begin with, Java was a *Dutch* colony, and a very old one; its opium farm had evolved in intimate connection with other institutions special to the island and deeply rooted there; and in sharp contrast to the rest of Southeast Asia (and other parts of Netherlands India), the vast majority of its customers were not laboring Chinese sojourners but native Javanese. These facts help us understand not only the Java opium farm itself, but also the crisis that overtook it and the new organization that eventually replaced it, the Dutch Opium Regie. Such questions of institutional character and evolution form the subject matter of this book.

book synopsis

Reconstructing the Java opium farm often resembled the work of a physical anthropologist, conjuring from a jawbone here and a leg bone there the whole body of an early man or woman. For though the opium farm was pervasive in much of Java, evidence of it retrievable by the historian today is uneven and scattered. Compounding this problem is the fact that many people who were involved in the opium farms took care to obscure certain things: opium farm profits and the membership of opium farm kongsis, or syndicates, were

5. Butcher, "Revenue Farming and the Changing State," pp. 18, 21–24.

business secrets among the Chinese; deals between opium farmers and native officials (or Dutch ones) were also confidential, of course. Moreover, Dutch officials in Java were not keen to reveal to their superiors in Holland (worse yet, to the scrutiny of Parliament) too many details about how opium revenues were really made. As a result, many things about opium farms came to light only inadvertently—when one kongsi sued another in the colonial courts, for example; or when scandal or default prodded the ordinarily taciturn Dutch to investigate the affairs of a native official or an opium farmer.

My reconstruction of the opium farm is therefore built from hundreds of fragments—an opium farm ledger book from Madiun residency, a court case in Japara, a spy's telegram sent from Surabaya, a newspaper clipping, a piece of family lore. Because of this, the "opium farm" emerging in this book is in one sense an abstraction, an abstraction of the same kind as, say, Java Man. Built from facts, it describes no *particular* opium farm at any *particular* time.

Source material

Yet there are clear parameters. In much of the western third of Java (the residencies of Bantam and the Priangan), the opium trade was generally forbidden. Here there was a black market in opium, to be sure, and a handful of legal outlets, but no opium farms. Opium farms existed everywhere else on the island, however. They were strongest in central and east Java, the most densely populated regions and the homeland of the Javanese. Similarly, the decade of the 1880s generated the greatest concentration of materials for a study of the opium farms. But documentary sources from earlier years are abundant enough to corroborate the more detailed reconstruction possible for this period. The opium farm as I describe it existed in mature form for a period of about thirty years beginning around 1860, and many of its characteristics had endured for decades beforehand.

The vast majority of my sources come from the accumulated files of the Dutch minister of colonies, which now slumber in the Netherlands' national archive system. These files contain richly detailed and varied documents, a vast lode of information that the Dutch meticulously stored but seem seldom to have consulted retrospectively. A great many of these documents were shipped to Holland on the occasion of making one or another modification to the Indies opium regulations. Until 1869 such changes were made in The Hague. After that the governor general was authorized to make

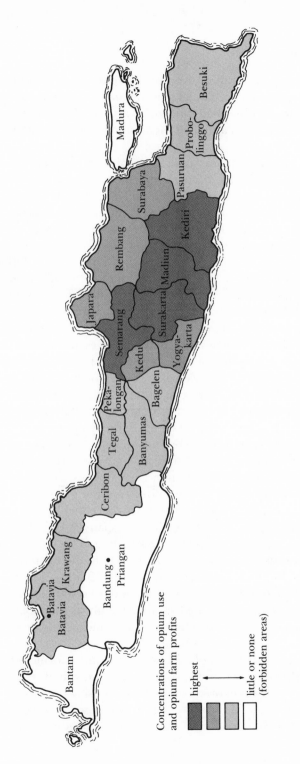

Concentrations of opium use
and opium farm profits

highest ←————————→ little or none
(forbidden areas)

Java: residencies, showing concentrations of opium use and opium farm profits

them himself, in Batavia; even so, he routinely sent copies of his policy revisions to the colonial minister and often appended to them reports and data that had guided his actions. The minister (or his staff) reviewed them and filed them, sometimes responding, sometimes not.

In less routine instances a call for information went out from The Hague. One such case occurred in 1892, when a member of the lower house of Parliament, Levysohn Norman, revealed to his colleagues an opium-smuggling scandal in Java. Caught unawares, the minister of colonies wrote to the governor general for an explanation. The governor general passed on the request to the director of finance, who in turn wrote to Chief Inspector of Opium Affairs Charles TeMechelen requesting complete details. TeMechelen gathered all available documents about the case, including transcripts of the interrogations of each participant, and sent them to the director of finance, who forwarded them via the governor general to Holland. They now rest in the archives, filed permanently in the massive Exhibitum, or file, dated August 9, 1892, No. 76.

Rising above the collective voice of the Dutch Colonial Service—whose members either wrote or otherwise generated and collected most of what now lies in the archives—is that of Charles TeMechelen. He was the central Dutch figure in opium farm affairs in the 1880s and early 1890s. His antismuggling campaign, and even more important, his evolving role as "house expert" in opium farm affairs, generated an uncommon fund of documentary materials about the farms. Many of the sources used in preparing this book were reports, memoranda, or letters written either by him or to him. His Opium Report of 1888 was the first relatively complete study of the opium farms ever done by the Dutch; and his collected papers include a wide range of materials relating to the operations of his task force, his personal career, and opium affairs in general. Other Dutch officials who preceded him, and who also took a special interest in opium, generated similar though smaller collections of documents. Christian Castens, director of means and estates in the mid-1860s, was one such official.

But voices other than official ones have also informed this book. Among them are those of private Dutch individuals who lived in Java—newspaper reporters and editors, missionaries, doctors, lawyers, planters, and writers—as well as Javanese literati and some of the island's common men and women (including seventy-nine opium smokers interviewed in 1890); and, occasionally, there is the voice of an opium farmer himself, although usually speaking in words chosen carefully for him by his Dutch lawyer.

Another important voice informing this book is that of Liem Thian Joe. Liem was a peranakan (locally born) Chinese newspaper reporter who, in 1931, salvaged from the office of the Chinese Council in Semarang much of what remained of its files and archives. (The Dutch were closing it down at the time.) From the documents he found there—the formal enactments of Semarang's Chinese officers and other "old writings," statute books, early Malay- and Dutch-language newspapers, and sundry publications put out by local Chinese organizations—as well as from his own fund of local lore, Liem compiled his anecdotal history of the peranakan Chinese community of Semarang, *Riwajat Semarang: Dari Djamannja Sam Poo Sampe Terhapoesnja Kongkoan* (The Story of Semarang: From the Times of Sam Poo up to the Abolishment of the Chinese Council). Liem is both scrupulous and celebratory in telling the story of his forebears, adhering to the facts as his sources reveal them—he often quotes them directly—but also leaving out embarrassing episodes that might "hurt people's feelings or reopen matters evidently forgotten by everyone."[6] His *Riwajat* reveals what he thought "worthy of being remembered." Among such worthy facts, and prominently so, is the connection between opium farming and the great men of the peranakan collective memory.

Piecing together the opium farm from its scattered remains also required some external, referential guidance. This involved finding, in Clifford Geertz's words, "a current (or recent) system that one has some reason to believe bears at least a familial resemblance to [that] . . . one seeks to reconstruct."[7] In this vein, one study that was helpful in connecting the opium farm's anklebone to its shinbone was Tien Ju-k'ang's *Chinese of Sarawak: A Study of Social Structure* (1953). Tien emphasizes the role of powerful patronage givers, who are also Chinese officers, in the social and economic structure of a Chinese community based in a colony that, by twentieth-century standards, was rather like a nineteenth-century one.

Among numerous printed sources from the period, one bears

6. Liem Thian Joe, *Riwajat Semarang: Dari Djamannja Sam Poo Sampe Terhapoesnja Kongkoan* (Semarang, 1933), "Permoela'an Kata."

7. Clifford Geertz, *Negara: The Theatre State in Nineteenth-Century Bali* (Princeton, N.J., 1980), p. 6.

singling out. This is the *Indisch Weekblad van het Recht*. A weekly magazine summarizing legal developments in the Indies and containing complete transcripts of recent court decisions, the *Weekblad* is especially useful in studying opium-related crime and the internal structure of the Chinese opium farm kongsis. It also illustrates a problem facing all students of nineteenth-century Java—the transliteration of non-European names. It was not unusual in the *Weekblad* for someone's name to be spelled in two, sometimes three, different ways in a single article. Other documents reveal that the problem was not haphazard printing. It is most likely that the *Weekblad* simply copied verbatim the spellings used in handwritten transcripts prepared and copied by clerks. The spelling of the names of Javan Chinese was particularly erratic, the result of applying nineteenth-century Dutch orthography to the spoken sound of the names. For English speakers this procedure produced more familiar results in the British Straits Settlements. Liem Kie Soen of Java, for example, would have been Lim Kee Soon in Singapore. I have followed the practice of using the commonest contemporary spelling.[8]

For Indonesian and Javanese words and place-names, when referring in the notes to a specific document identified by a title (for example, Staat aantoonende de hoogste opiumprijzen in de kitten der Residentie Pasoeroean), I have followed the original spelling. Otherwise I have applied modern usage: Pasuruan instead of Pasoeroean, Surabaya for Soerabaja. And, speaking of opium, candu for tjandoe.

8. Lea Williams has compiled a brief chart of Netherlands Indies equivalents of Kuo-yu surnames (with Chinese characters) in his *Overseas Chinese Nationalism* (Glencoe, Ill., 1960), pp. 207–9.

1

The Finest Tropical
Island in the World

In 1861 the British naturalist Alfred Russel Wallace visited
the island of Java. For three and a half months he explored its cities
and hinterland. In Buitenzorg (Bogor), the cool hill town south of
Batavia and seat of the governor general, he saw Dutch Java's famed
Botanical Gardens. They disappointed him. But Java itself did not.
As he passed through its countryside and saw its "magnificently
varied . . . mountain and forest scenery" he was startled by Java's
beauty and abundance. He marveled at the size and density and at
the productivity of its peaceable rural population.[1]

Like other English of his day, the much-traveled Wallace was
inclined to see in this evidence for the wisdom of Dutch colonial
administration.[2] On Java he saw good roads connecting the country
"end to end," harmonious governance in which European and native rulers worked together for the commonweal, and life and property secured "as in the best governed states of Europe." Among a
"semi-barbarous" people a modern civilization was spreading. Java
was, he concluded, "the finest tropical island in the world."[3]

In 1861 Java was secure within Holland's colonial embrace and
creating wealth for its masters. Money raised from Java's fecund

1. Alfred Russel Wallace, *The Malay Archipelago* [1869] (Singapore, 1983), pp. 85,
75.
2. See, for example, James William B. Money, *Java: or, How to Manage a Colony*
(London, 1861).
3. Wallace, *Malay Archipelago*, p. 76.

coffee gardens and sugarcane fields was paying off a huge war debt and subsidizing new national railways. The Dutch at midcentury thought of it as the centerpiece, the crowning jewel, in their expanding empire of islands in the Indonesian Archipelago. Except for Madura, which was administered as part of "Java and Madura," all the others were mere "Outer Possessions." But it had not always been so.

Holland's merchant adventurers first entered Indonesian waters around the turn of the seventeenth century. For them, Java was of only secondary interest compared to the spice-bearing islands of the Moluccas. But the passage to these distant sources of nutmegs, cloves, and mace was long and vulnerable. Considerations of practicality and security soon necessitated a foothold on Java. At first the Dutch East India Company (VOC) proceeded warily in establishing one, limiting itself to a few fortified trading centers in Java's harbor towns. But in 1619 Jan Pieterszoon Coen founded Batavia as VOC headquarters on the site of old Jakatra.[4] Batavia, in Coen's grand vision, was to be the capital of Holland's new Asian empire.

And so it became, but slowly. The company deliberately limited its presence on the island. Indeed, in the early years it had to defend its foothold against raids from the native state of Banten, in west Java, and in 1628 and 1629 against the armies of Mataram's Sultan Agung, who dominated most of the rest of the island. But having taken these first decisive steps, and having been forced to hold their ground at great cost, the Dutch became involved ever more deeply in the politics and commerce of Java. Weaker kings later in the century found the company, with its financial and martial resources, a useful ally against usurpers and other regional challengers. In return for their assistance, VOC officials periodically wrested from the kings of Mataram and other local rulers territorial concessions and trading privileges, one of the first of which was the monopoly to import and distribute opium.

This process of territorial accretion continued over two centuries and more, even as the power of the company waxed and waned. Slowly, treaty by treaty, domain by domain, the kingdom of Mataram was eaten away. The royal house was split in 1755; thereafter a sultan ruled from Yogyakarta, a susuhunan from Surakarta, each

4. The VOC had already established a post there in 1611. See M. C. Ricklefs, *A History of Modern Indonesia* (London, 1981), p. 28.

"A modern civilization . . . is spreading." Chromolithograph by Jhr. J. C. Rappard, in *Nederlandsch-Indie* (1881–83).

over a little kingdom in the island's heartland. Two even tinier quasi-autonomous domains further fragmented the royal core; they too had their own locally magnificent monarchs. The Dutch called all of them princes (*Vorsten*), their territories principalities (*Vorstenlanden*), and posted advisers at the two major courts. The early nineteenth century brought Napoleonic reformers and then British conquerors to Java. Under Lieutenant Governor Thomas Stamford Raffles, Britain held the island from 1811 to 1816, returning it to Holland after Napoleon's defeat at Waterloo. The last serious threat to Dutch hegemony erupted from Yogyakarta in 1825 with the rising of Prince Diponegoro. He capitulated after five years of rebellion, the bloody tides of which devastated central Java and its population. When the Java War was over the principalities were even smaller, and in them the vestigial remains of Javanese sovereignty were thoroughly ceremonial.

By this time the old company had long since faltered under a mounting weight of corruption and debt. In 1800 Java, along with other VOC possessions in the archipelago, had become a possession of the Dutch crown. Its fate thus passed from the hands of a mercantilist trading company into those of a nation that, in 1848, became a constitutional monarchy. Some Dutch now took a broader view of the colony. A few came to see it as a great national project, a profound responsibility giving luster and stature to the homeland. Eventually the Dutch would be moved to say, as Louis Couperus had someone say in his end-of-the-century novel of Java, *The Hidden Force*, "I think that we, in our colony, are great."[5]

But what, exactly, was the national project supposed to accomplish—aside from making money? And what really were Holland's imperial responsibilities? These questions fueled an enduring debate among a small circle of Dutch at home and many in the colony. A master plan or philosophy was never fully articulated. Instead, the Dutch governed Java in fits and starts in step with the urgencies of the day. As they did so, they called on broad sentiments that were rooted in the home culture, sentiments balancing responsibility with practicality and conscience with gain. Although their enterprise seemed to evolve willy-nilly, there was a guiding hand. This was the civilization itself, the new civilization that Wallace observed spreading in Java. Because they acted from within a highly confident Western culture, the nineteenth-century Dutch inevitably tried to mold Java in accordance with their own self-consciously rational and modern sense of things. This meant imposing order on Java's bewildering social and political complexities, some of them ancient, others the consequence of two hundred years of Holland's own interventions. The urge to tie up Java's loose ends can be seen in almost any colonial statute of the century and read from countless apparently unconnected actions of Dutch officials high and low.

But since no Dutch initiative could be carried out without the help of local collaborators, this urge was constantly frustrated. In its execution, each new scheme was changed by the participation of

5. Louis Couperus, *The Hidden Force* [1900], trans. Alexander Teixeira de Mattos (Amherst, Mass., 1985), p. 98.

Holland's Javanese and Chinese subjects, and in particular by their leaders. This is why no colonial program, law, or organ of government worked in practice as it appeared on paper. Despite the energy and momentum of the colonizing culture and its agents, the institutions of Dutch Java became models of accommodation and compromise. The facts of colonial demography made them so. ✦

The Dutch were preeminent on Java despite the fact that, numerically, they were barely present at all. Of Java's 18 million people in the 1870s, a scant 27,000 (0.15 percent) were Europeans; and this group included not only pure Hollanders but other Westerners and many people of mixed Indonesian and European ancestry. Socially, this tiny European-Eurasian minority formed one small-town community stretched thinly over the whole island. Following Diponegoro's rebellion it was virtually unchallenged as Java's political, racial, and economic elite.

A second group, seven times larger but still accounting for only 1.5 percent of the population, was essential to the Dutch enterprise. They were Java's resident Chinese, some 190,000 in number. The Chinese played an economic role of great importance in the colony and some were powerful government revenue farmers. They were, as a rule, an urban group like the Europeans. Under the authority of their Dutch-appointed officers, they clustered heavily in the Chinese quarters of the coastal cities and in Java's numerous inland towns and administrative centers—as, indeed, they were required to do.

The vast native population of Java formed a broad and rich base upon which these two historically foreign groups alighted. It was composed of many ethnic groups, including the Sundanese and Bantanese of the west, and some Madurese in the extreme east. But the vast majority were the Javanese, who populated the fertile rice lands of central and east Java. Most of these indigenous peoples inhabited Java's thousands of rural villages and lived under the wisdom and authority of their chiefs. It was they who provided the labor and produce upon which the economy of the colony was built. Their productivity made life profitable for Java's Chinese and, indirectly, paid for all the necessities and embellishments of the colonial state, even making it possible for Holland to subsidize the home economy. The Javanese habits of "submission and obedience," admitted Jean Chretien Baud, who was both governor general (1833–

36) and minister of colonies (1840–48), had made "many things possible here which elsewhere would be fraught with great difficulties."[6]

Each of these major groups represented distinct and complex communities with internal social structures of their own. A native aristocracy hovered above the indigenous masses, elevated by virtue of lineage and temporal authority and revered for their superior command of the civilized arts and manners. Wealthy merchants who were patronage givers and community benefactors—and Chinese officers—dominated Java's Chinese population. Among the Europeans, full-blooded Dutch held the reins of power and looked down their noses at "half-blood" Eurasians.[7]

The distinctions among Europeans, Chinese, and indigenous peoples on Java were not merely a matter of race, custom, and history. They were also fixed in the colonial law. Despite the commonplace confusion of genes in real life, legally speaking one was either European, "Native," or Chinese.[8] A person's racial status as one or the other determined where one could live, what taxes one paid, to which laws one was subject, before which courts one was tried and, if found guilty of a crime, how (and with what degree of harshness) one was punished. It even determined what a person could wear, for in colonial Java it was illegal, in the words of the 1872 statute, "to appear in public attired in any manner other than that of one's ethnic group."[9] A native could not dress up as a European, nor could a Chinese cut off his Manchu braid. Such laws, which made the colonial caste system conspicuous, as well as the natural inclination of individuals within the separate communities to display their status openly in distinctive dress and adornments, combined to

6. Quoted in R. E. Elson, "Sugar Factory Workers and the Emergence of 'Free Labor' in Nineteenth-Century Java," *Modern Asian Studies*, 20, 1 (1986), 140.

7. Writes W. F. Wertheim: "There was no question of equality between white man and half-blood." In his *Indonesian Society in Transition: A Study of Social Change* (The Hague, 1956), p. 139.

8. The Chinese, like all "Foreign Orientals"—a category that included Arabs and Indians—were subject to the laws and regulations as well as the legal institutions established for "Natives," but there were important exceptions to this, particularly with respect to taxes, commercial law, and the Chinese Officer System. As a result, Chinese were, in fact, recognized as a distinct group and discussed as such in official literature. Arabs and other Foreign Orientals totaled 8,383 and 14,573, respectively, in 1875. KVvNI 1875, Bijlage A, no. 3.

9. SvNI 1872, no. 111. See subsection "Vermomming." Wertheim, *Indonesian Society*, p. 138.

make nineteenth-century Java, visually, a colorful tableau of rank
and race.

The senior figure in this spectacle was the governor general. He
presided over the Dutch enterprise in Java and the rest of the
archipelago. A minister of colonies in The Hague appointed him to
exercise the sovereign rights of the Netherlands monarch in the
Indies and to preside over the administrative machinery of the
colony. It was his responsibility to see that colonial governance
adhered to the principles laid down in the fundamental law (Regeerings Reglement) and to respond to the wishes of crown and Parliament. Parliament was increasingly dominant, wresting control of
colonial affairs from the monarchy following 1848 and fixing the
colonial budget from 1867.

But Java was a long way from Holland and the scrutiny of the
minister and Parliament. Locally, the governor general often acted
in concert with an advisory board composed of high officials called
the Indies Council (Raad van Indie), and on the advice of his several
department chiefs and a Secretariat based in Buitenzorg. But he was
not bound to do so. Furthermore, the general unwillingness of
realities in Java to fit into the neat schemes of colonial planners in
Holland meant that the governor general had often to act independently of guidance from home. He was, therefore, a person of
substantial personal power. From his splendid official residence he
presided over a domain considerably larger and vastly more popu-
lous than Holland itself. Little wonder that among the colonial
Dutch, especially his jealous subordinates, his office was known as
"the throne of Buitenzorg."

Outside the capital, colonial governance was entrusted to members of a professional Colonial Service, the Binnenlands Bestuur.
These officials presided throughout Java's twenty-one administrative provinces, which, except for the principalities, were called residencies after the title of the senior local Dutch official, the resident.
Residents occupied imposing official dwellings in the provincial
capitals and presided over their smaller domains in a style and with a
personal latitude that mimicked that of the governor general. Beneath each resident was a hierarchy of other European officials,
many of whom were posted in outlying areas. Most important of
these were assistant residents, who headed one of the four or five
separate administrative subdivisions, or *afdelings*, making up the

Residency house. Chromolithograph by Jhr. J. C. Rappard, in *Nederlandsch-Indie* (1881–83).

residency. The resident and his assistant residents exercised a broad and loosely defined authority. They interpreted the rules and regulations of the colony for local application, administered the law, promoted special programs in which they were personally interested, and generally personified the state, often quite arbitrarily.[10] Each district also hosted a small cadre of *controleurs* and, some of them, assistant controleurs. In principle these young administrative apprentices exercised little authority, but it was their job to learn

10. Robert van Niel, "Government Policy and the Civil Administration in Java during the Early Years of the Cultivation System," Proceedings, Conference on Modern Indonesian History, July 18–19, 1975 (Madison, Wis.), p. 61. See also M. C. Piepers, *Macht tegen Recht: De vervolging der Justitie in Nederlandsch Indie* (Batavia, 1884), pp. 52–56, who criticizes the independence and petty despotism of the Colonial Service, especially the residents.

their territories intimately. As Wallace observed, it was the lowly controleur who "periodically visits every village in the district, examines the proceedings of the native courts, hears complaints against the head-men or other native chiefs, and superintends the Government plantations."[11]

In all Java (and Madura) in 1883 there were 22 residents, 93 assistant residents, and 151 controleurs on active service.[12] A few other officials and functionaries augmented the European corps in the larger towns—judicial officers, locally stationed military men, and the residency secretaries, for example. This was a strikingly limited official presence considering Java's population and, in fact, it represented only the highest levels of the regional administration. The Colonial Service did not govern Java directly. In imposing Dutch authority and in enforcing broad matters of policy it unquestionably prevailed. But matters of day-to-day governance were in other hands. Over the years this slight but dynamic Dutch administrative head had been grafted onto the broad shoulders of a vast indigenous administrative corps.

European and native government intersected at the level of the assistant resident. An assistant resident's afdeling was in most cases coterminous with the domain of a bupati, a native prince who stood at the pinnacle of the local social and political order. In Javanese lands bupati and their kin, as well as their subordinates in the indigenous government, were pryayi, noblemen, whose prestige in the eyes of the people sprang as much from their cultural excellence—as embodiments of high Javanese tradition—as it did from their official positions. To the Javanese mind the two were synonymous.[13] This pairing of European professional administrative officers with local princes of the realm was designed to bridge not only two levels of the colonial bureaucratic structure but also the disparate frames of cultural and historical reference which separated the Dutch view of things from that of the Javanese. Fully understanding this, Dutch regional officials prided themselves on their command of Javanese language and etiquette.

11. Wallace, *Malay Archipelago*, p. 73; van Niel, "Government Policy," p. 62.
12. RAvNI 1883.
13. Heather Sutherland, "Pangreh Pradja: Java's Indigenous Administrative Corps and Its Role in the Last Decades of Dutch Colonial Rule" (Ph.D. diss., Yale University, 1973), pp. 45–46. See Clifford Geertz, *The Religion of Java* (Glencoe, Ill., 1960), chap. 17, for a discussion of pryayi culture in the twentieth century.

The bupatis were descendants of the old provincial elite families of Mataram. As the political center of gravity swung gradually toward the Dutch during the VOC years, their ancestors had offered allegiance and services to the new European master, albeit sometimes under duress. The Dutch had found them useful collaborators, for they facilitated the delivery of coffee, rice, and other products that the company's economy depended on. For their part the bupatis reaped material rewards and privileges, not the least of which was the reinforcement of their preeminence in the Dutch-controlled lands. (Said the poet Ronggawarsita, reflecting on the Javanese experience: "to go along unthinkable, yet if one does not, one gets no share").[14] Borrowing a usage from home, the Dutch called them regents, their territories regencies. This was a durable collaboration, which, having evolved over some two hundred years, was fully institutionalized by the mid-nineteenth century in the native administrative corps (Inlandse Bestuur), or Pangreh Praja.[15] Within the afdeling/regency this collaboration was dramatized in the Dutch assistant resident's symbolic adoption of the regent as his younger brother.

The size of individual regencies varied considerably, but on the average a regent governed a population of some 180,000 people in the 1870s, most of them villagers. In addition to his personal staff and entourage, he was assisted by legal and religious officials, jaksas and penghulus, respectively, and by an administrative officer, the patih, who looked after the mundane aspects of government on his behalf. The regency was divided into several districts, each headed by a pryayi official called the wedana, and these districts were further divided into subdistricts containing about fifty villages each. An assistant wedana presided over each subdistrict; he was the lowest official in the pryayi hierarchy and maintained daily contact with

14. Quoted in Joseph Errington, "To Know Oneself the Troubled Times: Ronggawarsita's 'Serat Kala Tidha,'" in *Writing on the Tongue*, ed. Alton L. Becker (Center for South and Southeast Asia Studies, University of Michigan, 1989). Writing probably in the 1860s, Ronggawarsita spoke of the "insanity" of the times when seen from a traditional Javanese perspective.

15. Heather Sutherland, *The Making of a Bureaucratic Elite* (Asia Studies Association of Australia: Southeast Asia Publications Series, no. 2; Singapore, 1979), pp. 3–6, discusses the East India Company origins of the Dutch-pryayi accommodation. B. Schrieke, "The Position of the Regents from the Days of the Dutch East India Company to the Constitutional Regulation of 1854," *Indonesian Sociological Studies*, 1 (1960), 201–21.

village heads, *lurah*, and other local notables.[16] This pyramidal hierarchy was embellished at each level with staffs of petty functionaries, some of them young pryayi apprenticing for hoped-for careers in the corps, and with the retinues of hangers-on which were part of the trappings of pryayi prestige.

The Pangreh Praja was an indispensable part of the colonial administrative apparatus. The regent and his subordinates were, for the Dutch, the vital, intimate link between them and the masses of the countryside. The Dutch, of course, bent them to specific tasks: native officials collected taxes, arbitrated disputes, investigated crime, and facilitated economic schemes. But in a broader sense they were simply responsible for everything in their individual domains. They kept a watchful eye and in a variety of day-to-day activities helped maintain local peace and orderliness. Their residences and the ceremonial square (*alun-alun*) where they stood were the focal points of local power. As members of the pryayi elite, the native officials served as culturally sanctioned and personally revered symbols of authority whose local eminence served Dutch interests of peace, order, and profit.[17]

Profit, of course, had been the original Dutch incentive in the Indies, and it remained so when the East India Company transformed itself from a commercial into a territorial power. Typical of the economic exploitation of Java during the company years were a broad range of practices designed to harness the labor of native producers—and, indirectly, the land they worked—to bring such commodities as coffee, sugar, pepper, and rice to market. These practices involved numerous and diverse patterns of cultivation, collection, delivery, and payment, but considered collectively they had two common features. First, they required the active collaboration of the early regents and other native chiefs, whose traditional rights over the labor and surplus bounty of their subordinate populations the Dutch had finessed into a system of "forced deliveries." Second, virtually all these arrangements also required the participation of Java's resident Chinese community, who, as traders, bankers,

16. This is a simplified description of a complex and variable bureaucratic (and social) structure that is based on the Dutch-imposed standardization of the Javanese administrative corps in 1874. SvNI 1874, no. 73.

17. SvNI 1867, no. 114; SvNI 1886, no. 244; and SvNI 1874, no. 93; and Sutherland, *Making of a Bureaucratic Elite*, pp. 19–20.

and brokers, and as rice and sugar millers and supervisors and managers, facilitated the transformation of indigenous labor into exportable commodities, and who, in the role of revenue farmers, otherwise taxed Javanese bounty and delivered great sums to the VOC or its profiteering servants.[18] As a formula for exploiting peasant labor and resources, this adroit manipulation of Javanese feudal entitlements and Chinese acumen survived the demise of the company and achieved its most intensive application in the nineteenth century. The Dutch described it crudely but accurately in a familiar colonial saying. "The Javanese plows and sows," they said. "The Chinese gathers it in. And the European walks away with it."[19]

Under Marshal Herman Willem Daendels, who governed Java from 1808 to 1811 as Napolean's proconsul, something of the spirit of the new age in Europe was visited on the island. He built a great road from one end of Java to the other, and both he and his successor, the Englishman Raffles (1811–16), sought to impose European authority more firmly and thoroughly than ever before. Raffles's subjugation of Yogyakarta in 1812 brought new lands—previously appanages of the sultan—into the Western realm, and new fiscal boons as well: Chinese revenue farmers who collected tolls, ran markets, and sold opium in the sultan's territory now paid their fees to the government in Batavia.[20]

Raffles also experimented in colonial housekeeping of a more liberal stamp. It was his hope to "destroy the power of the regents and to bring the peasantry into direct contact with an enlightened Western government."[21] Part of his fiscal program was a capitation tax to be paid by individuals in cash. Landrent, as it was called, was designed to replace village-level levies in produce. Raffles's scheme failed in its main goal of loosening the feudal bonds between peasants and the chiefs, but, carried on by the Dutch after their return to

18. G. Gonggrijp, *Schets eener economische geschiedenis van Nederlandsch-Indie* (Haarlem, 1928), p. 36; Dionijs Huibert Burger, *De Ontsluiting van Java's Binnenland voor het Wereldverkeer* (Wageningen, 1939), pp. 15–22; and C.J.G. Holtzappel, "The Indigenous Basis of the Revenue Farming System in Java," paper prepared for the Conference on Revenue Farming, Research School of Pacific Studies, Australian National University, 1988.

19. In P. H. Fromberg, "De Chineesche Beweging en het *Koloniaal Tijdschrift*," 1912, in *Verspreide Geschriften* (Leiden, 1926), p. 487.

20. Clive Day, *The Dutch in Java* (New York, 1904), pp. 147–63 for Daendels, and pp. 165–202 for Raffles. Ricklefs, *History of Modern Indonesia*, p. 110.

21. John Bastin, *The Native Policies of Sir Stamford Raffles in Java and Sumatra* (Oxford, 1957), p. 68.

Landrent "tax" paid by individuals in cash

power in 1816, it had important repercussions for the village economy. Namely, it created an opportunity for middlemen—Chinese
and native chiefs—to advance cash tax payments on behalf of villagers in return for disposition over a portion of their harvests. This
intensified the monetization of Java's rural economy—a process
long since begun—and gave the Chinese merchant another entrée
to the village world and its agricultural bounty.[22]

A new scheme to make Java profitable was inaugurated in 1830, a
task now urgent in the wake of the treasury-exhausting expenses of
the Java War (1825–30). Known as the Cultivation System, it was
based on reapplying with vigor the principles of the forced delivery
system, which had never been wholly abandoned even during Raffles's time. Under the Cultivation System, native agriculturalists
were obliged to allot one-fifth of their land and labor to cultivate
crops that the Dutch could export profitably—coffee, sugar, indigo,
tea, tobacco, and a variety of others—and were called upon to cut
and haul wood and to labor on public works and in sugar factories.[23]

The Cultivation System was not executed uniformly. Typically,
local arrangements based on accommodations among Dutch officials, native heads, Chinese merchants, and villagers prevailed over
the grand design.[24] Nevertheless, the program brought significant
economic development to the island, with new dams, water courses,
sluice gates, and canals; and new roads as well as bridges, homes,
rest houses, and post stations.[25] The government poured vast numbers of copper pennies into the village world in the form of Cultivation wages and other payments, thus accelerating the monetization
of the rural economy.[26] Such development inevitably brought with
it an intensification of the colonial presence, most significantly in the
expansion of the Dutch and pryayi administrative corps, the latter
being essential to organizing land and labor to make the system
work. Paralleling this expansion was the growth in number and
importance of Java's Chinese officers, as the island's growing Chi-

22. Gonggrijp, *Schets*, p. 78; Bastin, *Native Policies*, p. 57. See also Peter Boomgaard, "Buitenzorg in 1805: The Role of Money and Credit in a Colonial Frontier
Society," *Modern Asian Studies*, 20 (1986), 34; and Peter Carey, "Waiting for the 'Just
King': The Agrarian World of South-Central Java from Giyanti (1755) to the Java
War (1825–30)," *Modern Asian Studies*, 20 (1986), 88, 97.
23. Elson, "Sugar Factory Workers," p. 142.
24. Van Niel, "Government Policy," pp. 61, 64–65.
25. Gonggrijp, *Schets*, p. 140.
26. Ibid., pp. 156–57.

nese population pressed inland to tap new opportunities for trade and enterprise which the Cultivation System stimulated.

The Cultivation years reaped steady financial rewards for Holland; between 1831 and 1866 some 672 million guilders were remitted to the Netherlands from Indies profits, where they were used to reduce home taxes, build railroads and fortifications, and redeem the public debt.[27] The system itself, however, gradually succumbed under a barrage of criticism leveled at its excesses—which some blamed for the rash of food shortages, famines, and epidemics that occurred in the late 1840s and early 1850s—and of increasing demands by Dutch capitalists for a colony open to exploitation by private enterprise, it having been demonstrated just how profitable Java could be.[28]

The period after 1860, therefore, witnessed a move away from forced cultures and toward the private capitalization of commercial agriculture. The Indies economy was being brought rapidly into the expanding pattern of world trade, as clipper ships and then steam vessels shortened the distance between Europe and Java, a trend that the opening of the Suez Canal in 1869 intensified.[29] Meanwhile the administrative and economic infrastructure that had been designed to serve the Cultivation System was refurbished and expanded to meet the needs of the changing colony. The construction of an islandwide telegraph network (in 1857) and development of a modern postal service (1862) were part of this, as was the beginning of railroad construction. New banks were founded to finance private enterprise—mostly agricultural—and on plantations and construction sites wage labor was gradually replacing customary corvee levies.[30]

The 1870 Agrarian Law resolved the issue of state versus private enterprise definitively in favor of the latter. This law, while reiterating the principle of the inviolability of native land by forbidding its sale on a large scale, gave private investors access to vast parcels of land suitable for plantations by permitting them to lease these parcels from villages for periods of seventy-five years. In addition,

27. Ibid., pp. 149–50. See Furnivall's discussion of the *Batig Slot*, the policy of using Indies revenues to contribute to home finances. John Sydenham Furnivall, *Netherlands India* (Cambridge, 1939), pp. 210–11.
28. See the discussion in Day, *Dutch in Java*, chap. 9, and Furnivall, *Netherlands India*, pp. 148–73.
29. Furnivall, *Netherlands India*, pp. 170–71; Gonggrijp, *Schets*, p. 149.
30. Gonggrijp, *Schets*, p. 160.

companies and private individuals could now acquire deeds to parcels of "free land" available for rail and train concessions, as well as for homes, warehouses, and factories in Java's expanding towns and cities.[31] In the wake of the 1870 law, private plantations, especially sugar plantations, spread throughout the island and enterprises of all kinds proliferated. Among those to seize the new opportunities for profit were the Chinese, who in addition to expanding and diversifying their traditional activities as merchants and contractors for services also joined Europeans in commercial agriculture.

Java's economic transformation during the nineteenth century was accompanied by a demographic one. The population rose dramatically. By 1873 the 5 million people Raffles's census enumerators had counted in 1815 had grown to almost 18 million.[32] The population had not only grown but had spread out, as peasant cultivators moved into open lands to the east of the principalities—in Kediri, for example—to make new rice fields and settle in new villages.[33] Dislocations caused by the Java War, regional economic hardship during the Cultivation years, population pressure in densely peopled districts, and new economic opportunities all contributed to this population movement. They also loosened a large number of peasants from village attachments and local authority structures. Thus, the size of Java's unattached "floating" population increased appreciably. Such a class of mobile individuals—peddlers, theatrical players, musicians, Islamic teachers and mystics, wandering knights and hero-brigands (*satria lelana*)—had played an important part in traditional Javanese society, especially as a medium of social communication between coastal towns, inland courts, and rural villages.[34] They had remained an important social element under the Dutch. Now, added to the more traditional sorts of wanderers and vagabonds were ever larger numbers of peasants who left their villages to seek work as plantation laborers and workers of all sorts in the expanding colonial economy. By the 1870s and 1880s large

31. Ibid., p. 164; Furnivall, *Netherlands India*, pp. 178–80; SvNI 1870, no. 118, contains the new lease regulations.

32. The Raffles figure is quoted in Gonggrijp, *Schets*, p. 175, as 4,499,250; according to the official census of 1873, there were 17,786,118 people in Java and Madura at that time. KVvNI 1875, Bijlage A, no. 3.

33. In his *Social History of an Indonesian Town* (Cambridge, Mass., 1965), Clifford Geertz discusses the growth of Modjokuto—his pseudonym for a real town in east Java—during this period. See p. 34 for a brief discussion of nineteenth-century migrations, and pp. 70–71 for the origins of the town itself.

34. Th. Pigeaud, *Javaanse Volksvertoningen* (Batavia, 1938), p. 35.

numbers of such individuals lived in crowded *kampungs* on the out-
skirts of local towns, or in company compounds set up to house
factory workers and field hands in the sugar regions.[35]

Growth of the "floating" population was just one measure, however, of the degree to which Java's rural population was increasingly
participating in the world economy. Driven both by opportunity and
by need, it was now common for villagers living in the expanding
orbit of sugar plantations and mills, coffee gardens and towns—
including many new ones sprouting along freshly laid railroad
tracks and roads—to earn cash as seasonal or part-time laborers as
well as by peddling firewood, grass, fruits and vegetables, or by
running small produce stalls (*warung*). As before, they also sold
some of their rice and smallholder crops such as coffee. Money
earned this way helped pay the landrent and was used to pay for
celebrations surrounding circumcisions, marriages, and religious
holidays, and for items of necessity and pleasure from sewing nee-
dles to opium.

In a larger sense, income from the money sector helped Java's
growing population keep pace with its basic needs in the 1870s and
1880s and permitted some to enjoy a marginal prosperity. (Rising
opium sales are one measure of this prosperity.) But the volatility of
the money sector also made the people of Java vulnerable. When the
money sector contracted—as it did severely with the collapse of
world sugar prices in the mid-1880s—subsistence for rising numbers of people in the countryside was all the harsher.

Intricately enmeshed within this evolving economy and society
was the opium farm, the largest and most lucrative of Java's Chinese-run revenue farms. Like all institutions of nineteenth-century
Java, it was the product of a long evolution. Some characteristics of
the farm were reminiscent of patterns developed in the days of the
Dutch East India Company. The practice of leasing important revenue farms to Chinese merchants, for example, was as old as the
company itself and, in fact, predated it. In the seventeenth and
eighteenth centuries Chinese held monopolies for road tolls and
river crossings, salt manufacture and sale, and had even held leasehold rights over the produce and manpower of numerous north
coast villages.[36] Although the formal structure of the opium farm

35. Elson, "Sugar Factory Workers," p. 148.
36. Burger, *De Ontsluiting*, pp. 15–22.

was not established until 1809 by Marshal Daendels, Chinese merchants had been manufacturing and selling opium in Java for much of the two preceding centuries under various arrangements with the East India Company and native rulers.[37]

In Daendel's system of 1809, merchants competed at a public auction for opium farm leases that gave them a monopoly for manufacturing and selling opium in a territory defined by the government. The government collected fees from the farmers and also profited by selling them opium, the importation of which the government monopolized. All further changes in opium farm structure were essentially improvements or variations on this simple plan.[38] As Dutch hegemony in Java became more pronounced during the nineteenth century, especially after the addition of large territories in central and east Java to the government lands at the end of the Java War—the new residencies of Banyumas, Bagelen, Madiun, and Kediri—the territory opened to government opium farmers also expanded. With the exception of regions chosen by the Dutch to be opium free (the Forbidden Areas, *Verboden Kringen*), all Java hosted Dutch-appointed opium farmers by 1832.

By the 1860s the opium farm had emerged as a key institution in the colonial state, interlocking with others such as the Chinese Officer System, the Pangreh Praja, and the Colonial Service. In the years of economic expansion following the end of the Cultivation System it achieved its maturest form and widest influence. Under Holland's stewardship opium had pervaded the finest tropical island in the world.

37. Jean Chretien Baud, "Proeve van eene geschiedenis van den handel en het verbruik van opium in Nederlandsche Indie," *BKI*, 1 (1853), 95, 100.
38. The first Dutch-established opium farm in Java, for the city of Batavia, was leased to Chinese captain Lim Beeng Kang in 1747. Three months later it was abolished, apparently because Lim's opium dens had become gathering spots for criminals. See ibid., pp. 125, 144.

2

Opium, Sinister Friend

Arab traders are generally credited with introducing opium to Asia. It reached Java centuries ago, exactly when and borne by whom it is not known. When Hollanders first appeared off the coast of Java in the late sixteenth century, opium was already an important article of regional commerce.[1] In their attempt to dominate the local trade during the ensuing century, Dutch merchants competed with English, Dane, and Arab. Finally in 1677 the Dutch East India Company secured a treaty from King Amangkurat II of Java guaranteeing the VOC a monopoly over the importation of opium into his kingdom, Mataram, as well as over its distribution internally. Another smaller kingdom, Ceribon, agreed to similar terms the following year.[2] This was the beginning of the Dutch opium monopoly in Java. Holland expanded it eventually to embrace all the Indies, and guarded it jealously until the colony itself was lost.

Dutch traffic in opium to Java rose considerably following the treaty of 1677, and J. C. Baud has calculated that from 1619 to 1799 the VOC introduced an average of 56,000 kilograms of raw opium

1. Jean Chretien Baud, "Proeve van eene geschiedenis van den handel en het verbruik van opium in Nederlandsche Indie," *BKI*, 1 (1853), 90.
2. On the subject of early competition among Europeans and Arabs for the Java trade, see the letter from Governor General Rijklof van Goens to Heeren XVII, February 13, 1679, in J.K.J. de Jonge, ed., *De Opkomst van het Nederlandsch Gezag over Java; Verzameling van onuitgegeven stukken uit het oud koloniaal Archief* (The Hague, 1873), 4:9. The VOC-Mataram treaty is in J. E. Heeres, ed., *Corpus Diplomaticum Neerlando-Indicum* (The Hague, 1907–38), 3:74–79.

into Java every year—officially.[3] Given the vulnerability of Java's coastline and the relatively ineffective policing apparatus of the company, we may assume that the true amount was much higher. Contemporary accounts reveal that opium was widely available in Java at the outset of the nineteenth century, especially in the northern coastal regions with their harbor towns, and in the densely populated principalities of Surakarta and Yogyakarta. Revenues from the official opium monopoly grew dramatically in the first quarter century, and Peter Carey writes that by 1820 there were 372 separate places licensed to sell opium in Yogyakarta, "namely nearly every major tollgate, sub-tollgate and market in the Sultanate."[4] (Princely opium addicts were observed among Diponegoro's retinue, and during the Java War many of his troops fell sick when the opium supply was disrupted.)[5] With the expansion of the administrative apparatus of the colonial state in the 1830s, especially as the Cultivation System grew and as the Dutch established official opium farms in much of inner Java, opium became even more widely available and its consumption spread rapidly.

Opium's penetration of Java was not even, however. The Bantanese of west Java and their Sundanese neighbors in the adjacent Priangan regencies were evidently little attracted to it. Dutch observers attributed this to cultural and religious values, especially to the stricter observance of Islam in these areas. They reinforced the local disinclination with an official ban. The Priangan and most of Bantam (Banten) were closed for opium sales early in the nineteenth century, and neither hosted an official opium farm.[6] Even though both regions contained a black market of variable liveliness, it didn't remotely compare with the volume elsewhere. When in the early twentieth century the Dutch legalized opium sales in Banten and the highlands, less opium was sold there than anywhere else in Java.[7]

3. Baud, "Proeve," pp. 92, 101–2, 158–59.
4. Peter Carey, "Changing Perceptions of the Chinese Communities in Central Java, 1755–1825," *Indonesia* (April 1984), 33.
5. Ibid., p. 35.
6. SvNI 1824, no. 44; Baud, "Proeve," p. 162. Bantam contained four opium depots, which were usually run by the Batavia farmer. See SvNI 1874, no. 229.
7. On smuggling in the Priangan, see Resident Preanger-Regentschappen to GG, April 23, 1900, no. 4213/28 in V 23/1/1904/21. The Java-wide pattern of opium consumption as of 1909 is summarized in "Overzichtskaart van het opiumverbruik op Java en Madoera onder Chineezen en Inlanders," October 27, 1909, in V 11/1/1911/30.

The richest opium markets were in east and central Java.[8] The opium farms of Surakarta and the residencies of Kediri, Semarang, and Madiun nearly always yielded the highest revenues. During the nineteenth century this is where the most powerful opium farmers held sway. Figures gathered in the early twentieth century confirm that opium consumption per person was consistently highest here. The neighboring coastal residencies of Japara, Rembang, and Surabaya, along with Kedu and Yogyakarta in south-central Java, also contained large opium-smoking populations. These territories were predominantly Javanese, indeed collectively they formed the Javanese heartland. The same area also entertained a lively Chinese commerce. It penetrated south from the mercantile towns of the north coast deep into the village world of the interior. Growing steadily throughout the century, this commerce was intimately connected with the competition for Java's opium market. It was here that opium farms reached their most mature form.

Residencies on the periphery of this core region—from Batavia to Pekalongan on the west, and to the east, Pasuruan, Probolinggo, and Besuki, as well as the island of Madura—contained enough opium users to support profitable opium farms throughout the nineteenth century. Although consumption per person was less here than in the core region, the use of opium was still relatively widespread. In addition, opium farms in these residencies were often held by the same individuals who dominated the more lucrative farms, with the result that they, too, were drawn into the arena of major opium farm competition.

Opium smoking was, then, a common feature of urban and rural life in nineteenth-century Java. Among the Dutch, who preferred gin, it was a vice associated only with the weaker "half-bloods," and "the bad ones" who "disappeared into the *kampung*s and the slums."[9]

8. On the subject of opium consumption in Java in the late nineteenth century, the three best sources are "Resume van de door de Hoofden van Gewestelijk Bestuur op Java en Madura ingezonden antwoorden op de hun gestelde vragen betreffende het opiumverbruik," in VKG 3/2/1885/K1, hereafter cited as Opium Resume, 1885; Charles TeMechelen: Rapport uitgebracht in voldoening aan 's Gouvernements Besluit dd 9 July 1885, no. 9 in V 22/8/1888/6, hereafter cited as TM: Rapport 1888; and a series of interviews conducted in central and east Java in 1890 with seventy-nine acknowledged opium smokers, which may be found among the Charles TeMechelen papers, TMC 422c; hereafter referred to as Opium Interviews, 1890.

9. Quotation from P. A. Daum, *Ups and Downs of Life in the Indies* [1892], trans. Elsje Qualm Sturtevant and Donald W. Sturtevant (Amherst, Mass., 1987), p. 195. In *Hidden Force*, Louis Couperus depicted such a person in Si-Oudijck, the unacknowledged son by a native mistress of a Dutch official. Si-Oudijck's dilapidated dwelling in the village is "permeated with the acrid odor of opium" (p. 119).

Javanese opium smokers. Courtesy Koninklijk Instituut voor de Tropen, Amsterdam.

Among the Chinese, however, it was popular. In the coastal cities and inland towns where they settled, wealthy Chinese men enjoyed the opium pipe in their homes and in private smoking clubs, while their poorer countrymen shared public dens and clandestine smoking places with the locals. Liem Thian Joe, the chronicler of the Chinese community of Semarang, writes that few wealthy Chinese were free from it, and that it was "a great honor" (*toa-lee*) for guests in a Chinese household to be offered opium.[10] Although individually the Chinese consumed considerably more opium than the indigenous population—indeed, most of the severest addicts then and later appear to have been Chinese—they made up only a minor part of the mass market. By far the larger quantity of Java's opium was consumed by the Javanese.

10. Liem Thian Joe, *Riwajat Semarang (Dari Djamannja Sam Poo Sampe Terhapoesnja Kongkoan)* (Semarang, 1933), p. 140.

By the 1870s opium was ubiquitous in the Javanese lands. Every village had its quotient of regular smokers as well as a larger number of people who used opium only on special occasions. Opium seems to have been especially attractive to Java's "floating" population: vagabonds, musicians, and theater folk, peddlers and artisans, and the swelling contingent of laborers who worked for wages—laying rails, plucking coffee, cutting cane, hauling produce and supplies— in the expanding private enterprise economy of the late nineteenth century. Among the pryayi, opium had long been a feature of hospitality and social life. Male guests in central Java were routinely entertained with opium at aristocratic festivities. In the humbler society of village and plantation, celebrations marking the end of the rice harvest or the beginning of the coffee-plucking season often included the sharing of opium among the men. "At a party in the village it is generally the custom," said a villager from Bojonegoro interviewed in 1890, "for the host to provide opium for those who enjoy smoking. The village leaders who may be present are regaled in this manner."[11]

The Javanese used opium in a variety of ways depending on their means and tastes. The essential product was candu, purified raw opium mixed with taste enhancers and adulterants. Wealthier individuals smoked fancy-grade candu in finely crafted pipes (badudan); commoners smoked a cruder blend using simple pipes and enjoyed cheaper preparations such as tiké, finely cut awar-awar leaves (ficus septica) laced with candu and sugar. Simple throwaway pipes were fashioned from papaya stems or otherwise homemade.[12] Many people also smoked tiké and opium-soaked tobacco rolled up in a maize leaf or made into a cigar or cigarette another way. Smoking was preferred, but opium could also be "eaten." Some Javanese spiked their coffee with it, others mixed it with their betel quid.[13]

Opium dens dotted the landscape, although they were only one of many venues where opium was consumed. From M.T.H. Perelaer's antiopium novel of the 1880s, Baboe Dalima, comes a description of one such den located in a Javanese town, the seat of a pryayi official. It stood just behind the mosque on the alun-alun, an insubstantial bamboo structure with low ceilings and dirt floors. Having paid the storekeeper, a customer received a slip of paper inscribed with

11. Opium Interviews, 1890, no. 5.
12. Ibid., no. 66.
13. TM: Rapport 1888.

Chinese characters indicating the amount of his purchase. This he presented to a female attendant in one of the den's twenty-four cubicles, each of which was furnished with one long, low bench, a *baleh-baleh*, and lighted dimly by a small oil lamp. "There on the baleh-baleh," Perelaer tells us, "lay a Javanese . . . stretched out full length, and half reclining on his side. He had taken off his head cloth, and his long black hair floated over the . . . pillow on the bench." The attendant then "advanced to the baleh-baleh, took some candu out of a small box, warmed it at the flame of the lamp, and then mixed it with a little very finely cut tobacco. Then she rolled it in her fingers into a little ball about the size of a large pea, put this into the bowl of the opium pipe, and handed it to the . . . smoker."[14]

Java's opium smokers seem to have been choosy about their candu. They distinguished between that which was pungent or bland, cool or hot, and sweet or bitter on the basis of taste and smell. Opium was imported to Java in its raw form and was processed into consumable products locally. An opium farmer's "chemist" could produce candu of varying tastes by altering the proportions of Bengal and Turkish opium being used, and by skillfully blending in additives such as burnt sugar, lemon extract, and *jicing* (the ash remains of already smoked candu).[15] Formulas for good candu evidently varied from region to region, depending on what was popular locally, and a clever opium farmer did his best to satisfy local tastes. In Surakarta, for example, many customers insisted on raw opium, and opium farmers obliged.[16]

To meet the local demand, opium farmers routinely manufactured a variety of products. One farmer in Pasuruan, for example, was observed in 1891 making four grades of candu of varying tastes and declining potencies. The lowest of these he used to mix with awar-awar leaves to make tiny balls (*gelengs*) of tiké that he sold for pennies apiece.[17]

The Javanese purchased opium with their earnings as plantation

14. M.T.H. Perelaer, *Baboe Dalima*, trans. E. J. Venning (London, 1888), pp. 189–92. Perelaer was trying to arouse his readers' indignation; therefore, in his text the pillow was "disgustingly filthy," the smoker "wretched," the den itself "a squalid, filthy little bamboo building."
15. TM to DF, September 16, 1887, no. 1171/4 Geheim in TM: Rapport 1888; and J. Haak, *Opiumregie met normaal tjandoe* (Semarang, 1889), p. 13.
16. TM: Rapport 1888.
17. Bijlage F1 to TM to DF, February 16, 1891, no. 169/12 in TMC H422d.

coolies and petty traders and workers, from selling the products of their fields, and after 1870 from their share in the rent money for leased agricultural lands. Some with special skills (such as puppeteers), or with a talent for business or a high position, made more, but most people had very limited money incomes. In 1885 an unskilled laborer in Java earned, on the average, 25 cents a day (more in some areas), and a skilled craftsperson could earn anywhere from 60 to 200 cents depending on the local economy.[18] It is not surprising that village opium-den holders in the 1880s reported that it was a rare person who had more than 20 cents a day to spend on opium.[19] Among seventy-nine opium smokers interviewed in 1890 in Bojonegoro, Rembang, Malang, and Jember, the range in daily spending for opium was striking—up to 100 cents in one or two cases—but the commonest daily expenditure was 5 cents, and only a few said they spent more than 10 to 20 cents daily on opium.[20] Five cents was sufficient to buy, on the average, a small wad of tiké, or some similarly adulterated preparation; 20 cents bought three more of the same. These are very modest amounts of opium. Other observational evidence from the farm years and official statistics collected later show that the vast majority of Java's opium smokers fell into this range. In Java, large numbers of individuals consumed very small amounts of opium.[21]

"Among the remedies which it has pleased Almighty God to give man to relieve his sufferings," wrote English physician Thomas Sydenham in 1680, "none is so universal and so efficacious as opium."[22] Today morphine continues to be clinically superior to

18. KVvNI 1885, p. 218. In 1888 the average daily wage for workers on independent coffee plantations in east Java was 37 cents; on government-run plantations in central Java it was 10 cents or less. See "Het loon van de Koffieplantende bevolking op Java in verbond met art. 56 van het Regeerings-reglement," *IG*, 2 (1888), 1818–33. Copper pennies (duiten) were the usual medium of cash exchange in the rural economy. Djoko Suryo, "Social and Economic Life in Rural Semarang under Colonial Rule in the Later Nineteenth Century" (Ph.D. diss., Monash University, 1982), p. 209, shows wages marginally higher, especially around Semarang itself.

19. TM: Rapport 1888.

20. Opium Interviews, 1890.

21. Directeur van Middelen en Domeinen to GG, August 16, 1866, no. 3238 in V 16/2/1867/1; TM: Rapport 1888; and *Verslag Opiumfabriek*, 1913, which shows that the Regie, from 1903 to 1912, consistently manufactured and sold more one-half mata (193 milligrams) tubes of candu (its smallest) than any other size, along with millions of gelengs of tiké. See the charts, p. 13.

22. Quoted in Jerome H. Jaffe and William R. Martin, "Opioid Analgesics and Antagonists," in *The Pharmacological Basis of Therapeutics*, ed. Alfred Goodman Gilman, Louis S. Goodman, and Alfred Gilman, p. 494 (New York, 1980).

newer drugs in relieving pain. One of its important characteristics as an analgesic is its universality; most types of pain respond equally well to morphine. Another is the relatively low level of mental clouding and behavior modification that results from therapeutic doses: "Morphine and related drugs rarely produce the garrulous, silly, and emotionally labile behavior frequently seen in alcohol and barbiturate intoxication."[23] Furthermore, morphine depresses the cough reflex and provides unparalleled relief for diarrhea and dysentery.[24]

The medicinal properties of morphine, borne in smoked candu, go a long way in explaining the appeal of opium to the Javanese. This is especially true in light of prevailing public health conditions in Java during the last century.[25] Given the physical environment in which they lived, and the absence of hygienic habits and medical facilities, nineteenth-century Javanese were extremely vulnerable to disease. Their insubstantial houses made of bamboo and grasses were small, cramped, and damp and harbored pests such as rats and cockroaches. Villages were usually built along rivers and swamps, around fish ponds and arable fields, all of which, writes Djoko Suryo, offered "a favorable environment for living disease agents and intermediate disease hosts, such as mosquitoes, flies, and other insects."[26] Water was almost always unclean and never boiled. Disease was constantly present. The people suffered chronically from fevers, and from malaria, diarrhea, dysentery, typhoid, chicken pox, and measles. In Semarang and central Java cholera epidemics occurred at the rate of one a decade, sometimes more frequently, and during these times the death rate soared. Improvements in communication and transportation during the late nineteenth century may have actually increased the incidence of disease, as epidemics spread swiftly along roads and rails. In addition, during the last quarter of the century the region experienced a succession of calamities which also increased the incidence and severity of illness— floods and droughts, followed by crop failures, food shortages, and famines.

Dutch provisions for public health were totally inadequate against

23. Ibid., p. 499.
24. Ibid., pp. 513, 503.
25. See Djoko Suryo, "Social and Economic Life in Rural Semarang," esp. chap. 5, "The Constant Problem of Health," upon which this paragraph is based.
26. Ibid., p. 246.

this onslaught. By the 1880s only 5 percent of the population had been inoculated against smallpox, and there was but one native paramedic, a *Dokter Jawa*, for every 345,000 individuals.[27] Practitioners of herbal medicine and Javanese healers who specialized in esoteric and magic cures also failed in the face of these conditions, and consequently it is not surprising that opium became a valued part of the Javanese pharmacopoeia. Put simply, opium relieved when other remedies could not.

Judging from the responses of the seventy-nine opium users interviewed in 1890, many smokers first tried opium as a remedy of last resort for one of several conditions: headaches; fevers and chills (including malaria); stomach aches, diarrhea, dysentery, and asthma; tuberculosis ("bloody coughing"); fatigue and anxiety.[28] Opium was also used for symptoms of venereal disease (*sakit perempuan*) and for pain caused by injuries such as sprains, dislocations, and broken bones. Opium smoke was blown into the mouths of the sick, and its ashes, mixed in a salve, rubbed into painful joints.[29] Because of its analgesic and other medicinal properties, ingested opium clearly provided relief from the pain associated with these conditions, and ameliorated many other symptoms as well.[30] In addition, among a population in which it was rare for a mature adult to be without aches and pains of one kind or another, regular opium smoking provided a more general analgesic effect. For many people, smoking candu took the edge off the routine physical discomforts of life.

Possibly this is the explanation for the frequent claim of Javanese opium smokers that they used candu as a stimulant (*obat tjape*). Despite the fact that morphine is generally acknowledged to cause drowsiness and, under favorable conditions, sleep, Javanese smokers persistently said that opium gave them energy and helped them

27. Ibid., pp. 254–55.
28. Opium Interviews, 1890. These interviews were conducted under the supervision of both Dutch and Javanese officials in Bojonegoro, Malang, Rembang, and Jember. Among the seventy-nine people interviewed were farmers, day laborers, vagabonds, peddlers, village headmen and officers, and gamelan players. The sample included two Chinese and two women. The subjects were questioned about the origins of their habit, their average daily consumption, the source of their money, and the activities of the local opium farm. In the case of cholera, opium was also the usual treatment for Europeans, usually a bottled remedy known as Bleeker's Opium Drink. See Isaac Groneman, "Cholera en Creoline," *Geneeskundig Tijdschrift voor Ned-Indie*, 1899; and the same author's *Kitab Pendjagaan diri dan obatnja waktoe ada penjakit Cholera* (Yogyakarta, 1901).
29. Opium Interviews, 1890, no. 58.
30. Because the human body develops a tolerance for morphine, the pain-relieving effect of steady doses gradually lessens, although it does not disappear altogether.

stay awake at night.[31] Men who engaged in difficult manual work often relied on opium, and plantation managers provided it to their coolies for this reason. Village watchmen and performers at all-night entertainments—shadow play puppeteers and gamelan musicians, for example—also relied on opium to keep them awake, as did people who had to sit up with sick parents or children. Evidently it was believed that one could escape cholera by avoiding sleep. One Javanese woman related, "I started smoking fifteen years ago. . . . It was during the cholera time. My husband and I went to buy two gelengs every afternoon so that we could stay awake nights to ward off the disease."[32] Although from a clinical point of view morphine does not act as a stimulant in humans, by removing the dull irritation of routine aches and pains opium would surely induce a *feeling* of vigor, alertness, and energy. All the more so when a few puffs of candu also brought with it a halo of momentary euphoria.

Pleasure was another important aspect of opium smoking among the Javanese. Many people smoked opium because it was delicious and it made them feel good. They said, "Someone who smokes opium feels strong, light and carefree."[33] The sensual possibilities of opium, especially the arousal of sexual feelings and fantasies, were not lost on the Javanese either. One young man said, "Opium made me feel very good and I saw beautiful women in my dreams who came and brought me opium."[34] In Java, bordellos were nearly always adjacent to opium stores and were synonymous with opium dens.[35] Many a young man first acquired the habit as a habitué of the local brothel.[36] ("Where *have* you been?" demands Semar of his son Petruk in a clown scene from a shadow puppet play of the 1880s. "I needn't ask! A young man of the present age sits in the opium den or the bordello.")[37] Said one young man in 1890, "I went with my friends to the dance maidens and started smoking there. The most

31. See Jaffe and Martin, "Opioid Analgesics and Antagonists," p. 499. The Blue Miao of Thailand also consider opium a stimulant. William Robert Geddes, *Migrants of the Mountains* (London, 1976).
32. Opium Interviews, 1890, no. 71.
33. Ibid., no. 1.
34. Ibid., no. 64.
35. Peter Boomgaard writes, "A *warung* in the Ommelanden around 1800 was a brothel-cum-opium den, doubling as a gambling-house and cockpit. It was there that the unmarried *bujangs* spent their money and got into debt." Peter Boomgaard, "Buitenzorg in 1805," p. 35.
36. TM to DF, 16 February 1891, no. 169/12 in Exh 9/8/1892/76; Opium Interviews, 1890, nos. 52, 53.
37. H. E. Steinmetz [Eckert] records such a wayang clown (*panakawan*) scene in his *Indische Brieven aan een Staatsraad* (Haarlem, 1888), p. 155n.

daring had the most successes with the girls."[38] Some men, however, complained that they began smoking opium at the encouragement of their wives, who sought to prevent them from taking second wives by diverting their sexual restlessness to the passive euphoria of the opium pipe.[39]

Among men there seems to have been an important social element to opium smoking: gathering in the dens and brothels; sharing a pipe with neighbors, relatives, or co-workers at a ritual feast; smoking and gambling into the early hours. It may be that opium was especially prized by the Javanese as a pleasure-inducing substance because it altered outward behavior so little. Unlike drinking alcohol, when smoking opium one could maintain decorum and be certain of one's composure. On the other hand, with the exception of those who made up the small but visible fringe element of prostitutes, dancers, and musicians, women do not appear to have engaged in social opium smoking.

Opium's attributes as a restorer of vitality, an aphrodisiac, and an inducer of euphoria are celebrated in Javanese literature of the nineteenth century. *Suluk Gatoloco* (Gatoloco's Story) is a long poem composed by a pryayi which champions the ancient Javanese mystic tradition over the more moralistic (and newer) teachings of devout Muslims, or *santri*. Its penis-shaped hero, Gatoloco, fortifies himself for doctrinal combat with Muslim pharisees by gulping down a huge wad of opium dross (jicing/klelet):

> At once the intoxicating power spread
> Right through his body . . .
> Therewith his strength was all restored.

Later he is serene, his heart "clear and bright."[40]

Despite the ubiquity of opium in the Javanese lands and testimonials to its powers in such works as *Suluk Gatoloco*, Javanese attitudes about opium were ambivalent. There also existed a considerable fear of and scorn for it in the society. Orthodox Muslims frowned on opium and preached against it, and in the traditional school of Javanese ethics and behavior, smoking opium was one of

38. Opium Interviews, 1890, no. 1.
39. Ibid., no. 6.
40. *Suluk Gatoloco*, trans. Benedict O'Gorman Anderson, *Indonesia*, 32 (1981), 126; 33 (1982), 38.

the five Thou Shalt Nots (*malima*), along with thieving, whoring, drinking, and gambling.[41]

Paku Buwana IV, ruler of Surakarta under Dutch suzerainty from 1788 to 1820, expressed this view in his long didactic poem *Wulang Reh* (Teachings on Right Conduct). He wrote:

> As for an opium smoker,
> his laziness is mixed with apathy
> The only thing he likes is
> facing a lamp while
> sitting on a bench with his leg up
> while holding leisurely an opium pipe
> . . . .
>
> When he becomes addicted, his body becomes thin
> the color, blue white
> . . . .
>
> His breath is panting
> coughing frequently,
> with mucus in his chest
>
> Avoid that:
> it is not proper for any of you
> Smoking opium is bad.[42]

What happened to the individual could happen to the state. Indeed, it already had. (Wrote Ronggawarsita, "Now the glory of the realm / is seen to be faded, / rules' regulation in ruin / for lack of examples.")[43] Paku Buwana IV's warning about opium may be read in part as a comment on the decline in the moral values of the Javanese court, which helped to precipitate, and accompanied, the political dismemberment and subjugation of the kingdom by the Dutch. The association between political weakness and a morally decadent elite ("laziness . . . mixed with apathy") was a recurring theme in Javanese thought. It was the basis for exhortations against

41. Philippus van Akkeren, *Een Gedrocht en toch de volmaakte mens: Suluk Gatolotjo* (The Hague, 1951), p. 55.

42. Paku Buwana IV, *Teachings on Right Conduct*, or *Wulang Reh*, trans. Martin Hatch and Suranto Atmosoputro, stanzas 139–42. Manuscript made available to author by Martin Hatch.

43. Quoted in Joseph Errington, "To Know Oneself the Troubled Times."

opium smoking in appointment documents by which the rulers of Mataram invested senior officials of the realm, and it surfaced periodically in literary works and in the reform efforts of individual rulers. In the eighteenth century, for example, Paku Buwana II resolved to prohibit "all his descendants from eating, smoking, or swallowing opium."[44]

The dichotomy of attitudes in *Suluk Gatoloco* and *Wulang Reh*— between a celebration of opium's pleasures and a recognition of its pernicious consequences—also found expression at a popular level. In shadow puppet plays, clowns wore opium pipes in place of swords and indulged in opium-related irreverences, sometimes referring to opium personally as *Mbok Lara Ireng*, Woman Black Sickness.[45] Opium's disastrous impact on a family budget was evidently also part of the conventional wisdom. "When I'm out of money," said Ngat, a coolie who spent 10 cents a day (12 duits) on opium, "my wife refuses to give me any of the money she makes batiking. If I ask money from her, I get a scolding instead."[46] Even as a miracle drug, the Javanese knew there was a price to pay—opium gave them hemorrhoids.[47]

Moreover, opium was addicting even at the modest levels consumed by most Javanese smokers.[48] Javanese were well aware of this. Many of the 1890 interviewees, for example, commented on having to increase their consumption after a time in order to sustain the desired effect. When they stopped smoking, they experienced withdrawal symptoms: "I felt so bad I couldn't stand it," one said; another said, "If I don't smoke for a day, I feel shivery and fatigued."[49]

For the Javanese, opium was indeed a friend, but a sinister one. The admonition to avoid it, characteristic of the courtly moral teach-

44. Carel Frederick Winter, "Verbod tegen het gebruik van amfioen, Soerakarta 1840. Oorzaak van dit verbod door Pakoe Boewon II," *TNI*, 2 (1840), 588. *Wulang Reh*, stanzas 252, 253. Resident Surakarta to DF, February 15, 1867, F in VKG 27/1/1869/17c.

45. Conversations with Sudibbyo Sastrowardhoyo, Onghokham, Joseph Errington, and others.

46. Opium Interviews, 1890, no. 1.

47. Mevrouw J. Kloppenburg-Versteegh, *Indische planten en haar geneeskracht* (Semarang, 1907), p. 45; Antonie de Mol van Otterloo, *De Opiumschuiver in het Hospitaal* (Utrecht, 1933), p. 83.

48. John C. Kramer, "Speculations on the Nature and Pattern of Opium Smoking," *Journal of Drug Issues* (Spring 1979). Kramer (p. 250) writes, "20 or 30 mg of morphine taken daily is marginally addictive while 60 mg is clearly so."

49. Opium Interviews, 1890, nos. 71, 5: TM to DF, 16 February 1891, no. 169/12 in Exh 9/8/1892/76.

ings, seemed to reach deep into society. Opium was nowhere universally accepted, and even in the areas where it was most common
many individuals avoided it. Occasionally a strong folk repugnance
to opium surfaced in the Javanese countryside. In the mid-1880s,
for example, the Dutch opium expert Charles TeMechelen spent
several days in Sokorejo, Madiun, a prosperous village of more than
one thousand families from which all opium smokers had been
banished by collective action of the inhabitants. To explain this
extraordinary state of affairs, TeMechelen noted simply that villagers shared a deeply held belief that the village would come to ruin
if it harbored opium users.[50]

It is impossible to gauge the extent to which the inhibitions expressed in these literary and folk traditions actually tempered the
use of opium. The oft-observed discretion with which many smokers, especially pryayi smokers, enjoyed their opium sprang not so
much from shame as from the need to protect oneself from the
watchful eyes of the local opium farm, or perhaps from the disap-
proving eyes of a Dutch resident. On the other hand the fact that
opium was nowhere universally used suggests that reservations
came into play, as does the popular association of opium with the
low-life realm of gambling, prostitution, and petty criminality.

For the most part, however, these reservations do not seem to
have acted strongly in inhibiting opium smoking among the Javanese. The reason lies most probably in two facts: first, for many
Javanese a small portion of opium made a positive contribution to
the comfort of their day-to-day lives; second, the vast majority of
Javanese opium smokers escaped severe addiction. They were simply too poor for it.

Morphine, an alkaloid of opium, was the principal narcotic in
candu.[51] A geleng, or wad, of average farm tiké—costing, on the
average, 5 cents—contained roughly 76 milligrams of candu. Based
on Dutch chemical analyses of farm opium made in 1889, this much
candu contained about 15 milligrams of morphine.[52] A 20-cent
purchase contained some 60 milligrams, or four times as much.

50. TM: Rapport 1888.
51. Kramer, "Speculations," p. 249. Opium also contains small amounts of co-
deine; see Jaffe and Martin, "Opioid Analgesics and Antagonists," p. 496.
52. Seventy-six milligrams equals one-fifth mata. "Proces-verbal: Op verzoek van
Mr. C. W. Baron van Heeckeren hebben wij ondergeteekenden Ant. C. Marcks en J.
Haak, Apothekers, een onderzoek ingesteld op zes zoogenaamde anti-opium middelen, 20 December 1889," in TMC H422d; J. Haak to W. P. Groeneveldt, June 17,
1892, in V 2/1/1891/39.

Taking into account fluctuations in price and in the quality of opium available, we may estimate that an average opium smoker consumed between 15 and 60 milligrams of morphine daily. Smoking opium, however, is an inefficient method of absorbing morphine: a portion is destroyed in burning, another remains in the ash, still more is exhaled. By some medical estimates, smokers absorb only one-tenth of the morphine in their opium.[53] But even if the absorption rate was considerably higher, most Javanese opium smokers ingested morphine at modest levels, well within (on the low side) and somewhat above (on the high side) dosages of morphine that might be administered for pain today.[54]

The level of addiction experienced by most Javanese opium smokers was, as a consequence, not debilitating. Almost all of them appear to have succeeded in controlling their habits. Indeed, they had little choice. The expendable income of Javanese peasants and workers varied from year to year. Prosperous years, like those of the expansion of private plantations in the 1870s, brought new money to the countryside, just as years of depression threw people back on subsistence farming. Incomes also fluctuated within any given year, reflecting the rural agricultural cycle that swung between dearth at planting time and abundance at the harvest.[55]

These variations in individual income permitted a modest increase in opium smoking at certain times and necessitated curtailment at others. Prices fluctuated over time, too, and smokers frequently had to adjust to more expensive (or more diluted) candu when farmers decided to pass on their rising costs or their business losses to their customers. Javanese opium smokers were therefore accustomed to externally imposed variations in their consumption. And what is perhaps most important, even when the resources of an entire household were expropriated to support someone's habit, virtually all opium users had purchasing levels beyond which they could not possibly go. In terms of the amounts of morphine in-

53. Kramer, "Speculations," p. 249.
54. Eight to 20 milligrams, according to Jaffe and Martin, "Opioid Analgesics and Antagonists," p. 509.
55. The most detailed information on the yearly pattern of opium sales comes from the Regie period, when the government kept careful monthly statistics. These detailed records corroborate the observations of officials and opium farmers during the farm period. See Resident Semarang to HIOR, June 29, 1907, no. 12695/49 in V 18/6/1908/1; the monthly Opium Regie reports for 1902 to 1904 in V 7/1/1905/18, V 7/1/1905/19, and V 7/4/1905/32; and TM: Rapport 1888.

volved, these levels were relatively low. Although the hunger for opium drove a few to crime and violence, the vast majority seems to have adjusted to these fluctuations and limitations with few apparent negative consequences.

In most cases this meant accustoming oneself to a lower morphine intake, a process involving temporary discomfort as the body adapted. At such times, people switched to cheaper preparations containing less candu, such as weaker tiké, or to such concoctions as candu ash dissolved in hot water.[56] Or they tried to make up the difference using a variety of cleverly made false candus and surrogates.[57] Of the latter, awar-awar (*ficus septica*), the main ingredient of tiké, was the commonest. But others were also known. In east Java, people mixed the crumpled leaves of the pulen tree (*fraxinus griffithi*) with tobacco and rolled them into cigarettes wrapped in maize leaves. These preparations did little more than mimic the flavor of candu and help to meet the psychological need for a certain number of familiar daily puffs.[58] On the other hand, some Javanese used marijuana, or ganja (*cannabis indica*), to replace or stretch their candu supply.[59]

Others adjusted to rising prices and cash shortfalls by attempting to quit opium altogether. This inevitably involved a period of withdrawal. Some who tried it eased the way with surrogates and cures, and with common sense. "Whenever . . . I had the urge to smoke again," said Sleman, a former mild addict, "I bought ten cents worth of salt, five cents worth of tamarind, and mixed these in water in two bottles. I took a swallow from time to time—and fled to the mountains to be as far away as possible from the farmer."[60]

To summarize, the characteristic form of opium consumption in nineteenth-century Java was the regular or intermittent smoking (drinking or eating) of very small amounts of morphine-weak opium preparations by large numbers of Javanese people. Their level of consumption depended on the circulation of cash in the countryside

56. See Isaac Groneman, *Een Ketjoegeschiedenis, Vorstenlandsche Toestanden II* (Dordrecht, 1887).

57. VR August 1902 in V 7/1/1905/19.

58. K. Heyne, *De nuttige planten van Nederlandsch-Indie* (Buitenzorg, 1927), 1:575; W. G. Boorsma, "Een Opium-surrogaat," *Teysmannia* 5:564–66. Pulen (poelen) was also known as *kadjoe kedhang*.

59. M.T.H. Perelaer, *Baboe Dalima* (Rotterdam, 1886), p. 383n41; this is the only source that mentions this, however.

60. Opium Interviews, 1890, no. 64.

and therefore fluctuated with general economic conditions. The repercussions of these facts for Dutch Java's opium monopoly were immense. First, the fact that the majority of opium users were native Javanese, for whose welfare the Dutch acknowledged some responsibility—rather than Chinese, who, the Dutch observed, looked after their own well-being all too well—injected into Holland's otherwise revenue-driven opium policies a small, nagging moral counterpoint. Second, the fact that the major opium market in Java was a dispersed one, made up of hundreds of thousands of individuals each of whom spent only pennies a day for opium, accounted in large measure for the pervasive nature of the institution that was designed to tap that market, the Java opium farm.

3

Opium Farms

Public ritual was an important part of the Dutch colonial style in Java. In a fashion mimicking the old state pageantry of Mataram, the Dutch made a spectacle of important occasions—the arrival of a new resident, for example, or the ascent of a regent—and in so doing acted out for spectators the social and political relationships that prevailed.

Befitting this tradition, the opium farm auctions were held in the audience hall (*pendapa*) of the residency's senior regent.[1] Here gathered all the dignitaries of the residency: the regents and lesser pryayi officials, Chinese officers, and members of the Dutch Colonial Service, all attired for an important state occasion and displaying their symbols of authority. The townspeople enjoyed a morning of excitement and color as the residency's wealthy and influential citizens convened to witness and participate in the auction. The resident himself, representing the Dutch government, was the presiding official of the auction. He would arrange to arrive last, escorted perhaps by a company of Javanese cavalry, and accompanied by a servant wielding his golden parasol of authority.[2] When he took

---

1. See Sutherland, *Making of a Bureaucratic Elite*, pp. 19–20, for the cultural significance of the *pendapa* and the regent's dwelling, the *kabupaten*.
2. See the photograph of Resident Pieter Sijtoff (Semarang) with his umbrella bearer on p. 114 of E. Breton de Nijs [Rob Nieuwenhuys], *Tempo Doeloe: Fotografische Documenten uit het Oude Indie* (Amsterdam, 1974), for the ambience of one resident's official presence.

his seat in the center of a long table facing the hall, the competition could begin.[3]

Reading in Malay, a clerk announced the terms for the competition; he identified the farm boundaries, indicated the amount of opium the government would provide the farmer, and mentioned the number of legal opium stores within the farm territory. He warned bidders against bribery, deceit, and fraud. (Witnesses remarked that participants, already familiar with the details, paid little attention to any of this.) An auctioneer then initiated the bidding.

Much was at stake. To the Dutch resident high bidding meant a hearty contribution to state coffers from his residency. This would be interpreted as an indication of the success of his administration, for in Batavia opium revenues were considered a general gauge of the prosperity of the realm and, it followed, the care of its management. For Chinese bidders the outcome meant control over the most lucrative of the government revenue farms and the patronage and prestige that went with it. Java's wealthiest merchants competed for the farms, which is the reason that the Chinese called the opium farm auction the *peperangan antara raja-raja*, or "the battle of the kings."[4]

A bid at the auction represented the amount that potential farmers were willing to pay yearly for the exclusive right to distribute and sell government opium within the farm territory, in most cases an entire residency.[5] This amount was the farm fee (*pachtschat* in Dutch, *padjek* in Malay). (It could reach enormous proportions. The Semarang farm fee was f26 million in 1881, for example, higher in later years; but even earlier in the century Semarang farm fees often approached a million guilders.)[6] Although the Dutch were wary of unrestrained speculation, they generally encouraged competition

---

3. Three descriptions of opium farm auctions are P. Meeter, "Opiumverpachting en Chineesche officieren," *IT*, October 8 and 15, 1889; *De Locomotief* (Semarang), December 6, 1872; and Piepers, *Macht tegen Recht*, p. 314.

4. Liem, *Riwajat*, p. 141.

5. At various times the farm territory was enlarged to include a cluster of residencies, or reduced to a subdivision of a residency—an afdeling or regency; but the usual unit was the residency.

6. For example, f903,000 in 1846, f960,000 in 1858. Farm fees could also dip remarkably; in 1870 the Semarang fee was only f320,000. See "Opium Rapport: Stad (en voorsteden) en Afdeeling Semarang," by Assistant Resident voor de Politie te Semarang (J.A.B. Wiselius), unpaged, 1882 in TMC, H422a; hereafter cited as Wiselius, Semarang Opium Rapport, 1882. The Koloniaal Verslagen (KVvNI) under "Verpachte Middelen" and appropriate appendices contain the annual opium farm revenues by residency.

among bidders. Residents were known to provide legitimate farm candidates with free transportation to the auction, and to serve champagne at pre-auction parties to loosen the inhibitions of potential big spenders.[7] Immediately after the bidding ended the resident cabled the auction results to the director of finance in Batavia; when the results from all the residencies were in, the governor general forwarded them to The Hague.[8]

The opium farm auctions did not occur without careful preparation. Chinese candidates studied the local conditions affecting potential farm profits and assessed just how far their own resources could be stretched in the upcoming speculation.[9] They acquired, if they could, certificates of solvency and good character from their respective residents—prerequisites for participating in the auction. Aspirant opium farmers at times even cabled the authorities in Batavia to ask about twists and turns in government policy.[10] Liem Thian Joe relates that in the days before the opium auction in Semarang, leading Chinese from all central Java converged on the city, flooding the Chinese quarter with house guests. This gave them the opportunity to test the waters for the upcoming competition. Since even among competitors it was to everyone's advantage to keep the bidding low, Liem says that in these pre-auction conferences the current farmer and his potential rivals explored possibilities for cooperating. When this succeeded, control of the farm could be brokered ahead of time, with the public bidding staged to reflect prenegotiated agreements. In such cases the "battle of the kings" still took place, but behind closed doors. (Escalating farm fees in the 1870s and 1880s seem to indicate, however, that this sort of collusion occurred less than the Dutch feared it did.) Failure to broker the auction ahead of time, on the other hand, might alert

7. "Nota: Amfioen" (unsigned) in VKG 1/5/1868/48. Ex-Director of Middelen en Domeinen (Means and Estates) C. Castens told a gathering of the Indisch Genootschap (Indies Society) of a previous director who had entertained one farmer millionaire with a trip through Java, all in an effort to loosen his pockets for an upcoming opium farm auction. Christian Castens, "De Opiumpacht op Java," *Verslagen, Vergadering Indisch Genootschap* (March 26 and April 9, 1872), p. 79.

8. See, for example, GG to MvK (telegram), November 29, 1873, in VKG 14/4/1874/11.

9. Meeter, "Opiumverpachting," p. 3, describes a notarial act in which auction tactics, a complex system of signals to encourage or discourage the designated bidder, are agreed on by kongsi members.

10. See the short unsigned and untitled article in *De Indier, Nieuwe Bataviaasch Handelsblad* (December 12, 1872), p. 968.

farm candidates to stiff competition ahead, and the need to seek partners with extra capital.[11]

For the Chinese, forming partnerships was among the most important aspects of preparing for the auctions. The Dutch required prospective farmers to have two formal guarantors who, along with the farmer, signed the farm contract and bound themselves to its obligations. In most cases these three men, the legal consignees of the farm, represented a much larger association of backers—the opium farm kongsi—who actually financed the farms.[12]

A typical farm kongsi had several members, each of whom held a certain share in the financial responsibilities and profits of the farm. The distribution of shares was agreed upon in secret notarial acts signed by kongsi members, acts that made the mutual commitments of the partners binding in the colonial courts.[13] To give one example, Tan Kam Long formed a kongsi to finance the Batavia farm in 1872. It had six members, all of whom signed a notarial act that assigned each a portion of 120 shares.[14] The kongsi partners appointed a treasurer to manage the kongsi and to see that its regular payments to the state were met; in most cases he was the official farmer. Should the farmer-treasurer renege on his responsibilities, the government could appoint another kongsi member—one of the guarantors—as farmer. And should one or several kongsi members declare bankruptcy or otherwise fail to meet their portion of kongsi obligations, the remaining solvent members were responsible for

11. Liem, *Riwajat*, p. 141; Meeter, "Opiumverpachting."

12. When discussing opium farm kongsis, I use the word *kongsi* in its general sense of a Chinese firm—*vennootschap* or *maatschappij* in Dutch: a formally constituted group of investors, frequently members of an extended family, organized to maximize the use of collective capital, and usually on a short-term basis. See Ong Eng Die, *Chinezen in Nederlandsch-Indie: Sociografie van een Indonesisch bevolkings groep* (Assen, 1939), p. 146; J.J.M. de Groot, "Kongsi," *ENI*, 2:283–84; and J. E. Albrecht, *Soerat ketrangan dari pada hal kaadaan Bangsa Tjina di Negri Hindia Olanda* (Batavia, 1890), pp. 48–50.

13. The use of notarial acts to formalize kongsi organizations is a clear result of the 1855 statute (SvNI 1855, no. 79), which placed Chinese residents of Dutch Java under Dutch civil and commercial law. Much about the opium farm kongsis was probably common knowledge among the Chinese community; for instance, when the farm kongsis settled their yearly accounts, claims by shareholders against the farm management were common grist for the gossip mill. See DMD to GG, August 16, 1866, no. 3230 in V 16/2/1867/1.

14. Oey Ekkiam vs. Khouw Tjenke, RvJ Batavia, August 4, 1876, in *IWR* no. 686, 1876. When intrakongsi squabbles reached the courts, the contents of the notarial acts became public. See the case of farm kongsi "Bie Hong," RvJ Batavia, November 11, 1886, in *IWR* no. 1331, 1888.

the entire amount, a good reason to choose one's kongsi partners with care.[15]

For their part the Dutch prepared for the auctions by collecting intelligence on the capabilities and resources of various potential opium farmers and occasionally negotiated with some of them beforehand.[16] Some kongsis had better reputations than others. Writing to the director of finance about one kongsi, Charles TeMechelen commented, "The trustworthiness of this kongsi and its proficiency in farm management is beyond doubt as far as I'm concerned, something that can hardly be said about so many others."[17] Two years later TeMechelen advised against accepting a high bid from another kongsi because of its connections with a notorious smuggling ring; besides, he added, the prospective farmer was inexperienced in farm management and still financially dependent on his father.[18] As eager as they were to encourage high farm fees, the Dutch did not accept any offer, but sought a combination of managerial expertise and financial strength. In the same way, wise kongsis would not seek a farm franchise at any price.

The Dutch authorities also tried to prevent the prolonged domination of any one opium farm, or a group of them, by one kongsi. This was another reason they encouraged competition among the Chinese for farm contracts.[19] In one such case the resident of Kediri advised the government to support any legitimate competition to Tan Kok Tong, the Chinese captain of Kediri who had monopolized the local farm for years and whose "colossal power" threatened would-be challengers.[20] In the same year the director of finance recommended government support for Surakarta farmer Tio Siong

---

15. See the case of Tan Kam Long, Landraad Batavia, March 10, 1874, and HGvNI, June 10, 1874 (appeal), in *IWR* no. 574, 1874; and Khouw Tjeng Ke vs. Oeij Ekkiam, HGvNI, April 3, 1879, in *IWR* no. 827, 1879.

16. For examples of this, see Resident Japara to TM, March 16, 1888, in V 27/11/1888/69; and Resident Pekalongan to TM, April 5, 1888, no. 55 in V 27/11/1888/69.

17. TM to DF, July 5, 1888, no. 1015 in V 27/11/1888/69. Han Liong Ing, holder of the Rembang and several other farms in the 1880s, was the leader of this kongsi. The career of Charles TeMechelen is taken up in Chapters 8 and 9, below.

18. TM to DF, October 21, 1890, no. 1737/4, in TMC H422e. For other examples of such intelligence gathering, see TM to DF, October 9, 1890, no. 1625/4; TM to DF, October 24, 1890, no. 1750/4 Geheim; and DF to GG, January 10, 1875, no. 259, all in TMC H422e. See also Rapport DF, October 5, 1889, W10 in Exh 9/8/1892/76.

19. See the comment of Resident Phitzinger of Madiun in his letter to DMD, October 1, 1866, L Geheim in V 16/2/1867/1.

20. Resident Kediri to DF, June 22, 1876, no. 3023/4292 in V 20/1/1877 (3/141).

Mo, a newcomer who had challenged the monopoly of a powerful kongsi in central Java.[21]

When it appeared that candidate farmers had conspired to keep the bidding low, or if the auction results proved unsatisfactory for another reason, the Dutch held a second public auction or accepted confidential bids.[22] This was not uncommon. In 1886, for example, twelve out of twenty opium farms went ultimately to candidates other than the original highest bidders. The refarming in that year reflected Dutch disappointment with the financial outcome of some of the auctions, as well as postauction worries about the managerial abilities and trustworthiness of some of the winning kongsis.[23]

Following final acceptance of a bid, a contract was drawn up between the new opium farmer, his guarantors, and Netherlands India. A typical contract included three articles: (1) the subject—the exclusive right to retail opium in a clearly defined territory;[24] (2) the duration of the contract—from one to three years; and (3) the price—the farm fee plus the cost of purchasing official opium from the government. Sometimes a contract included the ratio of Levant to Bengal opium the farmer was to receive and a list of all the legal opium stores in the territory.[25]

Because the Dutch repeatedly revised their opium farm system throughout the nineteenth century, in any given year the exact obligations of farmer and state were likely to be slightly different than in the previous or following term. Nevertheless, the basic arrangement between the two parties remained the same from the 1860s to the end of the century: in return for prompt and regular delivery of government opium, for the provision in some residencies

21. DF to GG, January 10, 1876, no. 259 in TMC H422e.

22. In 1871 candidate farmers conspired to submit no bids for the farm districts of Semarang, Surakarta, Yogyakarta, Kedu, Bagelen, and Banyumas as a protest against new farm regulations promulgated for 1872. See *De Locomotief*, December 15, 1871. See also DF: Konsideratien en advies, April 29, 1872, no. 6196 in V 20/8/1872/37.

23. See the chart titled "Overzigt van den loop der opiumverpachting in 1886 gehouden" in TMC H422e for the details of the 1886 farm auctions. In contrast, only two farms were refarmed in 1889. KVvNI 1890.

24. In 1864 the Supreme Court ruled that the Semarang farm territory included the entire harbor as well, even though this was not stated expressly in the farm contract. In practice this appears to be the case with other entrepot farm territories as well. See Case of Pak Kamisidin, HGvNI, November 3, 1864, in *IWR* no. 79, 1864.

25. For a Semarang farm contract, see C. Th. van Deventer, *Strafzaak Ho Tjiauw Ing; Pleidooi van den Verdediger* (Semarang, 1891), pp. 24–25.

of grounds and buildings,[26] and for the implied support of the colonial government in upholding and protecting the farm monopoly, farmers were obliged to meet their monthly obligations promptly, to keep orderly and complete records of their transactions, and to abide by the regulations of the farm system. Of these regulations a few were paramount: only official opium could be distributed via the farm apparatus; it must be processed before being sold, and sold only for cash; no more than 2 tahils (76 grams) of opium (later 1 tahil, or 38 grams) could be sold to any individual on any given day; and no opium could be sold other than in the official stores; finally, opium-free Forbidden Areas were to be honored by neighboring opium farmers.[27]

Of all the farmer's obligations to the government, the most serious was his obligation to meet his payments in full and on time. When farmers occasionally defaulted on their monthly payments, Batavia was tolerant as long as the defaults did not mount up. Farmers simply paid the fines stipulated for their lapses. But the Dutch dealt with cumulative failures more severely. Tio Siong Mo's Surakarta farm illustrates what could happen. Tio acquired his farm in 1874 and then again in 1875, this time for a three-year term. He began to lose money in January 1875, and his deficits mounted throughout the year. Tio's pleas that a portion of his obligation be deferred went unheeded, and in February 1876 the Dutch sued him. They dissolved his contract and sent him and his guarantors to prison for debt.[28] In another case a kongsi led by Tan Tjong Hoay—

26. This stipulation was added in 1861 (SvNI 1861, no. 102), probably a recognition of conditions already existing in most areas. In 1867 Surakarta farmer Carapiet Andreas (Ho Yam Lo's Armenian kongsi partner) successfully used it to force the government to provide free ground and buildings in Surakarta, despite the fact that the government owned none there. See Th. C. Andreas vs. NI, RvJ Semarang, September 11, 1867, in *IWR* no. 237, 1868; and Th. C. Andreas vs. NI (appeal) HGvNI, August 13, 1868, in *IWR* no. 302, 1869. Facilities provided by the state must have been skeletal, for records of farm expenditures regularly list additional costs for rent.

27. The basic administrative statements on the opium farm system were three Opiumpacht Reglementen: SvNI 1853, no. 87; SvNI 1874, no. 228; and SvNI 1890, no. 149. Revisions and additions occurred almost yearly, especially in the conditions (*voorwaarden*) for successive farm terms. These ordinances were included in the Staatsbladen (SvNI) and summarized under "Verpachte Middelen" in the annual Koloniaal Verslagen (KVvNI). See also Albrecht, *Soerat ketrangan*, pp. 35–38.

28. Tio Siong Mo to Tweede Kamer (lower house of the Dutch Parliament), February 1, 1876, in V 17/8/1876/74; DF to GG, April 13, 1876, no. 5076 in V 7/6/1876/32; DF to GG, May 31, 1876, no. 7364 in V 17/8/1876/74; and "Kort

which held farms in Batavia, Kedu, and Semarang in 1870 and 1871—accumulated a combined deficit of f722,418.80. The government at first agreed to a settlement in which the kongsi promised to pay off the debt in monthly installments. But when the kongsi partners quarreled over their individual obligations, the Dutch sued; five kongsi members, including Tan, were imprisoned for nonpayment of the remaining debt of nearly f600,000.[29]

Tan Tjong Hoay's experience illustrates how risky opium farming could be sometimes. For Tan the 1870–71 farm had been both financially and personally disastrous. In an attempt to meet his kongsi's obligations he sold off valuable properties, including his spacious family compound in Semarang. And in 1878, following the ultimate failure of his farm kongsi to settle its debts, Tan was forced to step down as Chinese major of Semarang.[30]

But the tables could be turned. Liem Kie Soen, the Surabaya opium farmer for 1871, successfully sued the government of Netherlands India for losses when he was forced to close his opium stores for two days because the government warehouse in Surabaya could not supply him with opium. Liem claimed that he not only lost two days' income, but that his business was permanently damaged by the shutdown. To the colonial courts the issue was clear: the government had reneged on a contractual obligation to an opium farmer. Batavia paid him nearly f150,000 in damages, costs, and interest.[31]

Once acquired, an opium farm territory was either managed as a discrete unit or subdivided into smaller farm territories each leased to a subfarmer. Such subfarming created, in fact and in law, a farm

---

overzigt van de opium pachten in Solo 1875–1877; Madoera 1881–1883, en Sumatras Westkust 1884–1886," a summary of significant farm failures drawn up for Charles TeMechelen sometime in the mid-1880s, in TMC H422e. Solo is the familiar name for the principality of Surakarta.

29. NI and Tan Ing Tjong vs. Tan Tjong Hwaij et al., HGvNI, January 24, 1878, in *IWR* no. 763, 1878.

30. Liem, *Riwajat*, pp. 142–44. Liem's chronology of the Tan Tjong Hoay affair is incorrect; he has Tan stepping down as major in 1873. Actually, his departure from office occurred during 1878. See RAvNI 1878 and 1879 (vol. 2). Liem Thian Joe is silent on the default case itself, saying simply that Tan lost heavily in the farms.

31. For details of the Liem Kie Soen affair, see the following correspondence: DF to GG, February 27, 1873, no. 3165 in V 3/7/1873/(26/1107); DF to GG, December 29, 1875, no. 16903; and DF: "Nota van toelichting," December 29, 1875, in V 21/2/1876/24; GG to MvK, January 7, 1878, no. 38/18; Verklaring: W.F.C. Eerens, March 1, 1878, no. 560; and Lim Kee Soen vs. Regeering, RvJ Surabaya, May 22, 1872 (summary of the Raad's arguments in awarding the settlement to Liem), all three in V 14/3/1878/(11/602).

within a farm. The subfarmer entered into a relationship with the farmer similar to the farmer's relationship with the state: in return for a monthly sum of money, he bought raw opium from the farmer, manufactured it, and then distributed it throughout his subsection of the farm territory at his own risk.[32] It was customary in Surabaya, for instance, for the farmer to subdivide the farm territory and release his franchise privileges to others. As Surabaya farmer, Liem Kie Soen kept one district, where he was Chinese lieutenant, for himself, and subfarmed the others. He provided his subfarmers with a portion of the official opium supply but otherwise took no hand in the management of the subfarms.[33] Tan Tong Haij's Kediri farm (1884–86) was similarly subdivided. Tan himself held the central Kediri area; the other regencies were each the responsibility of one of Tan's kongsi partners.[34]

The mutual obligations of farmers and subfarmers, like those of kongsi partners, were often formalized in notarial acts.[35] In a typical case Oeng Tjiang Tjwan agreed in a notarial act to lease a portion of the Surabaya farm from farmer Kwee Khee Soe for the sum of f7,000 per month and to pay a fine of f5,000 in case of default.[36] In another case Lim Tiong Yong contracted with Kediri farmer Kwee Swie Toan for a subfarm that included two opium stores; he agreed to pay f60 a day for one and f40 a day for the other and to offer a promissory note as security.[37] The advantage to the farmer of formalizing the farm-subfarm relationship by notarial act is illustrated in these two cases. Both subfarmers defaulted in their payments and both farmers subsequently sued them in the colonial courts, successfully, for breach of contract.[38]

For farmers there was another advantage to subfarming. Farmers

32. That subfarms were a routine feature of the opium farm system is acknowledged by inclusion of *onderpachters* as a distinct category in the frequent opium ordinances, for example in SvNI 1866, no. 117.

33. Assistant Resident voor de Policie to Resident Soerabaja, May 30, 1866, no. 1947 in V 16/1/1867/1.

34. Tan Soe Lien vs. Tan Tong Haij, HGvNI in *IWR* no. 1218, 1886.

35. After 1855 this was likely to have been nearly always the case. Java's Chinese took full advantage of the colonial legal structure in commercial affairs. This meant ratifying private transactions before a notary since a notarial act could be used as evidence in the courts.

36. Kwee Khee Soe vs. Oeng Tjiang Tjwan en Tjia Wiedjan, HGvNI, July 14, 1881, in *IWR* no. 945, 1881.

37. Lim Tiong Yong vs. Kwee Swie Toan, HGvNI, April 17, 1873, in *IWR* no. 521, 1873.

38. See the cases cited in nn. 36 and 37, above.

were legally responsible for all opium farm violations committed by their "representatives, agents, subordinates and employees,"[39] but not, the Indies Supreme Court decided in 1863, for the representatives, agents, subordinates, and employees of a subfarmer. Subfarmers, then, in the eyes of the law, were as responsible as farmers themselves in regard to violations of the opium farm regulations. Thus in the 1863 test case, subfarmers of the Surabaya farmer Lim Tekhiap were obliged to pay fines imposed because of illegal activities by their subordinates, and in 1867, in a similar case, Kediri farmer Tan Kok Tong avoided similar fines by proving (with employment documents, *piagem*) that those accused of illegal opium sales were employed by a subfarmer, not by himself.[40]

Having acquired an opium farm, or a subfarm, the farmer had to address the business of the farm itself: the manufacture of refined opium products, the sale of these products within the farm territory, and the protection of his monopoly. Virtually all opium farmers were wealthy men who invested capital in the opium farms as one among many enterprises. Not infrequently they held several farms at the same time. For these reasons management of the farm was commonly left to one or more professional managers (*kuasa pacht* and *gemachtigde*). It was these men who supervised the day-to-day operations of the opium farm, the first essential aspect of which was the manufacture of candu.

The profits of the opium farms, and the whole structure of influence and patronage which the farm system represented, rested essentially on the demand for opium among the population of Java. It was in the interests of the farmers, therefore, to provide opium products tailored to both the tastes and purses of opium smokers, and to do so in such a way as to maximize farm profit on each unit of raw opium that they processed. The crucial process was the conversion of raw opium—it arrived in sticky balls wrapped in papaver leaves—into candu, or refined opium. Depending on the efficiency of the manufacturing process, the quality of the original raw opium, and the level of adulteration in the final candu, a farmer could produce a yield of from 8 tahils (304 grams) of candu for the finest to 16 tahils (608 grams) for the crudest, from 1 kati (618 grams) of raw

39. SvNI, 1865, no. 86, art. 20.
40. Case of Lim Tekhiap, HGvNI, September 17, 1863, in *IWR* no. 15, 1863; and Tan Kok Tong, Tan Kok Liang, and Se We Soey vs. NI, HGvNI, February 7, 1867, in *IWR* no. 204, 1867.

Opium farmer–Chinese officer. From *Tijdschrift voor Nederlandsch Indie*, 15 (1853).

opium.[41] Farmers learned from experience just how much adulteration their clients would permit and adjusted their recipes accordingly.

The traditional method of refining raw opium in Java was both simple and inexact. Having removed the viscous raw opium from its papaver-leaf shell, workers scorched it over a flame, mixed it with water, and dripped it through a paper filter. It was then boiled in copper pots until it reached the desired consistency.[42] By the 1880s some larger opium farmers used steam-powered processing equipment. Han Liong Ing, for example, the Rembang opium farmer from 1887 to 1890, operated a steam-powered processing and packaging plant that employed twenty-three people.[43] Such modern equipment no doubt increased the uniformity of an opium farmer's product. Even so, opium recipes varied widely from place to place and even from day to day in the same facility. Charles TeMechelen observed the manufacture of one product in 1891 and related: "One takes a scoop of the one [ingredient], and a handful of the other; the mixture occurs without a single measurement or weight."[44]

Opium farmers ordinarily manufactured two basic sorts of candu. *Cako*, intended to be smoked pure with an opium pipe, was for the Chinese-pryayi market. It contained a high proportion of morphine-rich Bengal opium and was laced with a small quantity of sugar syrup. *Cakat*, prepared for the mass market, was made largely from cheaper and less potent Turkish opium and mixed with either a burnt-sugar or lemon-juice extract and a quantity of jicing (scrapings from a used pipe). Farmers blended cakat, a thin syrup, with finely chopped awar-awar leaves to make tiké, one of the most commonly consumed opium preparations in Java.[45] This is one

41. TM to DF, September 16, 1887, no. 1171/4 Geheim in TMC H422c; TM: Rapport 1888; and J. Haak, *Opiumregie*, p. 13.

42. J. Haak, a chemist who visited one such plant in 1889, pointed out that the process was wasteful of morphine at two points, scorching and boiling. Steam processing eliminated losses at the boiling stage because uniform temperatures were possible. Haak, *Opiumregie*, pp. 29–30.

43. TM to DF, September 16, 1887, no. 1171/4 Geheim in TMC H422c. Han's factory consumed 2 piculs (123.6 kilograms) of bamboo leaves—used to wrap tiké portions—40 katis (24.7 kilograms) of burnt sugar, 40 katis sugar syrup, and 24,000 tin boxes every month. In 1883 there were five steam-powered opium processors in Java. KVvNI 1885, Bijl. HH, no. 35.

44. TM to DF, February 16, 1891, no. 169/12, p. 27 in Exh 9/8/1892/76.

45. For candu processing, see DMD to GG, August 16, 1866, no. 3230 in V 16/2/1867/1; TM to DF, September 16, 1887, no. 1171/4 Geheim in TMC H422c; and TM: Rapport 1888, pp. 15–16 in TMC H422a. Farmers were sometimes un-

reason why the legion of Javanese peasants who smoked small amounts of tiké daily were vastly more important to the opium farm than the small number of well-to-do customers who preferred a more refined product.[46]

Manufacturing candu and tiké was, then, a basic element in an opium farmer's business. The efficiency with which he did it, and the skill with which he adulterated his products, affected the profits of the farm. A more important component of an opium farm, however, was the farmer's distribution network—his organization. It was the farmer's organization, distributing and selling farm opium and policing the farm's monopoly privileges, which brought opium and its bearers into the Javanese countryside.

A unique document permits us to examine one farm organization in some detail. It is a complete ledger for Djie Bok Hien's Madiun opium farm for May 1888.[47] Altogether Djie's farm contained 57 official opium stores and employed 293 people.[48] It was not subfarmed, but subdivided into five districts that corresponded to Madiun's administrative afdelings. Each of these had a separate management and budget. Atop the whole structure stood Sie Djong Gim. As Djie's superintending administrator (*kuasa pacht*), it was his responsibility to arrange for the transshipment of government opium from the Surabaya warehouses to Madiun and to apportion the monthly allotment among the five subdistricts. He also supervised the flow of opium revenues throughout the farm, receiving regular payments from the district managers and keeping the cen-

willing to accept confiscated clandestine opium, as stipulated by law, because it disrupted their Levant-Bengal ratio, and thus their formulas. See G. T. Rouffaer, *Indische Aanteekeningen gedurende mijne 1e reis (Nov 1885–Febr 1890)*, the section marked "Aanteekeningen over Opium," pp. 835–60, in Rouffaer Collection, KITLV H721. This is Rouffaer's handwritten notebook on several Netherlands India subjects. Hereafter cited as Rouffaer, "Indische Aanteekeningen."

46. On the relative profitability of tiké, see DF to GG, May 22, 1891, no. 7637, folio 10 in TMC H422c; TM: Rapport 1888; and TM to DF, December 11, 1888, no. 1693/4 ("Nota voor den Directeur van Financien betreffende de uitkomsten van de tijdelijke exploitatie en het beheer der Solosche opiumpacht voor Gouvernements rekening") in VKG 25/3/1889/T4.

47. "Staat Boelan Madioen Pacht," May 1888, in VKG 23/11/1888/F17. The section that follows is based entirely on this document unless otherwise cited. The ledger includes a "Staat Boelan" (monthly statement) for each of the five Madiun farm subdistricts, a "Recapitulatie" of major expenditures by category (salaries, rent, manufacturing supplies, post, and so on) and an "Overzigt" of farm sales from January 1 to June 30, 1888. It is drawn up in Malay.

48. The farm actually employed more people than this, including *mata-mata gelap*, secret agents.

tral books and treasury. All other important activities of the Madiun farm were organized and performed at the district level. A closer look at the farm organization in one district illustrates the main features and activities of the farm organization at large.

The Ngawi farm district was run by a manager, Tan Tjieng Yang. His staff in the regency capital (and the seat of an assistant resident) included an assistant manager, a treasurer, a secretary and assistant secretary, and a cashier. Attached to the farm office was a group of seven farm *mata-mata* (agents, or spies) and one *kepala mata-mata* (head agent), whose job it was to enforce the farm monopoly. There were also the employees of the local processing plant: two weighers, one foreman, and fifteen workers. These workers no doubt did other jobs as well, such as transporting opium to the district's eleven opium stores. Also on the payroll were one Javanese boy servant and two stall boys to care for the farm's horses.[49] The eleven opium stores in the Ngawi farm district were each manned by a Chinese branch manager, the *bandar*, and a weigher; four of them had mata-mata assigned to them. Of the employees of the Ngawi farm district, only some of the mata-mata and an occasional servant were Javanese.[50] The Ngawi farm organization was essentially a Chinese organization.

Ngawi's May 1888 ledger indicates something more of the routine activities of the farm organization. Expenditures are listed for purchasing raw materials for making and packaging opium products (tobacco, awar-awar leaves, charcoal, and rice wine, for instance—in Ngawi rice wine was part of the local tiké recipe); for making tours of inspection of the opium stores; for entertaining guests; for telegrams, stamps, ink, and stationery; and for a contribution to the poor, of 60 cents. The ledger also shows that mata-mata and workers received part of their wages in opium.[51] Although wages and salaries account, cumulatively, for the lion's share of the monthly budget, the largest single entries in the Staat relate to the crucial

49. Ledgers of other districts include additional employees such as coachmen, drivers, cooks, and water carriers.

50. The stall boys and perhaps one or two of the workers could have been Javanese; the "Staat" refers to them only by occupation. In other district staats where names of workers are given, however, they are exclusively Chinese.

51. *Rangsoen* or *rantsoenen* was the amount of opium farmers set aside for their own personnel. It was sometimes used as a bookkeeping heading to disguise illegal distributions of opium, or so thought Charles TeMechelen. TM to DF, April 3, 1892, no. 724/12 in Exh 9/8/1892/76.

areas of intelligence gathering and farm security: investigating violations of the farm monopoly and paying bounties for successful
detective work on behalf of the farm.[52] These two items, together
with wages paid to mata-mata, account for one-fourth of the Ngawi
farm district's operating expenses.

The Madiun farm organization was typical in its general characteristics. All farms were pyramidal in structure. At the top stood the
farmer himself, legal holder of the franchise and chief patron of the
organization; at the (official) bottom stood the employees attached
to the numerous local opium stores. But between top and bottom
there were a variety of intermediate levels. The relationship between these levels, and indeed whether they were of the subfarm or
district management variety, was affected by several factors. Among
these were the farmer's own strength as measured by his wealth,
influence, and patronage; the structure and membership of the
farm kongsi; the conditions affecting opium sales and farm operations peculiar to a particular region (coastal residencies and residencies with a high Chinese population posed special problems); and
the personal relationship between individuals active in the organization. A son, brother, or uncle, for example, or a kongsi member,
would presumably participate on more favorable or perhaps informal terms than a distant cousin or outsider. An opium farm might
therefore resemble—to emphasize the extremes—anything from a
highly centralized, systematically organized business on the one
hand, to a rickety scaffolding of subfarms on the other.

Two arrangements that illustrate the variety in opium farm structure are the terms by which opium changed hands within the farm,
and the level at which it was processed. In a subfarm the subfarmer
contracted to buy opium at a fixed price from the farmer, paid a
farm fee, and took full legal responsibility for farm activities within
his district.[53] A district manager, however, may have been simply an
employee of the farm. If so, he might either purchase opium from
the farm at an agreed-upon price and remit a percentage of the
profits (keeping a percentage for his own share),[54] or sell regular
opium allotments from the central farm on a commission-plus-
salary basis. Similar variety surely existed between the district dis-

52. Under the heading *tjari ketrangan dan beli pertjobahan*.
53. See the cases cited above in reference to subfarming, pp. 51–52.
54. This is how Ho Tjiauw Ing's Surakarta farm worked; see Resident Surakarta to
DF, January 9, 1889, no. 242/20 in MR 136, 1889.

tribution centers and the stores themselves. As for processing, candu was manufactured in no fewer than eighteen places within Tio Siong Mo's Solo farm of the mid-1870s, an extreme case.[55] By contrast, in the Yogyakarta farm of the mid-1860s, all official candu was manufactured in the royal city and distributed every ten days to sales agents in eighty-four outlying stores.[56] With the introduction of steam processing, centralized manufacturing probably increased. It seems probable, however, that in most cases the level at which opium was processed related more to the nature of intrafarm relationships. Processing in the capital for the entire territory indicated a more highly organized, centrally administered farm organization headed by a strong farmer.

Opium stores represented the lower level of the official opium farm organization. Their number and location were determined by the colonial administration and stipulated in the farm contract. At midcentury, Dutch officials had begun systematically reducing the number of these stores throughout Java, and by 1866 the number of officially recognized opium stores was only one-third what it had been in 1851—a reduction from 2,664 to 876.[57] The number reached its lowest point in 1874 and then began to rise again in response to the apparent failure of the reduction policy in circumscribing opium consumption (its avowed purpose) and in response to numerous petitions from farmers who said that an artificial reduction in the number of opium outlets hurt farm business (not to mention government revenues) by playing into the hands of black marketeers.[58] Nevertheless, by 1890 there were still fewer than one thousand for the entire island.[59]

These stores, located throughout each farm about 8 to 16 kilometers apart, represented only the midpoint in the progress of opium

55. DF to GG, May 31, 1876, no. 7364 in V 17/8/1876/74. An article in the Opium Reglement stipulating one central manufacturing plant and one central warehouse per residency (SvNI 1874, no. 228), like so many other opium regulations, obviously went unenforced.

56. Resident Yogyakarta to DMD, August 14, 1866, no. 2264 in V 16/2/1867/1; and "Staat van het aantal amfioenkitten of verkoopplaatsen op Java en Madura gedurende de jaren 1860, 1861, 1862, 1863, 1864, 1865, 1866," in V 16/2/1867/1.

57. DMD to GG, September 12, 1866, no. 3563, and "Staat van het aantal amfioenkitten, etc.," both in V 16/2/1867/1.

58. See, for example, Besluit, Resident Surakarta, July 16, 1875, no. 188/2484 in V 17/8/1876/74; Wiselius, Semarang Opium Rapport, 1882. Resident Japara to DF, February 9, 1892, no. 1350/18, Resident Semarang to DF, March 4, 1892, no. 2490/49, and Resident Kediri to DF, February 22, 1892 (no number), all in V 15/6/1892/26.

59. Anon., "Het getal opiumkitten op Java," IG, 2 (1888), 1927.

from the opium farmer to its final consumer. (In the Madiun farm there was roughly one official store for fifteen thousand people.) Although itinerants and others routinely used them as opium dens, such stores were actually distribution centers from which opium entered the urban Chinese neighborhoods and the Javanese village world.[60] In every opium farm residency there were hundreds, and in some cases thousands, of illegal opium stores and dens,[61] as many as thirteen thousand in Java and Madura in 1890.[62] Candu and tiké were also hawked from village to village and door to door by local vendors.[63] These clandestine outlets and those who operated them were most commonly known as *patungan;* hence, the phenomenon of myriad unofficial opium dens, stores, and peddlers operating beneath the level of the official farm stores was known as the patungan trade.[64] The patungan trade, or system, was the invisible base of the farm organization. It catered to the needs of the majority of Java's opium-smoking people and was the component of the opium farm system most familiar to the Javanese.

Like the farm organization, the patungan system was more various than uniform. A patungan opium den could be anything from an exclusive Chinese opium-smoking club to a one-room bamboo hut;[65] in Madiun, and presumably elsewhere, opium was readily

60. Wiselius, Semarang Opium Rapport, 1882.
61. In 1889 Resident P. F. Wegener of Semarang estimated that there were, and had been for years, approximately seventeen hundred such patungans in his residency. See Resident Semarang to GG, November 25, 1889, no. 16617/49 in VKG 1/2/1890/H1. The resident of Surakarta admitted in 1889 that his residency contained at least three hundred illegal opium dens. Resident Surakarta to DF, January 9, 1889, no. 242/20 in MR 136, 1889.
62. TM to DF, March 24, 1892, no. 651/4 in V 15/6/1892/26.
63. Tan Ting San wrote Charles TeMechelen in 1891 that in Rembang opium could be purchased "everywhere in the countryside" ("di mana mana desa dan kampong"). Tan Ting San to TM, undated (but from the context sometime in 1891) in TMC H422c.
64. Rouffaer, "Indische Aanteekeningen"; Resident Rembang to DF, February 20, 1892, no. 797/39 and TM to DF, March 24, 1892, no. 651/4 in V 15/6/1892/26. Patungans were also known as *brandon, tempilan, perembe,* and *titipan,* depending on local usage.
65. See the 1858 correspondence concerning Tan Tjong Hoay and C. Andreas's request that twenty-one houses in the Semarang Chinese camp where opium was available for the private, secluded enjoyment of well-to-do Chinese be freed of police harassment, in VKG 1/2/1890/H1. The authorities agreed. In 1889 the issue of these "gentlemen's societies" came up again. At that time signs saying "Opium House" (probably *roemah tjandoe* or *roemah madat*) hung outside their doors. According to Semarang Resident Wegener they had degenerated into "wretched, small and filthy hovels." Resident Semarang to GG, November 25, 1889, no. 16617/49 in VKG 1/2/1890/H1. Village smoking places, usually ramshackle huts, were called *bumbungan.*

available in common food stalls.[66] Local farm bandars employed hawkers to peddle their product in the villages. Given a discount on their opium purchases, and the opportunity to stretch their supplies by adding more adulterants, these petty traders often sold candu and tiké more cheaply than the official stores. In addition, farm employees receiving a portion of their wages in opium—mata-mata in particular—supplemented their incomes by peddling. Most clandestine dens were small buildings operated by a local Javanese or Chinese who purchased opium from the farm store and offered it to a regular clientele.[67] Government regulations limiting opium sales from farm stores to 2 tahils (76 grams) per person per day hardly touched the patungan trade; 2 tahils of candu represented, after all, 200 one-mata portions, or 600 or more gelengs of tiké![68]

The patungan trade penetrated areas closed to the official farm organization: the Forbidden Areas, private lands, and leasehold plantations. The availability of opium in the Forbidden Areas, even the prized Priangan regencies, was well known; and the presence of clandestine opium dens on private lands—and on the leasehold plantations which mushroomed after the Agrarian Law of 1870, especially those in central and east Java—was also common knowledge. Moreover, it was widely believed that the large number of laborers required to maintain commercial agriculture would flee any enterprise that did not provide opium. Many managers, therefore, arranged for the nearest farm store to supply regular amounts to a patungan agent located on plantation property. Some even participated actively in the trade themselves.[69] One Dutch admin-

66. TM to DF, October 9, 1890, no. 1625/4 Geheim in TMC H422e.
67. Rembang Resident A. C. Uljee offered the opinion that patungan traders were usually poor peasants who sold opium on commission for others to support their own addiction. Resident Rembang to DF, February 20, 1892, no. 797/39 in V 15/6/1892/26. On patungans, see also Resident Pekalongan to DMD, May 30, 1866, no. 1514 in V 16/2/1867/1; Wiselius, Semarang Opium Rapport, 1882; and Rouffaer, "Indische Aanteekeningen," p. 853. Chemist J. Haak found that opium purchased from patungans in small quantities was inferior in quality to opium purchased directly from the farm store. Haak, *Opiumregie*, p. 14. See also the case of The Kong, a patungan opium peddler in Japara accused of adulterating opium given him by the farmer to sell. Landraad Japara, October 7, 1878, in *IWR* no. 804, 1878.
68. See Cirkulaire DMD, May 14, 1866, no. 1865 in V 16/2/1867/1, in which C. Castens recommended this limitation in the interest of squelching the patungan trade ("de heimelijke kolportage van opium"), and the ordinance that made it policy later the same year, SvNI 1866, no. 117.
69. The firm of Rijk Grosskamp of Surabaya was reputed to have computed the salaries of its plantation personnel on the basis of income generated by clandestine opium sales on its various properties. TM to DF, October 3, 1891, no. 850/12 in V 11/4/1892/130.

istrator familiar with local conditions in the coffee plantations of Pasuruan predicted doomsday should the plantation patungan traffic be harassed or abolished. Parcels located some distance from the farm store, he said, would fail because their workers would flee. Smuggling would flourish and with it widespread official corruption; all this would precipitate a fatal economic crisis.[70] Although there was some disagreement on this issue, most men on the spot agreed that the plantation patungan trade should be countenanced in the greater interest of Java's developing commercial economy.[71]

Just how important the patungan system was to opium farmers is illustrated by a letter from Tan Ting San to Charles TeMechelen in 1891. Tan represented a kongsi planning to bid on the Rembang opium farm of 1892 and bluntly asked if the future farmer, like the present one, would be permitted to maintain as many clandestine opium dens as he wished. If assured that the resident would continue to wink at the patungan trade, Tan said, he would pay a higher farm fee than the current farmer.[72]

The patungan trade was, in fact, the lifeblood of the farm. Patungans did what the official farm organization could not do—they forged the final link in the opium-distribution chain. For the farmer, the patungan system, if permitted by the authorities to flourish—as it was for most of the nineteenth century—was an efficient and inexpensive means of reaching as many consumers as possible, far less expensive than maintaining a comparable number of official stores.[73]

But much that went on in the patungan trade was beyond the farmer's reach, for here the legal and the clandestine markets overlapped. Given opportunity and incentives, peddlers who hawked

70. Assistant Resident Malang to Resident Pasuruan, March 17, 1890, no. 15/10 in V 11/4/1892/130.

71. See the comments made by members of the Blitar Agricultural Society (Blitarsche Landbouwvereeniging) at their meeting of September 10, 1887, in Blitar, Kediri. "Bespreking van de opium quaestie en de invoering van het licentie-stelsel door de Blitarsche Landbouwvereeniging, 10 sept 1887, Blitar," *Tijdschrift voor Nijverheid en Landbouw in Nederlandsch-Indie*, 36 (1888), 50–53. On opium sales and plantations, see the reports of M. Stoll (Assistant Resident Malang): Assistant Resident Malang to Resident Pasuruan, February 17, 1890, no. 12/10, and March 17, 1890, no. 15/10 in V 11/4/1892/130; and March 21, 1891, no. 27/10 in MR 348, 1891. Also TM to DF, October 3, 1891, no. 850/12 in V 11/4/1892/130. A specific case of a clandestine opium den located on a private estate in Buitenzorg and supplied via the farm is discussed in HIOR to DF, September 30, 1902, no. 2478/R in VKG 7/10/1903/015.

72. Tan Ting San to TM, undated (1891), in TMC H422c.

73. Resident Semarang to DF, March 4, 1892, no. 2490/49 in V 15/6/1892/26.

the farmer's opium might easily augment their supplies from another source, as could local den holders. The patungan trade was a
petty trade. Far more so than at the farm level, prices fluctuated with
competition, varying from place to place and day to day. Exchange
by barter and selling opium on credit were more common. It was for
the purpose of exercising surveillance over the patungan trade and,
to the extent possible, controlling it, that farmers employed mata-
mata. It was their job to penetrate the patungan world and to see to
it that the profits therefrom flowed toward the farm.

Opium farm mata-mata were variously policemen and detectives,
thugs and criminals. They were the farmer's men, his operatives. He
employed them to enforce his monopoly and to protect his interests—both licit and illicit. For this reason, they frequently appeared
working hand-in-hand with local Javanese authorities investigating
suspected smugglers and black marketeers and providing evidence
against them in court; and just as frequently—for the same reasons—they also turned up as extortionists and enforcers, using the
threat of an opium frame-up to neutralize or punish enemies of the
farmer or his representatives.[74] In many areas mata-mata routinely
paid visits to farm customers who, having lapsed in their regular
purchases, were suspected of buying on the black market. Although
forbidden by law, it is obvious from the scandal they created that on
such occasions farm mata-mata often searched both the bodies and
the homes of suspects and victims with little regard for their privacy
or modesty.[75] Opium farmers hired mata-mata for their local
knowledge, cunning, and their abilities at *silat*, the Javanese art of
bodily self-defense (and aggression). Most of them were Javanese.[76]

74. Mata-mata frequently turn up in transcripts of court cases involving opium
violations. See Case of Gouw Asek, RvJ Batavia, May 23, 1866, in *IWR* no. 156, 1866,
and the case of E. A. In 't veld Francis, RvJ Batavia, August 24, 1872, and HGvNI,
October 18, 1872, in *IWR* nos. 483 and 496, 1872. The threat of being "framed" for
illegal possession of opium by farm operatives is one of the most familiar stories told
of opium farm activities.

75. See Tio Siong Mo's petition to the Dutch Parliament (Tweede Kamer, lower
house), February 1, 1876, in V 17/8/1876/74 and DF to GG, May 31, 1876, no. 7364
in V 17/8/1876/74, on the subject of Tio's bold assertion that farm operatives regularly did, and should, perform investigative functions including house searching
and frisking in opium cases. Also TM to Resident Japara, December 31, 1882, no.
2694/10 in TMC H422a and TM to DF, February 16, 1891, no. 169/12 in Exh
9/8/1891/76.

76. Liem, *Riwajat*, pp. 98–100, recalls farmer Tan Hong Yan hiring toughs—silat
specialists ("jang poenjaken kepandean silat dan brani")—to protect his opium shipments en route, and comments on farm use of Javanese mata-mata to combat

Like the patungan trade, a network of mata-mata was an institutionalized feature of the opium farm system.[77]

The farm organization—both the official one and the patungan
system on which it depended—represented, then, a pyramidal network of commercial and personal relationships harnessed to reap
the profits of selling opium in Java. It was blessed with monopoly
privileges, and it penetrated to the most basic levels of society. How
much money farmers really made from their farms was never revealed. Certainly the sums that farmers paid to the state—representing who knows what part of their true gains—often reached
staggering proportions; and the collective memory of the Javan
Chinese attributes most of the fortunes of its nineteenth-century
Chinese heroes—men like Ho Yam Lo, Tan Hong Yan, Be Ing
Tjioe, and Oei Tiong Ham—to opium farm profits.[78]

As economic institutions of pervasive influence opium farms generated wealth in many ways. But even when viewed strictly, as
discrete businesses, opium farms were certainly attractive investments for individuals with capital. The initial investment, especially
if one combined with others in a kongsi, was not so intimidating as
the yearly farm fees might suggest. This is because the fees were
paid on a monthly basis; the opium that farmers bought from the
government was also paid for monthly. In good times the initial
expenses for taking over the processing facilities and inventories
from the previous farm, and for the first allotment of government
opium, could be recovered reasonably quickly from daily receipts.
The rest of the farm capital lay in buildings, inventories, goods,
tools, and implements, which could be sold or leased to an incoming
farmer when the farm changed hands again. The first part of any
farm term was always the most difficult. Outgoing farmers routinely
sold off their left-over opium at low prices and thus saturated the
market for the first months of a new farm tenure. When this surplus

---

Javanese black-market activities. A Javanese short story, "Tjandoe Peteng Toewin
Panjegahipoen," about farm days, tells of one Djarat's recruitment as a mata-mata by
the local farm bandar. Djarat, a silat expert, succeeds in foiling a smuggling attempt
by a down-at-the-heels priyayi, Den Dira. In G.W.J. Drewes, *Eenvoudig Hedendaagsch
Javaansch Proza* (Leiden, 1946), pp. 61–71. Translated for me by Onghokham.

77. Mata-mata accounted for a large proportion of black-market opium confiscations. See Th. C. Andreas vs. NI, RvJ Semarang, September 11, 1867, in *IWR* no. 237,
1868; TM: Rapport 1888; DMD to GG, August 16, 1866, no. 3230 in V 16/2/1867/1
and Resident Surakarta to DF, January 9, 1889, no. 242/20 in MR 136, 1889.

78. Liem, *Riwajat*, pp. 98, 100, 121, 151, 181.

dissipated, however, and the new farmer's organization (perhaps incorporating some of the old one) was established and running smoothly, an opium farm could be quite profitable.[79]

Nevertheless, opium farming was not a simple business. As we have noted, opium sales fluctuated with the yearly peasant and plantation agricultural cycles and with general rises and falls in economic prosperity over the years. Natural disasters such as floods and crop failures also affected sales, as did the fortunes of local plantation enterprises.[80] Farm profits also depended on other variables, including the skillful manufacture of candu and tiké, the efficiency of farm management, and the local knowledge and trustworthiness of farm employees. Profits rose proportionally with sales to Javanese, and farm agents actively promoted opium sales among the peasantry.[81]

The most vexing and complex variable affecting opium farm profits, however—the one that determined the price a farmer could ask for his products as well as the share of the market he could command—was the problem of supply. Official allotments to farmers were usually insufficient to meet the demands of the market, and they were expensive besides. This is why many opium farmers supplemented their official opium with "unofficial" opium. For his farm to succeed a farmer had either to suppress competition from clandestine dealers in his territory—the work of his mata-mata—or meet it by introducing cheaper opium himself, in effect becoming a smuggler, too. Opium farmers customarily tried both. Under the guise of protecting the state monopoly, opium farmers exploited both their own organizations and the administrative and legal apparatus of Dutch Java to gain control over the distribution of *all* opium in their territories, legal or not. Smuggling was therefore an integral part of the opium farm system.

79. On the topic generally, see the fifty-page report TM to DF, May 31, 1889, no. 640/4 Geheim in Exh 9/8/1892/76.

80. Tan Tong Haij, Kediri farmer (1875–77), claimed that the 1875 *moddervloed*— prolonged wet season, flooding—in Kediri placed unreasonable strain on his ability to meet his farm commitments. GG to MvK, November 1, 1876, no. 1810/24 in V 20/1/1877/(3/141).

81. Local farm bandars and low-volume patungan operators, it appears, engaged in promotional activities far more than did farmers themselves and their immediate subordinates. For a committed antiopium Dutchman's characterization of mata-mata in the role of promoter, see the story of Singomengolo in Perelaer, *Baboe Dalima*, pp. 81–92.

4

Smuggling and the Black Market

The opium poppy (*papaver somniferum*) was not cultivated in Java.[1] In the nineteenth century virtually all the official opium consumed there originated in Turkey and Persia or in British Bengal. The Indies government purchased it through private Dutch merchants in the Levant, at the Calcutta auctions, or from agency houses in British Singapore,[2] and doled it out at regular intervals to Java's opium farmers from warehouses in Batavia, Semarang, and Surabaya.[3]

1. Suggestions that opium might be cultivated in Netherlands India were made from time to time, almost always with reference to Britain's lucrative Bengal monopoly, but the archipelago lacked the necessary combination of climate, altitude, and terrain for successful large-scale production. See A.J.W. van Delden, "Beschouwingen over het denkbeeld om in Ned. Indie van Regeeringswege opium te produceeren," *Blik op het Indisch Staatsbestuur* (Batavia, 1875), pp. 274–84.

2. Among the agency houses that purchased Levant opium for sale to the Netherlands for the Indies market in the 1870s and 1880s were Levantsche Vereeniging Rotterdam, A. Lavino and Co., Dulith and Co., and E. A. Wissing. For more detail on aspects of this trade, see G. W. Koning, Levantsche Vereeniging Rotterdam to MvK, August 21, 1875 in VKG 24/8/1875/L20; Dulith and Co., A. Lavino, E. A. Wissing, and N. Wissing to Koning, July 29, 1882 in V 6/9/1882/63; and MvK to GG, April 13, 1887, no. 39/597 in V 13/4/1887/(39/597). For transactions in Bengal, see van Delden, *Blik*, p. 276, and Frederic Martin, *The Statesman's Yearbook* (London, 1874), pp. 657–58. On buying in Singapore, see Consul-Generaal (Netherlands) Singapore to GG, January 30, 1886, no. 113 in V 8/3/1886/4 regarding the purchase of 900 piculs by an agent of the Dutch Trading Company (Nederlandsche Handelmaatschappij, or NHM).

3. See the chart titled "Hoeveelheden Levantsche opium [*tiban*] die gedurende het jaar 1870 maandelijks aan de pachters moeten worden verstrekt," included in GG to MvK, March 2, 1870, no. 335 in V 12/4/1870/24.

Monopolizing the importation of raw opium to Java was the single long-term administrative measure taken by the Dutch to control the amount of opium that reached the population. In theory, using the monopoly to limit the amount of official opium meant that less opium would be available for consumption. Moreover, by charging farmers an inflated price for official opium and encouraging high farm fees, Dutch authorities argued that opium would be too expensive to spread widely among the masses. Therefore, except for a brief period from 1855 to 1861 and again from 1870 to 1872, Batavia placed limitations on the amount of opium that was available to each farm. Opium farmers received an arbitrary allotment (based on an uninformed estimate of the market) for which they paid an inflated price.

It was a weak policy. In supplying too little opium the Dutch created a demand for an alternative source. And in charging too much for it, they guaranteed profits for black-market suppliers. Furthermore, because the essential Dutch interest in opium lay in farm revenues, opium laws unrelated to prompt fulfillment of farm financial obligations were enforced weakly, not least because policing these regulations fell to indigenous Javanese authorities and to the opium farm itself. The combination of a flawed policy, a largely indirect colonial administration, and Java's long, vulnerable coastline created conditions ideal for a black market. Clandestine opium poured into Java.

It came by way of Europe, China, Singapore, and countless smaller states and entrepots. Like official opium, most of it came originally from the Middle East and British India; and most of it reached Java after having changed hands in Singapore and again in Bali. From Bali it penetrated Java. Here it both supplemented and competed with legal farm opium. "One may rest assured," wrote Christian Castens, the Batavia official responsible for opium affairs in the mid-1860s and one of the first to make a serious on-the-spot study of opium in Java, "that scarcely a day passes in which a significant quantity of [illegal] opium is not imported, if not here, then there upon the island of Java." Castens calculated that "the amount of such in a year's time far exceeds the quantity supplied by the government as legal opium."[4] In his estimation, 60 percent of the opium consumed in central Java was clandestine.[5] His assess-

4. DMD to GG, May 31, 1866, no. 2093 (Zeer Geheim) in V 16/2/1867/1.
5. DMD to GG, August 16, 1866, no. 3230 in V 16/2/1867/1.

ment was corroborated by other experts in later decades, and the weight of the evidence in retrospect also supports it. At least half of the opium consumed in Java during this period was officially illegal.[6]

Newspaper accounts, administrative records, and court transactions reveal how common opium smuggling was. The ease with which raw opium could be purchased in Singapore, China, or free harbors in the Indonesian Archipelago, and the equal ease with which it could be brought past the inefficient and overtaxed customs facilities of Dutch Java, made opium smuggling a reasonable risk for almost anyone.[7] Thus, alongside large shipments arranged by, or in competition with, opium farm interests and handled by professional merchant smugglers, came thousands of small parcels carried by others: small-time professional smugglers, amateurs hoping for a windfall, Europeans and Eurasians seeking a once-and-for-all solution to their debts, and many who simply carried clandestine opium for the private enjoyment of themselves and their friends. It came inter alia secreted in false-bottomed trunks, packed amid personal effects, and stuffed inside animal carcasses and fruit.

Most important were the volume shipments ordered by Java's wealthy Chinese merchants: opium farmers and their adversaries. Farmers and heavy-volume smugglers, if not one and the same, came from the same Javan elite. Because farm terms lasted a maximum of three years, there were always would-be or former farmers, some of them disappointed farm candidates backed by kongsis, who possessed the capital, client organization, and the know-how to compete with the farm. Several opium kongsis stayed in business irrespective of whether they held a farm or not. Opium smuggling was, in short, a routine part of Chinese commercial competition, another aspect of the "battle of the kings."

The geography of the Indonesian Archipelago and the variety of its political forms in the nineteenth century made possibilities for smuggling almost limitless. Sooner or later someone tried nearly every variation. Described here is the prevailing pattern of bringing

6. See, for example, Wiselius, Opium Rapport Semarang, 1882; and Assistant Resident Joana to Resident Japara, December 31, 1882, no. 2694/10 in TMC H422a.

7. As late as 1903 the chief of the Opium Regie, A. A. de Jongh, pointed out in a letter to the governor general both the impracticality (it was both expensive and an "impediment to trade") and the ultimate impossibility (opium was too easy to hide) of depending on customs to curtail illegal opium imports. HIOR to GG, September 18, 1903, no. 2554/R in V 13/1/1904/34.

clandestine opium into Java during the 1880s. It was a successful pattern because it exploited Dutch Java's geographical and institutional vulnerabilities effectively, and because it was flexible—it could be altered, simplified, or embellished as circumstances required.

Each smuggling venture began with the purchase of raw opium. The Chinese instigator of the venture in Java may have had direct connections in Singapore for this purpose, his relatives, for example. But most of them appear to have used the intermediary services of locally based trading houses that dealt in wholesale opium.[8] Armenian firms with offices in Surabaya dominated this trade.[9] They purchased opium via agents in Turkey, India, and Singapore for their Chinese clients and delivered it in Bali.[10] Chinese buyers settled their accounts with bills of exchange drawn on colonial banks, such as the Javasche Bank in Semarang, just as they would for any legitimate import.[11] Another group of middlemen handled smaller accounts for smugglers with limited operations or riskier credit, buying opium in bulk from Armenian or Chinese wholesalers and reselling in smaller lots to their clients.[12]

8. In an earlier period these firms evidently took advantage of an ordinance promulgated in 1854 permitting raw opium to be stored in Java's major entrepots—officially only for reshipment—to disguise their trade with local customers. SvNI 1854, no. 94. See Pahud de Montanges, "Nota betreffende de geschiedenis der opiumaangelegenheden in Nederlandsch-Indie van 1816 tot 1890," in V 29/9/1891/37, folios 12 and 13.

9. Assistant Resident Joana to Resident Japara, December 31, 1882, no. 2694/10 in TMC H422a; Assistant Resident Joana to Resident Japara, April 13, 1883, no. 622/10 in TMC H422b; Resident Bali and Lombok to TM, February 11, 1892, no. 14 (Geheim) in Exh 9/8/1892/76. Among the Armenian trading houses that dealt in opium were Polack; Joakim; Johannes; Sarkies, Edgar; and Zorab Mesrope.

10. The 1879 account books of clandestine opium dealer Njo Tjiauw Ging show, for example, a f150,000 credit for what Charles TeMechelen interpreted to be opium transactions (such transactions were recorded in code). TM to DF, August 3, 1889, no. 199/12 in V 27/5/1890, no. 111.

11. Assistant Resident voor de Policie (Surabaya) to Resident Surabaya, March 22, 1865, no. 473 in V 16/2/1867/1. TM: Rapport 1888; and Wiselius, Opium Rapport Semarang, 1882. Assistant Resident Wiselius examined records of such transactions in the Javasche Bank (Semarang Branch) for the period January to June 1879, during which time f700,000 changed hands in opium transactions.

12. The McAllister, arriving in Buleleng, Bali, in May 1892, brought shipments of several chests of raw opium for Edgar, Zorab Mesrope, and one Hing Lee, and smaller quantities for five other Chinese dealers, most of whose names were romanized in the English rather than the Dutch manner (e.g., Ek Choon, Hoon Chiang), suggesting that they were agents of Singapore firms. From notes in TeMechelen's files, most likely an intelligence report, dated 1892 Buleleng in TMC H422b.

Bali was the ideal site for transshipping opium. In and out of its numerous natural harbors thousands of indigenous craft carried on a lively commerce in local island produce. Trade between Bali and Javan ports was heavy most of the year; the monsoon made sailing hospitable from April to December. This active waterborne traffic served as the perfect cover for shipping illegal goods. In the nineteenth century Dutch authority was exercised in only certain of Bali's kingdoms, and there only lightly. In Buleleng, for example, a Dutch government territory and seat of an assistant resident from 1861, the opium farm regulations officially permitted the farmer to export large quantities of opium. From Bali, opium was transshipped to several outer-island ports as well as to Java.[13] Singapore trade statistics provide some insight into the volume of this trade. In 1885 some 1,092 chests of raw opium were shipped from Singapore to Bali. The Balinese themselves, presumably, could consume only a portion of this—although they too smoked opium—and allotments for other opium markets in the archipelago, such as Celebes, Riau, Sumatra, and Borneo, were listed separately.[14] Many, if not most, of these chests were destined for Java.

Throughout the years, several Balinese ports transshipped large amounts of opium, but Buleleng dominated the trade.[15] From 1879 to 1882 records compiled by the resident of Banyuwangi, Bali, and Lombok reveal that an average of 723 piculs (44,681.5 kilograms) of opium was shipped out of Buleleng to the north Java ports of Semarang, Japara, or Rembang every year, an amount equivalent to

13. The same *McAllister* mentioned above carried twenty-seven additional chests for clients in Makasar. See "intelligence report" Buleleng, 1892, in TMC H422b. On Bali and the clandestine opium trade in general, see TM: Rapport 1888; Wiselius, Opium Rapport Semarang, 1882; and Assistant Resident Banyuwangi (gekommitteerde voor de zaken van Balie en Lombok) to DMD: Nota betreffende den Smokkelhandel in opium, tusschen Boeleleng/Balie/Java en Madura, December 31, 1863 in V 16/2/1867/1. Also Lauts, *Het Eiland Balie* (Amsterdam, 1848), pp. 97–99. Among the other transshipment and manufacturing centers for clandestine opium were Riau, Benkulen, the Zutphen Islands, and the hundreds of small islands to the north of Batavia. Consul-generaal of the Netherlands in Singapore (W. H. Read) to DMD, January 13, 1866, no. 79; and DMD to GG, July 7, 1866, no. 2737 (Geheim), both in V 16/2/1867/1.

14. "Celebes en Onderhoorigheden," for instance, received 667 chests; an NHM shipment of 900 chests bound for Batavia is also included in this table, which was appended to consul-generaal Netherlands (Singapore) to GG, January 30, 1886, no. 113 in V 8/3/1886/4. On opium smoking in Klungkung, Bali, see Julius Jacobs, *Eenigen Tijd onder De Baliers: Eene reisbeschrijving met aanteekeningen betreffende hygiene, Land- en Volkenkunde van de eilanden Bali en Lombok* (Batavia, 1883), p. 114.

15. Assistant Resident Banyuwangi, "Nota"; DMD to GG, January 22, 1866, no. 318 in V 16/2/1867/1.

about half the official opium supply for all Java.[16] In Buleleng the Chinese major The Tjing Siang (1873–88),[17] for many years also the local opium farmer, carried on a thriving business in nonfarm opium. He kept an account with the Armenian firm of Polack in Surabaya and supplied some of the major smuggling kongsis on Java, even manufacturing candu for some of them.[18]

Another important opium middleman in Bali was Oei Soen Tjioe. Oei had procured from the rulers of Lombok the post of bandar, or chief port official, in Karangasem, a vassal state to Lombok in east Bali adjacent to Buleleng. He exploited this position fully in the exercise of the opium trade. To his clients he was variously procurement and shipping agent, candu manufacturer, and adviser, particularly on matters relating to the circumvention of Dutch regulations. For larger Chinese smugglers with their own network of operatives and clients Oei served mainly as a processor of raw opium. He specialized, however, in supplying opium to small clandestine importers on Java, those unable to acquire credit directly from the Armenian trading houses.[19]

It was in Bali, then, that a majority of Java's clandestine opium changed hands. Middlemen such as The Tjing Siang and Oei Soen Tjioe, several smaller operators, and European agents of the Armenian trading houses all engaged in opium transactions there.[20] Trusted Javanese boatmen were employed to carry the opium to Java. Upon presenting satisfactory identification these boatmen took delivery of the opium, loaded it on their vessels amid commonplace interisland produce—coconuts were a favorite for the Bali run—and where, as in Buleleng, harbor authorities were unavoidable, declared themselves out for Pegatan in south Borneo or some other permissible destination.[21] Their true destination was in

16. Resident H. Fitz Verploegh was making an educated guess about the destination. He is quoted in DF to GG, July 18, 1884, no. 12417 in VKG 3/2/1885/K1, no. 7. During these years official allotments of opium for Java and Madura averaged 1500 piculs (97,461 kilograms). See TM: Rapport 1888, Bijlage D.

17. The Tjing Siang was Chinese captain from 1873 and major from 1884. RAvNI.

18. TM to DF, February 19, 1889, no. 225/12 in V 8/7/1889/77.

19. On The Tjing Siang and Oei Soen Tjioe, see TM to DF, February 19, 1889, no. 225/12 in V 8/7/1889/77; and TM to DF, August 3, 1889, no. 899/12 in V 27/5/1890/111.

20. In 1892 both Edgar and Co. and Zorab Mesrope had European representatives posted in Bali. Resident Bali and Lombok to TM, February 11, 1892, no. 14 (Geheim) in Exh 9/8/1892/76.

21. For some reason Pegatan, a tiny, semi-independent native state of some ten thousand people on Borneo's south coast, was the favorite decoy port of destination for Javanese opium smugglers. "Pegatan en Koesan," ENI 3:245.

most cases the north coast of central Java, where they either slipped unwatched into a stream, or rested offshore until smaller craft could unload them under cover of darkness.[22]

Documentary sources compiled in Bali, Semarang, and Joana in the early 1880s provide us with a more intimate look at this trade. Of fifty-five boatmen who took on sizable quantities of opium in Buleleng in 1883 and who declared Pegatan as their destination, fifty-three were plying craft owned by people residing in Rembang or Joana, most of them Javanese; thirty-one of these boats carried Chinese passengers from Joana, Rembang, Kudus, or Pati. Together they bore 672.3 piculs (41,548 kilograms) of candu and raw opium.[23] A list compiled in 1879 by the harbormaster in Joana of Javanese boatmen who carried opium from Bali (although declared for Pegatan) during April to October names twenty-nine individuals who brought 179.43 piculs (11,088.7 kilograms) of clandestine opium to Joana alone.[24] Although some boatmen may have worked for themselves, most of them plied the Bali route on behalf of Chinese merchants. For example, in 1881 one boatman named Asro imported opium on behalf of four separate kongsis; in one, he and a local village head (lurah) held shares in common with a Chinese; in another he participated with two Chinese shareholders; and in the other two he simply handled the shipment for others—a total of 85 piculs (5,253 kilograms) of opium altogether. More typical is Haji Jahja, from the same village as Asro, who imported 30 piculs (1,854 kilograms) for a Chinese kongsi based in Rembang and Joana.[25]

If apprehended too close to the coast of Java with their lucrative cargoes, it was standard procedure for these boatmen to display their pass for Pegatan and to plead that inclement weather, damage to the ship, or some other necessity had forced them to make for

22. By resting offshore at a safe distance the "floating opium store-houses" could avoid harassment by government sea police; beyond the territorial limits (three English sea miles) they were untouchable. See SvNI 1879, no. 224; and TM: Rapport 1888.

23. Opgave: Uitklaringen naar Pegattan 1883 in TMC H422a. This document, in the form of a table, includes the following information: name of boatman, name of the owner of the vessel, residence of the owner, type of craft, amount of opium exported (categorized by Levant/Bengal, processed/raw), name and residence of passenger, and date of departure.

24. Bijlage B to Wiselius, Opium Rapport Semarang, 1882.

25. Ibid. This table, compiled by Semarang lawyer Baron Sloet van Hagensdorp, lists the names of the chief smugglers, their accomplices, those who brought the opium ashore and where, the average suspected quantity of clandestine opium imported by each group yearly, and, if known, the kongsi's agent in Bali. Presumably he had access to police files on recent black-market confiscations.

Java instead of Borneo. Take the case of one Pak Rassimin, Japara residency: apprehended by the colonial marines off the Karimonjawa Islands with nearly 7 piculs (432.6 kilograms) of candu, he explained that after purchasing raw opium from Oei Soen Tjioe in Bali, he had shipped out for Pegatan—a perfectly legal business transaction. Unfavorable winds, alas, had blown him toward the Java coast.[26]

Once along the coast, the vessels coming from Bali awaited the arrival of smaller craft to transship the opium ashore. An investigation into a major smuggling operation in Rembang in 1890 unearthed a wealth of information about this aspect of the trade. Participants testified that in early September of that year the Rembang opium farm received shipments of several piculs of clandestine opium.[27] The opium came aboard the usual type of craft from Bali. It was unloaded and hidden on the small offshore island of Marungan and subsequently brought ashore piecemeal, to be delivered at last to the home of Liem Kok Sing, key associate and manager of the Rembang opium farm.

To carry out the first part of the operation, Liem Kok Sing contracted the professional merchant-smuggler Haji Jahja.[28] Haji Jahja commandeered the necessary small boats and their crews, supervised the landing and hiding of the opium on Marungan, and managed three separate transshipments from Marungan to the Rembang coast. In a separate transaction Liem Kok Sing's aide and opium farm mata-mata Tan Soen Hwat hired a village guard named Sarban to complete the operation.[29] Sarban recruited a band of neighbors—including another village guard, a fish hawker, a day

26. Pro Justitia, Landraad Pati: Case of Pak Rassimin, January 30, 1882, no. 14 in TMC H422b.

27. The inquiry was conducted by the regent of Rembang R. A. Djojoadiningrat. Several key participants in the smuggling attempt categorically implicated Liem Kok Sing, although he denied being involved. The following account is based largely on the testimony of Haji Mohammad Jahja (Papriksaan Hadji Mohammad Jahja, October 3, 1890), Sarban (Papriksaan Sarban, October 5, 1890), and Sabirin (Papriksaan Sabirin, October 19, 1890). Copies of these statements, and of those of the other participants, are in TMC H422c (in Malay) and Exh 9/8/1892/76 (in Dutch). The "Marungan affair" and its repercussions for the Rembang farm are discussed in Chapter 9, below.

28. Haji Jahja was known by the authorities to be an agent for receiving and guarding smuggled goods. See TM to DF, November 25, 1890, no. 1934/3 in Exh 9/8/1892/76, p. 27.

29. Tan Soen Hwat had been implicated in a clandestine opium seizure in 1885. He joined the Rembang farm in 1887 as a mata-mata and was by reputation "a dangerous subject." See Papriksaans cited in n. 27, above.

laborer, and the lurah of Rembang village—to receive the shipments at the beach. The Haji's and Sarban's portions of the operation were totally separate. A local trusty of Liem Kok Sing named
Sabirin was the only person to participate in both stages. The Haji's
crews simply left him alone on the shore with the opium where he
awaited Sarban's men. He and Sarban, so they testified, then personally delivered the opium to Liem Kok Sing's dwelling.

Liem Kok Sing contacted both the Haji and Sarban because,
evidently, he already knew them to be useful in such operations.
They in turn recruited their help locally among friends and relatives
and paid them in lump sums with money advanced by their opium
farm connections. At least five of the participants had been implicated previously in similar affairs; three had been convicted.[30] This,
and the general ease with which the teams of accomplices were
recruited, indicates that the exercise was a familiar one. The Marungan operation illustrates the way in which, typical of all things
involving opium in colonial Java, the official and criminal worlds
overlapped. The opium farm, a sanctioned agency of the state,
employed professional smugglers to import illegal opium; a lurah
and two village functionaries were direct accomplices to the act, and,
it turned out, one member of Haji Jahja's team had recently been
employed by a special Dutch antismuggling task force.[31]

Importing clandestine opium required, then, the participation
and cooperation of several individuals and groups: the purchaser
himself and his personal clients; trading firms that extended credit,
and banks that provided facilities for the discreet exchange of
monies; agents and middlemen who specialized in executing the
transfer of opium from wholesaler to purchaser; boatmen and their
crews who shipped the opium to its Javan destination; and finally
the teams of men who brought it ashore and delivered it to its
purchaser. The process involved an informal coalition of individuals
and groups—Haji Jahja and Liem Kok Sing both had men they
could call on—who for the purpose of mutual profit each made one
single but essential contribution to the success of the larger venture.
Although some smuggling enterprises, especially those organized
by powerful farm kongsis, may have had permanent organizations
capable of encompassing the entire project, most smuggling ap-

30. TM to DF, November 25, 1890, no. 1934/3 in Exh 9/8/1892/76.
31. Papriksaan Ngariban, October 12, 1890, in TMC H422c.

pears to have involved ad hoc collaborations. Nevertheless, the web of interests which made smuggling a major enterprise in nineteenth-century Java was difficult to penetrate. Accomplices caught in the act and subjected to fines or imprisonment could rest assured, it was repeatedly alleged by those familiar with black-market operations, that their fines would be paid and their families maintained in their absence.[32] "[It] is generally taken for granted," wrote Charles TeMechelen in 1890, "that all and everybody [involved in smuggling] cling to each other like burrs . . . nothing can come between them."[33] TeMechelen himself learned the hard way—Liem Kok Sing had been his trusted friend for years.[34]

Clandestine opium came ashore all along the north coast of Java. The harbor of Batavia fed both its own hinterland and the Forbidden Areas of Bantam and the Priangan. Surabaya was the source of much of Kediri's clandestine supply and was linked by river routes to Madiun and Surakarta. Illegal opium also entered Java at Pasuruan and on the north shore of the East Hook. Small amounts penetrated from the south coast at places like Pacitan. The vast majority, however, was landed along the Japara-Rembang coast from Joana to Lasem. This region once thrived on trade and shipbuilding; as its prosperity waned in the nineteenth century, however, many of its sea-wise boatmen and fishermen turned to smuggling. By the 1870s and 1880s their success earned for the Joana-Lasem arc the nickname of Java's "opium funnel."[35] Major opium-smuggling kongsis had established themselves in Joana, Rembang, and Lasem. From the "funnel" clandestine opium flowed south through Blora to Surakarta, and via Kudus and Demak to Semarang, headquarters of some of the biggest opium farm interests.[36] Some of this opium remained to be consumed in the opium-hungry entrepot residencies of the coast such as Semarang and Surabaya, but most made its way inland, via roads, railroads, mountain passes, and village paths, to

32. See, for example, the comment in Resident Rembang to DMD, November 25, 1865, in V 16/2/1867/1.

33. TM to DF, November 25, 1890, no. 1934/3, in Exh 9/8/1892/76.

34. See Chapter 8, below.

35. Two occasions in which the nickname occurs are in Resident Rembang to DF, July 3, 1867, Y (Geheim) in VKG 27/1/1869 (17/C), and TM to Resident Japara, January 12, 1884 in TMC H422a. TeMechelen was assistant resident of Joana at the time.

36. DF to GG, May 22, 1891, no. 7637 in TMC H422c; Resident Rembang to DF, August 21, 1875, MI in V 22/5/1876/79; and TM to Resident Japara, December 31, 1882, no. 2694/10 in TMC H422a.

the inland marts of central and east Java, where client stringers of independent smugglers and patungan agents of the opium farms delivered it to its ultimate consumers.

Opium farmers and their associates were in an ideal position to engage in the clandestine opium trade. The combined resources of kongsi associates (many of whom lived in areas outside the farm territory and therefore had valuable extralocal contacts), as well as the farm organization and the personal influence of the farmer as a wealthy monopoly holder could all be brought to bear to expedite clandestine arrangements and to protect the participants.[37] Indeed, some farmers preferred smuggling to receiving full allotments from the colonial government. By fulfilling part of their needs legally and the rest via clandestine channels, they could lower their prices—to meet the black market—and at the same time keep the level of opium consumption, and the true value of the farm, a secret.[38]

Several specific cases of farm participation in clandestine opium activities surfaced during the 1860s to the 1890s. Hard evidence was difficult to come by, however, and only when blatant clandestine activities exacerbated other excesses did the Dutch move boldly against offending farmers. In one such case in 1852 a Pasuruan opium farmer was banished after his organization gained a notorious reputation for abusing the local population.[39] But such a decisive outcome was rare. Usually, when opium farmers or their relatives and business associates were discovered in compromising circumstances, they made successful alibis and after a brief flurry the matter was dropped. The futility of pursuing cases against major opium farmers was part of the conventional wisdom of the Colonial Service.

One Dutch administrator who did not heed the conventional wisdom was Christian Castens. As resident of Bagelen in the early

37. Circulaire aan Residenten (DMD C. Castens), December 31, 1866, no. 5081 in VKG 27/1/1869/170; Assistant Resident voor de Policie (Surabaya) to Resident Surabaya, March 22, 1865, no. 473, and Assistant Resident Pacitan to DMD, October 4, 1866, R (Zeer Geheim), both in V 16/2/1867/1.
38. See Konsideratien en advies van den DMD, July 21, 1866, no. 2903 in V 16/2/1867/1. This solves the apparent mystery as to why farmers frequently did not accept the full state allotments permitted them. See the chart appended to TM: Rapport 1888, which compares farm fees, maximum legal supply, and actual supply (what farmers requested from the state warehouses) for each farm territory in the 1880s.
39. E. de Waal, *Aanteekeningen over Koloniale Onderwerpen* (The Hague, 1865), p. 45.

1860s (1862–64) he assiduously collected evidence implicating several major opium farmers, including Be Biauw Tjoan and Tan Tjong Hoay, in a massive black-market opium farm operation in central Java. Be and his brother-in-law Tan were both Chinese majors in Semarang and headed the two most powerful Chinese families in central Java.[40] Be and his farm associates held several of the area's lucrative opium farms, including those for Bagelen and Banyumas residencies. They also exploited their collective resources and connections to import and distribute illegal opium, which they used to supplement their official allotments and to undermine neighboring farms held by rival kongsis.[41]

In an episode typical of the investigation of opium farm cases, Castens discovered, during an unannounced inspection, that the local Bagelen opium farm warehouse contained three times the amount of opium that should have been there. The local manager swore that all the opium was legal, but he could offer no evidence to substantiate his assertion that opium sales had sharply declined, as he alleged in explaining the surplus. The farm account books were missing (when the inspection began the farm bookkeeper suddenly took ill and excused himself); when they were finally produced they showed evidence of fresh revisions.

Resident Castens then appointed a commission of inquiry chaired by a local Chinese officer. The commission members dawdled over their work and rumors spread that the Bagelen farmer had bribed them with f10,000. At long last, and under duress, the commission confirmed an unexplainable 800 tahil (30.4 kilograms) surplus of candu, and revealed that the Bagelen farm had shipped opium illegally to Banyumas. Recalling the investigation, Castens wrote: "I had much trouble with the investigation of this affair . . . ; the people involved evaded the issues;—they didn't understand the questions, and gave answers that they later pretended to improve upon. In short, the most extreme slyness and conspiracy was at play."[42]

Despite this, the investigation bore fruit. In 1864 the governor

40. Liem, *Riwajat*, p. 104. The Bes and the Tans are discussed more fully in Chapter 5, below.

41. See DMD to GG, August 16, 1866, no. 3230 in V 16/2/1867/1; and C. Castens, "De Opiumpacht op Java," pp. 49–112.

42. DMD (Castens) to GG, August 31, 1866, no. 3405 in V 16/2/1867/1. Soon afterward Castens was promoted to director of means and estates in Batavia. Castens jokingly attributed his promotion to the behind-the-scenes machinations of Be, who was anxious to rid central Java of an unwanted irritant.

general, citing Be Biauw Tjoan's key role in the opium-farm smuggling ring, stripped him of his majorship. Be and several of his accomplices, including his brother Be Ik Sam, who was a Chinese captain in Bagelen, as well as the Chinese lieutenant of Banyumas, were fined heavily and henceforth forbidden to participate in opium farms as farmers, guarantors, subfarmers, or employees.[43]

Be Biauw Tjoan was by no means out of the opium business, however. With Be holding a major, although silent, interest, his kongsi continued to dominate opium affairs in central Java, bidding aggressively in the opium farm auctions and undermining competitor farms by flooding them with cheap black-market opium. In 1865, only a year after Be's dismissal, the new holder of the Bagelen and Kedu farms submitted a formal written complaint about Be's black-market activity in his territories;[44] and a full decade later Surakarta farmer Tio Siong Mo told the Dutch lower house in his extraordinary petition of 1876 of the Be kongsi's efforts to destroy his farm, efforts that ultimately succeeded.[45] Although some argued that Tio's farm was mismanaged—a charge largely true because most of the experienced farm operatives in Surakarta were Be clients and refused employment with Tio—Be's campaign against Tio was the talk of central Java. This time, however, Be Biauw Tjoan remained beyond reach. As Tio Siong Mo languished in debtors' prison, Be's power and prestige continued to rise. He was reinstated as Chinese major of Semarang in 1873 and continued in that honored post until his death in 1904.[46]

A smaller smuggling ring involving an opium farmer was also exposed in the 1860s. This was in Pacitan (Madiun residency), where the farmer, Tan Ing Soen, was also a Chinese lieutenant. Tan's partners in this enterprise were the regent of Pacitan, Raden Tumenggung (RT) Djogokario, and members of a local European family, the Coenraads, carpetbaggers who had entrenched themselves in Pacitan following the Java War. The ring had been orga-

43. KVvNI 1864.
44. Resident Rembang to DMD, November 25, 1865, in V 16/2/1867/1. See also DMD to GG, August 23, 1866, no. 3303 (Geheim) in V 16/2/1867/1, on Be Biauw Tjoan's Singapore interests, including, it was alleged, a share in the Singapore opium farm.
45. Tio Siong Mo, "Aan de Tweede Kamer der Staten-Generaal," February 1, 1876, and DF to GG, May 31, 1876, no. 7364, both in V 17/8/1876/74; and De Indier (November 21, 1874), p. 903.
46. RAvNI 1874–1904.

nized in response to the massive reduction in official opium allotments for Pacitan, Madiun, Surakarta, and Banyumas after 1861, and it made use of the government-contracted salt and coffee ships that plied Java's south coast and put in at Pacitan. Be Biauw Tjoan, it was alleged, used Tan's services to transport clandestine opium from Surabaya to Surakarta. The regent, a well-known opium smoker himself, used his official dwelling to store illegal opium and presided over a distribution network of lower pryayi officials and village headmen.[47]

Pryayi complicity in opium-smuggling ventures of this sort was not uncommon, especially in the principalities.[48] In the government residencies it was often in the interests of the regents and other pryayi officials to wink at illicit farm activities, if not to assist actively. In addition to various other tangible benefits of doing so, farmers reputedly provided vulnerable pryayi with free opium.[49] Cases of village-head involvement in smuggling activities were legion.[50] In some villages, shrewd headmen exploited their favorable locations to provide smugglers with safe transshipment routes and, in doing so, created a minor boon for themselves and their villages.[51]

Incidences of European and Eurasian participation in opium smuggling also surfaced. In a typical case, one E. N. Sieburgh, the black-sheep son of a highly placed member of the Colonial Service

47. A feud between the regent, R. T. Djogokario, and the Chinese lieutenant involving tardy payment of opium accounts and nonpayment of other debts led to the exposure of this ring. In an unusual move the Dutch dismissed Djogokario when the details came to light. See Geheim Oost-Indisch Besluit, November 25, 1865, T1, in VKG 25/11/1865/T1; Assistant Resident Pacitan to DMD, August 8, 1866, M (Zeer Geheim en Zeer Vertrouwelijke) and DMD to GG, August 31, 1866, no. 3405, both in V 16/2/1867/1. Onghokham feels that this affair was sufficiently memorable to have been included, albeit in allegorical form, in Ganda Atmadja's *Babad Pacitan.* See Onghokham, "The Residency of Madiun: Pryayi and Peasant in the Nineteenth Century" (Ph.D. diss., Yale University, 1975), p. 103.

48. In 1864, for example, the investigation of Be Biauw Tjoan's illicit activities was stymied in Yogyakarta by the protection of one or more members of the aristocracy. See DMD to GG, August 31, 1866, no. 3405 in V 16/2/1867/1. Opium-smuggling activities by members of the royal house of Paku Alam were investigated and confirmed in 1890. See Resident J. Mullemeister's Memorie van Overgave in MR no. 617, 1891. Surakarta resident A. J. Spaan reported in 1889 that the Surakartan aristocracy, even "zeer voornamd" persons, considered it ordinary to smuggle opium. Resident Surakarta to DF, January 9, 1889, no. 242/20 in MR no. 136, 1889.

49. DMD to GG, August 31, 1866, no. 3405 in V 16/2/1867/1.

50. See the several examples mentioned in TM to DF, April 13, 1892, no. 779/12 in Exh 9/8/1892/76.

51. One of these was Kenjeran desa on the beach east of Surabaya. It is described in Assistant Resident voor de Policie (Surabaya) to Resident Surabaya, March 22, 1865, no. 473 in V 16/2/1867/1.

and ex-partner of Chinese major Tan Tjong Hoay in a sugar milling deal, was implicated in opium smuggling in his new position as supercargo of the schooner *Charlotte*; he had concealed 800 tahils (30.4 kilograms) of candu in Javanese pots.[52] In another scheme, one that reached to the wineries of Germany, Th. Carel Andreas, scion of a locally prominent Armenian trading family, conspired to import opium in the false metallic bottoms of wine bottles, fourteen chests of them, marked "Chateau Lafitte."[53] Unemployed Europeans were among the most audacious of smugglers, mainly because they were protected by their caste from the embarrassment of frisking or having their homes searched, both routine procedures in opium investigations. No fewer than twenty-one Europeans stood trial in Semarang residency for opium smuggling in 1881 and 1882, including several women.[54]

Opium smuggling was scarcely new in nineteenth-century Java. Like any attempt to control and circumscribe trade in a valuable and easily portable article, Dutch efforts to monopolize the opium trade in Java had, from the outset, prompted efforts to circumvent the monopoly. But it was most probably during the period following 1860 that the importing and distribution of "unofficial" opium became a more or less routine feature of the farm system. In 1861 Batavia ended a seven-year experiment in which farmers were permitted to purchase from the government an unlimited supply of opium. During these seven years, the amount of opium supplied officially had more than doubled.[55] When worried officials once more clamped down on opium distribution and reduced the official supply by a fourth, opium farmers were faced with a demand they could no longer meet.

In the ensuing years of marked population growth and commercial development, farm fees rose consistently in spite of the fact that official allotments—though rising also—remained crimped below demand. Java's Chinese merchants obviously continued to view

52. DMD to GG, May 31, 1866, no. 2093 (Zeer Geheim) in V 16/2/1867/1; and SvD, E. N. Sieburgh, H198. Sieburgh had been employed on the staff of the director of means and estates for several years, then resigned; after seven years he took another minor staff position, this time in Semarang, from which he was dismissed for unethical activities in 1865, the year before the *Charlotte* affair.

53. See the various documents in V 11/12/1886/58 and VKG 1/3/1897/A4 for the details; and A. Machielse, *Opheldering in de zaak der Chateau Lafitte* (Surakarta, 1901).

54. Wiselius, Opium Rapport Semarang, 1882. See especially Bijlage E.

55. See the chart titled "Overzigt—Opiumpacht Java en Madura 1854 t/m 1866" in V 16/2/1867/1.

opium farms as profitable investments. As we have seen, one reason was that they could exploit their positions as opium farmers to do clandestinely what they could not do openly—import additional opium to distribute via the farm retail network. If they did not, as several astute observers of the farms pointed out, they could not possibly compete with the cheap black-market opium available elsewhere.[56]

A substantial nonfarm market in opium meant that farmers had to offer competitive prices. Because the price farmers paid the state for official opium was several times higher than the prevailing market price for raw opium in neighboring entrepots—in Singapore, for example—black-market opium was frequently available in Java for prices far lower than those of the farm variety. In the mid-1860s the residents of Japara, Surakarta, Kediri, and Kedu all declared that black-market opium was sold for from one-half to one-fourth the price of legal opium in their residencies.[57] Because farmers raised or lowered their prices in response to clandestine competition, farm retail prices varied enormously from store to store and from farm to farm. In 1873, to give one random example, one mata of farm candu cost only 12 cents in Semarang, but 32 cents in Batavia.[58] Such price disparities persisted to the end of the farm system and provide a graphic indicator of the strength of the black market.

Even if he supplemented his state allotments with cheap clandestine opium of his own, however, a farmer could not necessarily offer opium at the same price as the black market and still pay a high farm fee, purchase his legal opium, and maintain his organization. When Ho Yam Lo dropped his prices to black-market level in September and October 1875, daily sales in his Semarang farm quadrupled. Even with expanded sales like these, however, Ho soon realized that he could not continue to meet both the prices of his competition and his obligations to the colonial treasury; he raised

56. This argument was made repeatedly by DMD C. Castens. See V 16/2/1867/1. For others who concurred, see Assistant Resident voor de Policie (Surabaya) to Resident Surabaya, March 22, 1865, no. 473 in V 16/2/1867/1; Inspecteur Generaal van Financien (Motke) to GG, May 31, 1872, no. 10A in V 20/8/1872/37; and TM to DF, November 25, 1890, no. 1934 (Geheim) in TMC H422c.

57. MvK to Koning, May 5, 1868, no. 52 (Geheim) in VKG 5/5/1868/52.

58. For average retail farm prices for candu, see the annual Koloniaal Verslagen under "Verpachte Middelen" and the appropriate appendix. For an illustration of price fluctuations within a farm territory, see "Staat antoonende de hoogste opium prijzen in de kitten der Residentie Pasoeroean" in TMC H422d.

his prices again in November.[59] Farmers could not, then, respond to the challenge of the black market simply by importing clandestine opium themselves and lowering prices; their overhead was too high. Nor could they eliminate smuggling entirely; as the Dutch later discovered themselves, this required massive investment for the smallest of results. Given these limitations, farmers had to adopt a more complex ad hoc approach to dealing with the nonfarm market.

The key was controlling both legal and illegal opium. Farmers therefore, while sometimes smuggling themselves, did their utmost to inhibit and undermine (though they could never stop) smuggling by others. Farmers along the north coast, for instance, employed parapolice personnel at farm expense to patrol the coast and intercept unfriendly clandestine imports, and all farmers employed extensive networks of mata-mata to ferret out local black marketeers and ensure that the farm dominated the local market. These mata-mata worked hand-in-hand with local pryayi "police," and the results of their labors often turned up in the colonial courts, most especially the local administrative petty offense hearings called *politierol*. The mata-mata arm of the farm organization was absolutely crucial to farm success, for only with strong enforcement could farmers maintain a price structure adequate to pay their overhead and still claim a satisfactory share of the whole market.

Where the farm organization was relatively weak vis-à-vis the black market, mutually compatible accommodations between farmer and smuggler were occasionally necessary. For example, a farmer might buy off a black marketeer's supply at an inflated rate in return for a promise to cease selling in his farm territory; or a farmer and a clandestine distributor might agree to resolve their competition by "sharing the action," the clandestine distributor agreeing to purchase regular allotments of farm opium in return for remaining unmolested by farm mata-mata. Black marketeers might even be directly absorbed into the farm organization itself.[60] At the patungan level the line separating farm and nonfarm, legal and criminal, could be quite indistinct.

The conditions and environment of opium competition made

59. Wiselius includes a list of the Semarang farm's daily sales for the entire year 1875, excerpted from the farm ledger, in his Opium Rapport, Semarang, 1882.
60. Circulaire aan Residenten, December 31, 1866, no. 5081 in VKG 27/1/1869/ 17C; and TM: Rapport 1888.

other accommodations equally necessary. A farmer who imported clandestine opium to meet black-market competition in his own farm could easily be stuck with a surplus; prudence dictated that he order more than his calculated needs as a hedge against the risk of confiscation. Such overpurchasing led to two common farm irregularities. First, farmers conspired, to the detriment of the neighboring farm, to sell off their surpluses across farm borders; second, farmers routinely unloaded remaining surpluses in their own farm territories in the last month of their term, flooding the farm with cheap opium at the expense of the incoming kongsi. The price wars and glutted markets that resulted from these tactics had an important consequence for opium users. Namely, they made opium cheaper and more accessible. Selling the surplus entailed intense competition among patungan traders who, in an effort to maintain both their profits and their credit with patron suppliers, pressed harder and deeper into the villages.

An opium farmer's struggle against the black market forced him into a legally ambiguous role, a role in which he could not succeed in isolation. To advance his interests and thwart his adversaries effectively he needed a shrewd knowledge of the institutional soft spots of the colonial state, and the acquiescence—if not the active assistance—of both native and European officials. Moreover, the contest for the opium market cannot be understood apart from another one. This was the competition among Java's wealthy Chinese for wide-ranging commercial supremacy and social prestige, a competition that formed the most comprehensive aspect of the "battle of the kings." Understanding it requires a familiarity with the history and social structure of Java's Chinese community and with the special nature of the Chinese economic presence in nineteenth-century Java.

5

Opium Farm Chinese:
The *Cabang Atas*

The opium farm Chinese were a tiny but influential elite in colonial Java. They and their families and business associates were the *Cabang Atas*—the highest branch—of Java's Chinese community. They were, first of all, the richest and most successful of the Chinese. In addition, because the Dutch appointed the most prominent of them to be Chinese officers, they acted collectively as the exclusive buffer between the Chinese community and the Dutch government.

The wealth and power of the Cabang Atas stemmed fundamentally from its control over vast competitive Chinese commercial networks that dominated nearly all non-European economic activity in Java. Along the human links of these networks, reaching from the mercantile coastal cities into Java's rural villages, flowed a steady two-way traffic in which material goods, money, and credit entered the countryside in exchange for Javanese rice and other agricultural produce. Opium farms were enmeshed in this economy and played an important role within it. Holding an opium farm placed leaders of these networks in a domineering position over commercial activity within a wide area, often entire residencies. Closely related, therefore, to the competition for Java's opium market was a much broader one for the profits of the retail trade and control of the rice market.

Members of Java's nineteenth-century Chinese community were the heirs of a distinct Chinese-Indonesian culture that had been in

83

the forming for several hundred years. The first permanent Chinese settlements in Java had been established in the entrepots of the north coast sometime around the fourteenth century. Here settlers from Fukien Province (Hokkiens) and their local wives became the progenitors of the Chinese communities that the Dutch encountered in several Java harbor towns two hundred years later. The Dutch encouraged more Chinese to come to their outposts in these towns. In the following centuries, the Chinese community accommodated itself usefully both to Holland's expanding presence on Java and to the waning native kingdoms. Over time a stable overseas Chinese society developed, shaped by the dual process of intermarriage among the mixed-blood offspring of Chinese-Indonesian unions and the absorption of new immigrants from China.[1]

By the nineteenth century this society possessed a distinct culture called peranakan, derivative of both Hokkien and Indonesian elements.[2] Similar mestizo Chinese communities were forming simultaneously elsewhere in Southeast Asia, prominently in Thailand, Malacca, and the Philippine Islands, and through kinship and trade they were somewhat interrelated. But in its particular blend of Chinese and indigenous elements, Java's peranakan society was distinctive. In it "low" Malay, the lingua franca of Java's mercantile north coast, was the language of home and business; the political authority of the Dutch was taken for granted; and status accrued most abundantly to the commercially successful.

The early Chinese settlers and their descendants, in addition to participating in the Asian junk trade and interisland commerce, engaged in the milling of sugar and rice, the manufacturing of wine and candles, and a variety of crafts.[3] Chinese merchants and traders later became indispensable to the Dutch East India Company as middlemen; they brought the bounty of the land to Dutch trading posts and marketed company-imported goods from textiles to opium in the countryside.[4] Tax farms and other concessions leased

1. G. William Skinner, "The Chinese of Java," in *Colloquium on the Overseas Chinese*, ed. Morton H. Fried (New York, 1958), pp. 1–2; B. Hoetink, "Chineesche Officieren te Batavia Onder de Compagnie," *BKI*, 78 (1922), 10.

2. G. William Skinner, "Java's Chinese Minority: Continuity and Change," *JAS*, 20, 3 (May 1961), 356–57.

3. On the subject of the Chinese community in early VOC Batavia, see J. T. Vermeulen, "The Chinese in Batavia and the Troubles of 1740," *Journal of the South Seas Society*, 9, 1 (1953), chap. 1.

4. Donald E. Willmott, *The Chinese of Semarang: A Changing Minority Community in Indonesia* (Ithaca, 1960), p. 5; Liem, *Riwajat*, p. 80; Baud, "Proeve," pp. 99–100.

by indigenous rulers, among them collecting port duties and manufacturing and distributing salt, had become a boon to enterprising
Chinese before the company's arrival.[5] Similar monopoly concessions both in Dutch lands and the native states—including the leasing whole of coastal and inland villages and their inhabitants—
continued to be prize investments in company days and beyond;
opium farms were among the latest (from 1809) and most lucrative
of these monopolies.[6]

From the beginning the Dutch followed the Indonesian maritime
entrepot tradition of appointing dependable headmen to bear responsibility for the colonies of foreign traders who settled in their
port cities.[7] In selecting Chinese headmen, to whom they gave the
military titles of captain, lieutenant, and later major, the Dutch
sought to exploit the prestige and patronage of men who were
already established as leaders in their respective communities. This
account of the appointment of Batavia's first Chinese captain in
1619, from the company records, reflects both the qualifications and
the expectations the company had for its Chinese officers: "Inasmuch as there are now some 400 Chinese living here under our
protection, it is necessary to appoint a qualified person to maintain,
to the extent possible, order and law. For this purpose prominent
Chinese here have nominated one Bencon. It is therefore approved
that Bencon shall preside over the Chinese as a headman, charged
with settling civil affairs and referring all other serious matters to
us."[8]

Although for a long period the Dutch did not elaborate officially
on the functions and authority of Chinese officers, the role of the

---

5. Chinese frequently served as port officials, shahbandars, on behalf of indigenous rulers. See Liem, *Riwajat*, pp. 16–19, for a discussion of this and other activities
of Chinese in pre-VOC Java. See also Burger, *Ontsluiting*, pp. 10, 20.

6. See Burger, *Ontsluiting*, pp. 7, 9, 15, 16, 20. Liem, *Riwajat*, p. 83, describes how
the salt monopoly worked in the eighteenth century. See also "De Nota van de Kamer
van Koophandel en Nijverheid te Batavia over De Toelating der Chinezen," *De
Locomotief*, November 27, 1865.

7. The title captain (kapitan) is of Portuguese origin. See C. R. Boxer, "Notes on
Chinese Abroad in the Late Ming and Early Manchu Periods Compiled from Contemporary European Sources (1500–1750)," *T'ien Hsia Monthly* (December 1939),
462–63n23.

8. From Hoetink, "Chineesche Officieren," p. 10. Hoetink points out that on
several occasions in VOC Batavia Chinese officers were elected by their peers
(pp. 14–17). For an account of the career of So Bing Kong (Bencon of the excerpt),
see B. Hoetink, "So Bing Kong. Het eerste Hoofd der Chineezen te Batavia (1619–
1639)," *BKI*, 73, pt. 3 (1917), 345ff.

officers was quite concrete in practice. In 1745 a company resolution described their responsibilities as they were performed at that time. The captain, it noted, was to consult with his lieutenants about all matters requiring the attention of the authorities and to hold court weekly to settle civil quarrels among the Chinese on the basis of their own laws and customs. He was authorized to request space in the jail for the temporary detention of Chinese criminals (to await trial before Dutch magistrates), and he could call in the aid of the Dutch sheriff and bailiff to help apprehend troublemakers. Finally, the collective officers were charged with informing on troublesome elements among the immigrant Chinese so that they could be dispatched back to China. In sum, Chinese officers were to maintain civil peace among their own, refer criminal activities to the authorities, and generally exercise surveillance over the Chinese community.[9]

In return, the Chinese officers enjoyed the prestige of an official position. This was amply illustrated in extravagant public installation rites and the privilege of bearing a parasol of authority, which, symbolically, marked them as figures of dignity and respect. More concretely, appointment as an officer substantially augmented their influence among the Chinese community. In civil matters their decision had the weight of law, and in criminal matters they decided which Chinese bore the brunt of Dutch legal procedures.

As its territorial base broadened, the Dutch East India Company appointed additional Chinese officers in the Chinese communities coming under its control. Thus, in 1672 Kwee Kiauw became the first Chinese captain of Semarang.[10] Where the Chinese community was large, as in Batavia and Semarang, the Dutch appointed lieutenants to assist the captain.[11] Following the collapse of the company and the British interregnum, this pattern was repeated elsewhere as a Dutch administration embraced the island, and as greater numbers of Chinese moved on Dutch coattails into the interior. Expansion of the system was especially rapid in the early Cultivation years. In 1832 there were Dutch-appointed Chinese officers in only thir-

9. Generale Resolutien des Casteel Batavia, November 7, 1754, cited in Hoetink, "Chineesche Officieren," pp. 128–29. See pp. 72–78 for a description of Ting Ingko's installation in 1775 from the *Dagregister*.

10. Liem, *Riwajat*, p. 9.

11. Hoetink, "Chineesche Officieren," pp. 88–95, lists all the Chinese lieutenants of Batavia from 1678 to 1809.

teen cities and towns on Java, but by the end of the decade thirty-three localities boasted them.[12] By midcentury the system was fully developed. Batavia, Semarang, and Surabaya now had full staffs of majors, captains, lieutenants, and ward superintendents; a network of Chinese officers dotted the entire island. The collective officers in a given administrative unit came eventually to be known as the Chinese Council, or Kongkoan.

The Chinese Council controlled every point of contact between Java's Chinese community and the Dutch colonial regime. They were the human brokers through whom the statutes and policies of the colonizers were interpreted and implemented. For example, in the larger towns the council maintained a separate police force. Its job was to investigate crimes in which Chinese were involved and, in cooperation with local Javanese authorities, to pursue violators of government taxes and monopolies. In such investigations, Chinese officers were authorized to inspect the warehouses, shops, depots, homes, and other property of Chinese and other non-European suspects. In addition, Chinese officers, long responsible for arbitrating civil disputes, now sat officially as advisers in the colonial courts in all cases involving Chinese suspects. Officers were also frequently charged with collection of the livelihood tax, a 4 percent levy on income which was the major tax imposed on the Chinese (from which they and government revenue farmers were exempt), and were consulted about individual assessments if the tax was collected by an appointed commission. Lower-ranking members of the Chinese Council, members of the Orphans and Probate Court, were responsible for the disposition of the estates of those Chinese dying intestate, and were the legal guardians of orphaned Chinese.[13] The grip of the Chinese officers on the Javan Chinese community was secure.

The introduction in the 1830s of rules confining the Chinese to designated neighborhoods and severely restricting their movement throughout the island by requiring them to possess short-term travel passes further increased the importance of Chinese officers for both the Dutch and Chinese.[14] The Dutch imposed these regula-

12. RAvNI 1832 and 1839.
13. See SvNI 1855, no. 2, arts. 78–79; and J. E. Albrecht, *Soerat Ketrangan*, pp. 12, 13, 15, 22, 23, 25, 27, 29.
14. See C. Baks, "De Chinezen in Oostelijk Java, een demografisch onderzoek naar de penetratie over de periode 1815–1930," microfilm of typescript dated 1962, p. 11; and Liem, *Riwajat*, p. 87.

tions to complement the Cultivation System, whose promoters argued that controlling Chinese economic activity in Java's interior was necessary if Holland, and not the Chinese, was to reap the blessings of the plan. Cooperation of Chinese officers was necessary for enforcing the regulations; and not surprisingly it was during the early Cultivation years that the Chinese Officer System expanded rapidly to cover the entire island. Access to the interior markets, however, was becoming at the same time increasingly important for the Chinese. Now more than before they needed the favor of Chinese officers; officers were responsible for Chinese traveling in their regions, and when necessary they could intercede with both the Dutch and Javanese authorities where the lowly peddler could not.[15]

The same pass and quarter regulations also increased the importance of government revenue farms. The Dutch exempted farmers and their employees from the residence rules, though officially only on a temporary basis, and farmers could count on the liberal application of the pass regulations in the interest of state revenues. The revenue farms thus became the major vehicle by which Chinese merchants tapped Java's rural markets. Under a revenue farm umbrella Chinese lived and moved freely outside the officially designated neighborhoods. These dispensations were common to all revenue farms, but in the first half of the nineteenth century two farms were especially important: the market farm—the farmer collected sales tax in his market—and the opium farm. Baron von Hoevell estimated, in 1850, that some 14,000 Chinese lived in Java's interior under cover of the market farm, four Chinese for each of the country's 3,500 farmed markets.[16] In the same year there were 2,664 legal opium stores in Java and Madura. Based on von Hoevell's ratio, this suggests another 10,656 Chinese.[17] When the market farm was abolished in 1851, opium farms became the single major vehicle for coordinated Chinese influence and economic activity in rural Java.[18]

From early East India Company days on, success in business, acquisition of revenue farms and monopoly concessions, and ap-

15. Albrecht, *Soerat Ketrangan*, p. 10; Liem, *Riwajat*, p. 88.
16. "Nadeelen door de Chinezen in de dessa's op Java veroorzaakt," *TNI* (ed. Baron von Hoevell), 2 (1850), 216.
17. "Het getal opiumkitten op Java," *IG*, 2 (1888), 1927.
18. On the market farm and its abolishment, see SvNI 1851, no. 73; de Waal, *Aanteekeningen*, p. 303; and the entry "Pasar" in *ENI* 3:228.

pointment as Chinese officers went hand in hand. The first won recognition within the Chinese community; commercial success was in and of itself admirable, and successful merchants not only employed their countrypeople but benefited their communities in many other tangible ways. The profits of the first led to the exploitation of the second: the acceptance of the quasi-official position of government leaseholder. Chinese revenue farmers had a wealth of patronage at their disposal which greatly enhanced their social power among the Chinese; they were, as well, in an excellent position to curry favor with the colonial regime. Finally, appointment as an officer added prestige and the power of official authority. This was the path by which enterprising Chinese entered the Cabang Atas, the peranakan elite.

By the nineteenth century the Cabang Atas was a clearly recognizable class; sons of revenue farmers and Chinese officers married the daughters of other farmers and officers and became, often at an early age, farmers and officers themselves.[19] But at no time was access to the elite closed to the truly ambitious and talented. Successful newcomers or their sons frequently married into the dominant families; such mobility could be startlingly rapid. Indeed, Oei Tiong Ham, the last great opium farmer–Chinese officer, and the richest, was the son of a refugee from the Taiping rebellion. His father, Oei Tjie Sien, a supply officer with the Taipings, fled China for Java in 1858.[20]

The culture of the Cabang Atas in the nineteenth century had evolved over hundreds of years in step with political and economic changes in Java. In earlier centuries assimilation to Javanese ways had been more thorough than in the nineteenth century; some peranakans had become Muslims, married into the Javanese elite, and made their way upward as merchants and officials in the service of Java's kings and noblemen. But as opportunity came increasingly through good relations with the Dutch, the peranakans, like the pryayi, accommodated themselves pragmatically. As they did so, assimilation to Javanese society became less attractive, especially after the anti-Chinese bloodletting of the Java War.[21] Instead, the peranakans evolved a culture of their own. This unique accom-

19. Hoetink, in his "Chineesche Officieren," supports this view regarding Batavia's Chinese community; for other examples from central Java, see below.
20. Liem Tjwan Ling, *Raja Gula: Oei Tiong Ham* (Surabaya, 1979), p. 8. Willmott, *Chinese of Semarang*, p. 49.
21. Carey, "Changing Perceptions of the Chinese," p. 14.

Chinese men in Java. Courtesy Koninklijk Instituut voor Taal-, Land- en Volkenkunde, Leiden.

modation reflected the peranakans' existence as a partly Chinese community positioned in between white rulers and native subjects. A dramatic illustration is language. Malay, the neutral lingua franca of trade and administration—and for virtually all its other speakers on Java a "second language"—became mother tongue for many of them.

The urge to perpetuate a society distinctively Chinese remained strong, however, especially so—and perhaps exclusively so—among the men. Their ranks were constantly expanded and replenished by new arrivals. Moreover, in the nineteenth century it was also common for men of means to send their sons to China for education and apprenticeship in the home culture, and some were encouraged to stay on there.[22] When Be Ing Tjioe died in 1857,

22. Tan Tiang Tjhing, for example, sent his son Tan Hong Yan to China as a boy. Liem, *Riwajat*, p. 98.

three of his six sons were living in Java, three in China.[23] It was also among the men of the Cabang Atas that one found persons attuned to Confucian values and literate in Chinese.[24] Chinese men were obliged by the Dutch to dress in the Chinese style, but seem to have done so out of preference as well. On special occasions, peranakan men of means wore fine "Mandarin gowns."

The identification with China was kept alive in other ways as well. In religion the peranakans followed their own adaptations of "the old ways" of the home province. The wealthy ones—opium farmers and Chinese officers—endowed temples and imported from China statues of popular gods. Peranakans followed the traditional Chinese calendar of celebrations peaking at the New Year. Merchants and kongsis used Chinese characters for their "trademarks" (*caps*), and each Chinese officer was identified by his own special seal, an ideograph. Moreover, some Chinese families hired teachers to instruct their sons in the ancestral tongue, and later in the century there were traditional Chinese schools in the cities.[25]

In the long run, however, such efforts to sustain a Chinese identity were largely overwhelmed by the local environment. By the second half of the nineteenth century the majority of Java's peranakan Chinese who read the classics and other popular works from China, read them in Malay translations.[26] And indeed, as these translated works slowly gave way to a creative literature born of the Chinese experience in Java, it was a Malay-language literature.[27]

Within the family peranakan women were powerful agents for assimilation. Mothers and wives were invariably either indigenous (usually Javanese) or peranakan, almost never China-born. It is doubtful if more than a handful of them ever spoke Chinese; their languages, Javanese and Malay, inevitably became the languages of

23. One of Tan Hong Yan's sons settled in China. Ibid., p. 126.
24. Claudine Lombard-Salmon notes that among translators of Chinese works, several are Chinese officers. See her *Literature in Malay by the Chinese of Indonesia: A Provisional Annotated Bibliography* (Paris, 1981), p. 28.
25. Liem, *Riwajat*, describes one on p. 179. See also Leo Suryadinata, *The Pre–World War II Peranakan Chinese Press of Java: A Preliminary Survey* (Athens, Ohio, 1971), p. 5.
26. And Javanese. In the late nineteenth century, however, Malay translations overwhelmed Javanese ones. Claudine Lombard-Salmon, "The Contribution of the Chinese to the Development of Southeast Asia: A New Appraisal," *Journal of Southeast Asia Studies*, 12 (1981), 274.
27. Lombard-Salmon, *Literature in Malay*, pp. 28ff. In the last quarter of the nineteenth century some peranakan children began to receive Western education from tutors and missionary schools. Suryadinata, *Pre–World War II Peranakan Chinese Press*, p. 5.

childhood, home, and community. In other ways peranakan women followed local customs. The teeth of peranakan girls were filed at puberty and blackened at marriage; betel chewing was ubiquitous among them, and peranakan ladies treasured ornamental betel boxes just as pryayi women did.[28] Although mothers were fond of dressing their little girls in Chinese costumes for the New Year and other festive occasions, in everyday life peranakan girls dressed in the native fashion. As for women's clothing, it was distinctively peranakan, with sarongs and blouses and silk shawls recognizable locally as "Chinese," but much more of Java than of China. Indeed, on the rare occasion when a China-born woman did turn up in Java—earlier in the century, some of the wealthier men brought over concubines as "second wives," for example—their slacks and bound feet made them truly exotic.[29] Peranakan girls were expected to comport themselves dutifully and with extreme deference to their elders, which Liem Thian Joe attributes to Chinese custom, and they were cloistered from puberty until marriage. (So were pryayi girls.) Evidently, the wives of the prominent Chinese spent most of their time in the comfortable seclusion of family compounds. Wrote one female observer in 1892, "We rarely see them."[30]

Liem Thian Joe's unique chronicle of Semarang, *Riwajat Semarang*, celebrates the outstanding figures in the peranakan collective memory.[31] Tellingly, his nineteenth-century heroes are without exception both Chinese officers and opium farmers. In one striking passage he notes the death, in 1870, of Nonya (Mrs.) Be Biauw Tjoan.[32] Nonya Be was the most eminent peranakan woman of her day. Her grandfather, father, father-in-law, husband, brother, and son-in-law all held the prestigious position of Chinese major. It is not coincidental that they were all opium farmers as well. Their kongsis played a dominant, if not the dominant, role in opium affairs in central Java for much of the century.

Nonya Be's great-grandfather, Tan Bing, had immigrated to Java in the late 1700s. As Liem tells his story, he arrived poor in Semarang and engaged in petty trade until he had acquired enough capital to open his own store. His business expanded, and he leased

28. Liem, *Riwajat*, p. 114. See also Resident Kediri to DF, December 21, 1888, no. 70 in Exh KG 8/3/1888/V3. Tan Kok Tong's wife possessed a betel box valued at f25,000.
29. Liem, *Riwajat*, p. 90.
30. Therese Hoven, *In sarong en kabaai* (Amsterdam, 1892), p. 93.
31. Liem, *Riwajat*, "Permoela'an Kata."
32. Ibid., p. 142.

the teak-cutting concession and later still the lucrative salt monopoly. Then, like many successful Chinese entrepreneurs in Java, he invested in sugar milling. Tan Bing distributed his refined sugar to the towns and markets of central Java and gradually established shipping connections with Batavia, Ceribon, and Surabaya. His son, Tan Tiang Tjhing, later took over his various enterprises and in his subsequent career held the three most lucrative revenue farms in Java: the salt monopoly, the market farm, and the opium farm. In recognition of his success, the Dutch appointed the younger Tan lieutenant of Semarang in 1809.[33]

Following this appointment, Tan became captain and ultimately in 1829 Semarang's first Chinese major. His business interests included sugar, warehousing, and shipping in addition to the market and the opium farms. His son, Tan Hong Yan, a third-generation peranakan, became Chinese captain in 1828 and in the same year succeeded his father as opium farmer for all central Java.[34]

One of Tan Hong Yan's kongsi partners was Be Ing Tjioe. Be had been brought from China as a child by a successful peranakan dealer in tobacco and interisland shipping, into whose family he eventually married. He had served his first opium farm apprenticeship in 1824 as farm manager in Bagelen under Tan Tiang Tjhing and was named lieutenant and subsequently (in 1839) Chinese captain. By this time he was a full partner in Tan Hong Yan's central Java opium farm. Together Be and Tan built the first Chinese Council office in Semarang and staffed it with a professional secretary. In 1845 they cemented their commercial and civic partnership through the marriage of Be Ing Tjioe's first son, Be Biauw Tjoan—at twenty-one Java's youngest Chinese lieutenant—to Tan's daughter Tan Ndjiang Nio. Tan Ndjiang Nio thus became the illustrious Nonya Be. The elder Be and Tan were both ultimately named major, as was Be Biauw Tjoan himself in 1862, a position he held, save for the years 1865–72 (when Batavia stripped him of his rank because of his clandestine opium activities), until his death in 1904.[35]

33. Biographical information on Tan Bing and Tan Tiang Tjhing is from Liem, *Riwajat*, pp. 71, 72, 74, 76, 85, 86. Liem described Tan Tiang Tjhing as "an honest businessman (soedagar) with many influential friends (*sobat di kalangan pembesar negri*)" (p. 74).

34. At the time Java was subdivided into three opium farm districts: west, central, and east Java.

35. The *Riwajat* does not mention Be's temporary dismissal, probably because it was a regrettable episode unworthy of memory. Liem's style is anecdotal. References to the Bes and others are scattered haphazardly throughout the narrative; the infor-

For nearly half a century Be Biauw Tjoan was the doyen of the Cabang Atas in central Java. He stood at the center of the Be-Tan family partnership. He, his brother Be Ik Sam, and brothers-in-law Tan Tjong Hoay and Tan Tjong Thoen were among the dominant competitors for the opium farm leases of the 1860s, 1870s, and 1880s.[36] Be's business interests included other revenue farms, shipping, warehousing, and rice, and his investments reached at least as far as Singapore, where he owned property and, it was alleged, a secret share in the Singapore opium farm.[37] Like other successful Chinese merchants in Southeast Asia, he was fond of the lavish gesture: when his father died while visiting Batavia, Be contracted the private ship *Koningin der Nederlanden* for f10,000 to bear his remains back to Semarang for burial.[38] His more conspicuous charities included contributions to the war-ravaged inhabitants of Fukien, his ancestral homeland, and a shipload of rice for the famine-stricken Austro-Hungarian Empire in 1888.[39] Closer to home he continued the annual distribution of alms at Chinese New Year, an act begun by his father-in-law, Tan Hong Yan, which had thereafter become the customary charity of Semarang opium farmers; and he was the patron of several public institutions. One such was the Chinese orphanage he helped to endow with a contribution of f500 in 1864.[40] For a son-in-law, Be selected Liem Liong Hien, of a Grise peranakan family, who became Chinese lieutenant in 1858. Liem proceeded along the by now well-traveled path and became an opium farmer (in association with his father and brother-in-law) and a Chinese major.[41]

---

mation for this paragraph was compiled from pp. 72, 76, 86, 91, 101, 102, 103, 107, 132, 179.

36. Ibid., p. 141. They did not necessarily act in unison. Be Biauw Tjoan, for instance, was not party to Tan Tjong Hoay's disastrous 1872 farm. See Chapter 3, above.

37. *De Locomotief*, February 29, 1864; DMD to GG, August 23, 1866, no. 3303 in V 16/2/1867/1; Liem, *Riwajat*, p. 102; C. Castens, "De Opiumpacht op Java," and Tio Siong Mo, "Aan de Tweede Kamer der Staten Generaal," February 1, 1876, in V 17/8/1876/74; DMD to GG, August 23, 1866, no. 3303 Geheim in V 16/2/1867/1.

38. Liem, *Riwajat*, p. 126.

39. *De Indier* (December 6, 1873), p. 1039; *De Locomotief*, June 29, 1904; and Liem, *Riwajat*, p. 160. For his contributions to China Be was awarded the title of mandarin fourth class by the emperor of China.

40. Liem, *Riwajat*, p. 122; and *De Locomotief*, November 25, 1864.

41. See "Overzigt van den loop der opiumverpachting in 1886 gehouden," in TMC H422e. During the farm term 1887–89 Liem was party to the Bagelen and the Batavia, Krawang, and Bantam opium farms.

The wealth of the Cabang Atas was conspicuous. Aside from endowing charitable institutions and temples, the great opium farmer–Chinese officers of Semarang built luxurious family compounds nested in gardens laid out in the Chinese style, with fish ponds and ornamental mountains and caves made of coral. The Be family compound was known as Kebon Wetan, or the Eastern Garden; across the river was Kebon Barat, the Western Garden, home of the Tans. Within them the good life of the peranakan elite was lived—great feasts and parties. During the days of Be Ing Tjioe and Tan Hong Yan, Liem tells us, gentlemen Chinese drank rice wine together and entertained themselves writing poetry and listening to Chinese drummers and to the Javanese gamelan, good times recalled in the couplet "Bearing *arak* from Kebon Barat / Later I am drunk in Kebon Wetan."[42] At the end of the century Louis Couperus described the Chinese quarter of Pasuruan in east Java, and how, after rows of cramped shop houses, "The street widened and became suddenly more impressive: rich Chinese houses loomed up softly, like white villas. The most striking was the gleaming, palatial villa of an immensely wealthy retired opium farmer."[43] That opium was the source of such wealth evidently troubled the peranakans not at all. Many of them, after all, enjoyed opium themselves and offered it to their guests at home. Opium meant good fortune, an association illustrated well by another opium farmer of the Tan family who named one of his daughters, born in a particularly profitable year, Tan Apioen.[44]

The Be-Tan family group was one of a small number of peranakan family constellations which dominated Java's opium farms from midcentury on. In the farm term of 1887–89, for example, three such groups controlled, at the outset, thirteen of Java's twenty opium farms. The Be-Tan group held four farms: Batavia, Krawang, Bantam, and Bagelen. Three lucrative farms in central Java—Semarang, Yogyakarta, and Kedu—were held by a rival

42. Liem, *Riwajat*, p. 103: "Bawa arak dari Kebon Barat/Achirnja maboek di Kebon Wetan"; see also pp. 85, 150, 141. Tan Kok Tong, Chinese captain of Kediri and a major opium farmer of the 1880s, owned four gamelans. Resident Kediri to DF, December 21, 1888, no. 70 in Exh KG 8/3/1888/V3.
43. Couperus, *Hidden Force*, p. 71. I have changed one word in the English translation, replacing "opium dealer" with "opium farmer." The Dutch is *pachter*. In Couperus's novel, Pasuruan is called "Labuwangi."
44. Private communication from a relation of Miss Tan's; *apioen/apiun* is the common Malay variant of *opium*.

Semarang-based group headed by Ho Yam Lo, a self-made businessman who entered farm contracting in the 1870s in partnership
with the Armenian family Andreas, and who by the 1880s was one of
the wealthiest Chinese in Java,[45] a fact that was confirmed by the
appointment of his son Ho Tjiauw Ing as a Chinese lieutenant in
Semarang in 1887. By 1889 the Ho group, hoping to succeed where
two smaller kongsis had failed, had acquired the Surakarta and
Madiun farms as well. The third distinct group was headed by Han
Liong Ing, the Chinese lieutenant of Berbek, Kediri. This group,
called the "Kediri kongsi," held the farms in Ceribon, Tegal, Pekalongan, Rembang, and Japara, and had close familial ties with two
more, Chinese captain Tan Kok Tan's Kediri farm and The Tjaij
King's Besuki farm. Each of these constellations had one, usually
several, Chinese-officer members, and in fact only two farm kongsis
during this farm term had no Chinese officers as either farmer or
guarantor.[46]

Opium farm–Chinese officer constellations like the Be-Tan and
Ho groups in Semarang and the Kediri kongsi were, in fact, the tips
of vast social and economic networks. Each constellation represented a complex web of economic interests, family liaisons, and
both cultural obligations and contractual ones. Collectively, in the
sum of myriad interlocking individual investments and commercial
activities, the members of these constellations conspired to dominate commercial life in as wide a region as possible.

Broadly viewed, these constellations were hierarchical, like the
opium farms. At the top stood the group patrons, senior Chinese
officers, opium farmers, and farm guarantors. Beyond them were
lesser members of the opium farm kongsi, subfarmers, and lower-
ranking Chinese officers, including relatives and protégés of the
major patrons. At yet another level stood those in a direct, personal

45. Liem, *Riwajat*, p. 141.
46. Membership of the 1887–89 farm kongsis was compiled from the following
sources: "Overzigt van den loop der opiumverpachting in 1886 gehouden," in TMC
H422e; DF to GG, May 5, 1888, Z (Geheim) in V 13/7/1888/4; DF to GG, December
18, 1888, D7 in VKG 25/3/1889/T4; C. Th. van Deventer, "Toelichting tot het door
de Chinesen Ho Tjiauw Ing, luitenant-titulair zijner natie te Semarang, Liem Kie
Djwan, kapitein zijner natie te Djokjakarta, Ho Tjiauw Soen, luitenant zijner natie te
Djokjakarta, en Goeij Som Han te Semarang aan hun gesamenlijke crediteuren
aangeboden gerechtelijk accord," October 12, 1889, in V 22/2/1890/63; KVvNI
1891–92; and "Opgave van den opiumpachters met hunne borgen aan wie uitstel is
verleend voor de betaling van hun achterstand," in Exh 9/8/1892/76. Chinese officers are listed yearly in the RAvNI under Gewestelijke Bestuur.

relationship (receivers of credit, employment, or other sorts of patronage) to the core group, or to the kongsi as a corporate group; beyond these were hundreds of others who in smaller amounts, and several links removed from the center, enjoyed the patronage of the constellation in the form of credit, employment, or influence. Employment in the farms themselves was a major form of such patronage, but all sorts of economic activity was financed ultimately via the patronage of the dominant opium farm interests. Reaching out from the center of these constellations was a wide and diversified network of patrons and clients, along the chain of which the wealth of the few financed the enterprise of the many.

It was into the outer reaches of these patronage networks that many of Java's new Hokkien immigrants were absorbed, initially perhaps in menial capacities by employers with the same surname.[47] The most clever and energetic among them, having begun in some lowly activity, might attract the attention of a more influential patron, be placed with the farm organization, make a good marriage (if not for himself then for his children), and ultimately advance to affluence and prominence.[48] It was the truth inherent in such rags-to-riches experiences, and the more general ability of the peranakan patronage constellations to absorb newcomers and give vent to talent and vigor, which made assimilation to peranakan culture, and mobility within it, the most desirable path for the newly arrived Chinese immigrant.[49]

These constellations were not mutually exclusive. Marriages and the interests of business, usually intricately connected, bred a degree of overlap. Within them factions formed and dissolved in response to circumstances and opportunity. Nor were they permanently constituted. At the lower levels a good deal of slippage undoubtedly occurred in response to the changing fortunes of dominant patrons, particularly when opium farms changed hands. Nevertheless, such

47. Willmott, *Chinese of Semarang*, p. 301, points out that in Semarang it has been only recently that Chinese have not assumed a family relationship among all Liems, Bes, and so on; hence a newcomer with a common surname could be assured of assistance on the basis of presumed common ancestry. See Liem, *Riwajat*, p. 121. This assistance was crucial; newcomers, for example, had to acquire employment, and quickly, in order to qualify for a residence permit. See Albrecht, *Soerat Ketrangan*, p. 5.

48. See the story of one such *parvenu* in "Een Chineesch parvenu op Java," *TNI*, 1 (1853), 357. Though unnamed in this brief account, the subject is undoubtedly Be Ing Tjioe.

49. See G. William Skinner's comment in "The Chinese of Java," p. 2.

constellations represented clear focuses of economic power and
patronage. They were recognized as such among the Javan Chinese,
most of whom were, however indirectly, affiliated with one of them.
Indeed, doing business in many parts of Java required that one be so
affiliated.

The range of economic activities over which these constellations
presided was wide. They included other government revenue farms,
commercial agriculture, and light industry. Intimately connected
with these interests were widespread Chinese commercial networks.
It was Chinese traders who brought the surplus riches of peasant
Java into the urban marts and carried, alongside opium, countless
items of necessity and appeal—everything from textiles, fuels, and
metal implements to mirrors, thimbles, ribbons, and beads—into the
countryside where they were sold in rural shops and peddled in the
villages. The most significant feature of this trade was its penetration
beyond urban centers into the heart of rural Java. Here, in the
uncountable petty transactions of the village world, lay an important
source of peranakan wealth and social power. Not only did these
transactions insure a steady flow of rice toward the urban marts, but
they also supported a large network of clients, an army of individuals
whose private interests dovetailed with, and even depended on, the
strength of the constellation as a whole and that of its dominant
patrons.

Holding an opium farm was the first and major step toward
achieving commercial dominance in a given residency, but other less
lucrative government revenue farms also played an important role.
The minor farms included the right to collect certain special taxes,
fees, and tolls, and the exclusive claim to certain kinds of produce
(wood and jungle products, for instance) in specified areas. By
midcentury many of these monopolies were confined to limited
residencies or districts, and the once-important market farm had
been abolished completely.[50] Several others, however, including the
cattle- and pig-slaughtering monopolies, prevailed throughout the
island, and in many residencies certain important river crossings
and the monopoly of birds'-nest harvesting continued to be farmed
out to the highest bidder. Almost invariably, most of these farms in a

50. Confined to the Batavia or the Batavia-Bantam-Krawang region were the
wayang fee (for theatrical productions), jungle harvesting, the local tobacco tax, the
trade tax (neringen), Chinese head tax (hoofgeld), and most bridge and ferry tolls. See
de Waal, Aanteekeningen, pp. 402–27.

given residency were held by members of the same kongsi or patronage constellation that controlled the opium farm.[51]

The water-buffalo farmer (*kerbau pachter*), as the holder of the
cattle-slaughter monopoly was popularly known, collected a tax on
all cows, oxen, and water buffalo slaughtered within his residency.[52]
He was also charged with enforcing government restrictions on the
slaughter of several categories of protected animals and was expected to inform the authorities of cases of cattle theft. In practice,
he and his cadre of employees exercised surveillance over the cattle
population of the entire residency. For this purpose, and for the
convenience of the fee-paying population, the buffalo farmer maintained his officially sanctioned representatives everywhere in the
residency.[53] The pig farmer either slaughtered pigs himself or received a permit fee from individuals who slaughtered their own
animals.[54] Like the water-buffalo farmer he was required to post at
least one representative in every district, a good indication of widespread Chinese presence, since the Javanese eschewed pork.[55]
Holders of the pawnhouse leases claimed the exclusive right to lend
money at pawn for sums under f100. Ordinarily leased to individuals, from 1870 to 1880 pawnhouses were farmed as a monopoly.
Officially designated pawnhouses were scattered throughout every
residency. Of 922 in Netherlands India in 1874, 913 were held by
Chinese.[56]

Finally, the monopoly of harvesting birds' nests from Java's limestone caves was leased to the highest bidder in many parts of Java.
The birds'-nest farmer made arrangements with local villages to
carry out the arduous task of nest collecting. (Although not nearly as
pervasive as the other farms, the birds'-nest farm had a special

51. For various confirmations of this point, see Resident Banyumas to DF, July 8,
1867, L-K (Geheim) in V 7/12/1870/2; KVvNI 1875, p. 158; DF to GG, May 31, 1876,
no. 7364 in V 17/8/1876/74; TM to DF, October 4, 1888, no. 1387/12 in TMC
H422a; and TM to DF, February 16, 1891, no. 169/12 in Exh 9/8/1892/76.

52. For full-grown animals, 150 copper pennies (duiten); for calves, 100.

53. See de Waal, *Aanteekeningen*, pp. 239, 230, respectively.

54. From 100 to 200 copper pennies per animal.

55. De Waal, *Aanteekeningen*, pp. 394–95. Until 1864 pig farmers also monopolized the sale of pig flesh in their territory. See SvNI 1863, no. 137.

56. De Waal, *Aanteekeningen*, pp. 338–42. During the 1860s there were thirty-
three official pawnhouses in Madiun, fifty-five in Rembang, and thirty-seven in
Semarang. KVvNI 1875, pp. 164–65. See also Jan T. M. van Laanen, "Between the
Java Bank and the Chinese Moneylender: Banking and Credit in Colonial Indo-
nesia," in *Indonesian Economic History in the Dutch Colonial Era*, ed. Anne Booth, W. J.
O'Malley, and Anna Weidemann (New Haven, 1990).

connection with the opium farm. Harvesting birds' nests required ascending rickety bamboo ladders to pluck the valuable nests from the walls and ceilings of the caves; opium was considered so neces-sary to inducing courage to make the ascent that, even in areas where the government controlled nest collecting directly, nest pluckers were provided with free opium. Opium was also an essential part of the ritual offering to the cave spirits which preceded each harvest.)[57]

To their holders, the value of the minor revenue farms was mea-sured not in terms of the revenue they actually produced but in terms of the unhampered access to the interior enjoyed by farm employees. This access increased the reach of the controlling group and thus favored all its economic interests. At the same time it brought greater security to the opium farm by helping to keep rival Chinese out of the farm territory. "It has long been customary," wrote opium farmer Tio Siong Mo in 1876, "that the opium farmer take the cattle farm as well; this is absolutely necessary for the unrestrained exploitation of the opium farm. An opium farm that tolerates the presence of another farm, the cattle farm, in [its] territory can be certain of its own demise. The authority, for in-stance, to search homes, and the prestige the farm acquires from this and similar [privileges] count for little if one finds beside oneself in every desa another person with identical claims."[58] Tio knew from experience. He lost the pig farm to Be Biauw Tjoan's Hok Bie kongsi in the 1875 farm term, and the cattle farm to Be in 1876.

57. De Waal, *Aanteekeningen*, pp. 433–34, 438, 442. In the Priangan the regent of Bandung paid f2750 for the monopoly, and in Bagelen, Pacitan, and Yogyakarta the Dutch held the privilege for themselves. The connection of nests and opium was so close that when the government attempted to create a Forbidden Area in Treng-gelak, Kediri, the birds'-nest farm there had to be abolished. On the subject of the harvesting of birds' nests, see also C.J.P. Carlier, "Beschrijving van de Vogelnestklip-pen te Karang Bollong," *Tijdschrift voor de Indische Taal-, Land- en Volkenkunde* (1853), 304.

58. Tio Siong Mo, "Aan de Tweede Kamer," in V 17/8/1876/74. The Dutch recognized the complementary nature of the farms and always held the minor revenue farm auctions after those for the opium farm, a tactic designed both to inflate farm fees and to preserve tranquility in the countryside. They knew that losing kongsis at the opium farm auctions tried via the smaller franchises to gain access to their competitors' territories, and that opium farmers were extremely reluctant to let them do this. See KVvNI 1875, p. 158. This report records the unusual decision to award the cattle farm to the opium farmer for a smaller fee than bid by a competitor kongsi, for the specific purpose of strengthening the opium farm and preventing black-market competition within the territory.

Possession of these farms made it all the easier for Be to bring down
Tio's Surakarta opium farm later that year.[59]

Other investments highly favored by wealthy Chinese were government contracts. These included contracts for transporting state-
controlled commodities, selling salt, pruning the state forests, and
provisioning government institutions such as army encampments,
jails, and schools. The Cabang Atas dominated the bidding for these
contracts, and even where European bidders won the contract—
frequently the case with coffee-transport and salt contracts—Chinese undoubtedly subcontracted for the actual work. Like the farms,
many of these contracts not only generated direct profits for their
holders but also put them in a position to penetrate Java's agricultural heartland. Employees of the coffee-transport contractor, for
example, carried government coffee from inland warehouses to the
coastal shipping centers; they thus enjoyed unhindered movement
along the interior traffic arteries. The salt-distribution contractor
presided over a network of Chinese-manned salt stores which criss-
crossed the island. Employees of the various contractors, like those
of the farmers, could engage in a plethora of auxiliary activities.
Acquisition of these contracts was therefore yet another aspect of the
"battle of the kings." It was important for the dominant opium farm
interests that few of these contracts fell into the hands of rivals.[60]

The development of private commercial plantations following the
1870 Agrarian Law expanded possibilities for this kind of contracting. Individual plantations now contracted for construction, transport, and provisions. The Chinese were quick to take advantage of
such opportunities. Because exemptions from residence and travel
rules were granted in the interest of agriculture and industry as well
as the government revenue farms, such contractors, though they
did not enjoy the same legal authority as the farms, enjoyed considerable freedom of movement.[61]

In addition to revenue farming and contracting, wealthy Chinese
invested in a variety of other enterprises and, where it was permitted,

59. DF to GG, May 31, 1876, no. 7364 in V 17/8/1876/74. *De Locomotief*, December
15, 1865, carried a story, for example, of the confiscation of sixty katis of black-
market opium from an agent of the cattle and pig farms.

60. For lists of the various government contractors, see the annual KVvNI. In
1885, for example, the salt and coffee contracts are listed in Appendix PPP, the
forest-pruning contracts in Appendix FFF.

61. SvNI 1866, no. 57.

real estate. For example, peranakans financed the manufacturing and processing of rice wine, bread, oil, leather, and, most important, sugar.[62] In the 1870s and 1880s nearly half of the private sugar mills in Java were Chinese owned.[63] Many of Java's "private domains"— large landed feudal estates dating from the time of Raffles—were in Chinese hands; and after 1870 several wealthy Chinese, among them the dominant opium farmers and their associates, joined Europeans in taking advantage of the new opportunities offered by the Agrarian Law of that year by investing directly in commercial plantation agriculture. (Like the Europeans, they sometimes borrowed from Dutch-owned banks to do so.)[64] Ho Yam Lo, for example, had sugar lands and a mill in Probolinggo and held long-term leases on indigo and cotton lands in Pekalongan and rice land in Semarang.[65] Be Biauw Tjoan, Tan Kok Tong, and Oei Tiong Ham were among the other opium farmers who were known for their plantations and sugar mills.[66]

An 1871 statute permitting "non-natives" to rent smaller parcels of agricultural land from indigenous proprietors provided an additional investment opportunity for Chinese capital. Between 1880 and 1884, 470 Chinese (compared to 262 Europeans) took advantage of the opportunity.[67] Finally, wealthy peranakans owned a multitude of small properties—houses, shops, warehouses, and the like. Many of these properties were in the island's Chinese neighborhoods, but a substantial number lay outside. Farmers routinely maintained permanent properties in the interior to house their agents. Perusing the government property-tax records in the 1860s, C. Castens discovered that Be Biauw Tjoan owned properties in nearly every afdeling in central Java,[68] and a list of Tan Kok Tong's

62. See the compilation of Chinese commercial activities in Oudgast, *Onze Oost* (Amsterdam, 1897), p. 19.

63. KVvNI 1885, Appendix BBB; KVvNI 1875, Appendix RR.

64. Djoko Suryo, "Social and Economic Life in Rural Semarang," p. 178. See the contracts in V 22/2/1890/63. Among the banks were Handels Vereeniging, Amsterdam; Koloniale Bank, Surabaya; and the Internationale Crediet- en Handelsvereeniging, Rotterdam.

65. "Een pachtgeschiedenis," *IT*, December 3, 1889.

66. TM to DF, February 16, 1891, no. 169/12 in Exh 9/8/1892/76; and KVvNI 1875, Appendix R, no. 19.

67. See KVvNI 1885, p. 77, for the statistics; SvNI 1871, no. 163, for the statute.

68. Castens, "De Opiumpacht op Java." Castens does not name Be specifically in this article; rather he speaks of "one of the largest opium entrepreneurs in Java." We know from his private correspondence, however, that it was Be Biauw Tjoan he was investigating.

real-estate holdings compiled in 1888 revealed that Tan owned an imposing number of properties in Madiun and Surabaya residencies as well as in his home residency of Kediri. In Kediri he held the deed to seventy-three properties, only seventeen of which were in the official Chinese wards.[69]

Around and beneath the collective activities and investments of the Cabang Atas—the opium and other revenue farms, government and private contracts, commercial agriculture, and real estate—there was a lively Chinese retail trade. In return for manufactured goods (including opium) and credit, the Chinese brought village produce, particularly rice, into the marketplace. This general process was the sum of a multitude of small, discrete economic activities, transactions between Javanese villagers and small traders on the one side, and Chinese shopkeepers, moneylenders, and rice and produce dealers on the other. Copper pennies—both official cents and the older, ubiquitous duits—and credit were the primary media of exchange in this rural economy. The Chinese were essential to the circulation of the first and to the availability of the second.[70]

The circulation of copper pennies was the commonest popular manifestation of the gradual monetization of Java's rural economy—a process begun centuries before, but an increasingly pervasive one in the nineteenth century after the introduction of the land-rent tax and with the growth of wage labor. With copper pennies Javanese peasants purchased necessities such as seed and farming implements and other items of petty trade; with pennies, too, they bought the frills for their feasts and entertainments. The small quantities of candu and tiké which formed the base of the patungan trade in opium were also bought and sold for pennies; likewise, revenue farmers levied crossing tolls, slaughter fees, and all the other petty exactions of the countryside in pennies.

Although Javanese peasants sent a wide variety of goods to market—among them firewood, fruits and vegetables, and dry-season crops (*palawija* such as cassava, maize, groundnuts, and soybeans)—

69. Opgave: Property of Tan Kok Tong in Kediri; this is a list of seventy-three properties including their location, date of deed, tax assessment, and estimated real market value. In V 23/11/1888/F17.

70. A duit was worth approximately f0.006 in the 1880s. See M. T. H. Perelaer, *Baboe Dalima* (Dutch edition), 2:391n108. The duit, though no longer minted after 1843, remained the prevailing and preferred currency in the countryside of central and east Java well into the twentieth century. See P. Creutzberg, "Geldwezen in Indonesie in de 19e en begin 20e Eeuw," unpublished manuscript, pp. 24–25.

their fortunes were tied fundamentally to rice. Rice was the central commodity of the rural economy, and much Chinese activity in the countryside was designed to bring it into the Chinese-dominated marketplace. Chinese rice-gathering activities in Java had a long history, but like the spread of cash and other aspects of the island's economy, they intensified in the nineteenth century.[71] It was no accident that the growth of the rice trade, the partial monetization of the rural economy, and the full-scale development of the opium farm system occurred hand in hand. Indeed, as the strongest and most pervasive arms of the peranakan patronage constellations and their kongsis, opium farms were an invaluable asset in controlling the flow of rice in a given region; they also functioned as important credit institutions in financing the trade in peasant-grown commodities.

In the village world the collection of rice and other produce by Chinese was inextricably bound to moneylending and credit giving. At the bottom of the peranakan patronage hierarchies stood the rural Chinese trader—perhaps an employee of the opium, cattle, or pig farms, or the transport contractor, or salt distributor.[72] He may have been a local opium farm store manager, a mata-mata, a part-time patungan opium dealer, an itinerant craftsman, or one of the thousands of Chinese who by right of precedent lived permanently in one of Java's rural villages.[73] It was such individuals who entered into commercial relationships with village chiefs and farmers. A gap between expenses and cash income seems to have been an inescapable aspect of the peasant economy. Javanese therefore borrowed

71. Although the produce and rice trade in the interior was virtually a Chinese monopoly, Arabs, Europeans, and Eurasians also occasionally engaged in similar middleman activities. Burger, *Ontsluiting*, pp. 74, 76, 89.

72. A unique view of the internal structure of Chinese rural trade can be found in Tien Ju-k'ang, *The Chinese of Sarawak: A Study of Social Structure* (London, 1953). Tien's Chinese traders operated—in the late 1940s, the period of his fieldwork—in an economic and demographic environment in many ways similar to Java of the century before; Sarawak was, for instance, a lightly governed, economically under-developed colony. Most interesting is Tien's discussion of the credit relationships between members of Chinese patronage chains that connected urban *daokehs* (usually Chinese captains) and petty rural traders. Tien's study of the Sarawakian Chinese suggests what may have been the internal commercial and social relationships within nineteenth-century Java's opium-farm-based but economically diverse patronage constellations. See esp. pp. 42, 44, 65, 66, and chap. 9, "The Problem of Power."

73. Witness Sim Ju Hing, a farm mata-mata who lived as a *numpang*—a classification of villager who lives with another family, earning his keep by performing specific duties for his hosts—on the desa property of Javanese Martodimejo in Ponorogo, Madiun. See Onghokham, "The Residency of Madiun," pp. 198, 241.

small sums from the Chinese—to pay their taxes and debts; to buy seed or rent a draft animal; to hire someone to help prepare the fields; to sponsor a ritual celebration; or, for local hawkers and roadside stall-keepers, to do a day's business in fruits, vegetables, fish paste, sugar, and tobacco. Many of these loans took the form of an advance (in money or goods) on a rice delivery promised at the following harvest, or of a straight loan at high interest with unripe rice offered as security.[74] There were numerous variations, but the result was nearly always the same: unable fully to pay off one loan before needing another one, peasants found themselves committing a steady flow of rice upward through the Chinese patronage constellation.[75]

A correspondent of the *Soerabaja Courant* provides us with an extreme example. Although tainted by sinophobia, his story illustrates a process that, to varying degrees, affected many rural villages. In this vignette, a low-level employee of the opium farmer—perhaps a servant or small-time patungan dealer—establishes himself in a village. With farm backing and the cooperation of the village headman he begins buying up local produce. The village subsequently becomes the site of an official opium store, complete with a local bandar, a client of the residency opium farmer, and his helpers. The opium store soon becomes the hub of a growing local commerce, as the bandar and his agents advance opium, cash, and goods against

74. Van Laanen, "Between the Java Bank and the Chinese Moneylender"; Djoko Suryo, "Social and Economic Life in Rural Semarang," p. 179.

75. Comments about and observations of Chinese moneylending activities frequently appear in administrative correspondence dealing with opium affairs and Chinese problems in general. See, for example, Liem Hok Djien to MvK, August 25, 1889 (trans. L.W.C. van den Berg), in VKG 17/10/1889/G16; Assistant Resident Malang to Resident Pasuruan, March 21, 1891, no. 27/10 in MR 348/1891; and TM to DF, February 16, 1891, no. 169/12 in Exh 9/8/1892/76. See also "Nadeelen door de Chinezen in de dessa's op Java veroorzaakt," *TNI* (1850), 2:217; "De Chinezen als geldschieters der Javanen beschouwd," *TNI* (1859), 2:58–61; "De Chinezen op Java," *De Indische Mail* (1886) 1:195–98; and "Bespreking van de opium quaestie en de invoering van het licentie-stelsel door de Blitarsche Landbouwvereeniging," *TNLNI* (1888), 36:51. The picture of Chinese domination of rural trade which emerges in these sources was corroborated at the turn of the century by the findings of the official commission assigned to investigate indigenous poverty in Java, the so-called *Welvaart Onderzoek*. For a summary of the findings of the commission regarding the Chinese and rural trade, see C. J. Hasselman, *Algemeen Overzigt van de uitkomsten van het Welvaart-Onderzoek gehouden op Java en Madoera in 1904–1905* (The Hague, 1914), pp. 12, 121, 124–25, 321, 338–39. Hereafter cited as Hasselman, *Welvaart Onderzoek*. Djoko Suryo, "Social and Economic Life in Rural Semarang," p. 198, says that the coming of rails helped Chinese to dislodge remaining indigenous traders from the rice trade.

the discounted value of unripe rice to be repaid with full-grown rice at harvest time. Ultimately, by virtue of debt relationships and the self-interested collaboration of the headman, he and his agents virtually own the village. A steady stream of rice is guaranteed. With this the bandar pays his own debts to patrons higher up in the constellation, thus assuring himself of new supplies, goods, and credit.[76]

The extent to which Java's peasant population found itself indebted to the Chinese cannot be stated with statistical accuracy. It is clear, however, that such indebtedness increased throughout the century, and that by the 1870s and 1880s it was common in central and east Java. This seems to have been an inevitable outcome of Chinese penetration inland, for controlling the flow of Java's village bounty was a prime objective of the "battle of the kings."

The concrete manifestation of the Chinese presence in nineteenth-century Java was a network of opium stores and dens, slaughterhouses, pawnhouses, salt stores and depots, produce warehouses and ferries, plantations and mills, homes, shops, and stalls. These, either in isolation or clustered together in, say, a subdistrict capital—the seat of an assistant wedana—were the focal points of a Chinese presence that was, economically speaking, pervasive. Revolving about these nodes were all the multifarious economic activities of the patungan world, the primary goal of which was to tap peasant agricultural productivity.

It is obvious that colonial laws designed to confine the Chinese to ghettos in the coastal cities and inland towns did not eliminate them from the village world. Instead, these laws enabled certain powerful Chinese to gain a domineering influence over the Chinese population who lived and worked there—first, by allowing them to monopolize the revenue farms and contracts that conferred exemptions from those laws; and second, by permitting revenue farmers to exploit their quasi-legal authority, in theory restricted to the investigation of monopoly violations, to harass competitors and to reinforce their local presence generally. The additional fact that most opium farmers were high-ranking Chinese officers and that lower-ranking officers were, in many cases, their relatives and clients made their position nearly impregnable. Farmer-officers had a formidable battery of legal and social weapons at their command.

76. H.E.E., "Nederzettingen van Chinezen in de Binnenlanden," *De Indische Mail* (1886), 880–83.

But no one Chinese constellation could dominate a residency completely. It often happened, for example, that one group controlled the opium and cattle farms while another the pig farm or the transport contracts. In addition, the 1866 statute that itemized and strictly defined the Chinese neighborhoods in Java explicitly exempted Chinese residents who were, at the time of promulgation, established outside the camps: they and their heirs could remain permanently where they were.[77] Thousands of Chinese were thus recognized as part of the permanent demographic status quo of rural Java. The quickening pace and more diversified nature of economic activity following the 1870 Agrarian Law also increased opportunities inland for Chinese investors, contractors, and laborers. There was, therefore, always an entrée for rivals, always a black market in opium, and alongside this, always a relentless competition for the profits of inland marketing and trade. Therefore, as the kings battled in the auction hall, their corps commanders and legions warred among the towns and villages of the countryside.

77. SvNI 1866, no. 57, art. 4. The statute specifically includes in this exemption those Chinese who lived "in the desas." See Resident Surakarta to DF, January 9, 1889, no. 242/20 in MR 1889, no. 136, for Resident Spaan's comment on permanent Chinese settlers in Surakarta.

6

Channeling Influence:
Chinese, Pryayi, and Dutch

Competition among Java's leading Chinese merchants for opium farm leases and for lesser revenue farms was the most visible aspect of an intense competition waged at all levels in Java's society. To compete successfully the opium farm Chinese had to make their influence felt at every level—in the village, in the residency capital, and in Batavia. Doing so meant accommodating to the powers and ways of the village world, as well as to the pryayi administrators who presided over it, and to the Dutch Colonial Service, whose members administered Java on behalf of the Netherlands. It also meant exploiting the institutions that welded these diverse elements together, one of the most important of which was the colonial court system. It was typical of nineteenth-century Java that opportunities for such accommodation existed in abundance. The integration of elite Chinese, Javanese, and Dutch interests was among the key institutional features of its plural society.

Successfully waging the war for markets in the village world meant coming to terms with its masters, the regents and their pryayi subordinates. Regents, heirs of the ruling regional families of the preceding era, and now Dutch clients, variously ruled and administered their districts at the head of an administrative corps of hereditary noblemen. In pyramid form the pryayi hierarchy of regent, wedana, and assistant wedana, fleshed out at each level by lesser functionaries, clerks, and apprentices, formed the link between the headmen of the villages and the overarching Dutch administration.

Local affairs were entirely in their hands. Intimate in the knowledge of their districts, they translated local irregularities into administrative and judicial action. Law and order in the village world was their responsibility. The farm Chinese needed their cooperation.

This was especially true because the struggle for the opium market, and other markets as well, was intimately involved with the world of rural crime and crime detection. There was, first, the black market in opium. Controlling the black market was an essential task of the opium farm organization, but they could not do it alone. Second, almost any officially sanctioned Chinese activity in the interior provided an opportunity to engage in a related criminal activity. Opium smuggling by the opium farm was the most important of these, but there were others. Where inclined, water-buffalo farmers were in a good position to mastermind cattle thefts, for example, and pawnshop keepers were the logical fences for the stolen goods of thieves and brigands. Finally, the usual routines for investigating crimes in rural Java, whether used by farm mata-mata or local pryayi police, lent themselves to a regime of deliberate harassment of unwanted competitors. Indeed, Javanese conventions for dealing with crime in the countryside, and the way in which these conventions meshed with the institutions of Dutch colonial authority—the colonial courts in particular—created an environment in which Chinese influence could be brought to bear with great effect.

Java's colonial courts displayed the ambivalence typical of nearly all institutions in nineteenth-century Java. This ambivalence sprang from the Dutch attempt to impose an ever-more-thorough political and economic presence in Java while at the same time maintaining the balance of interests and relationships on which their authority had come to rest. Insofar as they concerned native Javans and the Chinese, the courts were essentially an arm of the European administration: they existed to enforce the laws and statutes that embodied government policy and in this respect were clear tools of colonial despotism. On the other hand, in their structure and day-to-day operations the courts were an important instrument of accommodation. In indirectly ruled Java, the interests and sensibilities of Holland's client partners, the native aristocracy and the Chinese elite, were, at least in part, provided for by the courts.

These courts reflected directly the social caste system of the colony. Europeans—including Eurasians and the occasional native or Chinese granted European legal status—were tried before courts composed entirely of other Europeans, all of whom were legal officers, and they were subject to legal codes nearly identical to those of the Netherlands. Depending on the seriousness of the offense, they appeared either before a Dutch judge in the residency court or before a panel of legal officers in one of Java's three Councils of Justice.[1]

Javanese and other "natives" and "Foreign Orientals," including the Chinese, were tried in the native courts, a hierarchy of councils and tribunals from the district to the residency level which were manned by indigenous dignitaries and officials but chaired, except at the lowest levels, by members of the Colonial Service or by Dutch judges. In the native courts, offenders were tried and sentenced according to indigenous law, custom, and tradition—insofar, that is, as these applied to the offense at hand and did not conflict with "generally recognised principles of fairness and justice."[2] Local squabbles and disputes among natives were heard and settled by the wedana. At a higher level, regents (or their patihs) held court for cases involving the infringement of community rules—neglectful maintenance of paths or water sluices, for example, or failure to perform village services.[3] The lowest native court that handled criminal cases, offenses against government statutes, and, in general, infringements of "law and order" were the police courts—called police roll—in which Dutch administrative officers, either residents or assistant residents, meted out arbitrary justice on the advice of local Javanese or Chinese authorities. Finally, the most serious offenses involving natives were tried before the Landraad, a council of indigenous dignitaries and advisers chaired by the resident or a Dutch circuit judge.[4] At the top, a supreme court sat in Batavia to supervise the entire judicial structure. The supreme court heard cases in which the state itself was a party, and acted as final review and appeals court for decisions made in all courts from the Landraad upward.[5]

1. *Raad van Justitie*. The three councils were located in Batavia, Semarang, and Surabaya. See W. C. Veenstra, "Rechtswezen," *ENI* 3:392, 394.
2. Quoted from Veenstra, "Rechtswezen," p. 393.
3. Regents could impose small fines and jail sentences for such infringements. See M. C. Piepers, *De Politierol* (Batavia, 1868), pp. 6, 7; Veenstra, "Rechtswezen," p. 395.
4. Landraad-type circuit courts also existed to hear the weightiest cases. They differed from Landraads only in being chaired by a judicial officer instead of an administrative one. As judicial officers gradually took over all Landraads toward the end of the century, the circuit courts became less important and were ultimately abolished in 1901. See Veenstra, "Rechtswezen," p. 396; also SvNI 1901, no. 13.
5. Veenstra, "Rechtswezen," p. 394.

Although the European and native courts were designed in theory to be distinct, in practice they overlapped considerably. In the first place, the European courts acted as the appeals court for Landraad cases. Also, any case involving a complaint or a contest between people of different castes—that is, between a native and a European—was tried in the higher of the courts, that is, before a Dutch tribunal based on Dutch law. Furthermore, the definition of "local law, custom, and tradition" on which cases in the native courts were to be decided was left ambiguous. Did it mean Moslem law or local custom? When applied to Chinese, was it the Chinese Imperial Code or local peranakan usage? These questions, left unresolved, meant that Dutch police judges and Landraad chairmen were more likely to act independently of indigenous expert opinion. In any case, many legal offenses in colonial Java, including opium violations, could not be decided on the basis of traditional laws and customs, for none was applicable. Finally, certain groups enjoyed a special legal status: indigenous aristocracy, including many pryayi officials, were exempted from the police roll and could be called before the Landraad only by dispensation of the governor general; and after 1855 many sections of the European civil and commercial codes, including those relating to debt, insolvency, and bankruptcy, were declared applicable for Java's Chinese.[6] Violations of some laws, therefore, subjected them to the native courts, of others, to the European courts. These ambiguities in Java's dual system of justice partly accounted for the success with which the opium farm Chinese exploited it.

Two offenses accounted for nearly all violations of the opium farm monopoly which reached the courts. These were, first, the possession and, second, the sale of nonfarm opium. Which colonial court had jurisdiction in such cases depended on the defendant's racial status and on the severity of the offense. Severity, in turn, was defined entirely by the amount of illegal opium involved. In the native courts, cases involving less than 1 tahil (38 grams) of candu— after 1877, 1 kati (618 grams)—were tried by the police judge; larger amounts, before the Landraad.[7]

For the opium farm the police roll was the single most important court. Statistics gathered between 1878 and 1880 show that 96

6. Ibid., p. 392.
7. See SvNI 1877, no. 24. For the purpose of determining jurisdiction and sentencing, the weight of the confiscated opium—whether in a raw state, candu, tiké, or otherwise—was converted into a farm candu equivalent by a local farm-appointed committee of inspection.

percent of all opium-related cases coming before the native courts in Java—some 14,175 in all—were tried at the police roll level, the Landraad accounting for a mere 4 percent. The number of such cases coming before the European courts, judging from figures collected in Semarang, was small by comparison. Ten or so such cases reached the Semarang Council of Justice each year, and its jurisdiction included all of central Java; only a few more were heard at the individual residency courts. From these and other statistics collected at the same time, three important characteristics of opium-related crime and its prosecution emerge.[8] First, an average of 35 percent of police roll opium cases involved Chinese offenders; the rest, native Javans, mostly Javanese. Second, a full 80 percent of such cases involved unlawful possession of opium, a charge requiring much weaker evidence than unlawful sale. And third, the vast majority of these cases involved quantities not only smaller than 1 kati, indicated by the fact that they came under police roll jurisdiction, but smaller than 1 tahil, or 100 mata.[9]

The commonest opium-related crime, therefore, was the illegal possession of a small quantity of candu by a Javanese; the next commonest was the illegal possession of a similarly small quantity by a Chinese. We may conclude, then, that the police roll, before which these cases were tried, was a crucial institutional element in the opium farm's effort to fight the black market at its base by dominating the rural patungan trade. As such it was also an effective coercive tool that helped the farm-controlling Chinese constellation make good on its broader commercial claim to the whole farm territory.

The Dutch resident, or more commonly the assistant resident, held police roll twice weekly, often on the verandah of his official dwelling. Here gathered the local pryayi and their police subordinates, all the relevant complainants and witnesses, the Moslem and Chinese advisers, and other interested parties, including local representatives of the opium farm. The jaksa, an indigenous legal official,

8. Resident Japara to DF, April 19, 1880, no. 1834/10; Resident Semarang to DF and DJ, May 12, 1880, no. 1641/3; and "Verzamelstaat van het aantal overtredingen van het opium pacht reglement [SvNI 1874, no. 228] welke op Java en Madura van 23 feb 1878 tot 23 feb 1880 zijn aangebracht," all in V 15/6/1883/51; and Wiselius, Opium Rapport Semarang, 1882.

9. This was pointed out by the director of finance, who complained that the new ordinance of 1877 (SvNI 1877, no. 24), designed to expand even further the role of the police court in prosecuting opium cases, had been pointless because most opium cases had always involved quantities beneath 1 tahil (38 grams). See DF to GG, January 11, 1879, no. 410 in V 3/5/1879/38.

acted as clerk of the court and prepared a summary of the results of the pryayi investigation in each case for the presiding official. Based on this report, the assistant resident interrogated the defendant and witnesses, heard the advice of the Moslem adviser or Chinese officer, consulted expert opinion (of the local opium chemists, for instance), and finally reached a decision. He found the defendant guilty or not guilty and imposed a sentence. His decision was unappealable.[10]

Before 1866 public whipping was among the commonest punishments meted out at the police roll. After that, police roll sentences ranged from a few days in the local jail to three months' unpaid labor on public works. Offenders could also be fined up to f25— after 1877, f100—and jailed for failure to pay.[11] Such sentences, petty though they may seem, were formidable in terms of the local rural economy and were made even more so by the fact that suspects frequently spent days or weeks detained by the wedana or police *mantri* pending completion of their investigations—that is, before their cases were heard.[12]

Police roll justice was arbitrary and occasionally brutal. Based on the discretion of the presiding Dutch official, almost anything could be construed as an offense against public order.[13] Thus alongside those prosecuted for theft, arson, and opium and gambling violations, others were punished for selling charms, "insanity," sleeping under the trees, seduction, overtaking the resident's carriage, and wizardry.[14] In addition, despite the 1866 ban, the physical abuse of

10. For an intimate glimpse of police roll proceedings, in this case in Joana, see Proces-verbaal: Vonnis Rechtspreken, Raad van Justitie Semarang, December 28, 1885, in V 27/7/1886/99.

11. In 1866, 62,659 people were whipped for police roll violations. See Piepers, *Politierol*, Introduction and pp. 22–24, 27; and TM: Opium Rapport 1888.

12. For a discussion and examples of such "preventive detention," see Laps, "Eenige losse opmerkingen over Amfioen-overtredingzaken," *IWR* no. 514, 1873; Fromberg, *Verspreide Geschriften*, pp. 411, 468–69. A mantri was a low-level native official who performed a specific function. A police mantri investigated crime and helped prepare cases for the local court.

13. Statistics regarding police roll cases collected in 1886 reveal that alongside twenty-three other categories of violation (including theft, arson, begging and panhandling, assault), most were listed under either "Other Offenses" or "Willful Offenses." See Bijlage F of TM: Rapport 1888. In Semarang, for instance, the number of cases listed under "Other Offenses" was six times higher than the next highest category. Of violations listed specifically, opium offenses accounted for a high percentage, especially in central Java.

14. See the list of 104 miscellaneous offenses that had been punished by police judges in "Verzameling qualificatien van vergrijpen ter policierol gestraft," *IWR* no. 176, 1866.

suspects under police roll interrogation still occurred well into the 1880s.[15]

The police roll was therefore a true instrument of colonial despotism. The Dutch intended it to be so, having retained it amid much criticism and debate when the system of justice in the Dutch Indies was overhauled at midcentury. Its defenders argued that the public exercise of arbitrary authority was important to the protection of Dutch interests and to the maintenance of a strong presence.[16] For on-the-spot members of the Colonial Service, the police roll was faster, cheaper, and more effective than the higher native court, the Landraad, where legal niceties such as rules of evidence had to be observed, and where the recourse of appealing to a higher court left a loophole for offenders with shrewd, and well-paid, Dutch counselors, a loophole of which the Chinese took special advantage.[17]

The thinness of the Dutch administrative presence in Java, however, and the legendary workload of its officials, made police judges almost thoroughly dependent on the investigations carried out by their pryayi subordinates. Time alone, not to mention the more difficult problem of penetrating the intricacies of crime and rivalries in the village world, meant that an assistant resident, as police judge, had to rely almost entirely on the conclusions and judgments of his native advisers. This meant in practice that the police roll, although it may well have acted in Dutch interests in a general way—that is, as a concrete, local manifestation of Dutch authority—could be used by others in a more specific way. Persons in a position to influence the outcome of local criminal investigations could frequently manipulate the courts in their own interests, legitimate or otherwise. The farm Chinese were among those who most successfully adapted and exploited the conventions for dealing with crime in the village world to do so.

In colonial Java, solving crimes was largely a pryayi responsibility. The regents, wedanas, and assistant wedanas who formed the upper level of the pryayi administrative structure were charged by their

15. For an example of routine petty violence at police roll hearings, see the case of Charles TeMechelen himself, whose violent excesses were reviewed by the Semarang Council of Justice. Proces-verbaal: Vonnis Rechtspreken, Raad van Justitie Semarang, December 28, 1885, no. 38 in V 27/7/1886/99.

16. For the debate surrounding the police roll question, see Piepers, *Politierol*, pp. 4, 5.

17. Note the comments in Resident Surakarta to DJ, May 5, 1880, no. 1472/P; and Resident Kediri to DJ, April 24, 1880, no. 2270/28, both in V 15/6/1883/51.

Dutch patrons with producing clear, unambiguous solutions, *ket-rangan*, to crimes that disturbed the prized and reassuring rural calm or threatened colonial revenues. The assistant wedana was the pryayi official most immediately responsible for pursuing a criminal investigation in his subdistrict. When a village headman summoned him to the site of an offense, he officially took over the investigation. It was his job to notify his pryayi colleagues of the crime, to lead house-searching activities (in cases of theft or black-market opium, for example), to confiscate evidence, to hold suspects, take eyewitness reports, and record accusations—in short, to conduct a complete legal investigation. His ketrangan, officially known as a provisional investigation, was used by the assistant resident to determine whether the case should be heard in court and at what level. At a later stage, the jaksa would use it as a basis for prosecuting the case before either the police roll or the Landraad.[18] Such ketrangan were therefore central to the efficient resolution of local disturbances and the prosecution of crime. For this reason, pryayi careers could depend on the success with which they prepared them.[19]

Success in producing ketrangan depended ultimately on a pryayi's links with the village world beneath him. These he maintained through his subordinate clerks and police mantris, who in fact performed much of the work that went into conducting a preliminary investigation. In turn their success depended on the cooperation of local village headmen and of a distinct class of village-world figures who specialized in criminal affairs, the *jagabaya*.

Jagabaya distinguished themselves from ordinary villagers by their supravillage experience and an aptitude for intrigue. As practitioners of the magical and martial arts, and adepts of the science of invulnerability, they attracted young disciples in the same way as the more orthodox Islamic teachers.[20] Their métier was crime, both its perpetration and detection, and their services were for hire. Thus

18. A more thorough investigation was supposed to occur before the trial. Except in the most serious cases, however, the original investigation report was the crucial one.

19. On the phenomenon of ketrangan and their importance, see *Onderzoek naar de Mindere Welvaart der Inlandsche Bevolking op Java en Madoera*, VIIIb: *Overzicht van de Uitkomsten der Gewestelijke Onderzoeking naar 't Recht en de Politie* (Batavia, 1912), 2: Slotsbeschouwingen, pp. 120, 122, 123; hereafter cited as *Mindere Welvaart Onderzoek*. Hasselman, *Welvaart Onderzoek*, p. 254; and MvO, L.Ch.H. Fraenkel, Resident Rembang (October 1901–July 1907) in V 5/3/1908/36.

20. See Benedict Anderson's discussion of the important social role of such figures in modern Java in his *Java in a Time of Revolution* (Ithaca, 1972), pp. 5, 9.

they frequently appear alongside other local functionaries as village police (*kapetengan*), appointed by headmen to protect villages from banditry and arson, and as detectives and "secret police" in the service of headmen, pryayi officials, and Dutch administrators. As such they often acted as ketrangan makers, specialists in producing airtight, and frequently false, solutions to criminal investigations which the Dutch required of their native subordinates. As kapetengan, jagabaya commonly enjoyed the use of communal property and were exempted from routine compulsory services. As "secret police" and detectives, they might be paid collectively by villagers or work individually for cash rewards and bounties.[21] They were viewed by the general population with fear, suspicion, and awe, as both heroes and villains, an ambiguity demonstrated by the fact that kapetengan were frequently required to swear a special oath to refrain from criminal activities within their home village. Better, went the conventional wisdom, to have a jagabaya as an ally than an enemy.[22]

The social environment of the jagabaya was much broader than that of the ordinary villager. Jagabaya gathered in opium and gambling dens and consorted among the fringe elements of Javanese society—dancing girls, prostitutes and pimps, traveling show folk, magicians and con men, fences and thieves, and the bands of bandits that preyed on the countryside.[23] It was their familiarity with these elements and their equal familiarity with the village world that made them such valuable resources. Jagabaya were therefore enlisted in the service of not only the native and Dutch authorities but also a variety of other individuals and groups whose interests penetrated the village world. Chief among these were the Chinese. Agents

21. *Mindere Welvaart Onderzoek* VIIIb, Deel II, p. 128.

22. The terms *kapetengan*, *djogobojo*, and *djogodesa* (as transliterated by the Dutch) were all used to describe those who held official or semiofficial positions as police within the village structure. Other terms associated with such figures in a less specific way were *bromotjorah*, *blateran*, and *weri*. See, for instance, Onghokham's discussion of the role of weri (which he translates as "spies") in nineteenth-century Madiun. Onghokham, "The Residency of Madiun," pp. 294–95. On jagabaya, see "Historische Nota over de dessabesturen op Java," KVvNI 1877, Bijlage N, p. 5 (based on observations made in 1864); J.H.F. Sollewijn Gelpke, "Dessa bestuur op Java," *IG*, 1, 2 (1879), 142; "Desa, Desa-hoofd, Desa-bestuur," *ENI*, 1905, 1:440–43; *Mindere Welvaart Onderzoek*, VIIIb, Deel II, pp. 116–17; and Hasselman, *Welvaart Onderzoek*, pp. 249, 254.

23. See Djoko Surjo, "Social and Economic Life in Rural Semarang," p. 268, on the *kecu*, or bandit gangs.

recruited from among the jagabaya class were key participants in the struggle between competing Chinese patronage constellations for control of Java's rural markets.

As opium farm mata-mata, jagabaya worked alongside Chinese mata-mata to play an aggressive role in finding black marketeers in the farm territory and bringing them to court. Tacitly condoned investigative excesses by mata-mata—including coercion, brutality, and invasion of privacy—and the colonial laws that punished possession of nonfarm opium by fines and hard labor, gave Chinese opium interests a great deal of leverage in the village world. Farm-initiated court proceedings could be used not only to punish legitimate black-market violators but to harass competitors of all sorts. The clandestine opium "setup," in which farm mata-mata or local police "discovered" a small cache of illegal opium planted in someone's house, was the commonest form of such harassment. Victims of such ploys could easily find themselves placed on a labor gang for from three months to over a year.

The actions of the farm and its personnel in these efforts deviated little from the prevailing conventions for solving crimes in the village world. Frisking, house searching, and the preventive detention of suspects were the stock in trade of all Java's rural detectives, from regents to the local kapetengan.[24] Farm personnel made routine use of all these techniques; in fact, the authority to do so was considered by the Chinese to be a firm, though unwritten, part of the farm contract.[25] The setup, in which an individual was framed to appear guilty of a crime he did not commit, and frequently convicted on the basis of craftily contrived evidence and false testimony—the work of jagabaya and village-wise Chinese mata-mata—was a classic device of harassed headmen and pryayi under pressure to present their superiors with ketrangan. Likewise, the fabrication of cases for purposes of revenge, and covering up one's own complicity in criminal affairs by foisting the blame on another, were hardly confined to the

24. See Piepers, *Macht tegen Recht*, p. 197.
25. In 1876, when Batavia forbade farm employees from both frisking and house searching (a ban that later evidence reveals was without effect), Surakarta opium farmer Tio Siong Mo wrote: "The authority to inspect the bodies of natives and Chinese, and to search their houses, is so old, and flows so naturally from the native's conception of the mutual interests of farmer and Government, that they are indeed considered an ongoing proviso of each farm contract." Tio Siong Mo, "Aan de Tweede Kamer der Staten-Generaal," February 1, 1876, in V 17/8/1876/74.

Chinese; complaints about these activities were general to the administration of justice at the village level throughout central and east Java.[26]

Opium farm activities in the field of crime and crime detection differed markedly from the norm, however, in one important respect: in concert they were directed toward the attainment of a specific residencywide goal, the furthering of the commercial interests of the prevailing Chinese patronage constellation. To bring cases into the colonial courts, farm interests could not rely solely on their own agents. Farm mata-mata had to maintain a close working relationship with local kapetengan and the police mantri who served directly under pryayi officials. The fact that Javanese mata-mata, kapetengan, and police mantri were frequently recruited from the same jagabaya group—that is, were most likely acquaintances if not comrades—generally facilitated such cooperation. In addition, the farm routinely subsidized these elements and their pryayi superiors by providing salaries, bonuses, and bounties in return for their efforts on behalf of the farm.[27] When, in the 1870s, special low-ranking European officers were assigned to troublesome residencies to assist local authorities in combating opium smuggling, they and their native subordinates also became the object of farm largesse. As a result, almost all farm-related cases prosecuted in the police roll and higher courts, though initiated by opium farm personnel,[28] involved the active participation of local kapetengan, police mantri, and pryayi.

Successful prosecution of such cases involved participation of yet

26. See MvO L.Ch.H. Fraenkel, Resident Rembang, October 1901–July 1907, in V 5/3/1908/36; *Mindere Welvaart Onderzoek*, VIIIb, Deel II, pp. 122–23; and Hasselman, *Welvaart Onderzoek*, pp. 251–56.

27. Discussion and examples of farm subsidy of indigenous functionaries and officials can be found in an untitled article in *De Locomotief*, September 2, 1864; Resident Bantam to DMD, September 23, 1866, F III (Zeer Geheim) in V 16/2/1867/1; DBB (director of the Colonial Service) to GG, January 21, 1876, no. 627 in V 22/6/1876/79; Piepers, *Macht tegen Recht*, p. 166; Resident Rembang to DF, July 17, 1882, Y in TMC H422b; Proces-verbaal: Vonnis Rechtspreken, Raad van Justitie Semarang, December 28, 1885, no. 38 in V 27/7/1887/99; H.B., "De Chineezen op Java," *De Indische Mail*, 1:195–98; Resident Rembang to DMD, September 27, 1866, no. 3752 in V 16/2/1867/1; and Resident Semarang to GG, November 25, 1889, no. 16617/49 in VKG 1/2/1890/H1. An interesting case arose in Bagelen in 1871 when Chief Jaksa Mas Ngabehi Atmodirono made excessive demands of the opium farmer in return for his cooperation, demanding not only money but control of the water-buffalo farm. See GG to MvK, March 11, 1872, in VKG 30/5/1872/W8.

28. Of 2,497 confiscations of clandestine opium in Surakarta in 1887, 2,003 were prompted by farm agents. See TM: Opium Rapport 1888.

another group, local farm-appointed and paid "chemists" who
formed inspection committees. These committees acted as official
consultants in black-market opium cases. They determined whether
or not the opium was of farm origin or not, on the basis of the smell,
taste, and color of the confiscated opium when subjected to a
flame.[29] Their reports formed an important part of the ketrangan in
opium cases. Considering the farms' relatively primitive methods of
manufacturing candu and the equally primitive techniques of chemical analysis used by these committees, their conclusions were most
certainly arbitrary and based on the farm's interest in the case. Yet
judges were required to seek their opinion; it was frequently the
only solid legal evidence that could be brought to bear to determine
a suspect's innocence or guilt. The inspection committee was thus
another part of the apparatus by which the farm exploited the
colonial legal system for its own ends.[30]

Records of farm-related investigations and court cases reveal the
way in which farm and nonfarm forces cooperated in the pursuit of
farm interests. In a typical case, the Japara subfarmer dispatched his
local agent Tjoa Boen Sing to search the home of one The Kong, a
patungan dealer suspected of receiving and selling nonfarm opium.
When Tjoa discovered evidence that The Kong had opened, then
resealed, the opium boxes supplied him from the subfarmer, Tjoa
called in the assistant wedana, who confiscated the evidence and
prepared the report eventually used by the jaksa to prosecute The
Kong before the Landraad. Crucial to the ketrangan was the report
by the local inspection committee who certified that The Kong's
boxes contained nonfarm opium, even though, as it later turned
out, they had not even opened them.[31] A similar case in Madiun
involved the Javanese Hirokromo. Most probably on a tip from a

29. In a sample opinion, the inspection committee in Joana declared that candu
found in the possession of one Troenodiwongso appeared too dark and crude and
smelled too sour to be the farm product ("roepanja kassar dan item; boanja ketjoet").
See Landraad Joana, Case of Troenodiwongso, October 20, 1879, in *IWR* no. 863,
1880.

30. A few astute administrators and judges succeeded in proving the inspection
committees incompetent. See the case of Proijodiwongso Sennen before the Kudus
Landraad, March 6, 1880 (in *IWR* no. 879, 1880), in which Landraad chairman J. J.
Smits successfully conspired to have the local committee pronounce a candu sample,
purchased only moments before from a farm bandar, to be from the black market on
the basis of its color and smell. See Case of Tjoa Ijan, Landraad Blitar, September 19,
1881, in *IWR* no. 955, 1881; Haak, *Opiumregie*, pp. 21–23; and Hoofdinspecteur
Opium Regie to MvK, February 9, 1907, in VKG 12/2/1907/E3 no. 16.

31. Case of The Kong, Landraad Japara, October 7, 1878, in *IWR* no. 804, 1878.

local farm mata-mata, he was arrested in his village by three police mantri who found him in possession of four packages of candu. He was taken to the wedana, at whose request the local Chinese chemists examined the confiscated opium. They confirmed that Hirokromo's candu had come from the Rembang, not the Madiun farm.[32]

Cases involving bigger fish and higher stakes demonstrated a similar coalition of forces at work. In 1873, for example, an attempt to smuggle more than a picul (61.8 kilograms) of contraband opium into the Semarang farm territory by an unemployed European named J. W. Scipio and a Semarang merchant named Lie Soei Tien was foiled by the combined efforts of the Semarang farm, pryayi, and the local Dutch administration. Having heard of the plan, Demak farm mata-mata Oei Djing Sang rendezvoused in the Chinese ward of Demak with a Javanese police mantri and his four subordinates. Here they awaited Scipio's carriage. When it arrived, they stopped and held it while the local farm bandar fetched the nearest European official to inspect the carriage. (Scipio's European status entitled him to this courtesy.) He soon arrived accompanied by the jaksa, the assistant wedana, and the wedana's clerk, all of whom witnessed the discovery of seventy-five packages of opium among the baggage, and all of whom later testified in the Council of Justice against Scipio and Lie.[33]

For opium farm interests, then, Javanese collaboration was essential to the investigation and prosecution of farm-related crime. Such collaboration was self-interested on both sides, for the pryayi, too, had something concrete to gain by protecting the local farm. Specifically, by means of gifts, bounties, loans, and salaries, the opium farm Chinese helped subsidize the regal manners and customs expected of pryayi by tradition—manners and customs that their own dwindling resources failed to support. In doing so, especially by providing a source of patronage, the Chinese helped to shore up the strained pryayi social structure.

In the Javanese world, a pryayi's role as the natural administrator of his realm blended with a broader cultural role. Javanese looked to

32. Case of Hirokromo, Landraad Madiun, December 30, 1879, in *IWR* no. 867, 1880.

33. Scipio and Lie each claimed the opium belonged to the other. Case of J. W. Scipio and Lie Soei Tien, Raad van Justitie, Semarang, January 31, 1874, in *IWR* no. 560, 1874. It is indicative of the influence of Be Biauw Tjoan, who dominated the Semarang farm, that not one member of the Semarang Chinese community stepped forward to provide bail for Lie Soei Tien.

the pryayi for human manifestations of the ideal Javanese. He was to display refinement, taste, and generosity, and to enact in his day-to-day life an aristocratic grandeur that exemplified the best of Javanese culture and that echoed the finest moments of Javanese history. The regents, representing the Javanese social pinnacle in the government lands, lived on the grandest scale, but other pryayi officials in the hierarchy mimicked, albeit on a smaller scale, the same taste for refined opulence and were bound by the same culturally defined social obligations.[34] These included sponsoring celebrations (providing food, entertainment, and lodgings) for countless special occasions, ranging from important stages in their own careers to commemorating the Dutch monarch's birthday—an event that their client status obliged them to celebrate. The Javanese expected charity of them, as well as support for indigent relatives and education for nephews. Very much in character, regents maintained large households staffed with servants and were openly hospitable to family guests and visiting dignitaries of all kinds, a generosity of which the Dutch took full, unabashed advantage.[35] It was all very expensive.

Traditionally such a life had been supported by the pryayi claim to a portion of the produce and manpower of their districts. Cultivation percentages, bonuses paid to regents in proportion to their district's contribution of export crops, were a modification of these traditional claims tailored to meet the needs of the Cultivation era. But when these ended with the dismantling of the Cultivation System itself, salaried pryayi administrators were less able to maintain the regal life. After midcentury a series of Dutch reforms gradually removed from the pryayi their remaining special resources: landed appanages and the right to personal labor services.[36] In addition, as Heather Sutherland has pointed out, the general tightening up of the administrative network which occurred as pryayi were incorporated in an ever more thorough fashion into an evolving and deepening Dutch presence reduced the area in which the official could extract even voluntary contributions of produce or labor from the

34. See Sutherland, *Making of a Bureaucratic Elite*, p. 25, especially her description of an assistant wedana, "a powerful and probably revered man to the population of his subdistrict. To them he was *ndoro sten* ('lord' assistant) and they would dismount and walk when they passed his house . . . and squat by the roadside and *sembah* should he pass them by."
35. On the way of life of regents and pryayi officials, see ibid., pp. 21–22.
36. SvNI 1867, nos. 122, 123, 125; and SvNI 1882, no. 136.

people.[37] To fill the gap as the century wore on, regents and other pryayi were increasingly prone to exploit their traditional claims to contributions and gratuities from the people by practices either vaguely or openly extortionary, and to rely on borrowed money.[38] For borrowing money, farm Chinese were among those who were prepared to offer more than favorable terms.[39]

As a result, higher native officials were frequently deeply in debt to the opium farm Chinese. These loans were more in the nature of considerations than business transactions and were not customarily recorded in notarial acts or promissory notes; they were also commonly disguised as another sort of transaction—a particularly popular ploy being the "purchase" by a Chinese of a gamelan or other property, for the continued use of which the pryayi seller paid a monthly "rent."[40] Precise figures about such indebtedness are therefore almost uniformly lacking. Investigations into the private affairs of regents, however, which occasionally occurred when their official performance diverged from Dutch expectations, revealed that they were nearly always substantially in debt to Chinese.[41]

Alongside loans, pryayi received gifts from the farm Chinese. Like their Dutch counterparts, pryayi officials were the recipients of *tanda hormat* and *sumbangan*—tokens of respect and customary of-

37. Most important in this respect was the Java-wide reorganization of the native administrative corps which occurred in 1874 (SvNI 1874, no. 73) and in which locally various administrative patterns, and the plethora of titles and ranks that described them, were standardized. The pattern described here, and the terminology, are those of the post-1874 period. See also SvNI 1867, no. 114; SvNI 1886, no. 224.

38. Sutherland, *Making of a Bureaucratic Elite*, pp. 22–23.

39. The worsening financial plight of the pryayi was often commented on as the nineteenth century wore on. See, for example, the article in *De Locomotief*, December 23, 1864, "Bezoldiging van Inlandsche Ambtenaren," the first sentence of which reads, "The Javanese are being robbed." See also Groneman's *Een Ketjoegeschiedenis*, a novel about a debt-ridden pryayi who takes to brigandage to redeem his pawned heirlooms. Other indications include advertisements, such as the one in *De Locomotief*, October 17, 1867, announcing the auctioning of Javanese treasures, in this case a gamelan.

40. See C. Snouck Hurgronje (Adviseur van Inlandse en Arabisch Zaken) to GG, March 14, 1905, no. 21 (Geheim) in V 21/9/1905/29.

41. See, for example, DBB to GG, May 5, 1888, no. 2601 (Geheim) in V 16/7/1888/6 (Case of RM Tirto Noto); Resident Rembang to GG, March 7, 1889, C (Geheim) in MR 1889, no. 287 (Case of RTP Karto Winoto); DBB to GG, May 9, 1888, no. 2636 (Geheim) in V 9/7/1888/4 (Case of RT Ario Soeria Ningrat); and C. Snouck Hurgronje to GG, March 14, 1905, no. 21 (Geheim) in V 21/9/1905/29 (RT Ario Soeria Ningrat). Pryayi also tapped other sources for loans, among them wealthy Arabs, plantation owners, and their own colleagues and subordinates—not untypically by deducting part of their salaries; see the case of RT Ario Soeria Ningrat, above. Also, Piepers, *Macht tegen Recht*, p. 167.

ferings—in some cases including their personal opium supplies.[42]
These loans and gifts played an important part in helping to keep
up the appearance of regality and meeting social expectations. More
important in reinforcing the pryayi structure, however, were the
various ways the farm acted to subsidize the pryayi corps. These, as
we have noted, included regular payments, frequently at the district
level and below, to encourage police work on behalf of farm interests. Large confiscations of nonfarm opium, for instance, brought
sizable bonuses for the participants; and local farm bandars were
known to express their gratitude tangibly for even the smallest
effort.[43]

The payment of such bounties and subsidies reinforced the pryayi
structure by providing a source of patronage. Pryayi officials could
disburse bounty and subsidy money downward among their subordinates, most of whom received their regular salaries from the government, and in doing so strengthen traditional ties of personal
loyalty. A particularly large bounty paid to Rembang regent Raden
Djojoadiningrat in 1890—in this case by the state—illustrates how
such money could be used. Djojoadiningrat distributed a total of
f8,120 in varying amounts to his patih, an assistant wedana, two
sunshade bearers (f470 apiece!), the headmen of two villages, a
police mantri and an irrigation inspector, four other lower police
and judicial functionaries, and an unspecified number of other
Javanese. Only some of these people had played a part in the actual
confiscation of clandestine opium which earned Djojoadiningrat the
bounty; he used the money for the more general purpose of reinforcing his personal position as head of the local pryayi hierarchy.[44]

The harmonization of interests which characterized opium farm
Chinese and pryayi relations found a parallel in those between the
Chinese and the Dutch. At this level, too, the farm Chinese succeeded in taking advantage of certain distinct features of Java's
colonial society to protect and further their interests.

42. DMD to GG, August 16, 1866, no. 3230 in V 16/2/1867/1.
43. TM to Resident Japara, December 31, 1882, no. 2694/10 in TMC H422a.
44. D. Dikkers (ambtenaar tijdelijk ter beschikking gesteld aan den Hoofd Inspecteur voor de opium aangelegenheden) to TM: Nota, undated (1890 by context), in
Exh 9/8/1892/76. This reference is unique in that it is the only one I know that
provides an actual list of how bounty money was disbursed. Several references from
the period point out that opium farm bounties were paid more swiftly and surely than
state ones. See the letter to the editor in *De Locomotief*, December 29, 1865; and
Resident Madiun to DMD, October 1, 1866, L (Geheim) in V 16/2/1867/1.

The first and greatest strength of an opium farmer was the revenue he provided the colonial treasury. This was considered so crucial to generation after generation of officialdom that it effectively undermined any sincere effort to deal with what were thought by some to be the negative social and physical consequences of opium smoking. Opium underwrote a significant portion of Holland's colonial enterprise. It was the farmer who effectively transformed raw opium into a fund of millions.[45] Over the years, therefore, a tacit assumption prevailed: how opium revenues were made was less important than how much reached the colonial coffers. This assumption, of which both opium farmers and local Dutch officials were well aware, related closely to two others, highly important to individual careers in the colonial service: that opium revenues reflected general prosperity, and that general prosperity was a reflection of prudent and wise administration. It therefore profited an official's career, so it was felt, if his residency or district provided abundant farm revenue. This is one reason that residency-level officials were often satisfied to give free rein to the farmer and his organization.[46]

A second reason that residents and their subordinates in the colonial service gave the farmer free rein was that farm activities, no matter how flagrantly in violation of the statutes, rarely constituted a danger to public calm or safety.[47] The officially illegal patungan trade, the black market, and illicit trading in clandestine opium by

45. F. W. Diehl, "The Opium-Tax Farms in Java, 1813–1914," paper presented to the Conference on Indonesian Economic History in the Dutch Colonial Period, Australia National University, 1983, analyzes the contribution of opium income to the colonial treasury. For the period 1848–66 he concludes, "It constituted 16.8% of the revenue collected in the Indies alone, but it covered 31.9% of the day-to-day local cost of the administration" (p. 7). Of the years 1876–1915, "when the colonial accounts ran into deficits totalling f295.3 million, the opium revenues amounted to f703.3 million, in the absence of which, the total deficit would have been f998.6 million. Thus opium reduced the potential deficit by 70%" (pp. 8–9).

46. See P. Meeter's comments on the reactions of members of the colonial service at an opium farm auction as "their" parcels came up for grabs. Meeter, *Opiumverpachting*, p. 3.

47. Exceptions did occur. In 1881 the assistant resident for the police in Semarang reported cases in which armed bands of smugglers clashed openly with the combined forces of farm mata-mata and the police. Wiselius, Opium Rapport Semarang, 1882. One also reads occasionally of such crimes as murder and arson associated with opium intrigue. See, for example, the case of Lie Yong Gwee, manager of the Pati branch of the Japara opium farm, who was fired on by three relatives of a Javanese who had been sentenced to forty days hard labor on a black-market opium charge instigated by Lie. Lie survived; his assailants were punished with fourteen years' hard labor. Pro Justitia, Landraad Pati, February 14, 1884, no. 20 (a,b,c) in TMC H422e.

farmers did little to prick the reassuringly tranquil surface so prized by the Dutch. Always eager to avoid a public scandal and to avoid projecting a negative image of their districts, not even the most conscientious officials, as one forthright resident put it, "feel constrained to meddle in such matters."[48]

The excessive workload facing members of the Colonial Service also militated against vigorous regulation of opium farms. As the century wore on, governing Java became both more complex and more bureaucratic; rules, regulations, guidelines, and circulars proliferated, multiplying paperwork at all levels ("living, eating and sleeping with pen in hand," as one observer described it).[49] Many officials felt, quite simply, that there were more important demands on their time than opium affairs and expressed this distinctly in the glib, shallow, perfunctory responses most of them made to periodic opium circulars emanating from Batavia.[50] Having read a series of such reports in 1867, a staff member in the Colonial Ministry in The Hague commented: "One seldom discovers the slightest trace of either knowledge or interest in opium affairs in their reports. Residents display . . . a feeling of powerlessness, and are convinced that the black market and farm secrets are impenetrable and thus that matters must be permitted to continue as they are."[51]

Finally, the frequent transfer of residents and assistant residents made the imposition of reform and regulation on such deeply rooted institutions as the opium farms, whose presence was permanent and whose character meshed congruently with local conditions, an all but hopeless task.[52] All of these factors favored Chinese farm interests because they created an atmosphere in which the local Dutch administration was predisposed to let farmers have their own way.

But farmers could not rely entirely on this acquiescent environ-

48. Resident Kediri to DMD, September 27, 1866, 02 (Geheim) in V 16/2/1867/1.
49. Couperus, *Hidden Force*. An official's wife puts it another way: "My husband has ceased to be a human being, my husband has ceased to be a man, my husband is an official." Both quotes from p. 74.
50. See the responses of Java's Residents to DMD C. Castens's 1866 opium questionnaire, Circular no. 1865, in V 16/2/1867/1.
51. Advies Bureau A: Maatregelen in Midden Java tegen den smokkelhandel in opium, August 7, 1876, in V 22/6/1876/79. See also the comments of Director of Finance de Roo in DF to GG, July 28, 1884, no. 12417 in VKG 3/2/1885/K1, no. 7; and those of Charles TeMechelen in TM to DF, August 3, 1889, no. 899/12 in V 27/5/1890/111.
52. On the effect of frequent administrative transfers on opium reform programs, see DMD to GG, August 16, 1866, no. 3230 in V 16/2/1867/1.

ment. Zealous officials were not unknown, and negotiations with the government on matters crucial to the farm occurred on a regular basis. Beyond that, farmers had occasionally to seek both compensation and redress from the authorities, and they sometimes faced the threat of legal prosecution. In such instances, farmers moved actively, lobbying with the administration and defending their interests in court. Fully understanding the implications of Java's racial caste system, farmers made shrewd use of European intermediaries, and Java's best Dutch lawyers counted opium farmers among their clients.

In the mid-1870s opium farmer Tio Siong Mo, for example, waged an all-out campaign to save his faltering and besieged opium farm in Surakarta.[53] Tio's farm income, depressed by flood and drought and chipped away by a black-market assault led by Be Biauw Tjoan, dwindled beyond the point at which he could continue to meet his contractual monthly payments. He then applied for relief in the form of lower payments and an exemption from his accumulated fines. For his various negotiations with the government Tio employed the well-known advocate C.P.K. Winckel,[54] who pleaded his case both publicly and privately (with residency officials, the director of finance, and the governor general), drew up his correspondence with the government, and when faced with dissolution of the farm contract, defended him in court. When the governor general finally issued an order to dissolve Tio's farm, Winckel assisted him in drafting a last-minute petition to the lower house of the Dutch Parliament in which he accused the Indies government of openly favoring the far more influential Chinese consortium led by Be Biauw Tjoan.[55]

Tio Siong Mo lost his case. But Dutch lawyers who represented farm interests were frequently more successful. Java's advocates were expert in manipulating loopholes in the colonial legal structure and in stretching the interpretive possibilities of laws to the limits. They also took full advantage of the appeals process, appealing Landraad convictions—where one's local reputation might be

53. See Chapter 4, above.
54. Director of Finance Sprenger van Eijk, in a letter to the governor general, called him "notorious," presumably because of his opium farm Chinese clients. DF to GG, May 31, 1876, no. 7364 in V 17/8/1876/74.
55. Tio Siong Mo, "Aan de Tweede Kamer der Staten-Generaal," February 1, 1876, in V 17/8/1876/74. Officials in Batavia thought the petition "far from seemly." DF to GG, March 22, 1876, no. 3899 in TMC H422e.

decisive—to the more legalistically minded European courts to clear their clients. Tan Tian Lie, for example, employed Dutch advocate F. H. Gerritzen in 1873 to sue the government for losses in his Madiun farm which were caused, he alleged, by tardy provision of government opium and interference in the activities of his farm by local pryayi. Gerritzen took the case all the way to the supreme court and won.[56] Similar cases were not uncommon. Likewise, farmers and other Chinese entrepreneurs under suspicion of smuggling did not go without legal aid. In an important case, Bali smuggling master and sometime opium farmer Oei Soen Tjioe employed D. Mounier, a Surabaya advocate, to sue the government for the return of his commercial books and correspondence, which had been confiscated by authorities in 1889. Mounier, a frequent defender of suspected smugglers, succeeded, and a disgruntled Batavia returned the evidence.[57]

Perhaps the most prominent Indies lawyer involved in farm and opium affairs was C. Th. van Deventer, later known as an outspoken promoter of Ethical colonial policies. During his Semarang legal career he represented several opium farm clients. In 1890, when the major kongsis faced bankruptcy and loss of their farm leases, he advised and appeared on behalf of the two strongest opium consortiums in central Java, the Ho group of Semarang, now headed by the late Ho Yam Lo's son Ho Tjiauw Ing, and Han Liong Ing's Kediri kongsi.[58] Van Deventer's services included using his influence as well as providing legal appearances. In late 1889 he wrote personally to the governor general on behalf of Ho Tjiauw Ing and his associates, calling them upstanding citizens of official importance.[59]

Europeans also served farm interests in other intermediary roles. Ceribon farmer Oei Tiang Djie, for instance, employed a retired

56. Tan Tian Lie vs. Regeering, HG, April 3, 1873 in *IWR* no. 520, 1873.
57. Procureur Generaal HG to GG, January 18, 1889, no. 118 in V 10/6/1891/42. Mounier appeared, for instance, on behalf of The Toan Hwat, a supercargo of the vessel *Bandjermassin* in his smuggling trial. See Pro Justitia, Raad van Justitie, Surabaya, September 21, 1889, in TMC H422b.
58. On van Deventer's role on behalf of these clients, see Resident Uljee of Rembang's comments in "Aanteekeningen op het vonnis van den Raad van Justitie te Semarang dd 13 juni 1891 No. 8 in hooger beroep gewezen van een vonnis van den Landraad te Rembang dd 28 maart 1891 No. 7 in zake Lie Hong Joe" in Exh 9/8/1892/76.
59. C. Th. van Deventer to GG, October 14, 1889, in V 22/2/1890/63. See van Deventer's comment about his Chinese clients (his most "congenial," he writes) quoted in *Leven en Arbeid van Mr. C. Th. van Deventer*, ed. H. T. Colenbrander and J. E. Stokvis, 1:167 (Amsterdam, 1916).

sheriff named A. L. Edwards to manage all his relations with the government; and, although rare, European-Chinese farm kongsis also existed.[60] Both the Andreas and Johannes families, Armenians, joined in farm consortiums in the 1860s and 1870s in Tegal, Surakarta, and Semarang.[61] It is likely that in these cases the capital was largely Chinese and that the European "front"—in these cases the European partner was the official farmer—was designed to facilitate a smooth liaison between the farm and the authorities. In 1867, for example, Th. Carapiet Andreas, the farmer in Surakarta, won a major concession from Batavia when the government was obliged by a decision of the supreme court to provide the farm with free grounds and buildings.[62]

Liaison between farm interests and private Europeans provided another link between peranakan opium interests and the colonial ruling class. Chinese and Europeans might be business partners; several such partnerships appear after 1870 in the exploitation of long-term leases to native land for commercial purposes. Some Chinese owners of plantations and processing plants hired professional Europeans to run them.[63] In some cases the general interests of some European or Eurasian families were connected with the fortunes of a particular Chinese. This may have involved mutual investment in various enterprises, and also indebtedness of one sort or another. The liaison of the Coenraad family in Pacitan with opium farmer and Chinese lieutenant Tan Ing Soen, which included partnership in clandestine opium dealing, is an example. When their mutual criminal activities were exposed, the Coenraads lobbied privately on Tan's behalf.[64]

The common nonchalance of Dutch administrators about the activities of opium farmers was further encouraged by an environment among the residency elite in which the exchange of favors was raised to the level of *adat* (accepted and honored custom).[65] Both

60. Resident Ceribon to DF, November 19, 1878, no. 7649/45 in V 16/10/1880/1.
61. Resident Tegal to DMD, June 8, 1866, no. 1083/23 in V 16/2/1867/1; Th. C. Andreas vs. NI, Raad van Justitie Semarang, September 11, 1867, in *IWR* no. 237, 1868; and *De Indier*, November 21, 1874, p. 903.
62. Raad van Justitie Semarang, September 11, 1867, in *IWR* no. 237, 1868; and Th. C. Andreas vs. NI, HGvNI, August 13, 1868, in *IWR* no. 302, 1869.
63. Metger (Semarang agent for Internationale Crediet en Handelsvereeniging "Rotterdam") to Mr. [Master of Law] C. W. Baron van Heeckeren, July 1, 1889, in V 22/2/1890/63, which includes a list of Ho Tjiauw Ing's employees in his sugar mills and coffee gardens.
64. DMD to GG, August 31, 1866, no. 3405 in V 16/2/1867/1.
65. Steinmetz, *Brieven*, p. 49.

Dutch colonial administrators and their Javanese counterparts lived in a social atmosphere in which their respective positions encouraged them, if it did not require them, to live beyond their means.[66] The colonial good life in Java—including maintaining huge households, lavish entertaining, and Java's renowned hospitality—was in part subsidized by means of social customs that permitted well-heeled Chinese supplicants to curry favor with the Colonial Service. Many of these activities can be grouped under the general name of sumbangan (contributions). The receipt of sumbangan by pryayi officials was sanctioned by Javanese tradition. Regents, for instance, were entitled to sumbangan on special occasions and routinely received unsolicited gifts from people with specific requests to be granted or general interests to further.[67] By the nineteenth century the sumbangan custom had long since permeated the European official class and was particularly characteristic of interelite relations. Opium farmers were among those who made masterful use of its possibilities.

One of the commonest forms of sumbangan was the offering of gifts to Dutch officials on festive occasions, for which the multicultural calendar of the Indies offered innumerable opportunities. Each Chinese New Year, for example, officials received tanda hormat (tokens of respect) from supplicant Chinese, gifts that might range in extravagance from Manila cigars and European liquors to expensive silks, gems, and jewelry "for the Mevrouw."[68] Birthdays of administrators and members of their families, as well as Christian holidays, offered similar opportunities to please the administration. A second form of sumbangan was the lending on a long-term basis of such items as furniture, carriages, and horses to newly appointed officials. In some residencies permanent furnishings of the resident's official dwelling—gilded mirrors, chandeliers, and draperies—were owned by wealthy farm Chinese, who "loaned" them to each successive occupant.[69]

66. "Oudgast," for example, comments, "Europeans in India are for the most part lavish spenders. Either they just don't know the value of money, or overestimate their resources." Oudgast, *Onze Oost*, p. 63. See also DMD to GG, August 16, 1866, no. 3230 in V 16/2/1867/1. Even Louis Couperus's model official, Resident van Oudijck, could not live within his means. See *De Stille Kracht*, p. 32.

67. Sutherland, *Making of a Bureaucratic Elite*, p. 23.

68. See DMD to GG, October 9, 1866, no. 3910 (Zeer Geheim en Vertrouwelijk) in V 16/2/1867/1; Piepers, *Macht tegen Recht*, pp. 161–62; G. J. Putnam Cramer, "Het opiumgebruik en de sluikhandel in opium op Java en Madura," *IT*, December 10, 1889. Opium farm account books sometimes included entries for gift giving. See TM to DF, August 9, 1891, no. 714/B in TMC 422c.

69. Piepers, *Macht tegen Recht*, p. 163; Steinmetz, *Brieven*, pp. 51–52.

Providing the expensive accoutrements of the colonial good life
was a specialty of the opium farm Chinese.[70] Witness this snide but
knowledgeable account, attributed to a Rembang official well ac-
quainted with local goings-on, about "Richard," the son of Liem Kok
Sing, chief managing officer of the Kediri kongsi:

> "Richard. Come here, my lad. Come here Indispensable. Listen, little
> man who does and sees everything, as if his eyes were binoculars.
> Richard, I need a team of horses."
> "So, do you really? Ah yes! Horses? That hadn't occurred to me.
> You'd like some horses? I'll take care of that, and they'll be good ones, I
> promise you."
> The horses came, and they *were* good.
> (Some time later) "Richard, the poor little horses have nothing to
> eat."
> "What! Nothing to eat? Merciful heavens! I'll tidy that up. There'll
> be feed, and the best."
> And the feed arrived. Richard provides everything that people
> want.[71]

Another related form of sumbangan was the routine providing of
food and supplies, either free or at discount, to the resident's and
other official households. Liem Thian Joe, for instance, writes of
nineteenth-century Semarang residents receiving daily provisions
of eggs, chickens, beef, pork, vegetables, rice, and fish—all fancy
grade—on the opium farmer's account.[72] Unsecured low-interest
loans to friends and relations of officials (prodigal sons, newly arrived nephews) were yet another form of sumbangan. Finally, the
habit of Indies Europeans of purchasing heavily on credit from
Chinese shops, a habit Chinese did little to discourage, also helped
to subsidize the petty opulence of the life of the ruling elite.[73]

70. See Assistant Resident Joana to Resident Japara, December 31, 1882, no.
2694/10 in TMC H422a; also "Opheffer's" account of an opium farmer's eagerness
to provide him with horses. G. L. Gonggrijp, *Brieven van Opheffer aan de redactie van het
Bataviaasch Handelsblad* (Maastricht, 1913).
71. "Opium Snippers," *Weekblad van Neerlandsch-Indie* (J. A. Uilkens, ed.), June 7,
1891, no. 32, pp. 1702–03.
72. Liem, *Riwajat*, pp. 148–50. Liem corroborates Dutch accounts of the sumbangan system and the special part opium farmers played in it.
73. Oudgast, *Onze Oost*, pp. 63, 72. On p. 60, Oudgast describes the "lain boelan"—
"another month" or, loosely, "maybe next time"—system of settling accounts, or
rather not settling them, between European ladies and Chinese provisioners. See also
Piepers, *Macht tegen Recht*, p. 160.

Before the auction. Chromolithography by Jhr. J. C. Rappard, in *Neder-landsch-Indie* (1881–83).

Moreover, lavish entertainments put on by the Chinese some-times provided welcome touches of unrestrained luxury. Therese Hoven describes one such affair in Surabaya, hosted by the Chinese major there to celebrate his seventy-first birthday. Some eight hun-dred guests watched a fireworks display and a grand parade of floats at his expense, and then feasted on boeuf pressé with sauce re-moulade, endless Chinese and Indies treats, plus champagne and "every possible wine and liquor." Tellingly, Hoven observes that whereas the rich Chinese invited Europeans to parties like these, the Chinese were never invited in return.[74]

The quintessential sumbangan institution in colonial Java was the auction. It was customary for officials to auction off their private

74. Hoven, *In Sarong en Kabaai*, p. 117.

possessions and household furnishings—from flowerpots and tea-
spoons to carriages and cattle—at the end of each posting. Such
auctions offered a final opportunity for an official's subordinates,
associates, and other well-wishers to demonstrate their respect by
purchasing items at highly inflated prices. On such occasions common teacups reportedly brought as much as f500, and native officials from regents to lowly mantris pledged a month's salary to buy
the discarded bric-a-brac of the residency house.[75] The higher the
position of the departing official, the larger and more dignified the
crowd and the more grandiose the bids. Because of this the auctions
of departing residents were carnival affairs, when all European and
native officials congregated in the residency capital and speculation
about the bidding became the subject of gossip throughout the
residency. Normal caste conventions were suspended at auction
time, and the customarily sacrosanct inner chambers of the resident's official dwelling were opened for everyone's inspection. As
one slightly horrified observer recorded, "Natives, Chinese and
Arabs uninhibitedly make themselves comfortable on sofas and bed-
steads [and] rummage through the drawers of the dressing table."[76]
Auctions were commonly preceded by a champagne reception, and
hosts were observed on such occasions to be unusually hospitable to
the wealthy Chinese.[77]

The high bids at such auctions were not purely voluntary. Native
officials, whose salaries hardly enabled them to make such gestures,
were expected to make a sumbangan; skilled professional auc-
tioneers exploited the public sensibilities of the Javanese to commit
them to bids beyond their means, to be paid in some cases by
deductions from their government salaries. For opium farm interests, ostentatious bidding served two related purposes: it was a
public demonstration of their good character and generosity and at
the same time served as a hint to the incoming official (who would be
fully informed about such matters) of what he might expect should
his relations with the farm be as felicitous.

75. Steinmetz, *Brieven*, pp. 51–52.
76. Ibid., p. 46.
77. For other accounts of such auctions see Piepers, *Macht tegen Recht*, pp. 170–75;
and Perelaer, *Baboe Dalima*, pp. 281–87. See also DMD to GG, October 9, 1866, no.
3910 (Zeer Geheim en Vertrouwelijk) in V 16/2/1867/1. Advertisements for upcoming auctions frequently appeared in *De Locomotief*. These advertisements are perhaps
the best indication of the size and luxury of official households, even those of
controleurs.

The casual environment of mutual obligation engendered by the sumbangan custom could be augmented, when occasion required, by direct bribes. The line between sumbangan and open bribery is indefinable; at some point, however, the give and take of adat became impropriety, while at another, graft. Sumbangan were an accepted feature of Indies life, sanctioned by custom and openly talked about. Direct bribery was not. The giving and receiving of bribes was therefore a private affair, the invisible base of the sumbangan iceberg. Critical observers of the farm system felt certain, however, that such bribery played an important role in relations between opium farmers and some officials. In his important report of October 9, 1866, C. Castens cited several cases of direct bribery with which he was familiar from his experience as resident of Japara and Bagelen, and reported to the governor general that no fewer than eighteen residents agreed that bribery played a significant part in opium farm affairs.[78] Commenting on Castens's report, the Indies Council simply acknowledged, "We have lived with bribery for a long time."[79]

The receipt by an official of a particularly well-timed and extravagant gift from an opium farmer was therefore a common item of Indies gossip. M.T.H. Perelaer drew upon such club talk for his portraits of Resident and Mevrouw van Gulpendam, the ambitious official couple who were the villains of his antiopium novel *Baboe Dalima*. The van Gulpendams solicited bribes from farmer Lim Yang Bang in exchange for squelching an investigation into the criminal activities of the farmer's son; their judicious support of Lim won for Resident van Gulpendam, whose opium revenues surpassed all others, a Dutch knighthood.[80] Perelaer's portraits of the van Gulpendams and the farm Chinese are full of indignation and are more in the nature of caricature. It is therefore interesting to note that Liem Thian Joe, who read *Baboe Dalima* when it was

78. DMD to GG, October 9, 1866, no. 3910 (Zeer Geheim en Vertrouwelijk) in V 16/2/1867/1. Though Castens described several cases of bribery that he accepted as being true, he mentioned no names.

79. Advies, Raad van Nederlandsch Indie, June 14, 1867, no. 12 in V 27/1/1869/17C. Piepers, *Macht tegen Recht*, p. 163, noted that in Batavia of the 1860s the resident was known among natives and Chinese as *toewan seriboe*, the residency secretary as *toewan seratoes*, and the registrar of the Landraad, his predecessor, as *toewan sepoeloeh*; that is, Mister Thousand, Mister Hundred, and Mister Ten, denoting, it was alleged, the price of doing business.

80. Perelaer, *Baboe Dalima*. See chaps. 6, 25, and 26 for depictions of graft in action.

serialized in an early Malay-language newspaper, credited Perelaer
with an accurate knowledge of the "ins and outs of Chinese life, the
extravagance of the farmers, and their methods of currying friendship with influential officials."[81] Never one to understate the influence of his peranakan forebears, Liem's comments nevertheless
suggest that the exchange of favors between colonial officials and
farm Chinese was common knowledge among the Chinese as well,
an object of interest and the subject of tales that became part of the
peranakan oral tradition.

If highly placed officials were susceptible to the blandishments of
farmers, low-ranking police and customs functionaries—who by
caste belonged to the ruling class but whose incomes made a comparable material life a vain hope—were all the more so. Such subordinates were recruited from among the poorer, less reputable Europeans and the Eurasian population, the loose ends of colonial Java's
racial elite, and they were nearly universally considered untrustworthy by their superiors.[82] It was widely known that low-ranking police
and customs personnel supplemented their incomes by accepting
additional stipends from opium farmers, ostensibly for their vigor in
protecting the legal farm. In fact, payoffs to sheriffs who served with
the police establishment in Batavia, Semarang, and Surabaya purchased anonymity for urban low life, clandestine gaming houses,
opium dens, and bordellos.[83] Typical of the stories told of such
personnel is that of the customs officer posted on the north coast at
the mouth of a small river and charged with preventing clandestine
imports. Despite a meager salary (for a European) of f480 a year, he
managed to stash away some f40,000 in silver money, which was
discovered hidden in his house after he died unexpectedly of cholera.[84]

At every level, then, from Batavia to the residency capital, from
the residency capital to the seat of the regent, from the regency seat
to the wedana's court, and on down to the village itself, the farm
Chinese found collaborators in the pursuit of their interests. The

81. Liem, *Riwajat*, pp. 139–40.
82. See Resident Serle's comments in Resident Bagelen to DMD, September 25,
1866, J (Vertrouwelijk) in V 16/2/1867/1.
83. See Resident Pekalongan to DMD, September 27, 1866, A (Geheim) in V
16/2/1867/1; and Piepers, *Macht tegen Recht*, pp. 167–68.
84. Cramer, "Het opiumgebruik." C. Castens wrote of subordinate functionaries
who possessed fortunes, "who would never dare explain how they acquired them."
DMD to GG, August 16, 1866, no. 3230 in V 16/2/1867/1.

success with which they exploited both the formal machinery of the Dutch establishment and other less formal aspects of the colonial administration and status system, not to mention the realities of the village world, illustrates the flexibility of Java's colonial institutions and the interdependence of the elites who, at whatever level, presided over them.

Like its sister institutions, the opium farm had a life of its own that, although constrained and partially shaped by Dutch policy, defied the rigidification of the statute book. The observable divergence between policy and practice which resulted was treated with absolute nonchalance by most colonial Dutch, but it irritated Dutch policy makers and worried many others who feared the consequences of an unrestrained proliferation of opium among the people. In doing so it spurred countless attempts during the century to formulate an opium policy that would bend the opium farm more closely to the officially stated goals of the government.

7

The Quest for the
Perfect Vice Tax

In Java, the Dutch never entirely abandoned the East India Company's view of opium as a lucrative commercial product. Well into the twentieth century revenues remained the dominant and constant variable in opium policy decisions. As a result of the full development of the opium farm system in the nineteenth century, however, and in response to changing attitudes regarding the aims and responsibilities of colonialism, other concerns emerged. One of these was the morality of the opium trade. Another was enforcement; indeed, as the Dutch presence widened and deepened, the problem of controlling the black market assumed an increasingly dominant part in formulating policies about opium.

In 1803, only nine years after the commissioners general of the dying Dutch East India Company had pressed their servants in Java to expand their opium sales to the limit in the interests of trade, the first strong voice was raised against the exploitation of opium profits in the Indies.[1] Speaking for the six commissioners whom the Dutch government (Batavia Republic) appointed to consider the question of colonial reform following the collapse of the VOC, Sebastiaan Cornelius Nederburgh recommended that "all measures that local circumstances permit be employed to lessen the use of opium upon the island of Java, and, if it is possible, to eliminate it altogether."[2]

1. Baud, "Proeve," p. 149.
2. "Rapport der Commissie tot de Oost-Indische Zaken," May 31, 1803, quoted in Baud, "Proeve," p. 133; Day, *Dutch in Java*, pp. 134–44; Bastin, *Raffles*, pp. 13–16.

Although war in Europe intervened before the recommendations of the commissioners could be put into action, their condemnation of opium, and their vision of a government policy that addressed itself to suppressing, if not eliminating, the opium habit, found adherents throughout the rest of the century—in the Colonial Service, the Indies Council, and in an occasional governor general, colonial minister, or member of Parliament. These voices were never to be the dominant ones, but the sentiment they expressed, a sentiment that blended with a more general one that viewed native welfare as one of Holland's colonial obligations, formed a constant counterpoint to the prevailing concern of the state, the quest for colonial revenues and profit. As a result, the attempt to design an opium farm system that was at once both lucrative and ethical was the goal of generation after generation of Dutch colonial officials.

After 1848 colonial policy writ large was Parliament's responsibility. Parliament provided the Indies with its first fundamental law in 1854 in which it laid down the general principles and rules to be followed in the governance of the colony. Furthermore, following 1867, Parliament held the colonial purse strings, and in the context of annual debates on fixing the colonial budget it took a greater interest in some of the colony's more mundane affairs. Colonial opium policy, however, seldom attracted their attention. The opium farm system provided important revenues and contributed to the *batig-slot*, the annual contribution from Indies revenues to the home Treasury. These revenues were simply taken for granted, and an occasional raised eyebrow over a particular practice or abuse to the contrary, Parliament left the regulation of the opium farms and the revision of opium policy to the colonial minister.[3] He

---

During his lieutenant governorship Raffles observed that the "use of opium . . . has struck deep roots into the habits, and extended its malignant influence to the morals of the people." He attempted to restrict opium sales to the principalities and the cities of Batavia, Semarang, and Surabaya, but was thwarted by his superiors in Calcutta. See Baud, "Proeve," pp. 156–57. See also Carey, "Changing Javanese Perceptions," p. 39, regarding opium farms and tollgates in the Yogyakarta sultanate.

3. An exception occurred in the late 1850s and early 1860s in response to a program of supplying opium farmers unlimited amounts of relatively inexpensive opium. This had been initiated by Governor General Duymaer van Twist (1851–56) in 1855 in the hope that it would encourage opium farmers to abandon the clandestine trade. They did so, but when the sale of official opium nearly doubled in five years' time, critics of the system rallied and lobbied for its abandonment. Pahud de Montanges, "Nota," folio 15; W. K. Baron van Dedem, *Eene bijdrage tot de studie der Opiumquaestie op Java; de Officieele Litteratuur* (Amsterdam, 1881), p. 7; de Waal, *Aanteekeningen*, pp. 5–21.

in turn relied heavily, almost exclusively, on the advice of his governor general and other officials in Batavia. Opium policy was therefore, generally speaking, drafted in Batavia and approved in The Hague. After 1869, at Colonial Minister Engelbertus de Waal's urging, the governor general was made responsible for the routine management of opium farm affairs.[4] Thereafter, although the governor general sought the consultation and approval of the minister for his particular policies, the formulation of opium farm policy was a local Indies affair. This was to remain the case as long as the farm system itself was accepted as the preferred method for gathering the profits of opium for the state.

In Batavia the opium farms and their regulation were the responsibility of the director of finance, a senior official who presided over the colony's elaborate revenue-gathering apparatus.[5] He was responsible for the ongoing review of policy. Whether self-inspired or nudged from above or below, the drafting of revisions and reforms in the farm rules fell to him. When considering important policy changes, most directors solicited the opinion of those colleagues in the Colonial Service who were posted in the residencies. Basing his decisions on such consultations, his own predilections, and the advice of his staff, the finance director then drafted a proposal that he submitted to the governor general. The governor general in turn sought the advice of the Indies Council and occasionally of the department heads. Before 1869 the governor general then wrote his own opinion and dispatched it (along with the finance director's original proposal, the collected opinions of the council, department heads, and residents) to The Hague for the approval of the colonial minister and the royal imprimatur. After 1869 the governor general, having accepted the original proposal or amended it, simply promulgated it as a statute on his own authority.

The particular shape of Dutch opium policy at any given time, therefore, was informed by many opinions, among them those of the finance director, the governor general, and other top officials in Batavia. If the colonial minister held particularly strong views, his

4. Pahud de Montanges, "Nota," folio 32, and the documents in VKG 27/1/1869/17C. De Waal himself had prepared a study of the opium question which formed the first part of his *Aanteekeningen*, published in 1865.

5. Before 1867 the director of means and estates was responsible for opium farms. See Furnivall, *Netherlands India*, p. 189. For the purview of the Finance Department, see the director's report in the annual Koloniale Verslag.

opinion also influenced the making of policy. More important, however, was the collective opinion of the Colonial Service, for they regularly advised Batavia on changes in the opium farm regulations. Because of their familiarity with local conditions their opinion weighed heavily. As a result, both the conventional attitudes of the colonial Dutch about opium and the environment of accommodation that existed between Chinese and local Dutch administrators greatly influenced the formulation of policy and the content of the farm regulations.

Where opium was concerned Dutch colonial administrators appear to have acted in a vacuum, and pragmatically, for only rarely does one of them refer to a scholarly or scientific authority, or even to such a well-known literary work as Thomas De Quincey's *Confessions of an English Opium Eater*.[6] Occasionally an official showed some knowledge of opium-related events elsewhere, such as the Opium War in China.[7] Just as occasionally a resident or assistant resident displayed a familiarity with one of the opium studies done by noted Dutchmen, such as J. C. Baud's "Proeve van eene geschiedenis van den handel en het verbruik van opium in Nederlandsch-Indie [An attempt at a history of commerce in and the use of opium in the Netherlands Indies]" of 1853, E. de Waal's *Aanteekeningen over koloniale onderwerpen* [Notes on colonial subjects] of 1865, or those of W. K. Baron van Dedem in 1876 and 1881.[8] For the most part, however, the colonial Dutch drew upon a common pool of assumptions—the shared experiences, prejudices, stereotypes, and folk wisdom of the Indies European community—and advised their colleagues and superiors accordingly. The same set of attitudes also affected the way in which policy, once enacted, was interpreted and enforced by local officials, and partly explains the laissez-faire attitude of many colonial officials about opium and the farms.

6. Thomas De Quincey, *Confessions of an English Opium Eater* (London, 1822).
7. For an exception, see Resident R.J.W. MacGillavrij's analysis of Chinese measures against opium smokers and smugglers summarized in DF to GG, October 19, 1867, no. 16849/B in VKG 27/1/1869/17C.
8. Baud, "Proeve"; de Waal, *Aanteekeningen*; van Dedem, *Opiumquaestie*; and W. K. Baron van Dedem, "Nota over de opiumkwestie op Java, met naschrift en debat," *VIG*, November 3, 1876, pp. 103–22. Sometimes mentioned in the 1880s was Von Miclucho Macclay's article in *Natuurkundig Tijdschrift van Nederlandsch-Indie*, 35:246ff., in which the author reported the results of his experiments subjecting himself to morphine. Perelaer used this as a basis for his discussion of the same in *Baboe Dalima* and thus disseminated Macclay's findings to a wider Indies audience. Perelaer, *Baboe Dalima*, 2:383n57 (Dutch edition).

The average colonial Dutchman viewed opium as a routine, even necessary, part of native life. It was, as he saw it, a folk custom deeply rooted among Java's insouciant tropical folk, a simple pleasure for their simple lives. Used in moderation it was beneficial; opium energized peasant bodies for productive labor, and rested them following a day of field work or compulsory services. It also played an important medicinal role, for according to theories then prevalent opium neutralized the poisonous vapors in the torpid miasmic air of the tropics; indeed, native doctors (*dukuns*) as well as Chinese and European ones used it as both prevention and cure for a variety of illnesses. Furthermore, wasn't it unfair to deprive the childlike Javanese of a pleasure they did not have the moral development and self-discipline to resist? If one did, a native would surely find a surrogate just as bad if not worse. One of the commonest fears expressed by defenders of the opium monopoly was that should Holland forbid the Javanese their opium, docile, placid, and harmless opium smokers would soon turn into rowdy, troublesome drunkards. "Throw the opium devil out the window," as one resident noted, "and the drink devil walks in the door."[9]

The spectrum of opinion about opium among the Dutch ranged from a strong moral indictment to forthright advocacy. The consensus lay somewhere in between. It was a rare voice that openly advocated opium; but almost as rare were those who felt that opium smoking was so bad a custom as to warrant banning it altogether. "Anyone," wrote Minister of Colonies J. J. Hasselman in 1868, "who has lived for years amidst a population addicted to opium smoking, and who has had the horrors of its abuse before the eyes, must resolve to spare nothing that might contribute to controlling and suppressing the evil."[10] Few agreed. Most, while recognizing the evil

9. Resident Rembang to HIOR (Hoofdinspecteur Opiumregie), July 9, 1907, no. 7666/39 in V 18/6/1908/1. The composite opinion presented in this paragraph is a distillation of many random comments made by officials in their correspondence. For examples, see DMD to GG, September 12, 1866, no. 3563 in V 16/2/1867/1; Assistant Resident van het Zuiden en Oosten Kwartier der Ommelanden van Batavia to Resident Batavia, June 4, 1866, no. 712/5 in V 16/2/1867/1; Resident Kediri to DF, July 30, 1867, no. 2896 in VKG 27/1/1869/17C; DF to GG, May 7, 1872, no. 3979 in V 20/8/1872/37; Wiselius, Opium Rapport Semarang, 1882; and Assistant Resident Joana to Resident Japara, December 31, 1882, no. 2694/10 in TMC H422a. Published views paralleled those expressed privately. See, for example, Castens, "De Opiumpacht op Java"; van Delden, *Blik*, pp. 274–84.

10. Quoted in Pahud, "Nota," folio 31 in V 29/9/1891/37.

consequences of addiction, thought that what they observed to be the moderate consumption of opium typical of Javanese smokers was at worst a tolerable vice.

An 1885 survey in which residents were requested to state their views regarding opium smoking as a social custom confirmed this composite point of view.[11] The vast majority saw no harm in the casual, moderate consumption of candu and tiké. Resident P. F. Wegener of Semarang spoke for most of his colleagues when he replied that during his thirty-four-year career in Java he had seen nothing to corroborate the notion that moderate opium use was harmful. On the other hand, opium's addictive properties were common knowledge, and survey respondents, reflecting the long-standing popular view, drew a sharp distinction between moderate use and addiction.[12] An important, though weaker, auxiliary to the community consensus was, therefore, that while opium should not, indeed could not, be prohibited, neither should access to it be un-limited. The occasional pitiful case was evidence enough of opium's lethal potential. Both opium's addictive properties and the Dutch-perceived weakness in native character required that the govern-ment impose some external constraints. Conventional wisdom sug-gested, in short, a policy in which smokers might have their opium, but not too much of it.

The popular view, in short, provided a rationale for a state-controlled opium monopoly. It suggested a policy in which the state might freely enjoy the vast profits of an opium monopoly and, at the same time, act in an ethically responsible manner by exercising control over the gross supply of opium. Extremists to the contrary, a total ban was unnecessary, and in any case, because opium smoking was such a deeply rooted custom, impracticable. The popular view was, as a result, in large measure also the official view.

The official view diverged from the popular view in one impor-tant respect, however. Representing as it did the result of official consultation at several levels, including the Colonial Ministry, and ultimately (after 1867) requiring the approval of the Dutch Parlia-ment, the official view reflected to a greater extent the liberal princi-

11. A summary of the responses, upon which the bulk of this paragraph is based, can be found in Opium Resume 1885.

12. The 1885 questionnaire was designed to test the importance of the distinction. See also Advies, Raad van Indie, August 29, 1884, no. 13 in VKG 3/2/1885/K1/7.

ple of ethical responsibility. A state did not have the right to profit from a policy to the obvious detriment of its subjects.[13] In the evolving official view, opium became not really acceptable, only inevitable—a necessary evil that the state had a moral obligation to hold in check. "It is His Majesty's earnest desire," wrote Minister of Colonies James Loudon to the governor general in 1861, " . . . not only to prevent the further increase of [opium] use but also to curtail the already prevailing extent of this evil."[14] From the 1860s on this was not only a consideration of Dutch opium policy, which it had been since 1832, but its officially stated goal.[15]

The periodic clamor over opium policy focused, then, not on the issue of opium itself, about which there was substantial agreement, but on the more difficult problem of harmonizing financial and ethical goals. Until late in the century the opium farm was accepted, despite occasional attempts to replace it, as the most satisfactory basic scheme for the opium monopoly.[16] Debate raged, however, over the nature, operation, and regulation of the opium farms, and critics called for reform of those defects in the system that encouraged corruption and abuse.[17] How can we, went the essential question, regulate the opium farm system so that revenues rise and consumption falls?[18]

Throughout the farm period, the Dutch answer to this question remained fundamentally simple. Each major revision of the Opium Farm Regulations (Opiumpacht Reglement)—in 1853, 1874, and 1890—reconfirmed a commitment to the same approach.[19] In those parts of Java where religion, culture, and local circumstances militated against opium consumption, notably in Bantam and the Pri-

13. The "welfare of the natives" became an official concern of Dutch colonial policy in the fundamental law (Regeerings Reglement) of 1854, the first such act to be submitted "to the judgement of the national representative body."

14. MvK to GG, April 19, 1861, quoted in Pahud, "Nota."

15. Baud, "Proeve," p. 167.

16. Several critics of Batavia's opium policy did propose alternatives to the farm, but they did not pose a direct threat to the farms until the late 1880s. Among them was Inspector General of Finance P.H.B. Motke's 1872 proposal to create a state opium monopoly based on France's tobacco monopoly, and which resembled the later Opium Regie. See Inspecteur Generaal van Financien to GG: Vertrouwelijke nota, July 14, 1872, in VKG 4/9/1872/A14.

17. See DMD to GG, August 16, 1866, no. 3230 in V 16/2/1867/1, folio 7.

18. Not surprisingly the farm system came under attack most frequently when revenues fell as consumption increased. See Castens's discussion in "De Opiumpacht op Java," p. 49.

19. SvNI 1853, no. 87; SvNI 1874, no. 228; and SvNI 1890, no. 149.

angan but in several other smaller regions as well, the Dutch created Forbidden Areas. Here there were no opium farms, and the distribution of opium was illegal. In the rest of Java, where opium farms prevailed, the Dutch artificially limited the supply of official opium, subjected the farm to state regulation and supervision, and, in the interest of expanding revenues, encouraged competition among Chinese bidders at the farm auctions. The result, they continued to hope, would be a limited supply of expensive opium sold under government supervision to the ultimate profit of the Treasury. In theory it was the perfect vice tax.[20]

Each generation of Indies officials, in turn, attempted to make the theory work. They revised the rules and conditions governing opium farms and, when this failed to achieve the desired ends, revised the revisions. Farm terms were lengthened, shortened, and lengthened again. Territories were enlarged to include several residencies, then broken down again. The official opium supply was restricted, enlarged, then restricted again; the official price (which farmers paid the government for official opium) was raised, lowered, then raised again; the number of official opium stores was permitted to grow, then cut back severely, then permitted to grow again. Opium-free districts were proclaimed, established, then opened to the farm again. The patungan trade was ignored, made subject to regulation, then ignored again. At one time or another the government attempted to place a limit on the amount of opium one individual could purchase daily, to limit the number of candu factories, and to ban opium smoking outside the official stores. But all tinkering failed; except for the size of the farm territory, which was generally fixed as the residency, none of these issues was ever resolved.

Aside from the intrinsic contradictions of their policy goals, two other factors weighed heavily in the Dutch failure to devise a workable opium farm policy. These were, first, Dutch ignorance of the inner workings of the farms and the opium-smoking world in general; and second, the limited degree to which they could enforce their policies once they were promulgated.

20. W. E. Kroesen, member of the Indies Council, expressed it this way in 1867: "I consider the highest possible tax upon a recognized evil, the import and use of which cannot be imposed by force, as one of the most ethical of taxes that can be laid upon the people; . . . for he who smokes no opium is not subject to it." Advies van het Raadslid, den Generaal Majoor W. E. Kroesen, October 25, 1867, no. 2 in VKG 27/1/1869/17C.

The apparent thoroughness with which policy deliberations were carried on disguised what more astute observers knew to be an appalling superficiality. The Dutch remained abysmally ignorant of the opium farms. As a result, they based most of their projections regarding opium consumption and the supply and price structure on poor information. Policies based on these projections were inevitably unsatisfactory. This ignorance was due in large measure to the laissez-faire attitude toward opium and the opium farm which prevailed in the Colonial Service. Residents were notoriously lax in examining farm account books (which they accurately believed to be fictionalized ledgers), and in other respects turned a blind eye toward farm activities.[21] "[In] no other area," lamented Charles TeMechelen in 1888, "does one find greater ignorance among officials than in that of opium."[22] Self-interest encouraged this sort of "know-nothing" attitude, but so did another part of the conventional wisdom, which viewed the inner workings of the Chinese-controlled farms as impenetrably mysterious.[23]

Even at the lowest level Dutch officials seldom knew very much about opium and farm operations. Younger officials, controleurs and assistant residents, those most intimately associated with the people and local manifestations of such important institutions as the farms, were encouraged to devote their energies to questions related to Java's agricultural prosperity, this being in the broader Dutch view the backbone and hope of the colony. Too close an association with the opium farm, even in fact-gathering or reformist activities, involved a certain taint. Opium affairs were demoralizing and, as the director of the Colonial Service put it in 1884, "did little to prepare [young officials] for the higher administrative tasks that awaited them."[24] One could not make a career in the Colonial Service as an opium expert; and in the Colonial Service making a career was the singular incentive.

Resigned to the farm and its many irregularities, officials typically responded to questionnaires from Batavia as briefly as possible. "In reference to your circular of the fourteenth of last month," replied Assistant Resident P. Severijn of Pacitan, "I have the honor to

21. Rouffaer, "Indische Aanteekeningen."
22. TM: Rapport 1888.
23. See TeMechelen's comments in TM to DF, July 5, 1888, no. 1015/4 in V 27/11/1888/69.
24. DBB to DF, September 14, 1884, no. 1748 in V 23/1/1890/95.

inform Your Excellency that in my opinion no objections exist to adopting the proposed revisions."[25] Simply assenting was the easiest way to avoid lengthy explanations and to cast one's vote in favor of the status quo. Some lied outright. An independent inquiry in 1888, for example, uncovered more than a thousand clandestine opium dens and stores in a residency in which, only a short time before, the resident had assured his superiors that none existed.[26]

Just as colonial officials in the field kept their Batavia superiors in the dark regarding day-to-day realities of farm operations, such as they knew them, Batavia too, when corresponding with the ministry, kept its reporting as clinical as possible. Opium-related scandals and farm irregularities seldom entered the governor general's reports. The ministry, however, not to mention critics in Parliament, had alternative sources of information; as a result, on not a few occasions the governors general faced embarrassing questions about stories circulating in the Indies press, or passed via private channels, which had come to the attention of the home authorities. Minister of Colonies P. P. van Bosse, for example, learned from a Surabaya newspaper of opium farmer Liem Kie Soen's suit against the state for failing to provide official opium in the amounts required. "I have the honor to request Your Excellency," he wrote to Governor General James Loudon, "to inform me regarding this affair at the earliest possible moment, specifically regarding the causes for failure to deliver the requested opium."[27] A few years before, when C. Castens's reports about opium-related corruption among the Colonial Service aroused the curiosity and ire of Minister J. J. Hasselman, the governor general, instead of replying directly to the minister's questions, defensively attempted to deflect them by casting doubt on Castens's reliability.[28] As a general rule it was best that The Hague know as little as possible about the opium farms.

Bureaucrats at each level supplied their superiors with the barest acceptable detail, and at each level the farm system looked progres-

25. Assistant Resident Pacitan to DMD, June 4, 1866, no. 638 in V 16/2/1867/1.
26. TM: Rapport 1888. The resident was P. F. Wegener of Semarang.
27. MvK to GG, December 5, 1872, no. 3/1889 in V/5/12/1872/3/1889. This letter inspired an unbecoming round of finger pointing within the Batavian bureaucracy. See the documents in V/5/12/1872/3/1889 and V 14/3/1878/11/602. For a similar case, in which the minister inquires about a *De Locomotief* exposé of the local clandestine market, see MvK to GG, October 2, 1889, no. R 15/67 in VKG 2/10/1889/R15/67.
28. See VKG 22/4/1868/36.

sively more schematic and manageable. Ignorance was greatest in The Hague, and least (though still very significant) in the field. Not surprisingly, naiveté about the state's ability to supervise and regulate farm activities for the greater profit of folk and Treasury varied directly in proportion to ignorance.

The desire on the part of a few concerned officials to break through this barrier of ignorance prompted occasional official inquiries into opium and farm affairs. Certain that Dutch ignorance of such matters played into the hands of "the intrigues and cunning of the Chinese farmers and their henchmen," J. C. Baud commissioned a thorough investigation of farm affairs in 1841.[29] Two decades later, as director of means and estates, C. Castens pressed his Colonial Service subordinates for detailed information about the opium farms in their residencies. The replies he received, as we have noted, were of mixed quality; nevertheless he succeeded, largely on the basis of his own investigations throughout his career and the reports of a few trusted colleagues, in making himself the best-informed Dutch official in opium matters in decades.[30] In 1871 the inspector general of finance, P.H.B. Motke, conducted a similar special inquiry into farm affairs in central and east Java.[31]

Such inquiries inevitably pointed out the vast discrepancy between the farms of the statutes and the real farms, and almost as inevitably inspired major proposals to reform the system; each of these investigations, for example, led to such proposals, aspects of which were incorporated into the policy revisions of their respective days. The full reports, however, were relegated to the files when the investigations were over and remained largely unconsulted by succeeding officials. Published articles, like those of Baud and de Waal, were basically policy studies and, while they provided a perspective on past policy deliberations and were somewhat informative as well on the subject of opium, did not provide officials who may have read them with more than a glimpse of the farms themselves or of the

29. Pahud, "Nota," folios 9 and 10.
30. Testimony to Castens's expertise came from Bureau A of the colonial minister's staff in 1867 when bureau members wrote: "Regardless of one's opinion of this senior official, it cannot easily be denied that he, even as Resident, displayed great vigor and genuine familiarity with the complex opium question. For years Bureau A has learned the most from *his* memorandums in opium affairs." Advies Bureau A, January 19, 1867, in V 16/2/1867/1.
31. Inspecteur Generaal van Financien to GG, Vertrouwelijke nota, July 14, 1872, in VKG 4/9/1872/A14.

nature and extent of opium smoking as a custom in Java. As a general rule, each new generation of Batavia officials started fresh, with only the most superficial statistics, their own experience, and the usual conventional wisdom to guide them. Consequently, the Dutch were nearly as ignorant of farm affairs and the world of the Javanese opium smoker in 1880 as they had been in 1840.[32]

Ignorance, then, alongside a pervasive apathy and laissez-faire attitude about opium farms, contributed to the Dutch failure to achieve their long-term policy goals. Equally important, and closely related, was the limited extent to which the Dutch administrative apparatus penetrated the indigenous world. Batavia exercised direct control over only the top European rung of the administrative structure, the Colonial Service, and even here locally posted officials were inclined for a variety of reasons to turn a blind eye to the farmer and his customers. Beneath the Colonial Service, enforcement of farm regulations fell to the pryayi corps and the farm organization, both of whom had a vested interest in the status quo. The opium farm was well insulated from the regulations of Batavia; as an Indies institution, integrated and ingrown, it defied effective supervision.

All the deliberation and debate that went into the periodic revision of the farm rules, and the ongoing process of creating, revising, and reforming opium policy in Batavia, was largely irrelevant to the farms themselves. Farmers adjusted to the arbitrary manipulation of the quantity and price of official opium by maintaining alternative sources of supply, and adjusted when necessary to the imposition of new regulations and restrictions from Batavia. Token acquiescence was usually sufficient to satisfy the local Dutch administration, which was eager enough to keep up appearances but which also knew that the financial strength of the farm was more important to Batavia than the strict enforcement of policy. Residents might occasionally have their knuckles rapped for excessive laxness where the farm was concerned, but blame for farm irreg-

---

32. This ignorance prompted yet another call, this time from the lower house, in 1881 for a thorough investigation into "the harmful effects of opium use for the people of Java and what can be done about it." See MvK to GG, December 27, 1881, no. 18/2438 in V 27/12/1881/18/2438. Passing the directive along to the governor general, Colonial Minister W. Baron van Goltstein reflected the general opinion that such an investigation would turn up nothing, but that it was necessary nevertheless to accommodate the lower house, "providing," he added, "the inquiry was kept within limits . . . and required no extraordinary expenses."

ularities would rest finally on the Chinese, who were assumed to be corrupt. Falling revenues, on the other hand, were the residents' responsibility, and residents were loath to impose restrictions on the farm that might jeopardize its contribution to the Treasury.

Despite the protestations of purpose in the official literature, often repeated in the preamble to yet another circular or statute, and despite the perpetual talk in Batavia about suppressing the opium menace, Dutch actions on a day-to-day basis focused most directly and consistently on maintaining opium's central contribution to the Treasury. The director of finance, for example, kept close records of the yearly income by residency—farm fees and official purchases by farmers—but never until the 1880s collected even vaguely accurate statistics on opium use and users.[33] Governors general always forwarded the amount of newly promised opium revenue to The Hague immediately after the farm auctions but never mentioned the names of the new farmers, who were among the most powerful men in the colony. At all echelons of the bureaucratic hierarchy officials avoided falling revenues of any sort for fear they would be suspected of mismanagement. The pressure for profit, permeating the official class from top to bottom, showed official Dutch expressions of concern about the hazards of opium, however well meant in theory, to be largely insincere in practice.

Throughout the century the most persistent irritant to the Dutch—both those who hoped for an opium policy that suppressed the opium custom and those whose sole interest was in revenues—was Java's rampant smuggling trade, for smuggling led inevitably to the wider availability of opium in Java and at the same time undermined the government's monopoly. It came to be taken for granted that most other problems of the farm system could be solved if only smuggling—and the black market it supported—could be eliminated. The proponents of this view argued that appreciative opium farmers would be all the more likely to bow to the legal supervision of the state if the state adequately protected their monopoly; no longer having to compete with the black market, farmers could raise their prices and make opium the luxury that Holland's pragmatic

---

33. The figures published annually in the Colonial Report (KVnNI), for example, were compiled from information provided by opium farmers, reluctant in any case to divulge their real sales and profits, and subjected in each residency to idiosyncratic formulas for reducing them to a publishable average. See DF to GG, May 4, 1883, no. 7200 in TMC H422b.

humanitarians wished it to be. It was in this hope that the Dutch, from the mid-1870s on, increasingly focused their administrative efforts on solving this one difficult problem.

Before the 1870s, in keeping with the principle of indirect administration, the Dutch relied entirely on the pryayi corps and the opium farms themselves to police the black market in the interior, and on their own overtaxed Customs Service—charged with exercising surveillance over the importation of contraband goods—to intercept clandestine opium at the point of entry. The latter was so ineffective that opium farmers in coastal residencies maintained their own coast watches—strings of lookout posts stretching along the beaches. The Dutch encouraged both regents and their subordinates, and the personnel of the Customs Department, to pursue smugglers and black marketeers by offering substantial bounties for successful opium confiscations. But the cumbersomeness and tardiness of the reward process undermined its intentions and played into the hands of the opium farm and competitor smugglers, who were swifter and more faithful in making restitution for services performed.[34]

The ineffectiveness of these antismuggling efforts eventually stimulated recommendations from members of the Colonial Service for a European-led antismuggling effort. In the 1860s officials such as Assistant Resident B. J. van Dijk of Surabaya envisioned Dutch officers presiding directly over an organization of secret indigenous "coast watchers," posing as fishermen, patrolling the coast in a fleet of native boats; and a director of finance proposed posting an opium official in every residency to supervise a network of inspectors and adjunct inspectors in every district.[35] In 1872 ex–director of means and estates Castens published a similar proposal for a Java-wide opium inspectorate, and for the establishment of a secret police

34. The payment of government bounties was cumbersome because of the intricate formulas for payment required by statute, in which bounty portions were allotted by twelfths (in 1853) and sevenths (after 1866), and the difficulty of determining just who in each case among a welter of spies, informants, police, and pryayi officials deserved it; and they were tardy because ordinarily all legal procedures had to be completed, and the suspect confirmed as guilty, before any money left the Treasury. See SvNI 1853, no. 87, art. 26; and SvNI 1866, no. 117, art. 26.

35. Assistant Resident voor de Policie to Resident Surabaya, March 22, 1865, no. 473 in V 16/2/1867/1; DF to GG, October 19, 1867, no. 16849/B in VKG 27/1/1869/17C. See also Resident Yogyakarta to DF, August 7, 1867, no. 1006/10 in VKG 27/1/1869/17C; and Resident Pekalongan to DMD, September 27, 1866, A in V 16/2/1867/1.

force to investigate and master wholesale smuggling.[36] Batavia took no immediate steps in this direction, however. Instead they continued to attempt to make existing measures more effective by channeling more money into secret police funds, especially in north-central Java, and by supervising more closely the police work of pryayi officials. In Semarang, for example, reporting on anti-black-market initiatives became a required part of a wedana's monthly accountancy.[37]

In 1876, however, Batavia departed from past practice and moved to involve the European administration much more intimately in the fight against smuggling. Controleurs in Semarang, Japara, and Rembang were charged with investigating violations of the opium farm. As young Dutch officers of the lowest rank in the elite Colonial Service, controleurs often spent years in local, intimate postings before being promoted to assistant resident; as a result they were most familiar among the service with the workings of such institutions as the farms on a local level. Clothed in investigative authority, including that of searching private homes, controleurs would now bring that familiarity to bear in the interests of defending the state's opium monopoly. In addition, a new classification of European functionary was devised whose sole responsibility, unlike that of controleurs, was to combat opium smuggling. These opium hunters (opiumjagers), as they came to be called, were posted in the same residencies under the direct supervision of the resident and were invested with similarly broad investigative authority.[38]

Batavia's decision to give controleurs police powers and to involve them directly in the business of invigilating the black market was controversial from the outset. Proponents of the idea, such as Director of Finance Sprenger van Eijk, emphasized the key role a controleur could play in coordinating the investigative activities of the newly appointed opium hunters and the Javanese administration.[39] But controleurs were already notoriously overworked, and the residents of both Rembang and Japara complained that additional demands on their time would be detrimental to the performance of

36. Castens, "De Opiumpacht op Java."
37. Resident Semarang to DF, July 23, 1875, no. 2628/3 in V 22/5/1876/79; see also Resident Rembang to DF, August 21, 1875, MI in the same Verbaal.
38. SvNI 1876, no. 136. See V 22/6/1876/79 for the correspondence and deliberation that preceded this decision.
39. Sprenger van Eijk's arguments in favor of the plan are summarized in GG to DBB, August 26, 1876, no. 542/C in V 23/1/1890/95.

more essential administrative functions.[40] Besides, controleurs stood officially beside the chain of authority, which ran through the assistant resident directly to the regent. As apprentice administrators without authoritarian functions, they were in the best possible position to win the confidence and trust of the village population, a primary goal of the controleur years.[41] Engaging directly in opium investigations, including the loathed house searches, argued opponents of the plan, would greatly undermine a young official's pool of nascent trust.[42]

Despite such criticism the program was soon expanded to include four adjacent districts joining Surabaya and Kediri residencies—where traffic in clandestine opium was particularly troublesome because of the Chinese neighborhoods strung along the Kediri River—and a few years later to the entire residency of Kediri.[43] For the next nine years the position of controleurs in other residencies remained unaffected by the changes in Semarang, Japara, Rembang, Surabaya, and Kediri. In 1889, however, controleurs were made responsible for opium violations in all Forbidden Areas and in several more residencies.[44]

For all the hopes that successive directors of finance had for them, controleurs played a relatively minor part in the war against opium smuggling. Their other responsibilities did not, in fact, leave them sufficient time to devote to opium problems; and their superiors in the Colonial Service, who consistently opposed the program as a distortion of controleurship, did nothing to encourage anyone among them to engage in the "degrading" business.[45] As a result, the lower-ranking opium hunters played the more important role in

40. Resident Japara to GG, April 3, 1876, no. 1312/10 and Resident Rembang to GG (telegram), March 21, 1876, no. 187, both in V 22/6/1876/79.

41. See Furnivall's account of the evolution of the controleur position. Furnivall, *Netherlands India*, pp. 193–94. See also van Niel's comments in "Government Policy," p. 62.

42. See n. 40, above, especially the resident of Japara's letter.

43. See Resident Surabaya to GG, December 1876, no. 20535; and Gouvernement Besluit, September 2, 1877, no. 13, both in V 17/11/1877/21; and the exchange of letters between the resident of Kediri, the director of finance, and the governor general in V 16/11/1880/1.

44. Gouvernement Besluit, December 20, 1889, no. 1 in V 23/1/1890/95. Several new Forbidden Areas were created in 1889; see SvNI 1889, no. 157. The residencies were Bantam, Batavia, Krawang, Pasuruan, Besoeki, and Bagelen.

45. See the comments in DBB to GG, November 27, 1889, no. 6468 in V 23/1/1890/95; and GG to MvK, September 14, 1884, no. 90/i in VKG 3/2/1885/K1/no. 7.

Dutch attempts to bring antismuggling measures more directly under European leadership.

The years after 1876, and especially after 1880, witnessed a rapid though piecemeal expansion of the Opium Hunter System as, one by one, residents and occasionally opium farmers themselves petitioned Batavia for their services.[46] By 1890 nearly every residency hosted at least one hunter, and quite a few—among them Rembang, Japara, and Semarang—hosted several. Opium hunters were assisted by a small corps of mounted Javanese investigators called police mantri (*mantri politie*), who were their agents and who formed their link with the village world. Through them hunters maintained contact with the criminal element of rural Java via a network of local spies and informants paid for by secret police funds provided for each residency by the government in Batavia.[47] The Opium Hunter System that developed, therefore, consisted of a small corps of police mantri who worked directly under the leadership of a low-ranking European functionary. As such it was a significant departure from the traditional and still-prevailing pattern of exercising local authority through the pryayi corps. Police mantris and their contacts were clients not of a wedana or assistant wedana but of a European hunter, who was himself directly responsible to the residency Colonial Service. The Pangreh Praja was bypassed, and in theory a direct link was forged between the Dutch administration and the village.[48]

Opium hunters and their subordinates now took to the field against opium smuggling alongside the farm organization and the indigenous administration. Although they were intended to represent the direct interests of the state in the suppression of smuggling, the hunters soon fell into the well-established pattern in which

46. See DBB to GG, January 21, 1876, no. 627 in V 22/6/1876/79; Resident Surabaya to GG, December 19, 1876, no. 20535, and Resident Kediri to DF, May 28, 1877, no. 2349/3402, both in V 17/10/1877/21; Resident Ceribon to DF, November 19, 1878, no. 7649/45, and Resident Kediri to DF, April 3, 1880, no. 1763/2405, both in V 16/10/1880/1; and the documents concerning the Ceribon opium farmer's request for a hunter in his farm territory, also in V 16/10/1880/1. The Ceribon farmer was The Tjiauw Tjiaj.

47. Resident Japara to GG, April 17, 1883, no. 3166/10 in TMC H422b; and TM to DF, March 28, 1890, no. 463/3 in TMC H422d.

48. Native mantri also served under Dutch authority as warehouse clerks, on irrigation and salt-extraction projects, and in vaccination programs. These were all modern functions; the police mantri, however, were engaged in work traditionally performed by the pryayi corps.

opium farmers maneuvered potentially challenging forces to their own advantage. Contrary to the hopes of its proponents, the Opium Hunter System became another weapon in the internal war among the Chinese elite for control of the opium trade and other markets. Both the environment of local accommodation in Java, in which loyalties were often more highly influenced by personal interest than by caste or obligation, and certain structural features of the opium hunter program made this outcome inevitable.

For one thing the success of the program depended in large part on reliable information. Opium hunters could acquire this only via their mantri's contacts with Java's fringe society of jagabajas, petty criminals, patungan opium traders, and the like, these being the people most familiar with the passage of black-market opium into and throughout the local region. For the opium farm, penetration of this fringe society was essential for the protection of vital patungan markets and for the surveillance of the black market within the farm territory. The farm recruited mata-mata from among it members for precisely this purpose. Its well-developed contacts made it easy for the opium farms to feed useful intelligence to opium hunters, and otherwise to manipulate them. As a result, opium hunters and their mantri subordinates came to rely heavily on intelligence supplied from farm contacts and often worked hand in glove with farm mata-mata against black marketeers threatening the hegemony of the dominant opium farm kongsi.[49]

Aside from the problem of intelligence, the program tended to operate in the service of opium farm interests for other reasons as well. These related to the position itself and to the pay it commanded, both of which pushed hunters into the more appreciative arms of the farm. Opium hunters were recruited from among the lower fringes of Java's male European population. Many were Eurasian. In stark contrast to their colleagues in the elite Colonial Service, most hunters were poorly educated. They were paid meager salaries and often posted in such lonely places as the morassland of the north coast. Members of the Colonial Service found them "unreliable" and "untrustworthy." Because of this, and their general disinclination to meddle in farm affairs, they provided them little

49. See the case of Tan Soen Haij, in which the combined efforts of Djario, an agent of the opium hunter, and Tan Tjie Nging, a farm mata-mata, brought Tan to court, albeit not to justice. Case of Tan Soen Haij, Landraad Kudus, February 11, 1879, in *IWR* no. 843, 1879.

support. Although opium hunters were eligible for the generous bounties offered for successful confiscations of clandestine opium, the difficulty of achieving convictions in the colonial courts in opium cases undermined the potential effectiveness of this incentive. As a result, loans, bonuses, and expense money provided by the opium farm constituted an important fringe benefit of the job. In addition, farm-supplied intelligence could result in the occasionally successful bounty-winning arrest. Especially in territories where the farm organization was strong, opium hunters had every incentive to graft their efforts to those of the farm. In doing so the opium hunters merely succumbed to a long-standing and pervasive pattern of accommodation in which the Colonial Service, despite their disdain for the "unreliability" of the hunters, were also participants. In this regard, Perelaer commented that the occasional hunter who took up his task with zeal and made a genuine effort to pursue the smuggling activities of the farm itself, as well as those of its competitors, might find himself liable to dismissal for "lack of tact and discretion."[50]

The Opium Hunter System was nevertheless an important structural innovation in the exercise of European authority in rural Java. Police mantri, as candidate officials, stood outside the pryayi patronage hierarchy, their fates more closely tied to success within a European one.

In 1882 the director of finance revealed to the governor general that the government's best efforts to combat opium smuggling— and this had included augmenting secret police funds (controlled by residents) and beefing up or expanding the activities of the Customs Service in addition to the controleur and opium hunter programs— had had few practical consequences. The number of confiscations of clandestine opium, it was true, had nearly doubled during the five years since 1876, but, discouragingly, the total amount of opium confiscated had remained static and even dropped some; the size of an average seizure had fallen from just over 2 katis (1.236 kilograms) to just over 1, which suggests that the number of individuals

50. Perelaer, *Baboe Dalima*, 2:265–66n109 (Dutch edition). Perelaer cites a document provided him by an unnamed but "senior" official to support his comments about opium hunters. Similar conclusions were reached by others. See TM to DF, March 27, 1892, no. 677/4 in Exh 9/8/1892/76; and HIOR to GG, September 18, 1903, no. 2554/R in V 13/1/1904/34. This last document was based on an 1894 resumé of the collective opinion of the Colonial Service on the efficacy of the hunter program in retrospect.

participating in black-market transactions had grown.[51] In the same report Director L.J.J. Michielson conveyed the similarly distressing results of a newer campaign designed to cut off the flow of contraband opium at sea.

Officials in Batavia had long been divided as to the relative effectiveness of arresting opium smuggling at sea—prior to or upon the point of entry—or harassing its distribution inland. The innovations of 1876, although originally implemented in coastal residencies, were aimed basically at the inland traffic. Beginning in 1879 Batavia began to attack the problem from the sea side as well. In that year it became illegal, for the first time since 1854, to store nongovernment opium in bonded warehouses in Java's harbors or to bring it aboardship within three English sea miles of the coast.[52] The following year the government assigned four vessels from the government marines—a steamship and three auxiliary sailing craft—to enforce the law. Entrusted with the task of snuffing out the heavy traffic in illegal opium between Bali and Java's north coast was a career seaman, at that time commander of the steamship *Telegraph* (shortly thereafter the *Arend*), named William Jacobus van Santen.[53]

Vigorously assuming his new responsibilities van Santen became expert at recognizing the overequipped "fishing vessels" designed for the long and occasionally rough run between Bali and the north coast, and he was soon familiar with other peculiarities of the trade: favored routes and landing sites; the art of hiding opium aboardship; and other ruses and dodges of the veteran smuggler. So armed, he engaged the opium skippers and their onshore patrons in a two-year game of cat and mouse. In the seas north of Java's "opium funnel," van Santen harassed and hounded suspicious craft, demanding their papers and passes and searching for opium. With general disregard for the niceties of international law he forced opium-laden craft from international waters into the three-mile perimeter within which he was authorized to confiscate contraband cargo and to make arrests.[54]

One of van Santen's victims was Pak Rasimin, skipper of a large

51. DF to GG, May 11, 1882, no. 7505 in TMC H422b.
52. SvNI 1879, no. 224. European vessels of more than fifty tons were exempt.
53. For the details of van Santen's career, see his Staat van Dienst, GM 1, folios 127 and 415.
54. The fullest accounts of van Santen's work in the antismuggling campaign can be found in DF to GG, March 31, 1882, no. 5089, and GG to DF, October 11, 1882, no. 60, both in TMC H422b.

vessel that specialized in the Bali run. Van Santen overtook Pak Rasimin's vessel, which was carrying a large shipment of opium, in international waters above Japara, suspiciously distant from its declared destination of Pegatan in South Borneo. Van Santen then maneuvered him to within three miles of an island cluster in the Java Sea, Dutch territory, arrested him, and confiscated his cargo.[55] A similar case involved an opium-laden boat that van Santen inspected on two consecutive days. On the second day the boat was lighter by twenty-nine tins of candu. Van Santen, certain that the missing opium had been transshipped ashore, chased the boat into Rembang harbor—some twelve miles away—for the arrest.[56]

For a time tactics like these appeared to bear fruit. As early as October 1880 the resident of Semarang reported that van Santen's patrolling had been so effective that the Semarang farmer had abandoned his own program of coast watching.[57] By late summer 1881 van Santen himself was able to report that several well-known smugglers who specialized in the Bali route had stopped frequenting the funnel. As if to confirm his optimism, the price of black-market opium rose in central Java, and sales figures indicated that the farms were enjoying a larger share of the whole market.[58]

But van Santen's apparent success was largely ephemeral. By late 1882 he himself had concluded that his patrolling activities were fruitless and wasteful and should be discontinued. He changed his mind because of the three-mile rule. The colonial courts, especially the European Councils of Justice, steadfastly refused to convict suspects who had been coerced into Netherlands India territory for arrest, no matter how convincing the evidence that they were smuggling opium. Pak Rasimin, for example, convicted and sentenced by the Landraads in both Semarang and Pati (there had been a jurisdictional dispute), was acquitted by the Semarang Council of Justice because he had been illegally hounded into Dutch territory.[59] Following a year of wide latitude, van Santen's superiors advised him to

55. Pro Justitia, Raad van Justitie Semarang, June 26, 1882, in TMC H422b, Case of Pak Rasimin.

56. DF to GG, March 31, 1882, no. 5089.

57. Resident Semarang to DF, October 5, 1880, no. 8763/1 in TMC H422b.

58. GG to DF, October 11, 1882, no. 60, and DF to GG, March 31, 1882, no. 5089, both in TMC H422b.

59. Gezagvoerder 1e klasse "Arend," W. J. van Santen to Vice Admiraal Kommandant der Zeemagten Chef van het Departement der Marine in NI, July 22, 1882, no. 39 in TMC H422b; Case of Pak Rasimin, Pro Justitia, Raad van Justitie Semarang, June 26, 1882, in TMC H422b.

restrain himself. Now if a suspicious craft lay outside the three-mile limit, he only inspected it. If it was carrying opium, van Santen could do nothing but attempt to intercept it when it made for shore.[60] In response, the larger opium vessels—or floating opium warehouses, as the Dutch called them—now waited offshore, and local boats transshipped the opium to the beach, usually under cover of darkness. Van Santen and his small fleet were helpless against such tactics, and following the temporarily suppressive effect of van Santen's cavalier forays in 1881, the Bali trade soon revived.[61]

Even during van Santen's heyday in 1881 the quantities of illegal opium moving from Bali to the "funnel" were extraordinary. In his report of December 1881 Commander van Santen appended a list of all opium craft he had inspected from June to December of that year. These craft had carried the equivalent of 622 piculs (38,439.6 kilograms) of raw opium, more than 100 piculs more than the legal allotment for Semarang, Japara, and Rembang combined. Considering the likelihood that many smuggling craft escaped his attention, van Santen estimated that 1,000 piculs of raw opium had been imported into Japara in these seven months alone. Despite van Santen's policing, the vast majority of this opium, so he himself ultimately concluded, reached its buyers ashore. In fact, during the two years of his special assignment, for all his efforts Commander van Santen made only two significant confiscations, both of which occurred because opium skippers unwittingly entered the three-mile fringe around the Karimondjawa Islands.[62]

Van Santen's frustration stimulated a lively correspondence among Netherlands Indies authorities on the question of extending territorial waters in order to expand the area in which opium confiscations could be made. The upshot was a compromise statute that made contraband opium laws enforceable within a six-nautical-mile perimeter, but only for vessels registered in Netherlands India.[63]

Among the lessons of the van Santen episode was that the coastal

60. See W. J. van Santen to Vice Admiraal, etc., March 24, 1882, no. 18 in TMC H422b.
61. DF to GG, March 31, 1882, no. 60, and GG to DF, October 11, 1882, no. 60, both in TMC H422b.
62. Van Santen's report (December 31, 1881, no. 109) is quoted in DF to GG, March 31, 1882, no. 5089. See also DF to GG, May 11, 1882, no. 7505. Both documents are in TMC H422b.
63. See SvNI 1883, no. 171; the documents in V 1/2/1883/18; and the memoranda of the director of justice (May 18, 1883, no. 3983) and the minister of foreign affairs (May 29, 1883, no. 4641) in TMC H422b. One nautical mile equals 1,852.2 meters.

patrolling carried out thus far had been too limited; native boats
easily bypassed the government vessels and made their way ashore.
Besides, simply covering the "funnel" was inadequate; it was the
most important but by no means the only site for bringing clandestine opium ashore. In subsequent years the government, inten-
sifying its efforts, would cast its net more widely. Another lesson of
the period was that a way must be found to coordinate the offshore
efforts of the marines with the onshore efforts of the colonial administration, opium hunters, and the pryayi corps. Batavia did not
approach this problem directly. Rather, a solution of sorts evolved
willy-nilly during the 1880s. This solution began with the combined
efforts of the Japara opium farm and an ambitious assistant resident
to defeat the local opium smugglers. By the late 1880s it had developed into a wide-ranging, semi-independent, and eclectic task force
under the leadership of that same assistant resident, since named
"resident of the sea," Henri-Louis Charles TeMechelen.

8

Opium Czar
Charles TeMechelen

Charles TeMechelen was born in Rembang and, despite occasional periods in Europe, Java was his true home. He was Eurasian, the son of a Dutch tobacco planter and his Chinese-mestizo wife.[1] At his mother's knee he learned Malay, and from his rural boyhood companions he learned Javanese—so fluently that it was later said he spoke it like a Javanese nobleman. He prepared for the Colonial Service at Delft Academy in Holland and began his official career in 1864 as controleur in his home residency.[2] Nine years later he was transferred to the Priangan, again as controleur, and then taught Javanese and Malay to prospective officials at the Gymnasium Willem III in Batavia. In 1882, after a two-year furlough in Holland, he was appointed assistant resident of Joana District in the residency of Japara, just west of Rembang.

Throughout TeMechelen's life he was an avid, even a fanatic, big-game hunter, so much so that he is remembered today largely for his hunting exploits.[3] TeMechelen's posting in 1882 called on him to

1. Johanna Willemina Persijn, his mother, was described by G. P. Rouffaer as half Chinese, half Indische. G. P. Rouffaer, "Charles TeMechelen, In Memoriam," *Nederlandsch-Indie Oud en Nieuw*, 9 (1918), 305. Dr. Gerret Pieter Rouffaer met Te-Mechelen during his five-year journey through the Indies between 1885 and 1890. See Rob Nieuwenhuys, *Oost-Indische Spiegel* (Amsterdam, 1972), pp. 12, 555.
2. He wrote about his controleur days in "Eenige dagen het desaleven meegeleefd," *Tijdschrift voor de Inlandsche Taal-, Land- en Volkenkunde*, 25 (1879).
3. See the photograph of TeMechelen standing beside the severed head of a Sumatran elephant he shot in the Lampongs, in Nieuwenhuys, *Tempo Doeloe*, p. 137.

join this avocation with his formal vocation as a colonial official. Joana was a notorious smugglers' den, lying at the heart of Java's "opium funnel." As G. P. Rouffaer wrote years later, "Into this clandestine opium emporium came TeMechelen, the born Rembanger, the fluent Javanese-speaking policeman, and foremost . . . the passionate hunter."[4]

During his first several months in Joana, TeMechelen quickly became aware of the opium-smuggling operations occurring in his district and of the ineffectiveness of coastal patrolling by the marines. He also observed the inadequacy of the opium hunters, four of whom now served directly under him. As presiding judge at police roll hearings, TeMechelen was introduced in detail to the machinations of local opium black marketeers.[5] His report in response to the Java-wide opium survey of 1882—filed when he had been in Joana only eight months—was among the most thorough submitted by any colonial official. It displayed an unusual grasp of opium affairs and revealed TeMechelen's initial efforts to penetrate and understand the hidden world of illegal opium. In it he discussed frankly the role of Joana as a key distribution center for clandestine opium for all central Java and the methods of financing the contraband trade through Armenian agency houses in Surabaya. He also made his first concrete proposals to deal with the problem, including Dutch action to curtail the preparation and distribution of opium from Bali, and an intensified program of local coastal patrolling.[6]

The following April TeMechelen wrote his resident to make a strong case for improving the coastal patrol. Having seen the ease with which small fishing boats carried opium ashore from the larger opium vessels anchored safely beyond the three-mile limit, he requested funds to buy and man a small fleet of similar craft—small man-powered fishing vessels called *jukung*—to intercept the transshipments.[7] He argued that it was a particularly opportune time to

4. Rouffaer, "Charles TeMechelen," p. 308. Other details regarding TeMechelen's life and career may be found in his Staat van Dienst, folios 306, 505.

5. During an eight-day period the following spring, he noted in a report to his resident, TeMechelen tried no fewer than thirty opium cases as police judge. Assistant Resident Joana to Resident Japara, April 14, 1883, no. 632/10 in TMC H422b.

6. Assistant Resident Joana to Resident Japara, December 31, 1882, no. 2694/10 in TMC H422a.

7. Assistant Resident Joana to Resident Japara, April 14, 1883, no. 632/10 in TMC H422b. There are many kinds of jukung. In general, however, a jukung is a small craft made from a hollowed-out tree trunk, fitted with a bamboo mast and used for river traffic and coastal fishing. "Vaartuigen," *ENI* (2d edition), 1927 supplement, p. 433.

Charles TeMechelen. Courtesy Koninklijk Instituut voor Taal-, Land- en Volkenkunde, Leiden.

strike at the smugglers. Several local opium importers were deeply in debt to their Armenian financiers, he had learned. Only by successfully completing transactions then in progress could they restore the credit on which their trade was based. Sabotaging these transactions could put several black-market suppliers out of business.[8] The resident agreed, and in forwarding TeMechelen's re-

8. See Assistant Resident Joana to Resident Japara, April 13, 1883, no. 622/10 in TMC H422b.

quest to the governor general added his own support and stressed that the situation was urgent. In March and April alone, he noted, he had received intelligence from the resident in Bali that nearly 150 piculs (9,270 kilograms) of opium had been dispatched from Buleleng in vessels destined for Japara and Rembang.[9]

In response, Governor General Frederik s' Jacob, at the recommendation of the director of finance, authorized the creation of a special local antismuggling task force in Japara. He allotted government funds to purchase fourteen jukungs, to pay their crews, and to appoint seven additional police mantri to work exclusively in antismuggling work.[10] Under TeMechelen's direction the newly formed task force swung into action in June 1883.

It did so with the full support of the Japara opium farm. The Joana task force was in fact a joint farm-administration enterprise, and TeMechelen was later to attribute its initial success not to the thin funding from Batavia, whose official backing legitimized the project, but to the far more generous financial support of Ho Yam Lo, the Japara opium farmer.[11] The assistant resident and the opium farmer planned the task force together, and in the months following its creation Ho contributed an average f4,310 each month to supplement government funds for craft, crews, salaries, and intelligence. At year's end the farm contribution, for which TeMechelen provided strict accounting to Ho, had mounted to f30,772—a sum five times larger than that provided via official funds.[12]

Ho Yam Lo's initial investment in TeMechelen's project paid off handsomely. Ho calculated that from June to December 1883 in Joana District alone sales of farm opium exceeded those of the previous year by some f83,000, representing a decisive victory over the local black market. Charles TeMechelen used this and other promising signs—including evidence of a credit crisis among contraband importers, as he had hoped—to support a new plan for an expanded, centrally supervised antismuggling program that he submitted in January 1884. The partial measures taken so far under his direction had been so successful, he wrote, that "should they be

9. Resident Japara to GG, April 17, 1883, no. 3166/10 in V 6/10/1883/64.
10. DF to GG, May 4, 1883, no. 7200, and Gouvernement Besluit, July 4, 1883, no. 5 in TMC H422b.
11. TM: Rapport 1888.
12. Assistant Resident Joana to Resident Japara, January 12, 1884, no. 80/10 in TMC H422a.

accepted as the single and general method of attack, the proposed goal, namely making the illegal import of opium once and for all impossible, would be completely within reach."[13]

TeMechelen now envisioned a fleet of fifty-one vessels: three government steamships, twelve large sailing vessels (*cemplon*), and thirty-six smaller ones (jukung). Manned by sea police composed of police mantri and teams of armed men called *kemandahs*, these vessels would patrol the coasts in tandem with a swift steamer, creating a flexible dragnet that opium ships from Bali and their local accomplices could not evade.[14] To be successful, TeMechelen went on, such a task force would have to work across residency boundaries. The recent initiatives in Joana had forced some local smugglers to transfer their activities to neighboring residencies, which already had a smuggling trade of their own. Unsuccessful efforts to enlist the residents of Semarang and Rembang for a conference on joint antismuggling strategies, however, had discouraged TeMechelen about inter-residency cooperation, if, that is, the matter was to be left entirely to the residency-based Colonial Service. "Because of this lack of unity," he wrote, "it will be necessary . . . to entrust the execution of the proposed measures to one person . . . a senior official."[15]

Batavia agreed. In March it authorized the creation of just such an organization under TeMechelen's direction. While remaining assistant resident of Joana, he was now simultaneously assigned to supervise and coordinate all government efforts to combat opium smuggling at sea. He was authorized to rent vessels and to hire crews for them; three hopper barges were transferred from the harbor works at Batavia to form the steamer component of his squadron. Over all of these vessels and their crews TeMechelen was given complete authority. He was also charged with hiring and dismissing temporary police personnel.

TeMechelen's sphere of authority was thus considerably broadened. This was particularly true in terms of his new role as coordinator of government antismuggling activities. Unofficially he was to

13. TM, Assistant Resident Joana to Resident Japara, January 12, 1884, no. 80/10 in TMC H422a.

14. Kemandahs were issued a saber and revolver each. Cemplon (tjemplon) are large wood-hulled sailing vessels commonly used in central Java as freight ships. "Vaartuigen," *ENI* (2d edition), 1927 supplement, p. 444.

15. TM to Resident Japara, January 12, 1884, no. 80/10 in TMC H422a.

preside over the activities of opium hunters in the coastal residencies (officially they remained responsible to their residents), and as a central repository and conduit of intelligence, he was to exercise a supervisory capacity of sorts over all functionaries whose work involved opium smuggling: opium hunters, Customs auditors, and controleurs who were assigned to the Customs Department in Batavia, Semarang, and Surabaya. Where opium problems were concerned, he was to serve personally as the official link between members of the Colonial Service—residents in particular—and to report to his superiors in both the Finance Department and the Colonial Service on their composite efforts.[16] For the various collective activities now either formally or informally under his purview, Batavia budgeted nearly f381,000 for 1884 and continued to provide a like amount throughout the decade.[17]

Bureaucratically, TeMechelen's new position was ambiguous. As assistant resident of Joana he was a member of the Colonial Service and answerable directly to the resident of Japara. As such he claimed a well-defined place in the administrative hierarchy, with commensurate status. But in his new function he was under the direct supervision of the director of finance. Moreover, for the purpose of exercising his inter-residency responsibilities, he was accounted the status, although not the title, of resident. His instructions stipulated that his special authority applied only to activities and measures against opium smuggling at sea. On land, where the authority of the Colonial Service and the pryayi corps prevailed, his function was more clearly supervisory. Here, black-market confiscations were still to be made exclusively by the local police, and criminal prosecutions were to occur in the routine manner in the courts where violations occurred.[18] TeMechelen's allegiance to two departmental masters and the ambiguities surrounding the limits of his authority were to prove troublesome in subsequent years. For the moment, however, Charles TeMechelen simply joined the hunt.

He soon decided to track his prey to its source and deployed his new squadron to strike directly at the opium transshipment trade in Bali. Buleleng was the center of this activity. Here and in neighbor-

16. Extract uit het Register der Besluiten van den Gouverneur Generaal van Nederlandsch Indie, March 15, 1884, no. 8 in TMC H422a.

17. From a statement of expenditures labeled simply "Staat" and undated, but including figures through 1888, in TMC H422e.

18. Besluit, March 15, 1884, no. 8 in TMC H422a.

ing Karangasem, a vassal state of Lombok outside Dutch control, the Buleleng opium farmer presided over a thriving and perfectly legal business processing and exporting opium.[19] Skippers from Semarang, Japara, and Rembang carried hundreds of piculs of opium through Buleleng customs every year simply by declaring their destination to be a free port in the outer islands.[20] TeMechelen began a program of intense patrolling in the Buleleng roads, where all vessels were liable to search by his sea police. Upon identifying an opium-bearing vessel, one of his ships would escort it to its declared destination. This tactic succeeded in inhibiting opium shipments from Buleleng. Manufacturing and exporting operations soon shifted to Karangasem, however. Here departing opium craft had to be intercepted at sea, and beginning in September bands of Balinese instigated by the local farm manager, Oei Soen Tjioe, openly harassed task force vessels patrolling the coast. TeMechelen's efforts to negotiate with the vassal princes of Karangasem fell through, undermined (thought TeMechelen) by Oei, who threatened to drop the local opium farm—for which he paid the princes a fee of f25,000 to f30,000 each year—if they tolerated meddling by the task force. In December the princes issued an ultimatum against patrolling in their waters, and the Dutch backed down.[21]

Despite this setback, Batavia judged TeMechelen's 1884 efforts largely successful. Because of the Bali offensive the quantity of clandestine opium reaching Java that year had been significantly reduced.[22] But TeMechelen's dual assignment—for he was still assistant resident of Joana—raised difficulties of another sort.

Most immediately troublesome in the opinion of Rembang's resident, J. P. Metman, was the degree to which TeMechelen busied himself with his smuggling campaign. For four of the eight months following his appointment, TeMechelen was absent from his district, having abandoned its administration to an inexperienced controleur. Flushed perhaps with the excitement of the chase and his new status, TeMechelen became not only neglectful of his more mundane duties but, according to Metman, insubordinate as well.

19. For the rules governing the Buleleng opium farm, see Extract uit het Register der Besluiten van den Gouverneur Generaal NI, November 23, 1875, no. 5 in V 4/1/1876/5.
20. DF to GG, July 28, 1884, no. 12417 in VKG 3/2/1885/K1/no. 7.
21. TM to DF, August 28, 1887, no. 1039 in TMC H422e.
22. TM: Rapport 1888.

He failed to inform him of his comings and goings, and on one occasion ignored a directive to attend the installation of Joana's new regent, a flagrant discourtesy to his "Younger Brother" and the local pryayi. Metman concluded, and his superiors in Batavia ultimately agreed, that TeMechelen's joint appointment was irreconcilable with his responsibilities as assistant resident.[23] In May 1885, therefore, in response both to his successes and failures, Charles Te-Mechelen was discharged from his duties in Joana and transferred to Semarang (shortly thereafter to Rembang), where, with the title of resident, he took up full-time "the supervision of measures to combat opium smuggling at sea." He thus became Java's first, and only, "resident of the sea," not his official title but that by which he was soon popularly known.[24]

With his successful exploits in Bali in 1884 and his appointment the following year as resident of the sea, Charles TeMechelen entered the public eye. As his influence grew he came to be identified personally not only with the world of opium smuggling and the offshore battle against it, but with the opium farms as well. Te-Mechelen courted this identity. He saw clearly the opportunities inherent in becoming the government's primary authority on opium affairs. He accurately perceived the smuggling problem as but one piece of a larger problem in which smuggling, the opium monopoly, and government laws and policies were inextricably bound together. He tried therefore to make his influence felt in all of these spheres. At every opportunity he pushed the limits of his authority and widened his activities. He would become indispensable.

Among the most important of TeMechelen's contributions as resident of the sea was the compilation of the first comprehensive study of opium in Java. Commissioned in 1885 by Governor General Otto van Rees, TeMechelen was to investigate the nature and extent of the opium habit in Java and to recommend measures the government might take to combat it. The final product, three years in the making, was a wide-ranging, detailed report.[25] In it Te-Mechelen candidly described opium smoking as a social custom and

23. Resident Japara to DF, February 8, 1885, no. 12 Geheim in V 27/7/1886/99.
24. SvD TeMechelen, folio 505.
25. Cited throughout as TM: Rapport 1888. There are two copies of this report, one in the National Archives, another among TeMechelen's papers in the Koninklijk Instituut, Leiden.

examined the workings of the opium farm, including its unofficial aspects such as the patungan trade. He also dealt with the black market, particularly opium smuggling and his efforts to suppress it. In a final section he submitted his detailed recommendations for the reform of the opium farm system.

Not surprisingly, TeMechelen's report recommended stronger government support and funding for the antismuggling work under his direction, including the construction of a special antismuggling vessel and the centralization of all antismuggling efforts—on land and sea—under one office. In addition he proposed several reforms in the farm system which would eliminate the gulf between the farm of the statute books and the real ones, such as liberalization of rules governing patungan distribution and bringing the entire farm structure under closer state supervision. He argued strongly that the government should take over completely the manufacture of official opium—which could be made uniform islandwide and chemically coded to distinguish it from illegal opium—and distribute it to farm outlets along carefully controlled channels.

TeMechelen, in short, envisioned a reformed opium farm system supervised by a strong state agency. Under such conditions, he argued, the vice-tax theory would work: a minimum number of people would pay the maximum price for an article of luxury which, however undesirable, practically speaking could not be wholly eliminated. This was a point of view that TeMechelen was to advance repeatedly in the years to come, years in which the farm system itself came under increasingly strong attack. Under his direction, he declared, the interests of the state, the opium farm, and the people would at long last coincide.

His main task as resident of the sea, however, remained interfering with the passage of illegal opium into Java, and to this he devoted the major share of his attention. TeMechelen developed a network of informants with whom he kept in touch by telegraph in the key locations of the smuggling trade—the most important being Singapore, Surabaya, and Bali. Through his spies in Bali and Surabaya, TeMechelen could frequently obtain precise information about the departure of opium vessels from Bali—including their cargo, skipper, passengers, and both real and feigned destinations—and accurately predict when to expect them.[26] This tech-

26. See the telegram from Abdullah, TeMechelen's Surabaya informant, in Exh 9/8/1892/76.

nique became all the more important after 1886, when, because of the cost of operations in Bali, TeMechelen ceased regular coastal patrolling of the "funnel," hiring local craft and crews only when there was special indication that a clandestine shipment was under way. The increasing incidence of large shipments of contraband opium by swift Chinese-English steamers from Singapore also put a premium on intelligence. From 1887 on TeMechelen learned about several such shipments a year from the Dutch consul general in Singapore, who maintained a spy network among the steamship crews and dock hands and kept a close watch on Chinese visitors from Java.[27]

The new expanded task force continued to enjoy a subsidy from the Japara opium farm, although government funding now exceeded that from the farm. Ho Yam Lo, the original backer of TeMechelen's efforts, remained keenly interested. When the hopper barges provided by Batavia proved inadequate, for example, Ho continued to assign his personal steam cruiser, the *Oentoeng*, to patrol alongside the government steamers. Typical of task force–farm cooperation, the *Oentoeng* was skippered and staffed by employees of the opium farm but carried a team of TeMechelen's sea police.[28] Ho also reported to TeMechelen on the month-to-month results of their combined antismuggling efforts in terms of their effect on farm sales.[29] As TeMechelen's base broadened, both the Semarang and the Rembang opium farm kongsis joined in contributing financial and material support. In addition to the Ho group, TeMechelen developed close relations with Han Liong Ing's Kediri kongsi, which acquired the Rembang farm in 1884. Farm money was used to hire additional patrolling vessels, to pay crews and other personnel, and, undoubtedly, to fund the farm–task force intel-

27. TM to DF, August 3, 1889, no. 899/12. See Consul General to TM, October 17, 1889, no. 995 in TMC H422c, in which Consul General G. Lavino informs TeMechelen of the recent arrival of two Rembang Chinese, of the participation of another in a major contraband shipment, and of his suspicions of the complicity of the Semarang farm in a recent shipment of opium aboard the *Srimanggar*. See also TeMechelen's Dienstnota of January 24, 1891, and the appended telegrams in Exh 9/8/1892/76.

28. See the case of Pak Lasimah, whose opium-laden boat was overtaken by the *Oentoeng* in late 1883: Pro Justitia, Raad van Justitie Surabaya, February 24, 1885, in TMC H422b. In December 1886 the government took over the maintenance costs of the *Oentoeng* though it remained a farm vessel. TM to DF, August 9, 1891, no. 714/B in TMC H422c.

29. Rouffaer found such a letter among TeMechelen's files. See his "Indische Aanteekeningen."

ligence apparatus. TeMechelen periodically reported to the farmers on the disposition of these funds.[30]

About such cooperation Charles TeMechelen had no qualms. He saw no conflict between the interests of the state and those of the Chinese-run opium farms, as long as both acted in good faith. If the state offered adequate protection against black-market opium, opium farmers would not be compelled to engage in smuggling—so he reasoned. Even as anti-Chinese sentiments welled up powerfully in the colony in the 1880s, he dissented, maintaining that men such as Ho Yam Lo were victims of a "pernicious inclination" to stereotype all opium farmers as conscienceless profiteers. "I am convinced," he said speaking of his Chinese partners, "that there *are* honest farmers."[31] Using his task force in part to strike against their competitors, he too became a partisan in the "battle of the kings."

The unsatisfactory state of affairs in Karangasem, Bali, continued unabated until 1887. On several occasions TeMechelen's patrol boats were attacked by armed bands. Much to his anger, Dutch authorities in Buleleng adopted a passive attitude toward these harassments, having thus far contented themselves with a diplomatic complaint to the raja of Lombok borne by two lowly controleurs. Emphasizing the danger "to the prestige of our authority" when attacks by "the petty kingdoms of Bali" go unpunished, even unprotested, TeMechelen prodded the government into action.[32] In August 1887 he personally conveyed to the king Dutch concern over the actions of his unruly dependency. This protest was restated in November by the resident of Bali and Lombok, who, as a specially appointed government commissioner, was convoyed to Lombok along with TeMechelen by a squadron of five warships. Bowing to this show of force, the ruler, Ratu Agung-agung Ngurah, promised to close the ports of Karangasem to the opium trade, to dismantle the opium farm there, and to protect all ships in the roads of Karangasem from molestation by his subjects.[33] He promulgated an

30. In his dealings with the Semarang farm, TeMechelen worked through its European advocate/representative, Baron Sloet van Hagensdorp. See TM to DF, August 9, 1891, no. 714/B in TMC H422c.

31. TM to DF, May 31, 1889, no. 640/4 Geheim in Exh 9/8/1892/76. The emphasis is expressed in the original as follows: "ik heb de overtuiging dat er *eerlijke* pachters zijn."

32. TM to DF, August 28, 1887, no. 1039 in TMC H422e.

33. Also under consideration at the same conference was the legal status of Netherlands Indies subjects who resided in Lombok or its dependencies, and other issues of contention. See Extract uit het Register der Besluiten van den GG, November 4, 1887, no. 1/C in TMC H422e.

edict to this effect. Several months later TeMechelen reported that the raja's vassals had complied, encouraged to do so, he thought, by the presence of a warship, two task force steamers, and several small sea police vessels just off shore.[34]

Meanwhile TeMechelen moved to block the relocation of the Karangasem opium operations in neighboring Badung, another semi-independent Balinese state, whose ruler responded by promising cooperation with the task force.[35] As a result of the constant patrolling of his squadron in Bali waters, and of his initiatives in Buleleng, Karangasem, and Badung, TeMechelen succeeded in putting Bali's Chinese opium merchants on the run and in reducing significantly the role of Bali as a supplier of black-market opium to Java.[36]

As a special official with a temporary appointment, TeMechelen had both to claim success for his efforts and at the same time to argue for their continuation and expansion. To this end he acknowledged freely in his reports that large quantities of opium continued to bypass his task force. He attributed these failures to inadequate funding—which forced him either to concentrate his patrol vessels in one place or to spread them too thinly—and to the special inadequacies of the government-supplied steamers. These had been built as stone carriers for laying new harbor abutments at Batavia. They were too slow to catch the swift Singapore-based steamships that were increasingly active as the Bali connection was tightened;[37] and they were too deeply built to pursue native craft into shallow coastal waters, where on three occasions they ran aground. All too frequently large hauls of contraband opium reached the shore despite adequate advance warning because the task force's vessels were too slow to keep up with them or too clumsy to pursue. Beginning in 1886, therefore, TeMechelen began campaigning for swift, shallow-

34. TM: Rapport 1888; TM to DF, August 28, 1887, no. 1039 in TMC H422e; Resident Bali and Lombok to GG, August 27, 1888, Geheim in KG Exh 30/10/1888/B21; and the account of the episode in Alfons van der Kraan, *Lombok: Conquest, Colonization and Underdevelopment, 1870–1940* (Asian Studies Association of Australia: Southeast Asia Publications Series, no. 5; Singapore, 1980), pp. 32–35.

35. Resident Bali and Lombok to GG, May 12, 1888, F Geheim in VKG 9/7/1888/D10/46. For general background on Bali, Buleleng, and Karangasem, see the articles "Bali," *ENI*, 1:83–87, and "Karangasem," *ENI*, 2:195.

36. Oei Soen Tjioe, for example, having been thwarted in Karangasem and Badung, fled to Ampenan in Lombok. E. Cijre to TM, February 8, 1892, A in Exh 9/8/1892/76.

37. Ships owned by Chinese subjects of Britain in the Straits Settlements.

bottomed steamers built especially for task force operations, a campaign he took up again in his comprehensive Report of 1888 and in which he was to be repeatedly frustrated. The denial of his requests for special cruisers and for funds to enlarge his fleet of smaller boats permitted TeMechelen to throw responsibility for the bulk of task force failures back on the government.[38]

Inadequate funding was but one of TeMechelen's handicaps, although it was the one that the government could act most directly to correct. More vexing were institutional ones. The limitation of his official authority to activities at sea meant that the successful completion of every task force effort required the cooperation and participation of authorities ashore—for sharing intelligence, making arrests, and prosecuting cases in courts. All too frequently, TeMechelen complained, such cooperation was lacking. Even when it existed, the opium laws of the Indies, riddled with loopholes, usually provided an escape clause for suspected smugglers.

The general disinclination of residents to coordinate their efforts against opium smuggling with one another and with him plagued TeMechelen from the time of his earliest initiatives as assistant resident in Joana. Things did not improve as he rose in rank and responsibility. He complained to his superiors that on numerous occasions he informed residents of impending clandestine operations only to have them take no action, or to follow up clumsily by assigning the least suitable personnel to do the job. Residents complained in response that his intelligence was faulty and that his subordinates were untrustworthy. They preferred to rely on their own pryayi-based sources and to organize measures themselves, withholding on occasion important information from TeMechelen on grounds of security.[39] Moreover, local police sometimes withheld information so that, in the event of a major opium confiscation, bounty money need not be shared with TeMechelen's men. Yet another thorny issue was the extent to which TeMechelen attempted to exercise authority over opium hunters and other functionaries officially under the residents' jurisdiction.

Disputes like these sprang in part from professional jealousy.

38. See TeMechelen's discussion of the issue in TM: Rapport 1888.
39. TM to DF, January 11, 1888, no. 35/3 Geheim in TMC H422d; TM to DF, August 17, 1890, no. 1316/4 in TMC H422e. For an example of a cabled warning from TeMechelen to the resident of Japara, see TM to Resident Japara, September 8, 1890, no. 1458/12 in TMC H422c.

Although officially a resident himself, as resident of the sea Te-Mechelen was outside the ordinary hierarchy of the Colonial Service. His fellow residents were loath to share their authority with him. TeMechelen's headstrong behavior did not endear him to them, nor did his frequent accusations—for he did not keep his complaints to himself. Not a diplomat, by the end of the decade TeMechelen was feuding openly with the residents of both Japara and Rembang.

Such animosity at the residency level reflected a general mutual distrust that developed during the decade between the regular Colonial Service and TeMechelen's ad hoc task force. TeMechelen cited this animosity, which he attributed entirely to the wholly unjustified antagonism of the Colonial Service, in continuing to insist on the necessity of uniting all antismuggling efforts under his direct management.[40]

On those occasions when the successful cooperation of Te-Mechelen's sea police and land authorities did result in bona fide arrests and the confiscation of contraband opium, loopholes in the opium laws made convictions nearly unattainable. Smuggling cases of this sort involved large quantities of opium and were therefore heard first in the Landraad, where members of TeMechelen's task force, local police, and farm personnel would all contribute testimony against the accused. Not infrequently suspected smugglers were convicted in the Landraad, where local sentiments weighed heavily. Such convictions were almost inevitably overturned in the higher Councils of Justice, however, where Dutch advocates hired by the accused (and their patrons) argued legal points before a committee of their peers to overturn the conviction.

The legal weaknesses of the 1879 antismuggling law (SvNI 1879, no. 224) became apparent during van Santen's early patrolling activities and continued to thwart the antismuggling campaign thereafter. The extension of the three-mile perimeter to six nautical sea miles in 1883 applied only to vessels registered in Netherlands India; for steam vessels and craft registered in Singapore and elsewhere the three-mile limit remained valid. For this reason Java-based smugglers increasingly registered their vessels in Singapore during the 1880s.[41] Even when caught within the perimeter laden

40. See DF to GG, January 31, 1888, R Geheim in TMC H422d.
41. TM to DF, January 3, 1893, no. 7/12 in TMC H422b.

with contraband, skippers need only plead that foul weather or an emergency had forced them off course. Furthermore, the law was worded in such a way as to make a vessel's commander (*gezagvoerder*) legally responsible for clandestine opium aboard his ship. This was particularly troublesome in the case of larger steamships, where the Chinese supercargo (proprietor of the ship's hold) and passengers were really the guilty parties; they could be declared guilty only when they were caught entering the borders of a particular farm territory in possession of illegal opium. In addition, TeMechelen's sea police were frequently none too careful about legal technicalities when making seizures at sea; among other things, they had to rely on imprecise land sightings and depth readings to determine their distance from shore, a crucial factor in defining whether or not a violation had occurred.[42]

The presence of any one or a combination of the above factors in a smuggling case opened the door for acquittal; then the confiscated opium would be returned, the impounded vessel released, and the suspect courteously escorted from Java. To a letter in which he summarized many of these points for the director of finance in 1893, Charles TeMechelen attached the transcripts of eighteen important opium cases of the previous decade. Only three had yielded convictions.[43]

The case of The Toan Hwat was typical. The supercargo of the Netherlands India–registered steamship *Bandjermassin*, The was accused of taking opium aboard in Singapore and landing it on the island of Bawean. He was convicted by the Landraad there, fined f18,500, and sentenced to three years on a labor gang. The Surabaya Council of Justice heard the appeal, which was argued by a prominent Dutch advocate. The council overturned The's conviction, arguing that the Bawean Landraad had not determined that The owned the opium, only that he supervised the cargo and knew about it. Furthermore, under the 1879 law the commander of the *Bandjermassin*, not The, was legally responsible for the presence of the opium aboard his ship, and he had not been charged. Since The was guilty of no other violation, he was acquitted.[44]

42. See C. W. van Heeckeren (Landsadvocaat Semarang) to TM, December 10, 1889, no. 278 in TMC H422b.
43. TM to DF, January 3, 1893, no. 7/12 in TMC H422b.
44. Case of The Toan Hwat, Pro Justitia, Raad van Justitie Surabaya, September 21, 1889, in TMC H422b.

Being denied the final reward of the hunt so often exacerbated TeMechelen's impatience with due process. In cases involving key smuggling figures, therefore, he came more and more to advocate bypassing the court system altogether. By Article 47 of the fundamental law (Regeerings Reglement) the governor general was authorized to exile enemies of public *rust en orde* (peace and order) without benefit of trial. TeMechelen recommended that Article 47 be applied to Oei Soen Tjioe, mastermind of the Bali connection, and other well-known but shrewd operators against whom it would be difficult to build an airtight legal case. But Batavia invoked Article 47 with great reluctance, and such requests were almost always turned down. Oei was not exiled. In 1889, however, TeMechelen did succeed in orchestrating a movement to apply the article to Njo Tjiauw Ging and Njo Teng Yoe, father and son, leaders of one of the most extensive independent black-market operations in central Java.

The case against the Njos was the culmination of years of work and is a rare example of a successful collaboration between TeMechelen and a resident, Metman of Japara, in a smuggling case. TeMechelen himself gathered the evidence, which included eight confiscated books of correspondence, ledgers, and commercial transactions, and placed it at Resident Metman's disposal. Metman interrogated both Njos—using translations of the Njo books provided by the Japara farm—and, having concurred in TeMechelen's recommendation that they be exiled, passed it along with his endorsement to the governor general. The directors of justice and finance and the Council of the Indies all subsequently endorsed the proposal, agreeing that the case against them fully established that the Njos were indeed a threat to public rust en orde. The case was exceptional, however; an important factor in the concerted movement against them was the suspicion prevalent in Japara that the Njos had instigated the murder of the daughter of a Chinese opium farm mata-mata a few years before. The case had been thrown out of court at the time and could not have been raised in strictly legal proceedings against them. In the context of Article 47 deliberations, it added the necessary tone of overt criminality necessary to invoke the article. The Njos were banished to Ternate.[45]

45. Deliberations on the Njo case, including transcripts of their interviews with Resident Metman, may be found in V 8/7/1889/77.

In eliminating the Njos, TeMechelen cut off a major conduit of nonfarm opium into central Java, an act of some significance for Han Liong Ing's Japara and Rembang farms. As such it was very much in the spirit of the task force as it developed under Te-Mechelen's direction. The task force continued to receive an opium farm subsidy throughout the decade, although the amounts coming from the farms dropped when they were faced with financial trauma after 1886. TeMechelen later estimated that even then the Japara and Rembang farms continued to contribute an average of f18,000 a year to underwrite the costs of new recruits.[46] Although the state replaced the farm as the primary funder of the task force, Te-Mechelen's involvement with the farms deepened. He continued to see a strong government-supported opium farm as a key ingredient to a successful antismuggling policy. He viewed himself as an instrument to help bring farm and state interests together. In this vein he asked to be assigned to coordinate all of Java's opium farm auctions. Familiar with the farmers and other potential candidates, he could apply a consistent policy that would profit both state and farm. Although officials in Batavia rejected this idea, he did play an increasingly important behind-the-scenes role as government adviser on the selection of farmers and other farm matters. In 1886, when task force efforts in Bali were being jeopardized by the belligerent actions instigated by the Buleleng opium farm, TeMechelen encouraged the Semarang, Kediri, and Surabaya kongsis to eliminate the problem by buying joint control of the Buleleng farm. The potential partners fell out, but the attempt on TeMechelen's part to employ the resources of the farms to combat smuggling was typical of his approach.[47]

TeMechelen developed particularly close ties with two opium farm kongsis. His original benefactor had been Ho Yam Lo, who as Japara opium farmer had underwritten the original prototype task force. Ho kept the Japara farm until 1886, and in 1887 captured the Semarang and Yogyakarta farms. Han Liong Ing (the Kediri kongsi), who had held the Rembang farm from 1884, added Japara and three others in 1887. TeMechelen became most intimately involved with the Kediri kongsi. He was personally friendly with its

46. TM to DF, March 5, 1892, no. 521/12 in Exh 9/8/1892/76.
47. TM: Rapport 1888; and "Toelis Rembang," May 20, 1886, cited by Rouffaer in his "Indische Aanteekeningen."

managing officer, Liem Kok Sing, a man for whom he developed a
profound respect during a decade-long friendship and collaboration.[48] By 1889 these two syndicates had a near monopoly of the
central Java opium farms, and Charles TeMechelen's identification
not only with these particular kongsis but with the institution itself
was sealed.

TeMechelen's identification with the farm system and his collaboration over the years with specific opium farm kongsis drew him
into the fierce competition among Chinese patronage constellations
for opium farms and the broader commercial powers they brought
with them. Both his official role as leader of government measures
to combat opium smuggling and his unofficial role as "house expert" in opium affairs made him an important element in that
competition. In striking at the black market, almost always in collaboration with the farm, he helped protect the commercial monopolies of franchise holders; behind the scenes he was in a position to
credit or discredit Chinese individuals and kongsis who, as farm
candidates, sought the patronage of the state.

TeMechelen's close association with certain kongsis and animosity
toward others brought forth the inevitable accusations of favoritism
from Chinese interests who did not share his confidence.[49] To many
observers in the Chinese and European communities his ties with
the dominant farm interests appeared corrupt; under his protection, if not, as some alleged, with his active participation, his favor-
ites participated in the very contraband trade that he was charged to
eradicate. Resident W.C.J. Castens of Japara was one of those who
thought so.[50] When it was later revealed that on at least one occasion
the Kediri kongsi imported clandestine opium under his very nose,
these accusations seemed to have been borne out. Yet no evidence
ever surfaced to implicate him directly. Rather, it seems more likely
that TeMechelen lapsed into a kind of willful innocence about his
collaborators. After all, he saw his own antismuggling efforts as
making it possible for opium farmers to deal honestly, and Liem
Kok Sing and the others evidently convinced him that they did.

48. See TeMechelen's comments about Liem in TM to DF, August 17, 1890, no.
1316/4 in TMC H422e.
49. See Liem Hok Djien's description of a Han Liong Ing–TeMechelen conspiracy
in Liem Hok Djien to MvK, August 25, 1889, in VKG 17/10/1889/G16/72.
50. TeMechelen refutes this charge in TM to DF, August 9, 1891, no. 714/B in
TMC H422c.

TeMechelen's close involvement with certain kongsis contributed to the vague odor of ill repute that had attached itself to him and his task force by the end of the decade. Contributing to this was the unsavory reputation of the lesser-ranking members of his organization. By 1890 some 185 sea police served under TeMechelen in the task force, in addition to part-time boat crews and other personnel. The dependability and trustworthiness of the sea police were perennial problems. Most of the sea police were recruited locally from among the available loose manpower in the coastal residencies, from "the less cultured" classes as TeMechelen called them. This was the same pool from which the farms and independent smugglers sought their own accomplices, and there appears to have been a high degree of interchangeability between them. Much like jagabaya figures in village society, many of TeMechelen's sea police straddled the lawful and criminal worlds, realigning their allegiance from patron to patron in the wake of immediate opportunity.[51] This, and low pay—infrequently augmented by a government bounty—caused a rapid turnover in task force membership, which in turn worked against the formation of firm institutional loyalties. The task force, in short, did not attract a high-caliber recruit. Such that signed on were all the more likely to exploit their positions to the hilt. Sea police, armed and bedecked with authority—their boats marked as police vessels—were in an ideal position to engage in acts of caprice and extortion (of the mata-mata variety) against innocent fishermen and traders. How common such acts were is difficult to assess, but they were common enough to gain for the sea police an unbecoming reputation for petty harassment and villainy over the years.[52]

Charles TeMechelen's own manner and personality only reinforced this negative image. As an Indies figure he was exceptional. Unlike most of his colleagues in the Colonial Service—who liked to affect a pragmatic, businesslike approach to their work—TeMechelen was a flamboyant man who hated routine. He was a bit of a martinet—intemperate, litigious, and given to self-dramatization. His pure-Dutch colleagues patronizingly attributed these qualities to the fact that he was Eurasian, a *halfbloed*. This fact alone relegated him, socially, to the fringe of the ruling class, despite the high status

51. See TM to DF, November 25, 1890, no. 1934/3 in Exh 9/8/1892/76.
52. See Resident Japara to DF, July 16, 1891, no. 3870/169; Resident Japara to DF, July 27, 1891, no. 103; and TM to DF, August 9, 1891, no. 714/B, all in TMC H422c.

of his position. (In describing an archetypical resident, Louis Couperus wrote, "He himself had remained very Dutch and above all
hated anything that was halfcaste.")[53] TeMechelen was notoriously
contemptuous of natives, and in 1885 was sentenced to a three-
month prison term (suspended) for physically abusing police roll
suspects. Such brutality was also characteristic of the stereotypical
"Indo."[54] The world of opium in which he came to play such a
central part was, to the average Indies Dutch, equally eccentric; it
was mysterious and corrupt, and corrupting. TeMechelen's own
eccentricities, indeed his "racial impurity," blended in the public
view of him with the taint of the opium world. That is why, as his
reputation grew, it brought with it a local fame that was more than a
little tinged with notoriety, like that of his Chinese opium farmer
associates. In the public eye, the resident of the sea became the
opium czar.

Despite this, TeMechelen's efforts did not go unappreciated in
Batavia. Among his staunchest supporters was E. A. Rovers, who,
after having served for four years as a Finance Department inspector in Semarang (where he had frequent contact with TeMechelen),
was appointed director of finance in 1887. A personal friend and
hunting companion, Rovers particularly valued TeMechelen's services as a troubleshooter for his department, and he frequently took
sides with him against his critics in the Colonial Service. In recognition of the importance of TeMechelen's work, Batavia added an
assistant resident to his European staff in June 1887; and two years
later the ad hoc position of resident of the sea was formalized when
the Office of the Chief Inspector of Opium Affairs was established
under the Department of Finance. As chief inspector, TeMechelen's
realm of authority was still confined to the sea. Still under consideration, at his own and now Rovers's urging, was the proposal to place
the management of all opium matters under his personal direction.
This question, however, was soon subsumed in a larger one that
addressed itself to the survival of the opium farm system itself.

53. Couperus, *Hidden Force*, p. 123.
54. See Proces-verbaal: Vonnis Rechtspreken, Raad van Justitie Semarang, December 28, 1885, no. 38 in V 27/7/1886/99. On being a Eurasian in Indies society,
Wertheim makes the observation that "many Indo-Europeans were kept fully occupied by the effort to demonstrate as close a relationship as possible with the white
race." Wertheim, *Indonesian Society*, p. 139. Rouffaer, "Charles TeMechelen," comments on TeMechelen's distinctive Eurasian characteristics, as does Nieuwenhuys,
Tempo Doeloe, p. 137. Nieuwenhuys points out that even TeMechelen's penchant for
big-game hunting was typical for an "Indische Jongen," or "Indies Boy."

9

Crisis

The early 1880s were prosperous years for Java. Commercial agriculture continued to expand in the wake of the 1870 Agrarian Law, which had opened Java to private exploitation. Between 1882 and 1884 European and Chinese entrepreneurs built eighteen new sugar mills on the island, and coffee crops exceeded 1.25 million piculs (77,250 metric tons) a year. What brought affluence to the planter brought affluence to others. Contractors prospered by preparing buildings and grounds; provisioning the plantations, mills, and work crews; and by hauling produce from processing plant to port. They prospered as well by providing services to government, which was now pressed to build roads, rails, and telegraph lines to accompany the faster-paced development. Laborers prospered too, joining construction gangs, working the cane fields and coffee gardens, and toiling in sorting sheds and processing plants. Wages rose. In residencies such as Pasuruan, where both coffee and sugar flourished, a new prosperity was to be seen manifested in better dwellings, furniture, clothing and ornaments, and a rising population of cattle. All this meant heady profits for Java's opium farmers and for the conglomeration of interests with which they were intertwined. General prosperity increased the value of the opium farms and raised the stakes in the peranakan competition for commercial supremacy.[1]

1. Furnivall, *Netherlands India*, pp. 195–96; DF to GG, May 22, 1891, no. 7637 in TMC H422c; R. E. Elson, *Javanese Peasants and the Colonial Sugar Industry: Impact and*

180
Opium to Java

The opium farm auctions held in the autumn of 1883 for the three-year farm term beginning in 1884 could scarcely have been held in more favorable circumstances. Or so it seemed. In all but three of Java's farm territories farm fees rose appreciably. Altogether, Java's opium farmers bid an increase to the treasury of 1.7 million guilders over the previous farm term.[2]

There had already been hints of calamity, however. In the late 1870s a wind-borne leaf disease began blowing its way through Java's coffee bushes, leaving patches of denuded, barren plants in its wake. And in 1882 sugar planters in Ceribon found sereh disease in their cane fields; during the next eight years this dreaded blight made its way eastward until it had attacked sugar crops in nearly every residency of central and east Java.[3] Hoof-and-mouth disease appeared among Java's working cattle. In the meantime commodity prices for sugar and coffee on the world market had begun to decline.

The effects of this coincidence of misfortune hit Java in late 1884, when international sugar prices fell drastically. As German farmers flooded the European market with beet sugar, growing cane in Java became a losing proposition. By 1887 coffee harvests had dwindled to 254,000 piculs (15,697 metric tons), a fifth of the former yield. In the European sector of the colonial economy this resulted in the short-run failure and dissolution of many of the new plantations and enterprises. Banks heavily invested in agriculture suddenly faced bankruptcy. The closing of private plantations and processing plants and the reduced opportunities to earn money on government coffee plantations—where wages paid to workers in 1885 were half those of 1884—robbed many Javanese of their source of ready cash. Money became scarcer and scarcer in the village world. (Exacerbating popular fears, rumors spread that the government would declare the ubiquitous duits—the older form of copper penny—valueless.)[4]

Change in an East Java Residency, 1830–1940 (Asian Studies Association of Australia: Southeast Asia Publications Series, no. 9; Oxford: Oxford University Press, 1984), pp. 134–35.

2. Precisely f1,661,976. See TM to DF, May 31, 1889, no. 640/4 Geheim in Exh 9/8/1892/76.

3. "Suiker," ENI, 3:161; Djoko Suryo, "Social and Economic Life in Semarang," p. 212.

4. Furnivall, Netherlands India, pp. 196, 198–99; KVvNI 1887, p. 3; TM to DF, May 31, 1889, no. 640/4 Geheim in Exh 9/8/1892/76, and DF to GG, May 22, 1891, no. 7637 in TMC H422c. See also Elson, Javanese Peasants, pp. 137–39; and Djoko Suryo, "Social and Economic Life in Semarang," pp. 210, 217.

All this was to have dire consequences for the opium farms, but the effect was delayed. Only one opium farm failed during the mid-decade farm term.[5] The fortunes of others, however, began to fluctuate. In Madiun and Kediri the opium farms had to borrow to meet their commitments. Ho Yam Lo sold his villa and gardens in Semarang about this time, and Tan Boen In of the Kediri kongsi mortgaged his real estate. By 1885 the financial health of the Kediri kongsi was considered so shaky that only after Charles TeMechelen pleaded its case privately was it permitted to compete in the opium farm auctions for the next term.[6]

When it did, however, its members displayed the optimism that was characteristic of all farm candidates that year, taking leases on no less than five opium farms: Ceribon, Tegal, Pekalongan, Rembang, and Japara. At the same time, Ho Yam Lo's Semarang-based kongsi acquired the Semarang, Yogyakarta, and Kedu farms, and Be Biauw Tjoan's venerable kongsi took the Krawang and Bagelen farms, and that for Batavia (which included the contract for supplying the opium depots in Bantam). In Kediri, Chinese captain Tan Kok Tong kept the opium farm that he had held since 1881.[7] Despite the nagging economic depression, these revenue farmers felt that the future was sufficiently promising to place among the highest collective opium farm bids of the century: f13,031,400 a year.[8] It was in part the inflated farm fees of that year, depending as they did on swift economic recovery, that set the stage for the general farm collapse that soon began.

Chinese optimism in 1886 was not altogether unfounded. Coffee planters were predicting larger harvests with the gradual passing of the leaf disease; and opium farmers shared with many Europeans the hopeful belief that the sugar crisis was a momentary deviation caused by short-term speculation on the part of wholesalers. It would soon resolve itself, they thought, bringing higher prices once

5. This was Tan Soe Lien's Pasuruan farm. Reeling from the immediate impact of coffee failures in the highlands around Malang, Tan also faced severe competition from the black market and the staunch opposition of Pasuruan's entrenched Chinese officers who resented the intrusion of an outsider from Kediri (Tan was Chinese lieutenant of Ngrowo). When Tan fell f161,473 in arrears, the government dissolved his farm contract and leased the farm to one of his competitors. See TM to DF, May 31, 1889, no. 640/4 Geheim in Exh 9/8/1892/76; KVvNI 1890, p. 183; and RAvNI 1883.

6. DF to GG, November 4, 1886, V8 Zeer Geheim in TMC H422e; TM to DF, October 21, 1886, Geheim in TMC H422e; Liem, *Riwajat*, p. 151.

7. See Chapter 5, n. 46.

8. TM to DF, May 31, 1889, no. 640/4 Geheim in Exh 9/8/1892/76.

again. For its part the government had agreed to grant relief to sugar producers in the form of tax postponements. It was also laying rails in several residencies, promising new opium farm customers in the form of large numbers of laborers on the government payroll. In addition, farm candidates in 1886 shared expectations for a powerful move against opium smuggling by the state, expectations based on the establishment of Charles TeMechelen's task force in 1884. Indeed in 1885 the collective farms had offered to pay f900,000 more for their leases in 1886 if the government continued the task force and prolonged their farm terms one year.[9] The opium farmers were far too sanguine. The worst period of rural money scarcity was yet to come.[10]

The depression in the countryside peaked in 1887 and 1888. Crops grown for cash, including rice (harvested in surplus during these years) now fetched low prices in the marketplace, and new cash in the form of wages and rent only trickled in. To raise money, villagers flocked to the pawnshops, pryayi sold their heirlooms. (The number of people embarking on the pilgrimage to Mecca plummeted.) Many villagers reverted to self-sufficiency based on rice. The repercussions of rural depression for the opium farms, the financial health of which was an accurate gauge of the collective Chinese economy, hit full force beginning in 1887.[11]

In January 1887 four opium farms collected insufficient revenues to pay their monthly fees. By May of that year no fewer than ten farms had defaulted, including all five held by the Kediri kongsi. Tan Kok Tong's strong Kediri farm met all its commitments in 1887 but fell behind in early 1888; and in 1889 the slump finally caught up with Ho Yam Lo's opium farms, now controlled by his son Ho Tjiauw Ing. The younger Ho was forced into bankruptcy before the end of the year. By the end of the farm term in 1889, only four of Java's nineteen opium farms had survived unscathed, notably Be

9. Excepting Banyumas.
10. The 1886 coffee harvest of 817,000 piculs (50,490 metric tons), for example, seemed to portend recovery, but production fell to 254,000 piculs (15,697.2 metric tons) in 1887, rose to approximately 570,000 piculs (35,226 metric tons) in 1888 and 1889, then plummeted to 100,000 piculs (6,180 metric tons) in 1890. See "Koffie, Koffiecultuur," *ENI*, 2:273–74, for precise figures. See also TM to DF, May 31, 1889, no. 640/4 Geheim in Exh 9/8/1892/76.
11. KVvNI 1887, p. 3; KVvNI 1888, p. 4; KVvNI 1889, pp. 6–7; TM to DF, May 31, 1889, no. 640/4 Geheim in Exh 9/8/1892/76; and DF to GG, May 22, 1891, no. 7637 in TMC H422c. Elson, *Javanese Peasants*, p. 141, gives pilgrimage figures for Pasuruan. See also Djoko Suryo, "Social and Economic Life in Rural Semarang," pp. 212, 227.

Biauw Tjoan's. The cumulative debt of the others ran to the millions of guilders, and many of the once proud kings were humbled in a tawdry spectacle of bankruptcy proceedings and debtors' prison.

The failure of Java's opium farms on such a scale was both unpredicted and without precedent.[12] Although the inflationary trend in farm auctions in the midst of an economic slump had bothered some, no one in 1886 foresaw the tenacity of the depression. As it deepened, both the opium farms and the government were forced to scramble in response, the farms to keep their franchises—the retention of which was essential to their own recovery—and the government to protect their jeopardized revenues. As the house expert on opium affairs, Charles TeMechelen played a key intermediary role during the crisis. Recognizing the mutual dependency of the two institutions, he advocated a response that attempted to balance the interests of the state with those of the farm.

Believing that most farmers were making sincere efforts to meet their obligations under unprecedented circumstances, TeMechelen advocated a policy of leniency. His approach emphasized easing the financial burden on opium farmers by reducing their total commitments and by granting them long-term credit for the unpaid balances of their cumulative debts, provided they could offer security to cover them. In his opinion it would be unjust to force opium farmers precipitously into ruin by holding them to the letter of their farm contracts. It would be foolish as well. Opium farmers were in a better position to pay their debts if they retained their farms, even when operating at a loss. For one thing, their revenues could improve at any time; besides, possession of the farm assured them of access to outside credit. Furthermore, the state could not hope to recoup its losses in the colonial courts, where farmers and their Dutch lawyers could prolong the proceedings indefinitely. Finally, the array of candidate farmers was precariously thin. By pressing them too hard the state could quite unnecessarily destroy an important source of state income. Opium farmers, as the true experts, harvested Java's opium revenues for the Dutch. "Support of the opium farmers, in the full meaning of the word," TeMechelen wrote, "is essential."[13]

12. Isolated farm failures, such as that of Tio Siong Mo's Surakarta farm discussed above, had occurred, but never collective failure.

13. TM to DF, May 31, 1889, no. 640/4 Geheim in Exh 9/8/1892/76. In this letter, some fifty pages long, TeMechelen summarizes all the arguments he had been making in defense of his position since 1887.

In this spirit the initial response of Batavia to the spate of farm defaults in the spring of 1887 was the unusual step of renegotiating the farm contracts. All ten of the troubled farms were granted reductions in their farm fees ranging from 17 to 34 percent; the monthly obligations of most were reduced by one-quarter.[14] This was intended to place more realistic obligations on the farms so that they could reestablish their operations on firmer ground and henceforth make their regular contributions to the Treasury without difficulty. For all but two of them, however, this relief was not nearly enough.

In Surakarta, for example, veteran opium farmer Tan Tong Haij was in trouble again by July. When this happened, TeMechelen negotiated with him in an unsuccessful effort to raise security for the farm's growing debts. Tan offered the mortgages he held on two ships, but these were inadequate and none of Tan's kongsi partners came forward who commanded sufficient resources to cover the farm debt. TeMechelen then attempted to save Tan's position by subfarming the residency (to disperse Tan's financial obligation) and, when that failed, by contracting a new farmer who would agree to act as guardian of Tan's interests. When all these tactics miscarried, TeMechelen continued to urge Batavia against removing Tan. By March 1888, however, when still no security could be raised, TeMechelen at long last advised that Tan's contract be dissolved. When this occurred in May, Tan Tong Haij was in debt to the government for more than f1.5 million.[15]

A similar pattern occurred in Madiun, where opium farmer Djie Bok Hien enjoyed the full support of both TeMechelen and the resident. At their urging his farm fees were reduced a second time in January 1888. By April, however, Djie's default was still growing. While the resident pleaded on Djie's behalf with Batavia, TeMechelen began binding Djie's property to the government as security. When it was discovered that Djie was selling his surplus opium in his neighbor's farm territory—this at a time when he was no longer paying for his official supply—both TeMechelen and the resident advised dissolution. This occurred in January 1889, by which time Djie, too, was f1.5 million in arrears.[16]

14. Notes from TeMechelen's files on farm failures, filed loosely and marked "Bijlage F" in TMC H422e. Hereafter cited as Bijlage F.

15. TM to DF, May 31, 1889, no. 640/4 Geheim in Exh 9/8/1892/76; KVvNI 1891, p. 177; and Bijlage F in TMC H422e.

16. See GG to MvK, January 18, 1889, no. 5/1 in VKG 25/3/1889/T4. On the travail of the Madiun farm, see Resident Madiun to DF, July 26, 1888, no. 95 Geheim,

The Kediri kongsi, with its five opium farms, was in difficulty from the outset of the 1887–89 farm term. They received the 25 percent fee reduction negotiated in the spring of 1887; but like most other farms, they continued to fall behind each month. This kongsi in particular enjoyed TeMechelen's personal favor. It was an early and faithful supporter of the task force, and Liem Kok Sing, who managed farm business on behalf of its two strongest financial patrons, Han Liong Ing and Tan Boen In, was both a professional collaborator and friend. TeMechelen judged their opium farms to be among the best managed in Java.[17] TeMechelen chose Tan Boen In, for example, to operate the beleaguered Surakarta farm on behalf of the government during a short interim following the dismemberment of Tan Tong Haij's farm in March 1888.

During the crisis TeMechelen was particularly eager to prevent the ruin of the Kediri kongsi. As its default mounted, TeMechelen intervened on several occasions to plead leniency and to negotiate a further postponement of the kongsi's accountancy. The kongsi in return placed their abundant resources in property, mortgages, and promissory notes in bond as security.[18] By July 1888 the Kediri kongsi was still in serious trouble, so much so that TeMechelen thought they would suffer unthinkable losses without further government indulgence. In October Governor General C. Pijnacker Hordijk cabled the bad news to Holland: "Farmers Ceribon, Tegal, Pekalongan, Japara and Rembang, collectively one kongsi, have requested deferment for nearly three-quarter million."[19] The following month Tan Boen In, speaking for the syndicate, petitioned Batavia for yet another extension, which at TeMechelen's advocacy was granted in January. Thus bolstered, the Kediri kongsi limped through 1889.[20]

In Kediri Tan Kok Tong's farm was financially strong and backed by valuable real estate. Tan, "one of the richest Chinese in Java,"[21] met his farm obligations through 1887, but by the beginning of

and TM to DF, August 6, 1888, no. 1136/4, both in VKG 23/11/1888/F17; DF to GG, December 18, 1888, D7 in VKG 25/3/1889/T4; DF to GG, January 31, 1889, no. 1417 in V 11/3/1889/73; TM to DF, May 31, 1889, no. 640/4 Geheim in Exh 9/8/1892/76; and KVvNI 1891, p. 182.

17. TM to DF, July 5, 1888, no. 1015/4 in V 27/11/1888/69.
18. The value of which was assessed at f674,990. KVvNI 1891, p. 179.
19. GG to MvK, October 24, 1888, T20 in V 14/11/1888/15.
20. TM to DF, May 31, 1889, no. 640/4 Geheim in Exh 9/8/1892/76; Tan Boen In to GG (no date) in V 27/11/1888/69; and jottings from TeMechelen's files marked Bijlage F in TMC H422e.
21. TM to DF, June 1, 1888, no. 874/4 in VKG 23/11/1888/F17.

1888, finding himself in the same predicament as his fellow farmers, he also embarked on a round of requests for special consideration. TeMechelen, in the now familiar argument, urged Batavia to comply; the interests of the Treasury would be better served by supporting Tan while binding his property as security for his unpaid fees. Tan also enjoyed the full support of Kediri's resident, who joined TeMechelen and Rovers in convincing Batavia of the wisdom of his course. In January 1889 Tan reached accord with the government, agreeing to pay his sizable debt—more than f700,000 by the end of his term—in f75,000 yearly installments beginning in 1890.[22]

As the crisis worsened in the fall of 1888, the lenient policy adopted by Director of Finance Rovers on the advice of his friend TeMechelen came under attack in Holland, notably by the newly appointed minister of colonies, L.W.C. Keuchenius. In November he wired Governor General Pijnacker Hordijk to complain of "indefensible permissiveness" in the government's handling of the defaulting opium farms.[23] The fault lay with TeMechelen, he thought, who aside from acting beyond the bounds of his official mandate, entertained a far too positive view of the opium farmers themselves. "He views the farmers not as businessmen," complained Keuchenius, "but as firm supporters of the government. I view them as an evil which must temporarily be endured but which in truth is, even more than opium itself, a cancer upon the native population."[24] Reeling from the news that farm debts to the state now surpassed f3 million, Keuchenius advocated legal and administrative measures to force farmers, "without delay and without consideration," to pay up.[25] Keuchenius's urging, and the unhappy truth that TeMechelen's policy of leniency and support had not thus far contributed to a turnabout, probably accounts for the harsh stance Batavia took against Ho Tjiauw Ing when the several opium farms he had inherited from his father, Ho Yam Lo, began to crumble in April 1889.

Ho Yam Lo began the farm term with three farms—Semarang, Yogyakarta, and Kedu. In June 1888, the same month in which Ho

22. TM to DF, May 31, 1889, no. 640/4 Geheim in Exh 9/8/1892/76; KVvNI 1891, p. 177.
23. Since 1883 Batavia had thus far taken legal action against only one opium farm. In February 1888 Poa Soen Yang's Pasuruan farm was dissolved and released to his first guarantor and Chinese Lieutenant Kwee Liong Tiang.
24. MvK to GG, November 20, 1888, in VKG 23/11/1888/F17.
25. MvK to GG, November 23, 1888, no. F17 in VKG 23/11/1888/F17.

died, his son and sole heir Ho Tjiauw Ing acquired the Surakarta opium farm on the heels of Tan Tong Haij's failure there. The following February Ho took over Djie Bok Hien's farm in Madiun as well. Ho hoped that by acquiring two additional farms at bargain prices he could counteract the pinch his kongsi was feeling in its original farms, particularly in Semarang. This was not to be, and following harrowing losses in the initial months of 1889, Ho Tjiauw Ing petitioned the governor general for a deferment of his obligations. Pijnacker Hordijk immediately turned him down and instructed Finance Director Rovers either to collect or to move toward the dissolution of Ho's farms. When Ho could not pay his April fees (because current farm revenues were being used to pay off short-term private loans he had negotiated to meet earlier farm obligations), the government began executing his property. On the advice of his Dutch legal counselor, C. Th. van Deventer, Ho and his kongsi associates then declared bankruptcy and agreed to the voluntary dissolution of their farm contracts.[26]

In the same month, however, Ho Tjiauw Ing petitioned once more for government leniency. In a letter addressed directly to the governor general, he ascribed the failure of his farms to the impoverishment of "the majority of the population" of central Java, and to an accumulation of calamities and disasters. Invoking the millions that his father's successful opium farms had contributed to state coffers over the years, Ho asked whether it was now "just and fair to sacrifice him without mercy."[27]

Neither this personal plea nor an elaborate compromise debt settlement prepared by van Deventer persuaded Governor General Pijnacker Hordijk.[28] Pressured by Keuchenius, he was determined to press the government's considerable claim of nearly f2 million

26. TM to DF, May 31, 1889, no. 640/4 Geheim in Exh 9/8/1892/76; Advies Bureau A2, February 28, 1890, and Speciale Procuratie, October 7, 1889, both in V 22/2/1890/63; Ho Tjiauw Ing to GG, June 1889, in TMC H422e; and *Een Pachter-geschiedenis, IT*, December 3, 1889, nos. 2 and 3.

27. Ho Tjiauw Ing to GG, June 1889, in TMC H422e.

28. Hoping to create public opinion favorable to his proposed compromise, van Deventer placed a copy of it in *De Locomotief*, to which the newspaper's editor, Pieter Brooshooft, added a favorable comment. *De Locomotief*, December 9, 10, 11, and 12, 1891; see C. Th. van Deventer, "Toelichting tot het door de Chineezen Ho Tjiauw Ing, luitenant-titulair zijner natie te Semarang, Liem Kie Djwan, Kapitein zijner natie te Djokjakarta, Ho Tjiauw Soen, Luitenant zijner natie te Djokjakarta, en Goeij Som Han te Semarang aan hun gesamenlijke crediteuren aangeboden gerechtelijk accord," October 12, 1889, in V 22/2/1890/63; Colenbrander and Stokvis, *Leven en Arbeid . . . van Deventer*, 1:158.

against Ho Tjiauw Ing's bankrupt estate. Weighing heavily against Ho was the widespread suspicion that his bankruptcy was fraudulent, specifically that he had cheated his creditors by illegally passing large sums of money to his son just prior to his declaration.[29] When the government prosecuted him on these charges in 1891, van Deventer defended him with a plea that he described as "the best I have ever delivered." Van Deventer represented Ho as a well-intentioned, honest, and not overly bright man whose single fault lay in being unprepared to assume the enormous responsibilities of managing his father's vast enterprises, which in any case were already faltering at the time of his death. Presenting a strict accounting of Ho Tjiauw Ing's estate and his efforts to deal fairly with his various creditors, van Deventer won his acquittal.[30]

Ho's acquittal kept him out of prison, but the liquidation of his estate—the family fortune and the fruits of his father's spectacular career—proceeded forthwith. By 1893 the state had earned from the sale of his properties an amount roughly one-fourth of Ho's outstanding debt of f2 million.[31]

By 1890 the government was pressing similar claims against several others, many of whom had by this time declared bankruptcy, and just as many of whom, despite prolonged legal battles waged by their Dutch advocates, found themselves in debtors' prison by 1891. From others, Tan Tong Haij and Tan Kok Tong in particular, Batavia received yearly and biyearly installments and restrained its prosecutors as long as these negotiated payments were forthcoming. Tan Kok Tong's retention of the Kediri farm in 1890, permitted at

29. His son, Ho Sie Fat, it was alleged, had used some of it to buy back family property at the liquidation sales in August. See Advies, C.T.E. Leijds: Ontwerp geregtelijk accord namens de fallieten Ho Tjiauw Ing, Liem Kie Djwan, Ho Tjiauw Soen en Goeij Som Han aangeboden, November 2, 1889; and G. W. van Heeckeren (Landsadvocaat Semarang) to Resident Semarang, November 11, 1889, no. 256, both in V 22/2/1890/63.

30. An important issue with which van Deventer dealt in his argument revolved around the question of whether or not an opium farmer was—legally defined—a merchant (*koopman*), inasmuch as the law under which Ho was being tried for fraudulent bankruptcy applied specifically to merchants. Van Deventer successfully argued that opium farmers could not be construed as merchants on the grounds that: (1) the farm contract was an agreement to lease (*huur*), not buy (*koop*); (2) opium was not a legal article of trade (*koopwaar*); and (3) farm contracts were temporary, that is, one could not make opium farming one's "usual profession" (*gewoon beroep*). "Being an opium farmer," he noted, "is no more a profession than, pardon the comparison, being a Member of . . . Parliament." Van Deventer, *Strafzaak Ho Tjiauw Ing*, p. 27. See also Colenbrander and Stokvis, *Leven en Arbeid . . . van Deventer*, p. 158n2.

31. KVvNI 1893, p. 184.

TeMechelen's recommendation, greatly facilitated his ability to pay; when Tan died in 1890, his associates and heirs were able to pay off a large portion of his remaining debt and put up security for the remainder.[32] Despite liquidation and installments and the efforts of others, like Tan Kok Tong's legatees, to pay off their obligations in lump sums, the outstanding opium debt as of 1893 still approached f6 million, most of which the Dutch were never to collect.[33]

Nearly a million of this was chargeable to the Kediri kongsi. Having been granted substantial dispensations during the 1887–89 farm term, and having bound much of their personal property to the government as security, Han Liong Ing and his associates Tan Boen In and Liem Kok Sing applied for and received the necessary Colonial Service approval to compete for the Japara and Rembang farms for the one-year term of 1890. As always, Charles TeMechelen played an important behind-the-scenes role in smoothing the way.[34] In September Han submitted his successful bid. When the new farm term began, Han pledged to pay f25,000 a month against the balance of his cumulative debt in addition to his new commitments.[35]

It was TeMechelen's hope that by paving the way for another farm contract and negotiating a settlement in which the kongsi could pay off its debt gradually, Han Liong Ing and the government would both be in the strongest possible position. This hope appeared to be justified when Han successfully paid his overdue farm fees for 1889 at the beginning of 1890.[36] But the Kediri kongsi was in a more precarious financial position than TeMechelen realized. Han had borrowed heavily within the Chinese community, and as his own position weakened he found it necessary to borrow under very unfavorable circumstances. He thus had to satisfy both his

32. TM to DF, October 9, 1890, no. 1625/4 Geheim in TMC H422e; KVvNI 1893, p. 184.

33. KVvNI 1893, p. 184. The precise figure was f5,739,412.62.

34. See his telegram to the resident of Tegal appended to Resident Tegal to DF, September 13, 1889, no. 176, and Resident Rembang to DF, September 19, 1889, LA, both in Exh 9/8/1892/76.

35. By notarial act dated February 28, 1889. See TM to DF, January 20, 1890, no. 174/4 in Exh 9/8/1892/76.

36. Resident W. C. Castens of Japara alleged, on the witness of a kitchen maid of the Japara farm manager, that Han succeeded in doing so largely by selling back to the government, in the form of a discount on his soon to be supplied opium for 1890, a large supply of unused official opium that was in fact phony—a concoction designed to look and smell like candu but made from citrus extract, hence *candu jeruk*. See Resident Japara to DF, February 20, 1892, no. 1285/18 in Exh 9/8/1892/76.

public and private creditors simultaneously, and to do so solely from the revenues of two opium farms.

This was to prove impossible. At the end of May, Liem Kok Sing was obliged to approach Resident W.C.J. Castens of Japara and tell him that the kongsi could not pay May's installment. Castens, aware that earnings from the Japara farm were being dispersed to cover losses in Rembang and to pay off kongsi creditors in Kediri, Semarang, and Madiun, gave Liem fifteen days to pay up or lose the farm. The kongsi met this ultimatum only by more private borrowing. This merely postponed the inevitable. The following month Han came up short again, and in August the kongsi defaulted in Rembang. Rembang's resident, A. C. Uljee, a tough reformer who harbored no love for either Chinese opium farmers or TeMechelen, was not inclined to be lenient. He immediately called together potential candidates to take over the farm and moved to dissolve Han's contract. Han now channeled his limited revenues to save the Japara farm and let the Rembang farm fall. It was dissolved in November.[37] The collective debt of the Kediri kongsi approached f1 million, and Han and his associates joined the other peranakan opium kings in declaring bankruptcy and witnessing the liquidation of their fortunes.[38]

The final fall and disgrace of the Kediri kongsi in 1890 was accompanied by a shocking scandal. On September 10 the regent of Rembang, Djojoadiningrat, confiscated 14 piculs (865 kilograms) of clandestine opium. This opium, subsequent investigations showed, represented a portion of a larger cache that had been landed on the offshore island Marungan in late August and brought ashore piecemeal during the first week and a half of September. An investigation into the affair headed by Djojoadiningrat, who examined virtually all the participants in the landing and transshipment of the opium, pointed to Liem Kok Sing as the perpetrator of the illegal import and, by implication, the Kediri kongsi as the owner of the clandestine opium.[39]

37. Resident Rembang to DF, July 31, 1890, no. 131 (Eigenhandig vertrouwelijke), and TM to DF, November 25, 1890, no. 1934/4, both in Exh 9/8/1892/76; KVvNI 1890, p. 181.

38. KVvNI 1892, p. 172.

39. Exh 9/8/1892/76 contains a mass of documents pertinent to the Marungan affair. The Dutch vice-consul in Singapore reported that his informants also implicated Liem. See DF to GG, June 12, 1891, U2 Geheim in Exh 9/8/1892/76; see also pp. 72–73 above.

A. C. Uljee, resident of Rembang. Courtesy Mevrouw Koolemans
Beijnen-Uljee.

Djojoadiningrat's ketrangan was especially welcome to Rembang's zealous resident, A. C. Uljee. Uljee had already made a thorough sweep through Rembang's native administration, replacing corrupt and insubordinate native officials with choices of his own. He had personally chosen Djojoadiningrat to replace the previous regent, whom he had ousted.[40] As a zealous reformer with a fine eye for corruption, and as an autocrat sensitive to the prerogatives of his position, Uljee had long bridled at hosting in his residency the notorious task force and its flamboyant Indo leader—who as chief inspector was his equivalent in rank. His loyal regent now provided him with the evidence he needed to substantiate a long-held suspicion: that Liem and the Kediri kongsi were engaging in smuggling operations under the protective umbrella of Te-Mechelen's task force.

Uljee proceeded to use the Marungan affair to discredit Te-Mechelen and the task force. Recognizing that criminal prosecution of Liem Kok Sing would jeopardize the ability of the Kediri kongsi to settle its debts, he pressed instead for the dismissal of one of Te-Mechelen's subordinates. (Uljee charged the man with having conspired with Liem to confiscate a small portion of the Marungan opium as a diversion.) More generally Uljee used the Marungan example to illustrate the ineffectiveness of the task force and to discredit TeMechelen's judgment and leadership. The regent, he pointed out, not the task force, had made the confiscation and several other recent smaller ones.[41] Without accusing TeMechelen directly, Uljee homed in on TeMechelen's close relationship with opium farmers and the general notoriety of his efforts. "Everyone here," he wrote, "is convinced that [his] personnel connives with smugglers."[42]

As Uljee well knew and adroitly exploited, the Marungan affair was especially damaging to TeMechelen, who had loyally supported the Kediri kongsi and who had on more than one occasion singled out Liem Kok Sing for special praise. Less than one month before, TeMechelen had written his friend Rovers of his nine-year acquaintanceship with Liem, or simply "Kok Sing" as he called him in his private notes. "I have come to feel friendship for this Chinese," he wrote, "a great exception among his race because of the good qualities of his sharp mind and his fine character, and cannot without

40. See TeMechelen's list of 16 of Uljee's "victims" in TMC H422c; also the correspondence about Regent Kartowinoto's dismissal in MR 1889, no. 287; MR 1891, no. 745, contains the correspondence concerning the ouster, also Uljee-instigated, of the regent of Tuban, RT Pandjie Tjitrosomo.

41. See his comments in Resident Rembang to DF, March 26, 1891, no. 2 in Exh 9/8/1892/76.

42. Resident Rembang to DF, October 23, 1890, no. 50 Geheim in Exh 9/8/1892/76.

direct evidence believe that he is of bad faith."[43] Though he supported Liem to the end, maintaining that Djojoadiningrat's ketrangan was a frameup instigated by Uljee,[44] TeMechelen was forced to concede privately in November that Liem may have weakened under the pressures of the depression and his kongsi's grave financial losses. Perhaps in desperation he *had* "sought salvation in smuggling."[45] TeMechelen removed him from his farm post.[46]

When Liem Kok Sing and his kongsi associates declared bankruptcy in 1891, Resident Uljee urged a criminal prosecution. In March, having received an authorization from the procuror general, Uljee dispatched two agents to Kediri to arrest Liem. Liem escaped, however, and dodged the police for six months. Rumors as to his whereabouts proliferated: he was disguised as a Javanese in Pasuruan; he was hiding out with friends in Modjokerto; he had fled Java altogether for Amoy. While Liem held out, his son Liem Djing Kiong—Richard Liem, as he styled himself—negotiated with officials of the Justice Department in Batavia. Liem would give himself up, said Richard, if provided immunity from preventive detention. Liem felt certain he would be poisoned if incarcerated in the Rembang jail. When Richard's efforts succeeded, Liem Kok Sing gave himself up to the controleur in Kertosono. Uljee, now fearing that Liem might be acquitted in Landraad proceedings, recommended that he be exiled under the provisions of Article 47. But Liem, asthmatic and tubercular, died before the matter could be pursued any further.[47]

While Liem Kok Sing was still dodging the authorities, the bureaucratic correspondence between Batavia, Uljee, and TeMechelen burned with vituperation as Uljee and TeMechelen, both avid bureaucratic infighters, exchanged charges and counter-

43. See TeMechelen's jottings on his copy (from Rovers presumably) of Resident Rembang to DF, October 23, 1890, no. 50 in TMC H422c; and TM to DF, August 17, 1890, no. 1316/4 (Vertrouwlijk) in TMC H422e.

44. See jottings cited in n. 43, above; TM to DF, November 25, 1890, no. 1934/3 Geheim in TMC H422c.

45. TM to DF, November 25, 1890, no. 1934/3 Geheim in TMC H422c.

46. TM to DF, April 13, 1892, no. 779/12 in Exh 9/8/1892/76.

47. See the following correspondence in Exh 9/8/1892/76: Procureur Generaal to GG, February 23, 1891, no. 355 Geheim; Resident Rembang to Procureur Generaal, April 25, 1891, no. 9; Resident Rembang to Procureur Generaal, July 8, 1891; Procureur Generaal to Resident Rembang, July 8, 1891, no. 382; Assistant Resident Berbek to Procureur Generaal, September 2, 1891, no. 1; Procureur Generaal to GG, October 11, 1891, no. 1939 Geheim; and DJ: Consideratien en Advies, November 11, 1891, no. 8448.

charges. To Uljee's accusation that his personnel had aided and abetted smugglers, TeMechelen pointed to the members of Rembang's local establishment—a village headman and two local village guards—who had admitted to participating in the smuggling attempt. Since the local administration was Djojoadiningrat's special realm, he, not Liem, TeMechelen argued, should be the object of official investigation.[48] In June the feud spilled over into the Indies press. In a gossipy series of short articles in the Surabaya tabloid *Weekblad van Neerlandsch Indie*, TeMechelen was pictured as the knowing dupe, a partner in crime, of his "all powerful friend and confidant Liem Kok Sing."[49] Uljee and Djojoadiningrat, on the other hand, were lauded as honest and long-suffering public servants striving to rid Rembang of the corrupt pair.[50] TeMechelen was incensed. Certain that Uljee was behind the articles, he lodged formal complaints against him and in late July their feud was discussed in the Indies Council. Thoroughly exasperated, Governor General Pijnacker Hordijk wrote to Uljee in August pleading with him to resolve his differences with TeMechelen. It was, he said, an "urgent necessity" that he do so.[51]

News of the Marungan scandal had by this time reached Holland, official efforts to contain it in Batavia notwithstanding. In November Rotterdam's member in the lower house, H. D. Levysohn Norman, an outspoken expert on colonial matters who had been elected in 1888 following a brilliant career in the Colonial Service in Java, brought the affair onto the floor of the lower house. He challenged Minister of Colonies Keuchenius to inform the members about the involvement of opium farmer Liem Kok Sing, "the right hand of den Heer TeMechelen," in massive black-market opium adventures. Caught unawares, Keuchenius was forced to plead ignorance.

48. See his letter, TM to DF, November 25, 1890, no. 1934/3 Geheim in Exh 9/8/1892/76; and Dienstnota aan den Directeur van Financien (TM), May 29, 1891, no. 490/12 in TMC H422c.

49. "De zaak contra TeMechelen," pp. 1683–84. *Weekblad van Neerlandsch Indie*, ed. J. A. Uilkens, no. 32 (June 7, 1891). The articles appeared in nos. 30–34 of the *Weekblad*.

50. Rhapsodized the *Weekblad*: "Rembang's regent is vroom en goed, en aan zijn meester trouw." See "Opium Snippers," *Weekblad van Neerlandsch Indie*, no. 32 (June 7, 1891), 1707.

51. Advies: RvNI, July 24, 1891, no. 10 in Exh 9/8/1892/76. Specifically, TeMechelen accused Uljee's protégé, Assistant Resident G. Gonggrijp, of leaking details of the case to the *Weekblad*. No deliberate leak was necessary, however, for the whole scandal was being bandied about in club gossip at the time. See TM to DF, June 23, 1891, no. 552/12 and other related correspondence in Exh 9/8/1892/76.

"I would be pleased," he wrote coolly to the governor general in Batavia, "if you would inform me . . . what [this] is all about."[52]

Throughout the feud TeMechelen continued to receive the unqualified support of Finance Director Rovers and other members of Batavia's officialdom.[53] The Department of Justice, for example, dropped Uljee's case against TeMechelen's subordinates out of hand. This was small compensation, however. The Marungan case, as it spread from Rembang to Batavia, into the press, and finally to Parliament, was irreparably damaging both to TeMechelen's personal reputation and to his oft-argued position that state and opium farm could cooperate in pursuit of their mutual, as well as their individual, interests. The Kediri kongsi, in his opinion the best of the opium farmers—proficient, honest, and cooperative—was seen to be both bankrupt and criminal.

Had the Marungan affair occurred in isolation, it would have been merely another of Java's occasional opium scandals, generating a brief flurry and then dying down to be forgotten. Occurring at the end of a disastrous collective failure of Java's opium farms, however, and in the midst of a concerted attack on the farm system, in full flower by 1890, it weighed heavily against the farms. Although in the movement to abolish opium farms no one event or argument was individually decisive, the final failure and disgrace of the Kediri kongsi and the concomitant public discrediting of Charles TeMechelen helped push collective opinion irretrievably in the direction of abolishing the farms.

The general loss of credibility of the farm Chinese and their most forceful supporter was thus a signal consequence of the opium farm crisis. This development was paralleled by unprecedented strain within the peranakan patronage constellations themselves. The desperate need for revenue by the constellations' patrons affected each

52. MvK to GG, February 8, 1892, no. 5 in 8/2/1892/5. Levysohn Norman's informant in Java was Dr. Isaac Groneman. See pp. 203–4 below. Levysohn Norman also accused Director of Finance Rovers of having been swayed to support Te-Mechelen's position during a business-cum-hunting trip they took together aboard a task force cruiser in August. See DF to GG, May 30, 1892, no. 7777 in Exh 9/8/1892/76 for his reply. Following his first Colonial Service appointment in 1857, Levysohn Norman had risen rapidly in the Batavia bureaucracy. He became general secretary in 1873 and in 1877 was named to the Indies Council (Raad van Indie). "Levysohn Norman (Henry David) 1836–1892," ENI, 2:407.

53. GG to Resident Rembang, March 4, 1891, no. 36 Geheim in Exh 9/8/1892/76. See also Procureur Generaal to GG, December 24, 1891, no. 2876 in MR 1891, no. 1048.

individual in these complex networks of commercial and personal
relationships, especially as members of the patronage chain pressed
their respective clients to settle past debts. In a fluid economic
system depending fundamentally on the free flow of goods and
credit, this constituted a significant disturbance. It bred, in turn,
both intense competition for what money could still be made in
depressed Java—selling opium or otherwise—and disaffection with
the group patrons, whose resources were now diverted from funding the manifold enterprises of the group to staving off disaster at
the top.

The influx of new Chinese immigrants continued unabated during the crisis. Few of these newcomers found a place in the once
expanding but now contracting patronage constellations headed by
the peranakan elite. To the growing number of such unaffiliated
new immigrants—many of them not of Hokkien origin, but
Hakka—the old Hokkien-peranakan power structure in Java was
monopolistic, a closed society that denied them entry. One violent
manifestation of this new fissure was a revolt of Chinese newcomers,
singkehs, in Yogyakarta. In November 1889 more than one hundred of them conspired to murder the Chinese captain, the opium
farmer, and the opium hunter.[54]

In recent years singkehs had moved into Yogyakarta in substantial
numbers. Here pass and residential restrictions were hardly enforced, and Chinese newcomers sought a living as day laborers,
peddlers, and moneylenders. They either settled directly in the
villages or resided in Yogyakarta's growing Chinatown, moving
daily en masse into the countryside to ply their trades. Both the
sheer number of these new arrivals and their drive to earn a living
constituted a threat to Ho Yam Lo's opium farm and the Ho-
dominated commercial life of the principality, not least as petty
agents for opium black marketeers. This threat was all the more
dangerous in the troubled years of the late 1880s. Liem Kie Djwan
was Chinese captain of Yogyakarta; he was a close associate of Ho
Yam Lo and a guarantor of Ho's Yogyakarta opium farm along with
Ho Tjiauw Soen, grandson of Ho Yam Lo and Yogyakarta's Chinese
lieutenant. In an effort to flush undesirable singkeh competition
from the interior, Captain Liem, with the support of Resident B. van

54. *Singkeh* is the term commonly used among Javan Chinese to mean a newcomer
or, in contrast to mixed-blood peranakans, a full-blooded Chinese. The account that
follows is based on Isaac Groneman's letters of November 20 and 22, 1889, published
in his *Uit en over Midden-Java* (Zutphen, 1891), pp. 297–306.

Baak and the active assistance of an opium hunter named Ninaber, began enforcing the long-ignored pass and residency laws. "Unauthorized" Chinese were suddenly harassed, arrested, and presented to the jaksa for prosecution.

It was just such an arrest that precipitated the November 1889 outbreak. As Ninaber escorted three recently apprehended singkehs to jail, gangs of their compatriots armed with stones and sharpened bamboo sticks set upon them, rescued the Chinese, and pursued Ninaber, Liem Kie Djwan, and Njo Gai-sing, the caretaker opium farmer. All escaped.[55] Before dispersing, the Hakka singkehs vandalized Liem's house and attempted to destroy the local opium farm buildings.

This small uprising was a clear protest against the Cabang Atas. The social and economic structures over which they presided, now in crisis, were no longer capable of absorbing newcomers in the traditional fashion. The outbreak reflected both demographic changes—the Chinese community had doubled in forty years—and the internal deterioration of one of Java's strongest peranakan constellations.

The rural crisis and opium farm failures of the 1880s weakened the Cabang Atas both with respect to the Dutch and to the Javan Chinese community. In doing so it precipitated the end of the opium farming system itself. For one thing, the major kongsis had reneged on their government obligations and left huge unpaid debts. For another, the crisis severely strained the Chinese socioeconomic order. What is more, it is quite likely that as the major kongsis pressed their subordinates for cash, abuses long identified with Chinese commercial activities in the countryside intensified—matamata extortion and thuggery, usury, and black marketeering, all intimately tied to the opium trade. Moreover, all of this occurred amid other disturbing manifestations of hard times such as banditry, cane burning, and rebellion.[56] Little wonder that these phenomena coincided with a sustained critical movement against the abuses and faults of the opium farm system. In this atmosphere, the long-standing rationale for maintaining the farms appeared to have been proven false. Catching the Cabang Atas at their weakest moment, opponents of the opium farms pushed for their abolition, and won.

55. The Ho farm had by this time been dissolved.
56. See Djoko Suryo, "Social and Economic Life in Rural Semarang," pp. 265, 269, 290; and Elson, *Javanese Peasants*, p. 149.

10

Relentless War!
Against the Opium Farm

The collapse of the major opium farm kongsis in the 1880s was accompanied by a vociferous attack on the opium farms. This attack was led by journalists, Indies professional men, missionaries, and Dutch politicians, along with a few members of the Colonial Service, whose collective voice by the end of the decade had provoked a comprehensive debate about opium in the colony.

In the usual fashion, the debate began by focusing on the need to reform the opium regulations and to curtail smuggling. At the same time new attention was given to the addictive nature of opium and to its potentially pernicious influence on health and the public welfare. But the new critics soon identified the opium farming system itself as the main problem. The opium farm, they said, represented an *imperium in imperio*. It defied effective supervision and routinely acted in flagrant violation of the laws. Furthermore, the power and wealth of the opium farms corrupted the colony's governing institutions. The native administration and lower courts were most vulnerable. But, said the critics, even the European Colonial Service was not exempt.

These observations were hardly new. Many features of the farm system revealed by Java's new generation of critics were aspects of the system long recognized and, for the most part, ignored or tolerated as part of the traditional Dutch-pryayi-Chinese accommodation. They now appeared, however, in a new light, a more dangerous one. This was the result of several evolutionary changes in the political and economic structures of the colony which rendered awkward semi-independent institutions such as the farms, and of more immediate pressures caused by the economic depression of mid-decade. These included a rash of frightening local rebellions and a visible decline in native material life.[1] Some people, seeking an explanation for these phenomena, found the perfect scapegoat in the island's Chinese—purveyors of opium, rural loan sharks, and "owners" of villages. Fear for the Yellow Peril thus also became an important stream of anti-opium-farm sentiment.[2]

All of this helped bring to the fore a reformist spirit. This spirit was fueled by a paternal sentiment—Indonesians were "younger brothers" for whose care and well-being the Dutch were morally responsible—and, at the same time, by a creeping fear that short-sighted abuse of the Indonesian population for financial gain might lead to the overthrow of the Dutch. Reformers in Java therefore began to agitate for reduced native taxes and an expansion of irrigation works and other projects aimed at improving welfare for the masses.[3] As an obvious system of exploitation, the opium farms came in for special attention.

In Holland it was Willem Karel Baron van Dedem who initially raised the subject of opium and the opium farms as a major question of policy. Van Dedem, who had practiced law in Semarang for ten years before returning to Holland and entering politics, argued that the opium question was a *levens quaestie* for Holland and her colonies, a question that demanded, but had never received, thorough examination.[4] He first raised the issue in 1876 in a speech before the

1. The decade was full of rebellions. Onghokham has pointed out that in the second half of the 1880s millenarian movements were especially frequent in central Java: "According to the Jayabaya prophecies [the times] would coincide with the establishment of a new kingdom inaugurating a new golden age. In particular there would be an end to Dutch rule. . . . All over Java there was in the late 1880's a feeling that a new age was dawning." Onghokham, "The Residency of Madiun," p. 259.

2. The long-standing Dutch view of the Chinese was mixed. The Dutch admired the Chinese for their industry and depended on their mercantile and craft skills for an untold number of services. But they distrusted them. The Chinese were, as well— so went the popular view—excessively greedy, "worshippers of the Golden Calf" and "bloodsuckers of the Javanese." The events of the late 1880s seemed to confirm this stereotype, and the anti-opium-farm literature is, not surprisingly, full of sinophobia. For earlier examples of anti-Chinese sentiment, see V.D.L., "Zullen nu de Chineze van de opiumpacht worden uitgesloten?" *TNI*, 19 (1857, II), 60–61; "Een Chineesch parvenu op Java," *TNI*, 15 (1853, I), 357–60; and Castens, "De Opiumpacht op Java," p. 51.

3. E. B. Locher-Scholten, "Mr. P. Brooshooft, Een Biografische Schets in Koloniaal-Ethisch Perspectief," *BKI*, 123 (1976, II/III), 320.

4. Van Dedem was a member of the law office in Semarang that M. Th. van Deventer subsequently joined. See Colenbrander and Stokvis, *Leven en Arbeid . . . van Deventer*, 1:136.

Indisch Genootschap (Indies Society), a forum established in 1854 for the discussion of colonial issues which served as the unofficial Indies parliament in Holland.[5] Here van Dedem lamented that despite the fact that opium had been repeatedly condemned by observers of its use in Java, so much so that the government had adopted as one of its official goals the reduction of opium consumption, no thorough study had ever been made of the meaning of opium smoking for the masses of Java. Because of this, officials still faced the opium question in the dark. In their ignorance they prolonged the vain quest for a moral vice tax that had begun in 1832; a succession of schemes had succeeded in raising revenues but had failed to place limits on opium use. This, said van Dedem, was clearly on the rise. He asked: if opium was as evil as the cumulative evidence appeared to indicate, and if Holland's policies failed to place limitations on its use, shouldn't something be done?[6]

Van Dedem won a seat in the lower house of Parliament in 1880 and he soon distinguished himself on colonial subjects. Debates on the opium question during his first year as a parliamentarian further convinced him that "the Government [was] not well informed" on the subject of opium.[7] He therefore embarked on a series of studies himself, published in 1881 in the *Indische Gids* (Indies Digest), in which he traced the development of colonial opium policy during the nineteenth century, pointing out the haphazard evolution of policy based on shortsighted budgetary considerations and on misinformation. Whereas nearly everyone admitted the need to place opium policy on a sounder footing, he observed, no one, from the colonial minister to the residents, had taken the initiative to do so. As each waited for the other to act, opium affairs drifted on in the old unsatisfactory pattern.[8] As for the common assertion that opium smoking in Java was no more than the Eastern equivalent of spirits, van Dedem replied, "A glance beyond the borders of our Indian territory all too easily reinforces the fear that what our Government

5. W. K. Baron van Dedem, "Nota," p. 561; and Furnivall, *Netherlands India*, p. 273.

6. See van Dedem, "Nota," pp. 104–17. Details of his career may be found in "Dedem (Mr. Willem Karel van)," *ENI* (1st edition), 1:429–30, and in the "Verslag" of the Anti-Opium Bond (published in *Opium-Vloek*, 3 [1895], 1–2) immediately following his sudden death in 1895.

7. Van Dedem, *Eene bijdrage*, author's unpaged introduction. This monograph was originally published in two parts by the *Indische Gids (IG)*, 1881.

8. Ibid., pp. 41–42.

presently accepts for reality is really the *fata morgana* of a rare naiveté."[9]

Van Dedem did not pose a direct threat to either opium smoking or to the farm system. He suspected that the conventional wisdom about opium smoking in Java disguised a far graver phenomenon, and he rejected the myth that the farm system was the only satisfactory framework within which to seek solutions for the many problems opium raised for the colony. But essentially his goal was to stimulate inquiry and deliberation as a basis for a sounder, more rational and ethical opium policy. At his urging in the lower house, the minister of colonies, Willem Baron van Goltstein, reluctantly ordered Batavia to undertake a thorough investigation. This led to some productive fact finding on the part of a few members of the Colonial Service, Assistant Resident Charles TeMechelen among them. The thorough investigation for which van Dedem had called did not commence, however, until 1885, when it was assigned to TeMechelen, who had since become resident of the sea. His Report of 1888 was the result.[10]

TeMechelen's report did play a part in the deliberations over opium and the farm system, which by that time had grown vociferous. More important in that debate, however, were contributions from individuals whose points of view were far more critical than TeMechelen's. Many of them were self-declared enemies of the opium farm. Their strident reportage in a sequence of articles, pamphlets, and books created a climate of opinion in which the opium farm system became, by the end of the decade, nearly indefensible. Among the most important of these were M.T.H. Perelaer, a disillusioned ex-Indies military man; Pieter Brooshooft, a crusading publicist who took over the influential *De Locomotief* newspaper of Semarang in 1887; and Dr. Isaac Groneman, a longtime resident of Yogyakarta who was an expert on Javanese life and personal physician to the sultan.

Perelaer was already retired from a twenty-five-year career in the military, most of it in the Indies, and an established success as a popular writer of sketches, vignettes, and military exploits when he took on the opium cause. By this time the optimism of his youth had

9. Ibid., p. 70.
10. See W. Elout van Soeterwoude, "De opiumpacht in Nederlandsch Indie; Voordracht met debat en brieven van Mr. M. C. Piepers en Mr. W. K. Bn. van Dedem," *VIG*, October 8 and November 5, 1889, pp. 139–226.

given way to doubt and cynicism about white rule in the tropics, in particular Dutch rule in the Indies. To him the opium farms symbolized what was wrong. He began his campaign against the farms in 1884 with a short exposé about the attempts, all in vain, by a private plantation owner in Semarang to get government help in removing an illegal opium den from his property.[11] This piece was a prelude to his tour de force, the novel *Baboe Dalima* (Dalima the Nanny), published in 1886.[12] *Baboe Dalima*, in the tradition of its more literary predecessor *Max Havelaar* by Multatuli (Eduard Douwes Dekker), was an openly political novel. He called it an *opium roman*. And in case anyone missed his point, Perelaer spelled it out in capital letters in his Foreword: "RELENTLESS WAR! War *à outrance* against the opium farm, that scandalous source of income for we Dutch."[13]

Drawing heavily on the already substantial body of literature on opium in Java and his own several years' experience there, Perelaer painted a portrait of scandalous conspiracy and corruption. In his Santjoemeh residency (Semarang) the resident and the opium farmer joined forces to line each other's pockets at the expense of honest Colonial Service officers, the integrity of the administration, and the Javanese peasant.[14] *Baboe Dalima* contained shocking images: of farm mata-mata abusing and terrorizing innocent villagers; of local Javanese opium farm agents enticing fellow villagers to the opium den with a variety of sly inducements; of a prosperous village falling into economic and moral ruin as its members forsook their honest labors for the opium habit; and of the overall corrupting combination of opium, sinister profiteering Chinese, and greedy officials. Greeted by some as a scandal itself—one reviewer called it "that filthy book"—*Baboe Dalima* was an effective indictment of government opium policy, revealing in a graphic way what Baron van Dedem called "the shadow side" of the opium farm system.[15]

11. M.T.H. Perelaer, *De Spoliatie gepleegd door de Nederlandsch-Indische Regeering ten opzichte van het Particulier landbezit op Java* (Rotterdam, 1884); and *Het Oordeel de Nederlandsch Pers over "De Spoliatie"* (Rotterdam, 1885).

12. Perelaer, *Baboe Dalima*. See the review "Kritiek van M.T.H. Perelaer's opium-roman 'Baboe Dalima,'" *IG*, 2 (1886), 1085–92. An English-language edition (trans. E. J. Venning) was published in London in 1888.

13. Perelaer, *Baboe Dalima*, Foreword.

14. The original edition was footnoted in order to direct readers to Perelaer's nonfiction sources.

15. Nieuwenhuys, *Oost-Indische Spiegel*, p. 20. On Perelaer, see Nieuwenhuys, *Oost-Indische Spiegel*, pp. 197–99; *NNBW*, 5:465; and SvD Michael Theophile Hubert Perelaer, filed in the Archive of the Ministerie van Binnenlandse Zaken, The Hague.

Another opium novel, this one by Isaac Groneman, appeared the following year. Called *Een Ketjoegeschiedenis* (A Bandit's Tale), it was less ambitious than *Baboe Dalima* but was based on Groneman's more intimate knowledge of Javanese life and society.[16] *A Bandit's Tale* is about the misadventures of an improvident Javanese aristocrat with a compulsion to gamble and his two opium-addicted wives. Groneman was broadly concerned with the deterioration of Javanese society under the impact of Dutch rule and was a relentless critic of government policy that exposed the refined and retiring Javanese to harsh exploitation by Europeans and Chinese. In this novel and in scores of short articles that he published in Javan newspapers between 1882 and 1890, he underscored the relationship between Javanese poverty; the breakdown of stable society as witnessed by the rise of crime, banditry, and rebellion; and the destructive influence of the Chinese in village Java.[17]

Groneman's villains were the Chinese opium farm agents, pawnshop operators, petty traders, and loan sharks (*woekerers*) who poisoned village society with opium and drained the rural economy dry. Symbolic of all that was bad about the Chinese presence was the opium den, "that spider's web of our pernicious ally, who like a gigantic spider lures and traps the poor Javanese, then seizes him, clutches him and binds him and sucks him until he is tortured to death."[18] A colonial government could not, he asserted, continue to permit, or encourage for its own profit, such exploitation and expect the everlasting gratitude of its charges. Rather, warned Groneman, "the ruin of the Indonesian, especially the Javanese, can be *our* ruin."[19]

Groneman believed that Holland's loss would be China's gain. He was alarmed over the growth of Java's Chinese population and warned often of the "singkeh flood," speaking of the rising numbers of unassimilated Chinese newcomers to Java. Of the farm critics he most clearly voiced a distinctively racial fear. The hard-working, bright, ever-adaptable and highly self-interested Chinese were, he

16. Isaac Groneman, *Een Ketjoegeschiedenis*.
17. These were compiled in Isaac Groneman, *Uit en Over Midden Java*. Writing his anti-Chinese articles from Yogyakarta in the depression-ridden 1880s, Groneman brings to mind an earlier period. Peter Carey has remarked that the Chinese (many of them newcomers) became "targets of popular hatred when economic conditions in south-central Java started to decline sharply due to the droughts and harvest failures of the years 1821–25." In "Changing Javanese Perceptions," p. 33.
18. Groneman, *Uit en Over Midden Java*, p. 100.
19. Ibid., p. 313.

thought, "the people of the future." The Javanese were no match for them. ("Darwin," he noted, "has clearly explained to us how this occurs.") If Holland did not act to limit Chinese immigration and, more important, to dismantle the institutions that gave them such substantial influence, then "Java, following a not yet determinable interim, shall become a Chinese colony, in the beginning perhaps still administered by Europeans and manned by Javanese slaves in the service of the strong Chinese race."[20]

In voicing the fear of a Yellow Peril, Groneman was tapping a growing sentiment among Indies Europeans. This sentiment was encouraged by the increasing visibility of Chinese in both town and countryside, and by the sight of failed European plantations falling into Chinese hands for a song at mid-decade.[21] At the same time, Indies Dutch were reading and hearing about a national revival in China itself. China, wrote one opium farm critic in 1889, was no longer "une quantité negligeable. It has built a formidable fleet and has organized its army. Today it sends off its representatives to investigate the situation of its countrymen in the possessions of European powers. Tomorrow come the consuls. Thereupon it will promote the legal equality of the Chinese and European inhabitants. And where will it end?"[22]

Groneman submitted many of his articles to the Semarang daily newspaper, De Locomotief, whose editor after 1887 was Pieter Brooshooft, an outspoken critic of government policies. Founded in 1845 as the Semarangsch Nieuws-en Advertentieblad and rebaptized when the Semarang principality railroad concession was approved in 1863, De Locomotief enjoyed a wide readership among Dutch planters and businesspersons throughout central Java as well as in certain circles of the Colonial Service. Among Indies newspapers, De Locomotief was respected for the quality of its reporting and its independence from Batavia. As editor, Brooshooft was in a position to give vent to his own reformist ideas and to provide a platform for other critics of government policy and observers of the shadow side of Dutch Java. In addition to Isaac Groneman, the advocate C. Th. van Deventer often took advantage of De Locomotief's forum.[23]

20. Quotes from ibid., pp. 162, 161, 150, respectively. For more on Isaac Groneman, see Nieuwenhuys, Oost-Indische Spiegel, pp. 201–5.

21. Some of the properties later confiscated from bankrupt opium farmers were purchased at this time.

22. N. J. Struick, Opiumpacht of Opiumregie (The Hague, 1889), p. 62.

23. Locher-Scholten, "Brooshooft," pp. 315–16; Oudgast, Onze Oost, pp. 182–85. Nieuwenhuys discusses Pieter Brooshooft in Oost-Indische Spiegel, pp. 308–10, 312–14.

In late 1887 Brooshooft addressed a petition, signed by 1,255 people, to twelve prominent Dutch politicians. It advocated the formation of an Indies party to represent the needs of the Indies in Parliament. Accompanying the petition was a book-length critique of the colonial tax structure titled *Memorie over den toestand in Indie* (Memorandum on the State of Affairs in India), in which Brooshooft leveled an especially virulent attack on the opium farms.[24] Although in principle, he wrote, the farm system was designed to place limitations on opium consumption, in practice it did just the opposite. Knowing this full well, the government turned a blind eye in the interests of preserving its opium farm revenues. Brooshooft went on to describe in great detail the various means by which the farm protected its interests, including its own clandestine trading, the role of the mata-mata and the Chinese Inspection Committees, the farm subsidy of the native police and pryayi corps, the abuses of the police roll, and the patungan trade and illegal dens. TeMechelen's task force, Batavia's current hope, may well have reduced the amount of illegal opium entering Java, but the results had been largely ephemeral, he argued. Opium smuggling itself was not the disease, merely a symptom of a more deeply rooted institutional cancer. How might one at long last bring an end to the "moral, physical and financial" ruin of the Javanese perpetrated in the interests of state income by the opium farms? By "unconditional abandonment of the farm system" was his answer.[25]

Brooshooft's hoped-for Reform party did not materialize, but his *Memorie* had an impact on the evolving anti-opium-farm sentiment. Because it was detailed, documented, and more authoritative than the work of other farm critics—TeMechelen's charge that it was "dilettantish" notwithstanding—it was rapidly seized upon by other antifarm activists, who used it in their articles, speeches, and debates. The *Memorie* became one of the most frequently cited indictments of the farm system.[26] Several later leaders of the antifarm

24. Pieter Brooshooft, *Memorie over den toestand in Indie* (Semarang, 1888); see pp. 122–57. For his proposal to found an Indies Reform party, see the "Korte Verklaring," which precedes the *Memorie*, pp. i–iii.

25. Ibid., p. 156.

26. TeMechelen made his comment in a letter to Rovers, October 4, 1888, no. 1387/12 in TMC H422a. Rovers concurred; see his letter to the governor general of February 20, 1889, HI Geheim in MR 1889, no. 136. Brooshooft had access to inside information, specifically government reports on the Surakarta farm prepared in 1882. See Resident Surakarta to DF, January 9, 1889, no. 242/20 in MR, no. 136. In 1887 he tried, unsuccessfully, to cull privy details from TeMechelen. See TM to DF, February 2, 1889, no. 121/12 in the same Mailrapport.

movement, such as Liberal member of Parliament E. B. Kielstra and Jhr. Elout van Soeterwoude, were greatly influenced by it.[27]

The efforts of Perelaer, Groneman, and Brooshooft were accompanied by a growing chorus of amens voiced from many platforms, from newspaper articles in Java to parliamentary speeches in The Hague. A full-scale public debate occurred, in which missionaries weighed in with their opinions alongside officials, planters, and publicists.[28] As evidence accumulated and opinions converged, a consensus gradually formed among people in and out of public life that Holland's colonial opium policy was untenable.

In 1889 Elout van Soeterwoude, a retired and well-connected official with the Colonial Ministry who had become an antifarm advocate following a trip through British and Netherlands India between 1886 and 1888, succeeded in tapping this consensus in Holland to form the Anti-Opium Bond. This organization henceforward played the dominant role in agitating for an end to opium farms. By 1890 the bond boasted 510 members (440 in Holland, 70 in the Indies) and a governing board that included twelve members of Parliament, six prominent church and missionary figures, and leading editors, jurists, and academicians. Under Elout's editorship its official publication, *De Opium-vloek op Java* (The Opium Curse in Java), appeared for the first time in September 1890.[29] Here the various threads of antifarm sentiment coalesced; indictments based on guilt and righteous indignation blended with those inspired by racial fears and practical statecraft. The strident *Opium-vloek* presented the most comprehensive point-by-point case against the opium farm system to date.

Indictment of the status quo brought with it a renewed search for alternatives. J.A.B. Wiselius, who as assistant resident of Semarang had performed one of the more thorough investigations of local

27. See E. B. Kielstra, "Java's grootste ramp," *De Gids*, 52 (1888); Locher-Scholten, "Brooshooft," pp. 324, 326.
28. Among the missionaries was J. L. Zegers, whose converts in Indramayu included several Chinese and Indonesian opium smokers. Zegers spent three years compiling his *Het Opium-vraagstuk in Nederlandsch Oost-Indie* (Nijmegen, 1890). See M. Lindenbom, *Jan Lambrecht Zegers; Zendeling van Indramajoe 1870–1890* (Nederland Zending Vennootschap, n.d. [1919?]).
29. W. Elout van Soeterwoude, *De Opium-vloek op Java* (The Hague, 1890). Four issues with the shorter title *De Opium-Vloek* followed in 1891, 1893, 1895, and 1899. Annual reports (Verslagen) of the activities of the Anti-Opium Bond are published in the successive issues of the *Opium-Vloek*, which also include the names of members of the governing board. On Elout van Soeterwoude, see *NNBW*, 1:814–15.

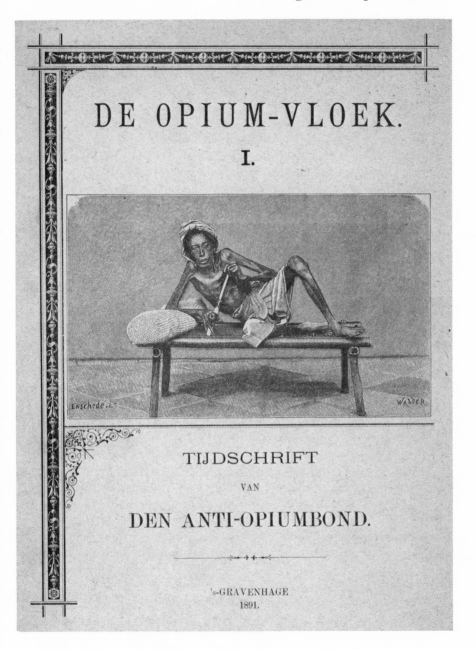

The Opium Curse. Magazine cover, 1891.

opium affairs in response to van Dedem's call for an inquiry in 1880, published a critical study of British opium policy in India in 1886. He found the British system well suited to India, but continued to view policy in Java in terms of making the opium farm system work.[30] This of course remained Charles TeMechelen's chief aim. By 1889, however, the vast majority of antiopium sentiment, echoing the view of the publicists, was even more strongly antifarm. Indeed, aside from a few missionaries, none of the important farm critics believed that a thorough ban on opium was possible in the immediate future. The search for alternatives therefore focused on devising a new sort of distribution system that would eliminate abuses associated with opium farms. Most important, such a system would hold Java's opium supply in check and eliminate the Chinese from the opium trade. A distribution scheme managed and staffed directly by the colonial administration, of the sort the French had implemented in Cochin China in 1881 (and which they called the Opium Regie), seemed most promising in all respects, and by 1889 opinion had coalesced in favor of some sort of Regie. Voicing the collective antifarm sentiment, the Anti-Opium Bond made an Opium Regie for Java a major plank in its program.

The idea of a regie was not new. Various sorts of government-run schemes had been proposed during earlier deliberations in the 1860s and 1870s, although they had never been taken very seriously; the assumptions made about the inevitability of the farm system were too deeply entrenched. But by the mid-1880s these assumptions were considerably loosened. Reintroduced, the regie idea now fell on more fertile soil. Both Groneman and Brooshooft became regie advocates, and in November 1888 Levysohn Norman, speaking in the lower house, proposed for Java a regie similar to that of France, a suggestion seconded in the upper house by J.E.N. Baron Schimmelpenninck van der Oye, a director of the Anti-Opium Bond.[31]

In 1889 two detailed proposals of just how such a regie might operate in Java were published. The most important of these, *Opiumpacht of Opiumregie?* (Opium Farm or Opium Regie?), was written by N. J. Struick, an inspector with the Finance Department in Batavia. Struick provided the first detailed description of the

---

30. J.A.B. Wiselius. *De Opium in Nederlandsch en Britisch Indie* (The Hague, 1886).
31. Kielstra, "Ramp," p. 32; Struick, *Opiumpacht*, Introduction.

Regie in Cochin China. There the French colonial government manufactured and distributed opium to wholesale outlets and then licensed local agents to service the retail trade. Struick pinpointed what he thought were the major weaknesses of the French system— mainly the low price of opium in Cochin China and the fact that opium retailers could increase their profits only by increasing sales—and went on to propose a modified version for Java. In his version both the wholesale and retail opium trade would be firmly in the hands of salaried state employees. In an article that followed and complemented Struick's, Indies army pharmacist J. Haak addressed the technical problems of manufacturing opium products for the Javanese market.[32]

In response to the public attack on the opium farms, and reflecting his own dismay over the collapse of Java's major opium farm kongsis, Colonial Minister Keuchenius grasped at the Opium Regie as a possible solution to the opium problem. He assigned W. P. Groeneveldt, a Chinese-language expert and a respected member of the Indies Council, to travel to Cochin China to make a thorough study of the French program. Groeneveldt did so in the early months of 1890 and submitted his report in August. On the basis of his detailed observations in the French colony and his intimacy with the situation in Java, Groeneveldt painted a highly positive picture of the possibilities for a regie.[33]

Groeneveldt's indictment of the farm system was especially effective because he was not an antiopium extremist. He believed that opium, used in moderation, represented no real harm to either individual or society, and that from both a moral and a fiscal point of view a vice tax was defensible. He asked, simply, as had Baron van Dedem a decade before, whether the farm system could ever achieve both the ethical and fiscal goals that the government had sought for so long. "The answer to this question," he replied, "must be an immediate and unequivocal 'No.'"[34] The fault lay in the conflict between the interests of the opium farms and those of the state. For instance, to protect their own profits, farmers were more or less

---

32. Haak, *Opiumregie.*

33. Groeneveldt, *Rapport over opium monopolie in Cochin-China* (Batavia, 1890). See also the brief article by Groeneveldt, "Opium Regie," in *Nederlandsch Indie onder het Regentschap van Kongingin Emma 1890–1898* (Batavia, 1898), pp. 227–28; KVvNI 1889; and the documents relating to the preparation of the report in V 15/9/1890/60.

34. Quoted from Groeneveldt's "Conclusion," reprinted in *Opium-Vloek,* 1:11. Hereafter cited as Groeneveldt, "Conclusion."

forced to import illegal opium and to encourage opium use among the people. Furthermore, the lion's share of opium profits, Groeneveldt argued, went to the farm and not to government. Could the farm system be reformed so that the interests of the state and its farmers more perfectly coincided? "I think this is impossible."[35] Nothing short of a state-administered monopoly would eliminate the abuses and conflicts of the past and thus permit the final achievement of Holland's dual aims. "As the image of the Regie gradually developed before me," he wrote, "as I came to know her in her success, in her failure, in her strength and her weakness, I was overcome with the firm conviction that it was she who could . . . bring us the deliverance we have thus far sought in vain."[36]

Groeneveldt's prototype regie was based on the French design, but it incorporated improvements of his own and of Struick's devising. In it the state would import, manufacture, package, and sell all the opium in the colony. The opium supply should be unlimited, Groeneveldt argued, but a strong land- and sea-based opium police would so obstruct the flow of illegal opium that the state could sell its product at high fixed prices. The high price of opium would make immoderate use impossible for most people. The initial costs involved in constructing a modern opium factory and of staffing an opium bureaucracy would, he thought, be offset in the long run by profits.

Groeneveldt's report, in short, proposed a radical institutional reform in the interest of meeting long-established but unachieved objectives. It reflected neither guilt nor racial fears; it addressed the opium question strictly as a matter of sound policy. Groeneveldt's solution was all the more palatable because it offered the hope that the Netherlands might enjoy its opium revenues even more abundantly without the farms and without the Chinese. The Groeneveldt report irrevocably tilted opinion within the government in the direction of a regie.

Three years intervened, however, before that opinion manifested itself in a parliamentary vote officially initiating an experimental Opium Regie. During the interim, the farm system was not without its defenders, and as a result 1891 and 1892 were the years of the Anti-Opium Bond's greatest activity. The bond wholeheartedly en-

35. Ibid., p. 23.
36. Ibid., p. 25.

dorsed the Groeneveldt plan. In its magazine and in frequent public meetings—often enlivened by Elout van Soeterwoude's primitive slide shows—it feverishly made the case against the farms and for the regie.[37] Individual members, meanwhile, such as Levysohn Norman and Schimmelpenninck van der Oye, kept the issue alive in Parliament. Typical was Dr. H.T.A.M. Schaepman's speech of January 1892 before the lower house in which, again invoking the image of Holland as a Christian motherland acting on behalf of her "younger brothers," he referred to the hoped-for adoption of the regie as an act of national rehabilitation.[38] More specific and just as damaging to the farm cause was Levysohn Norman's speech two months earlier in which he revealed to his fellow parliamentarians Liem Kok Sing's complicity in the Marungan smuggling scandal and Charles TeMechelen's close relationship with and behind-the-scenes lobbying for the Kediri kongsi.[39]

Among the major opponents in Holland of an Opium Regie were two former directors of finance (Batavia), H. R. Bool (1872–74) and L.W.G. de Roo (1883–87).[40] De Roo especially made himself the center of pro-opium-farm sentiment, debating with Elout before the Indisch Genootschap and publishing a succinct dissection of pro-regie thinking in 1892.[41] Adherents of the traditional policy, Bool and de Roo saw smuggling, rather than the opium farm itself, as the central problem. They argued accordingly that the government's efforts should be directed toward eliminating the black market. Once accomplished, an honest farm amenable to state regulation would provide the simplest and most expedient means of exploiting the opium monopoly and achieving the state's moral goals. Both felt that the establishment and administration of an opium bureaucracy would be more trouble and more expensive than it would be worth.[42] De Roo criticized the antifarm muckrakers as alarmists and

37. For a description of such a meeting, see the short article on p. 2 of the *Mail Courant van het Nieuws van den Dag,* February 6, 1892. At this particular meeting H.J.A.M. Schaepman held forth on "Our Colonial Policy and the Opium Question" to the enthusiastic response of his audience.

38. Reprinted in *Opium-Vloek,* 2:2.

39. MvK to Kongingin Weduwe Regenten, November 2, 1892, no. 39 in V 2/11/1892/39.

40. SvD H. J. Bool, P 295; SvD L.W.G. de Roo, N 233, 512.

41. L.W.G. de Roo, *De verkoop van opium op Java* (Nijmegen, 1892); L.W.G. de Roo, "Nota en voordracht over de opiumkwestie met debat," *VIG,* 1889, pp. 227–39, and 1890, pp. 2–64.

42. H. J. Bool, "De opiumpacht op Java," *Vragen des Tijds,* 15, 1 (1888–89), 75; Struick, *Opiumpacht,* p. 34.

scandalmongers and was particularly provoked by those who claimed to promote the Regie in the interest of protecting Indonesians from Chinese exploitation. It is Europeans, we Dutch, who exploit Java, he said frankly. Why do we not admit it and get on with it?[43]

In Batavia there was less excitement over the Groeneveldt report than in Holland. Here the views of Bool and de Roo found echoes in objections raised by the departments and by members of the Colonial Service.[44] Charles TeMechelen prepared a sixty-six-page report with eighty appendices condemning the proposal.[45] He felt that "the general pressure for reform" in the political atmosphere was prompting, in this case, an unnecessarily radical departure from past practice. He argued that few of the abuses of France's farm system in Cochin China, which had inspired the French regie in the first place, existed in Java. (Most farm critics disagreed.) And he asked: why should a policy, basically sound, be abandoned when reforms will suffice? Besides, he said, some features of the regie would create abuses far worse than those of the farms. TeMechelen was wary of the army of petty European bureaucrats who he imagined would step in to replace local Chinese opium bandars.[46] Like de Roo, he had no confidence that Europeans would act with any less self-interest than the Chinese. A regie, he went on, could only succeed if the government invested heavily, far more heavily than heretofore, in a comprehensive antismuggling campaign. There was nothing to indicate that it would now be prepared to do so. Finally, according to his complex calculations, the colony could expect to lose millions each year if it attempted to bring opium under its direct management.[47]

In his advice to the governor general, Finance Director Rovers also homed in on the possible evil consequences of abandoning the opium farms. "The condition of Indies finance," he began, "is highly alarming." In a point-by-point discussion of Groeneveldt's prototype, he restated many of the objections raised by TeMechelen, and then added several more of his own. One in particular that worried his department was that the state's regie would be forced to

43. De Roo, *De verkoop van opium*, pp. 37–38.
44. Groeneveldt, "Opium Regie," p. 227.
45. TM to DF, February 16, 1891, no. 169/12 in Exh 9/8/1892/76.
46. TM to DF, February 16, 1891, p. 36 in Exh 9/8/1892/76.
47. See ibid., Bijlage G, "Raming der Inkomsten."

accept illegal currency—the ubiquitous duits—in payment for opium, just as the farm did. Whereas the farm could release duits back into circulation, the state could not and would therefore lose even more money on the regie. He concluded that "the Regie is ugly and troublesome. In my view uglier and certainly in everyone's view more troublesome than the farm." But then, as if to confirm Te-Mechelen's worst fears about "the general pressure for reform," Rovers, his friend and staunch supporter, added: "But its heart is better, more honest; there beats in it something that does not beat in the heart of the farm. For me, this realization has turned the scales. Focusing less upon outward beauty and efficiency than upon inner worth, I have in the end, hesitatingly, come over to the Regie."[48]

Governor General Pijnacker Hordijk was similarly persuaded. Overriding the local consensus, he formally proposed that an Opium Regie be set up in Java and Madura. Having appointed Groeneveldt to study the technical problems of manufacturing, packaging, and distributing candu and tiké, he awaited parliamentary approval for the expenses of building a state opium factory and organizing a trial regie.[49] The appointment of Baron van Dedem as minister of colonies in the Liberal ministry of 1891 greatly increased the chances for approval. The opium issue was not a major one; the great political questions of the day revolved around domestic issues, schools, suffrage, and social legislation. Van Dedem's program as minister emphasized the separation of home and colonial revenues (decentralization), and called for public works—irrigation projects and railroads—to enhance the welfare of the indigenous population and, on this basis, lay the foundations of the future prosperity of the colony.[50]

Long a critic of government opium policy, van Dedem now made the Opium Regie part of this program. In the budget debates of 1892 and 1893 he patiently defended the costs involved, which by then had replaced the question of the opium farms themselves as the major issue. Both houses finally approved his budget in the spring of 1893. In September 1894 the Dutch Opium Regie re-

48. DF to GG, May 22, 1891, no. 7637 in TMC H422c.
49. Groeneveldt, "Opium Regie," p. 227.
50. Furnivall, *Netherlands India*, p. 230; "van Dedem," *ENI*; H. A. Idema, *Parlementaire Geschiedenis van Nederlandsch-Indie 1891–1918* (The Hague, 1924), p. 51; and W. J. van Welderen Baron Rengers, *Schets eener Parlementaire Geschiedenis van Nederland van 1849 tot 1901* (The Hague, 1948), 1:798–99.

placed the opium farm in the first trial residency, the island of Madura. In January 1896 the Opium Regie entered three residencies in east Java; and in 1897, following the successful outcome of these trials, Parliament gave the Opium Regie its final seal of approval and voted to replace opium farms with the regie throughout Java.[51]

The parliamentary decision to abandon the opium farm system in favor of a government-run Opium Regie brought Charles Te-Mechelen's career to an end. While the fate of the opium farms hung in the balance, he had continued to advocate his own solution to the opium question: a reformed opium farm system coupled with an extensive land and sea opium police with supraresidency authority.[52] He submitted a number of proposals for such a force between 1889 and 1892, the most extensive of which was his 1890 report in which he envisioned a land-side corps of four European inspectors, twenty-eight opium hunters (each assisted by an Indonesian police mantri), and two hundred Indonesian *oppassers* (policemen) acting in concert with the task force at sea—all under his direction.[53] Although Rovers supported the creation of such an organization, many residents, jealous of Colonial Service prerogatives in police affairs and burned by TeMechelen's often high-handed ways with local officials, voiced strong opposition.[54] The notoriety of the task force had left its mark as well; and, as governor general, Pijnacker Hordijk objected to TeMechelen's insistence on overall authority, for he feared its potential for strife between the task force and the Colonial Service.[55]

For all these reasons he did not approve the TeMechelen-Rovers proposal. Instead, in 1891 Pijnacker Hordijk authorized both Resident Uljee of Rembang and Resident Castens of Japara to establish

51. Parliamentary debates on the regie budget in 1892 and 1893 are summarized in *Opium-Vloek*, 2:100–126. Groeneveldt, "Opium Regie," p. 228.
52. His recommendations for improving the regulation and supervision of the farms, including the suggestion that the government take over opium manufacture, are summarized in TM to DF, September 16, 1887, no. 1171/4 Geheim in TMC H422e.
53. TM to DF, March 28, 1890, no. 463/3 in TMC H422d.
54. See DF to GG, September 10, 1890, no. 13638 in TMC H422d; also ex-Resident H. H. Donker Curtius's attack on TeMechelen in his letter to members of the lower house, December 1891, reprinted in his *Relaas van het Regent van Magettan ten Laste gelegde opium sluiken, en het daarna ingestelde onderzoek* (Surabaya, 1892).
55. First Government Secretary to DF, November 12, 1890, no. 2707 in TMC H422d.

their own smuggling-suppression programs—in effect, to replace task force operations in the very residencies where it was originally created and had always been most active.[56] This was a direct blow both to TeMechelen's hopes and to his personal esteem.

Another blow soon followed, or at least in his gloomy frame of mind TeMechelen interpreted it as such. In April 1892 Pijnacker Hordijk appointed a three-man committee, composed of Te-Mechelen and the residents of Surakarta and Surabaya, to study the whole opium-police problem in Indies society and to submit a definitive recommendation.[57] Both the formation of the committee and the choice of its members affronted TeMechelen. As the acknowledged expert on policing the clandestine opium trade, he saw no reason to form such a committee in the first place, and the selection of Surakarta's resident, O. A. Burnabij Lautier, a vociferous Te-Mechelen critic within the Colonial Service, made participating intolerable. Recalling the various and extensive studies and proposals he had already prepared over the years, he wrote to Rovers: "If in the view of higher authorities revisions and improvements were thought necessary, individual consultation with me about them would have been far more compatible with the deference to which I humbly claim the right, than bringing in others foreign to my field of expertise."[58] Insulted, he requested sick leave and sailed for Europe. Four years later, still in Europe, he submitted his resignation.[59] His departure from Java in the spring of 1893 coincided with the final votes in Parliament which rang the death knell for Java's opium farms and heralded the inauguration of the Opium Regie.

TeMechelen's era was a transitional one, a time of institutional readjustment and testing in which his voice was a conservative one, although he did not perceive it to be. The day was passing when semi-independent organizations could fit comfortably within the increasingly bureaucratized administration of colonial Java. This was as true of the task force as it was of the opium farms. Te-Mechelen chose not to adjust. Instead he fought his own rear-guard action against "the general pressure for reform" and, having lost, he quit. Had he stayed in the Colonial Service, it is most likely that

56. TM to DF, March 5, 1892, no. 521/12 in Exh 9/8/1892/76.
57. Extract Register der Besluiten van den Gouverneur-Generaal van NI, April 9, 1892, no. 16 in TMC H422d.
58. TM to DF, January 28, 1893, no. 198/3 in TMC H422d.
59. SvD TeMechelen, folio 505.

TeMechelen would have been entrusted with the management of the new Opium Regie.[60] Instead, he bowed out and devoted his retirement to prospecting and big-game hunting. He became the subject of lore, and upon his death in 1917 Rouffaer remembered him as "a romantic Indo . . . a charming piece of Java's past."[61]

60. Pijnacker Hordijk was apparently counting on TeMechelen's expertise in setting up the Opium Regie. When TeMechelen resigned, Pijnacker Hordijk was so angry he considered denying TeMechelen his pension by firing him. SvD Te-Mechelen, folio 505.

61. Rouffaer, "Charles TeMechelen," pp. 311–12. TeMechelen did not return to Java until 1906, having spent the intervening years in Germany and South Sumatra. He lived in Java until his death in 1917. TeMechelen was also known as a "Javanicus," someone expert in things Javanese. He published three works on Javanese theater: "Drie-en twintig schetsen van wayang stukken gebruikelijk bij de vertooningen der Wayang Poerwa op Java," *VBG*, 40 (1879); and shadow puppet play (*wayang*) texts in *VBG*, 43 (1882), and *VBG*, 44 (1884).

11

The Opium Regie
and Ethical Java

The anti-opium-farm crusade was part of a sweeping reorientation in colonial thinking which began in the 1880s. Observing that the Liberal policies of post-1870 Java had evidently failed to improve life for the Javanese, many of the Dutch began advocating new measures to foster native prosperity. Pieter Brooshooft's *Memorie* of 1888 was the first important political document of this trend.[1] Brooshooft called for a reduction in native taxes, an end to systematic exploitation (like the Chinese revenue farms), and for state-sponsored projects to improve indigenous agriculture. He also advocated local autonomy in colonial governance—for the Dutch, of course. These ideas found favor with the growing number of non-official Europeans in the Indies—planters, for example, and professionals, merchants, and employees of Western firms and enterprises. They found favor as well with humanitarian-minded politicians of the right (Anti-revolutionaries), center (Progressive Liberals), and left (Socialists) in Holland, and with Dutch industrialists who wanted to improve the purchasing power of Holland's Asian subjects.

Baron van Dedem's program as minister of colonies in the early 1890s responded to some of these sentiments. In 1899 C. Th. van Deventer brought them into sharp focus with his eloquent plea that Holland pay "a Debt of Honor" in restitution for its neglect of the colony and its people, and in 1901 Queen Wilhelmina officially

---

1. Brooshooft, *Memorie*.

lamented "the diminished welfare of the population of Java." Broos-hooft's pamphlet of the same year, *De ethische koers in de koloniale politiek*, gave a popular name to the program of welfare, efficiency, expansion, and autonomy which characterized Dutch colonial policy in the first decades of the twentieth century: the Ethical Policy.[2]

The Ethical years were marked by an expansion of state-sponsored education for Indonesians, great outlays for irrigation projects and other public works, and the promotion of popular credit facilities—these to replace Chinese moneylenders. The same years brought the definitive establishment of Dutch sovereignty throughout the Malay Archipelago, an act of imperialism that Holland's Ethici applauded, along with Brooshooft, as a "solemn duty."[3] They were also years in which racial lines were drawn more tightly than ever before, especially as the number of Dutch men and women in the colony rose and as a more purely European elite class formed. At the same time, the lines of authority were pulled ever more directly beneath the Dutch administration. Members of the Colonial Service now adopted an attitude of aloof paternalism toward Indonesians (with whose progress they were impatient) and of contempt for the Chinese.

Symbolic of the new spirit, the Opium Regie was a government department erected to right past wrongs. To its more idealistic promoters, it was an institution dedicated to expressing concern for the spiritual and material welfare of Indonesians. Although the regie fell short of such lofty aims, its innovations were profound nevertheless. The Opium Regie was one of the first fully developed institutions of Ethical Java.

Under the Opium Regie, all opium affairs were centered in the capital. In place of local farm-run opium factories, each producing its own distinctive candu and tiké, a government plant in Batavia now manufactured opium products of uniform quality and taste. In place of local opium farms and subfarms and their organizations, a Java-wide opium bureaucracy, staffed by pryayi and supervised locally by the Colonial Service, now sold regie candu and tiké through-

2. Queen Wilhelmina quoted in Amry Vandenbosch, *The Dutch East Indies* (Berkeley, Calif., 1944), p. 64; C. Th. van Deventer, "Een Eereschuld" (1899), reprinted in Colenbrander and Stokvis, *Leven en Arbeid . . . van Deventer*, pp. 1–43; Pieter Brooshooft, *De ethische koers in de koloniale politiek* (Amsterdam, 1901); on the Ethical Policy and its roots, see Locher-Scholten, "Brooshooft"; Furnivall, *Netherlands India*, pp. 225–37; Wertheim, *Indonesian Society*, pp. 65, 96.
3. Locher-Scholten, "Brooshooft," p. 337.

out the island. The factory and the bureaucracy were coordinated by a new government bureau within the Finance Department; it was headed by a chief inspector and staffed by four inspectors, an engineer, a mechanic, and a small army of minor functionaries and clerks.[4]

The inaugural years of the Opium Regie were taken up with technical and administrative problems. The regie's first opium factory commenced operations in Batavia in 1893. Here J. Haak led a team of engineers and chemists in solving the initial problems of manufacturing and packaging opium. Modern technology was brought to bear to produce candu and tiké of consistent quality and popular taste.[5] Haak, who in 1889 had made the first serious study of farm opium products, devised a candu recipe that was faithful to farm taste, color, and consistency. He then added a neutral chemical trace designed to provide a simple and foolproof means of distinguishing legal from illegal opium. Haak's factory candu was refined in up-to-date steam cookers. After that, specially made machines packaged it automatically in small tin tubes (ranging from 0.5 to 50 mata in size), riveted them shut with a metal eyelet, and stamped them each with the regie name and insignia.[6] Similarly blended, coded, and stamped, regie tiké was packed in hermetically sealed tin-foil capsules of one geleng each.[7] At the factory, regie workers packed the tubes and capsules in glass-topped wooden boxes— designed to thwart embezzlement—and shipped them monthly to each residency.

In anticipation of the entire Indies market, the Dutch replaced this provisional facility with a larger factory just outside Batavia in 1901. Here they manufactured candu and tiké on a vast scale, employing hundreds of Indonesian workers: 630 by 1905, more

4. See SvNI 1898, no. 78; and GG to MvK, July 2, 1903, no. 1458/2 in V 8/9/1903/20, which discusses the need for a larger bureau staff in anticipation of the regie appearance in all Java the following year.

5. The regie factory later manufactured morphine pills for the Chinese mining colonies in Bangka in the outer islands.

6. Haak, *Opiumregie*. The inventor of the chemical trace, Dr. J. de Groot, was decorated for his services in 1907. A. A. de Jongh to MvK, February 9, 1907, in VKG 12/2/1907/E3, no. 16. Regie tubes were available in the following portions, by mata: 0.5, 1, 2, 5, 12.5, 25, and 50.

7. See "Opium-verpakking: System 'Huizer,'" *Opium-Vloek*, 3:99–100; and Groeneveldt to GG, June 24, 1892, no. 7, and J. Haak to Groeneveldt, June 17, 1892, both in V 2/11/1892/39; and S. L. Huizer to MvK, January 22, 1895, in V 30/1/1895/21.

than 1,000 by 1913.[8] The Dutch took great pride in their new opium plant and it soon became an Ethical showplace. High Dutch officials invited visitors there to witness technology in the service of social progress.[9]

Prior to introducing the regie into a new residency, officials from Batavia consulted with the local Colonial Service and the outgoing opium farmer about supply and demand, the best locations for opium stores, and security.[10] Some opium farmers resisted the regie. Chinese captain Lim Tiang Hoei in Batavia, for example, took out a sheriff's writ to prevent regie people from entering his stores.[11] Some European owners and managers of private lands and plantations also fought it, objecting to the erection of official regie stores on or near their properties even in cases where patungan farm outlets had serviced these areas for years. In such instances Batavia fell back on old statutes, originally designed to protect the opium farm, to assert the regie's right to eminent domain.[12]

On the night preceding the Opium Regie's local debut, the government bought up the remaining farm opium. As regie agents gathered it from all the farm stores and deposited it in a government warehouse, a sign written in Dutch, Chinese, and the vernacular was posted above the new regie stores: "Government Opium for Sale Here."[13]

Under the Opium Regie each residency contained a central opium depot run by a European depot holder and an extensive network of official opium stores. There were at least as many of these stores as there had been legal farm shops before them; in Rembang, for example, there were forty-eight (soon expanded to fifty-eight),

8. See KVvNI 1905, p. 214; and Opiumfabriek, *Jaarverslag 1914* (Batavia, 1915), p. 3.

9. VR September 1901 and VR December 1901 (both in V 26/3/1902/27) report on the new factory and discuss the problems thereof. The December report complains of "a stream" of visitors, including several Indonesian teachers and the Rijksbestuurder (patih) of Surakarta.

10. These activities are described in the monthly reports (VR) of the regie; see, for example, VR December 1898 (in V 12/3/1902/24) about preparations in Surabaya.

11. VR September 1902 in V 7/1/1905/19.

12. See HIOR to DF, September 30, 1902, and HIOR to GG, July 18, 1903, no. 1948/R, both in VKG 7/10/1903/O–15; and SvNI 1836, no. 19, which asserted that prerogatives of private landowners did not prevail over those of the state's revenue-gathering agents.

13. J. E. Scheltema describes the changing of the guard in his "De Invoering der Opiumregie," *Bataviaasch Nieuwsblad*, October 1, 1902.

Opium factory of the Opium Regie. From *Gedenkboek voor Nederlandsch-Indie, 1899–1923*, Batavia, 1923.

two or more in each wedana's district.[14] Regie opium stores were manned by an Indonesian sales mantri who was completely responsible for the local retail trade. The sales mantri was aided by a helper. Sales mantri received opium from the central depot, sold it to their customers, recorded their daily transactions by type of product (candu or tiké) and portion (how many of each size tube they had sold), and remitted their cash proceeds to a native assistant collector,

14. Koesoemodikdo, "Soewatoe Timbangan jang Tiada Diminta," *TBB*, 30 (1906), 35; "Memorandum concerning the Opium Regie Service in Netherlands-India," in *Report of the International Opium Commission, Shanghai, China, February 1 to February 26, 1909* (Shanghai, 1909), 2:311.

one of whom presided over each regency/afdeling. Assistant collectors were the highest-ranking indigenous employees in the regie and served as intermediaries between individual sales mantri and the Dutch depot holder. They dealt out opium to the twelve or so stores in their districts, collected the proceeds, and gathered sales statistics.[15] The resident was in effect the manager of the regie in his residency. He was responsible for the efficient operation of the program and the supervision of the European and native staff. In practice, however, most of this work fell to controleurs.[16]

Beneath the opium stores each residency also included a network of licensed opium dens or, as the Dutch preferred to call them, consumption centers (verbruik-plaatsen). Regie rules permitted no opium to be sold in these dens. Smokers were required to purchase their opium at a regie store (which had no smoking facilities) and, if they wished, smoke it in a licensed den. Den holders made their money by renting out smoking utensils, providing awar-awar leaves and other condiments to mix with regie candu, and by selling the jicing scraped from the bowls of pipes used in their dens back to the regie.[17] The number of such dens varied considerably. Initially concerned with granting too many licenses, the regie soon faced the opposite problem. When opium den regulations were strictly enforced—by no means universally the case—den holders frequently found business so unprofitable that they asked to have their licenses revoked.[18]

The Opium Regie substantially expanded the Pangreh Praja corps. It provided new career opportunities for the growing number of young pryayi, many of them graduates of the expanding colonial school system, who sought "white-collar" jobs and the status of an official position. Not only were there new positions directly connected to the regie such as assistant collectors, sales mantri, and helpers (which in Rembang accounted for one hundred openings), but because new police mantris were now needed to replace opium farm mata-mata and opium hunters, the concomitant expansion of

15. VR August 1898 in V 12/3/1902/24; "Opium," ENI, 2:161–62; and monthly reports.
16. Shanghai Memorandum, p. 296. In Surakarta and Yogyakarta, where no regular Colonial Service controleurs were posted, the Dutch appointed special Opium Regie controleurs. See HIOR to GG, May 16, 1906, no. 1626/3, and GG to MvK, June 28, 1906, no. 899/15, both in Exh 3/8/1906/125.
17. See SvNI 1901, no. 62, and comments in various monthly reports.
18. See, for example, the discussion in VR May 1903 in V 7/1/1905/18.

Pangreh Praja police functions often created just as many more. In Batavia residency, for example, the Dutch created 120 new police positions to complement an Opium Regie staff of 97.[19]

Positions with the Opium Regie were roughly on a par with several others in the Pangreh Praja of the rank of assistant wedana and below, positions normally filled by the lower pryayi—a group distinctly elite but whose status and kin network were below that of the major regent families.[20] Most of the regie's initial employees appear to have been selected on the recommendation of locally influential pryayi who in the traditional fashion nominated their nephews and others to whom they were socially obligated.[21] Once hired, a Javanese employee's subsequent upward mobility in government service was not confined to the regie. The job of sales mantri was on a par with district secretary, and it was one notch below that of police mantri. Several sales mantri in the early regie years were promoted to police mantri and assistant collector, and some ultimately achieved the rank of assistant wedana.[22] Likewise, unsuccessful police mantri and assistant wedana might very likely find themselves dispensing opium as a sales mantri.[23] In one unusual case an assistant wedana who earned a reputation for "gross slovenliness" was dropped to coffee warehouse foreman and then to opium sales mantri before the Dutch gave up on him altogether and dismissed him.[24] Not all regie pryayi remained in the nether rungs of the Pangreh Praja. At least one later regent, Said of Blora (1913–26), began his career with the regie.[25]

The status of Indonesian employees of the Opium Regie as clients of the Dutch was unambiguous. It was only with great reluctance that the Dutch meddled in the old native civil service; reform-minded residents such as Rembang's A. C. Uljee, who cavalierly

19. Koesoemodikdo, "Soewatoe Timbangan," p. 35. Koesoemodikdo does not include helpers in his list of Rembang Pangreh Praja, most likely because he, reflecting the pryayi view, considered helpers to be of *magang* (apprentice) status, the significance of which will be discussed below. See also DF to GG, September 9, 1901, no. 17068 in V 17/10/1901/53.

20. See Heather Sutherland's comment on "higher" and "lower" pryayi in Sutherland, "Pangreh Pradja," p. 216n51. See also Sutherland, *Bureaucratic Elite*, p. 25.

21. VR December 1901 in V 26/3/1902/27; VR September 1906 in V 5/4/1907/19.

22. See the cases in VR December 1901 in V 26/3/1902/27; VR December 1903 in V 7/1/1905/18; VR April 1904 in V 7/4/1905/32.

23. See VR September 1907 in V 17/6/1908/10; VR February 1908 in V 28/9/1909/7; and several other monthly reports.

24. VR February 1906 in V 5/4/1907/19.

25. Sutherland, "Pangreh Pradja," p. 219n53.

weeded out native administrators with whom he was dissatisfied, were relatively rare.[26] Within new pryayi-staffed departments such as the regie, however, the Dutch exercised their prerogatives in matters of appointment, promotion, and demotion far more decisively. The recommendations of trusted Pangreh Praja still carried weight, but the Dutch were the clear and final arbiters. Furthermore, though the regie organization was designed to dovetail with the base of the Pangreh Praja structure, it was a fundamentally different sort of structure. Unlike their colleagues in the native administration whose roles and duties were traditionally more holistic than specific (this despite Dutch efforts to define them by statute), assistant collectors, sales mantri, and helpers were in effect the employees of a modern rationalized bureaucracy. Their functions were well defined, and they earned promotion or demotion largely on the basis of successful performance of them.

Not all of the Dutch took their appointing responsibilities so seriously as this suggests, however. The old taint associated with opium and the farms survived the transition to the regie, especially among some members of the Colonial Service. Regie officials regularly complained that residents posted their least desirable native candidates in the regie. The volume of such complaints suggests that a disproportionate number of incompetent, sickly, and irresponsible men found themselves working for the Opium Regie, all the more so because, for young pryayi, the regie held much less allure than the native corps with its traditional aura of prestige. They avoided it if possible. This problem was the subject of a special regie circular to residents in 1905, which was repeated in 1907 at the chief inspector's request. He feared for the reputation of his department. It would be disastrous, he said, should aspirant native officials come to feel that placement in the regie was the opposite of distinction.[27]

Although it may have been less attractive to aspirant native officials than the administrative corps, the regie offered an entrée into the desirable world of government service nevertheless. Besides, the regie did not harbor the incompetent for long. Regie work required the ability to keep accounts and to file reports—in short, a funda-

26. On Uljee, see p. 192 above.

27. Circulaire, GG to Residents, September 6, 1905 (Bijblad op het Staatsblad van NI, no. 6350, 40, 1907); VR November 1904 in V 7/4/1905/32; VR May 1906 in V 5/4/1907/19.

mental literacy. (This was now being provided for in a burgeoning network of native schools.) It also required deference to Dutch conceptions of propriety and decorum. Sales mantri could be dismissed for the slightest discrepancy in their accounts, and frequently were.[28] Old vices such as opium smoking, long tolerated in the Pangreh Praja despite official disapproval, were out of the question for young pryayi who sought careers within the changing colonial environment.[29] In the Opium Regie, and in other Ethical programs such as the People's Credit Service, disapproval often meant dismissal. And because the promotion ladder of the regie overlapped with that of the formal civil service, aspiring native officials ignored Dutch standards at their peril.

The position of Javanese employees of the Opium Regie illustrates a significant institutional change in Java involving the relationship between the Pangreh Praja and the Dutch administration. The native ruling class had long been subordinated to Dutch ends; the Pangreh Praja itself had evolved largely in response to the application of traditional Javanese patterns of social organization and government to the achievement of these ends, hence the sobriquet "government pryayi." But as the colonial presence deepened and became more complex, especially after the mid-nineteenth century, the Dutch began to exert pressure in the form of administrative reforms (such as the 1874 Java-wide standardization of the native administration) and negative incentives (denying the Pangreh Praja their traditional claims to the labor and produce of their districts) to reshape the corps and to make it subordinate not only to their ends but to their preferred means: an efficient, modern, salaried bureaucracy.

The first decade of the twentieth century witnessed an acceleration of this process. In addition to new departments such as the Opium Regie, in which pryayi were held accountable to increasingly well-defined standards, the whole question of Pangreh Praja reorganization came to the fore. The traditional method of recruitment into the Pangreh Praja, in which young pryayi apprenticed

28. Regie files are full of such incidents; almost every month one or more sales mantri or helpers would be dismissed for slight discrepancies in their accounts or minor infractions of regie regulations.

29. Several sales mantri who had acquired their positions via the influence of the regent of Demak were immediately dismissed when officials discovered they were opium smokers. See VR December 1901 in V 26/3/1902/27.

themselves (as magang) to native officials for years before receiving their first minor appointments, came in for special attack among the Colonial Service. Following a decade of debate and consideration it was formally abolished in 1910. The old system was replaced by a new one in which young pryayi began their official careers as assistant clerks (*hulp schrijvers*) following a period of education in a government school.[30] Aspiring officials now had to meet minimum educational standards and entered the bureaucratic ladder not as members of a local official retinue but as clients of the state.

Young Indonesians, in a sense, now apprenticed themselves to the Dutch, by attending their schools, adapting to their values, mimicking their social behavior, and seeking entry into their service. Students, assistant clerks, and regie helpers were the new magang, a modern variant of those who sat at the feet of a respected native official to learn the accepted modes of behavior in the world and, by mastering its requisite skills, to prepare for their place within it. For their part, the Dutch now increasingly assumed the role of patron. The whole Ethical program, with its concern for welfare, education, and cultural uplifting, symbolized the adoption of this relationship. One small example in practice was the care with which Javanese employees of the Opium Regie were reassigned in the wake of an opium-store closing. Another, and more striking, was Dutch unwillingness in many cases to close unneeded opium stores if doing so stifled mobility in the native corps. Some opium stores now existed because Javanese civil servants depended on them for their livelihood and prestige.[31]

Removing the official opium trade from the hands of the Chinese and entrusting it to Javanese civil servants under Dutch supervision met some of the goals of the antifarm movement and the Ethical spirit. It lessened for a time the exposure of village Java to intensive Chinese commercial activities, moneylending especially, and it ended the role of the opium farm organization as an enforcer of Chinese commercial monopolies in the countryside. Opium smuggling, however, was still a problem.

Regie opium was the most expensive in the world. In 1903 it was ten times the price of opium in the Singapore market.[32] As a result

30. See Sutherland's discussion of this period in Sutherland, *Bureaucratic Elite*, pp. 67–69.

31. VR April 1907 in V 17/6/1908/10; VR February 1908 in V 28/9/1909/7.

32. See HIOR to GG, September 18, 1903, no. 2554/R in V 13/1/1904/34; and HIOR to DF, August 24, 1907, no. 2794/R in V 18/6/1908/1.

the Java opium market remained a seductive field for the black marketeer. Clandestine opium continued to flow into Java, although China replaced India as the source of most of this. Particularly common from about 1905 on were opium powders and pills of Chinese manufacture which were peddled in Java as antiopium medications.[33] Singapore remained the major transshipment point for illegal opium, which increasingly came directly to Java hidden aboard Chinese-English steamers. The significance of Bali as an interim manufacturing and redistribution center had by regie days waned dramatically.

Aside from imported opium, there was a considerable illegal traffic in regie opium. Regie records reveal that on the average more than two-thirds of the opium violations under the regie involved the illicit trade in licit opium. Especially in the early years, in imitation of the opium farm markets, the price of regie opium fluctuated dramatically from region to region. This encouraged speculation in regie opium, and regie tubes moved regularly from low-priced regions to high-priced ones. Even after prices were stabilized in Java in 1907, regie opium in the outer islands continued to sell for considerably less than in Java, generating another opportunity for those willing to accept the risks of the black market.

The 1892 committee that had been formed to study the question of a comprehensive opium policy produced in its final report a round indictment of both the Opium Hunter System and the task force, just as Charles TeMechelen feared it would.[34] The committee's findings reflected the general disrepute into which both programs had fallen by the late 1880s. Regie planners therefore swept away not only the opium farms but also the ad hoc programs and agencies that had grown alongside them. Both the hunter system and the task force left its own legacy, however. Under the Opium Regie, police mantri assigned to opium work were appended directly to the local pryayi administration. And the use of steam-powered cruisers to intercept contraband opium shipments, task force–fashion, became a routine Regie activity.

As the regie entered each new residency, the Dutch dismissed the opium hunters, mantri, and lesser opassers who remained. Simultaneously they expanded the regular police by attaching several new

33. Reports of these "medications" proliferate in regie monthly reports from about 1905. See, for example, VR and VS March 1906 in V 5/4/1907/19.
34. See HIOR to GG, September 18, 1903, no. 2554/R in V 13/1/1904/34, in which the committee's conclusions are summarized.

police mantri and subordinate officers (probably the same people in many cases) to the regular native administration, particularly at the wedana and assistant wedana levels. These new officers were now responsible for the protection of the opium monopoly in their districts.[35] Though police mantri now labored in the service of the Ethical regie, their work was little different from that of the farm mata-mata, opium hunters, and local police whom they replaced. Their primary objective remained suppressing the black market and channeling the local opium trade toward the regie. By and large police mantri adopted the familiar modus operandi of their predecessors. In consultation with local sales mantri they pursued suspected smugglers and black marketeers, frequently people who had simply stopped visiting the opium shop, and they relied heavily on a network of underground informants and the crime specialists of jagabaya society. The old tricks and ruses of rural detective work—threats, frameups, agents provocateurs, and contrived ketrangan—were still very much a part of the day-to-day opium world. Now isolated from the legal opium trade, the Chinese were especially vulnerable to the excesses and caprices of the new opium police.[36]

Under the regie legal cases involving violations of the opium laws were still tried locally before the police roll and Landraad (although the latter were increasingly chaired by bona fide judicial officers) and still depended largely on ketrangan prepared by the local pryayi. In one respect, however, there was a significant change. The legality or illegality of confiscated opium submitted as evidence could now be determined with exactitude. The farm-appointed Chinese Inspection Committee, which had played such an important role in biasing the outcome of opium cases in favor of the farm, was a thing of the past. Regie chemists now examined all confiscated opium in the regie laboratory in Batavia, where a simple test determined its true origin.[37]

The testing of all confiscated opium in Batavia served another purpose. Along with samples of suspicious opium, residents submitted to Batavia reports summarizing the circumstances of each con-

35. SvNI 1898, no. 298; HIOR to GG, September 18, 1903, no. 2554/R in V 13/1/1904/34.
36. VR February 1903 in V 7/1/1905/18; and J. F. Scheltema, "The Opium Trade in the Dutch East Indies," *American Journal of Sociology*, 13 (July–September 1907), 236–37.
37. The regie's monthly reports include a breakdown by residency of all opium samples tested during the month, with results.

fiscation. This information was used to pinpoint smuggling "hot spots." On the basis of such information the regie could act to strengthen the corps of police mantri in these areas and, in cooperation with the local Colonial Service, conduct a black-market offensive. This occurred, for instance, in Kudus, Lasem, and Pati in 1903 when the regie launched a wave of house searches and arrests to put Chinese smuggling kongsis there out of business.[38]

The Opium Regie took over much of the work of the task force directly. In the manner pioneered by Charles TeMechelen, the regie patrolled the coasts of north Java, the Surabaya Straits, and Bali with its fast steam-powered cruisers, the first two of which had been built to TeMechelen's specifications and delivered in the spring of his departure from Java. To these were added two more in subsequent years. These pursuit vessels—the *Cycloop*, *Argus*, *De Valk*, and *Wachter*—concentrated primarily on escorting suspect Chinese-English steam vessels on their trips through Java harbors, often meeting them far out at sea and remaining with them until they left Netherlands Indies waters. This patrol-and-convoy technique depended for its success on the supply of intelligence, mainly from Singapore, which the regie collated in Batavia and relayed in code to its captains, customs authorities, and residents. Abandoned by the regie, however, was TeMechelen's substantial fleet of small sail-powered jukungs and the sea police who manned them. Opium Regie officials judged the fleet and its unruly kemandahs to be of doubtful effectiveness; they dismissed the sea police and put the boats at the disposal of individual residents. By 1903 only a handful remained in service.[39]

The regie's monthly reports chronicling the movement of its cruisers in pursuit of clandestine importers reveal a record of nearly continuous frustration. Time and time again when the regie received information about contraband opium aboard a specific vessel, one of its patrol boats would meet it, convoy it into Netherlands Indies waters, and inspect it, only to find no opium whatsoever. Such inspections usually proved fruitless unless regie and Customs authorities had information about exactly where on the ship the

---

38. See the monthly VS for the spring of 1903 in 7/1/1905/18.
39. HIOR to GG, September 18, 1903, no. 2554/R in V 13/1/1904/34. In this long report the chief inspector summarizes the history of the opium police. Each month the regie staff prepared a separate report addressed solely to problems relating to smuggling and the black market (VS).

opium was hidden. An incident in 1909 illustrates the problem. When the captain of the *Tjipanas* permitted an unusually thorough inspection of his entire ship, Batavia police uncovered ninety-seven tins of opium hidden in such places as a chest of rice in the fireman's cabin, the sleeping quarters of several crew members, the machine and engine rooms, beneath the floor of the engine room in a pocket of water (the result of a leak), and behind a false wall in another cabin.[40]

Regie officials recognized the inadequacy of the patrolling program, but by 1903 it was already the consensus that to intercept completely the flow of illegal opium into Java would require exorbitant expenditures.[41] The regie fleet was therefore not enlarged, even as the territory of the Netherlands Indies expanded into the entire archipelago. Instead, its cruisers—at mid-decade deployed to monitor clandestine opium shipments in the Celebes as well as in Java and Bali—gradually took on a variety of auxiliary nonregie tasks. They transported government goods and personnel, and in 1908 the *Cycloop* spent several weeks on a geological expedition to Krakatau.[42] Such ancillary activity further reduced the fleet's effectiveness as a deterrent to smuggling. In 1909 the regie vessels were transferred to the direct jurisdiction of the government marines, though they still patrolled regularly on behalf of the regie.[43] The Dutch had by no means given up on opium smuggling. Increasingly, however, they took other sorts of initiatives, diplomatic in nature, to interdict the traffic in opium before it reached the Indies. Changes in the Southeast and East Asian political landscape made this possible.

Most important, the expansion and tightening up of European authority in Southeast Asia made it more and more difficult for freewheeling Chinese merchants who specialized in the opium trade to find a safe base from which to operate. The advance of Dutch hegemony and direct civil government throughout the islands that surround Java brought with it tighter control over outlying ports, especially as the regie replaced older opium farms in these territo-

40. For this episode, see VS July 1909 in V 28/12/1910/32.
41. HIOR to GG, September 18, 1903, no. 2554/R in V 13/1/1904/34.
42. See, for example, VS August 1908 in V 28/9/1909/7.
43. Shanghai Memorandum, p. 296. The memorandum reveals that the Dutch budgeted about 2.3 percent of their opium revenues for antismuggling and police costs (p. 316).

ries as well. Lombok was the first "outer island" to host the Opium Regie in 1897, this immediately after the establishment of Dutch sovereignty there. Bali was added a decade later. The most important development in this respect, however, occurred in 1910, when the British dismantled the Singapore opium farm, along with those in Malacca and several of the Malay states, and replaced them with a regielike Opium Service. Vigorous British-initiated police activity now intercepted large quantities of opium before its owners could export it to Java.[44]

On the diplomatic front, regie officials attempted to enlist the cooperation of shipping companies and neighboring governments. The Dutch consul general in Singapore had been active in this respect for a long time. In 1909 he began direct consultations with the shipping companies whose steamers routinely visited Indies ports. The most notorious of these was the "Java-China-Japan Line" plying between South China, Hong Kong, Singapore, and Java; its Chinese crew members regularly harbored opium aboardship for contacts in Java. The *Tjipanas* was one of theirs. Because the company received a subsidy from the Indies government, it agreed to place Chinese regie spies among the crew.[45] A year later regie chief A. A. de Jongh attempted to enlist the cooperation of authorities in the South Chinese treaty ports and colonies to cut off the flow of Chinese opium to Java, most of it in the form of powders and pills. During his official visit in 1910 to Macao, Canton, and Hong Kong, where he conferred with British governor Sir Frederick J. D. Lugard, de Jongh tried to track down the source of "Foek Loeng" opium powder, a brand widely known throughout Asia.[46]

While Foek Loeng proved to be frustratingly elusive, de Jongh's consultations were illustrative of a new cooperative spirit among Asia's colonial powers in addressing what was increasingly called "the international opium problem." For example, the Dutch showed off their Opium Regie to investigative committees from four neighboring states: in January 1904 members of a committee appointed by the American Philippine Commission visited the regie factory

---

44. VR, VS June 1909 in V 28/12/1910/32; and VR, VS April 1910 in V 19/9/1911/36.
45. VS June 1909 in V 28/12/1910/32.
46. See his extensive report, HIOR to GG, December 2, 1910, no. 2243 in V 15/2/1911/C4. American and Japanese authorities, he learned, had also complained about proliferation of Foek Loeng.

(which they found to be "the most complete of its kind in Asia") and interviewed the bureau chief;[47] in 1908 the consul general of French Indochina solicited information about the regie to use in the reexamination of France's colonial opium program. British officials also studied the regie as they prepared to dismantle the opium farms in the Straits Settlements and Malaya; and the king of Thailand sent an official to inspect the regie as well.[48]

In 1909 the Dutch participated with twelve other nations in the first International Opium Conference in Shanghai, largely an American effort.[49] At the conference regie chief de Jongh presented a highly self-serving view of the Opium Regie, emphasizing the Forbidden Areas and Holland's intent to curtail the opium habit.[50] In the joint declaration published at the end of the conference, the participants agreed to take measures to suppress the production and use of opium, to accept in principle that opium consumption for other than medicinal purposes should be either banned or strictly supervised, and to make an all-out effort to inhibit international opium smuggling. Opium smuggling, after all, not only contributed to the abuse of the drug, especially in China, but it also cut into the revenues of Dutch, British, and French colonial establishments in Asia.

The Shanghai conference was the first of a series of major conferences on the international drug trade. Holland was to be an active participant in these conferences and hosted two of them in The Hague, in 1912 and 1913. The declared intention of the Hague conferences was to pursue via international diplomacy the progressive suppression of the abuse of opium, morphine, cocaine, and their derivatives along the lines initially sketched out in Shanghai. Dutch participation in these deliberations, however, was motivated by more than international humanitarianism. W. G. van Wettum, the Dutch representative to the 1912 convention, was an inspector

47. See Bureau of Insular Affairs, *Report of the Committee Appointed by the Philippine Commission to Investigate the Use of Opium and the Traffic Therein* (Washington, D.C., 1905), pp. 8–9, and 123–27, which contain the interview with Chief de Jongh. Quote from p. 39.

48. See VR February 1908 in V 28/9/1909/7; VR, VS December 1910 in V 19/9/1911/36.

49. John Palmer Gavit, *Opium* (London, 1925), p. 14; and *Report of the International Opium Commission, Shanghai, China*, pts. 1 and 2 (Shanghai, 1909). See also V 6/7/1908/8/1276.

50. Shanghai Memorandum.

with the Opium Regie; in conference deliberations he resisted the urgency of the humanitarians and reformers and attempted at every turn to protect Dutch commercial interests in the drug trade.[51] The apparent inconsistency between Holland's role as host of the Hague conferences and the actual position Holland took in the preparation of international accords reflected a similar anomaly in the policy and practice of the Opium Regie in Java.

Although the Opium Regie was much more amenable to supervision than the farms had been, a large discrepancy still existed between the regie of the statute books and the real regie. Nowhere was this more in evidence than in the patterns of opium distribution beyond the regie shop. In theory all individuals purchased their opium directly from the sales mantri and smoked it in a licensed den or in their own homes; in some cases individuals might legally purchase opium from the mantri on behalf of a neighbor or neighbors—the so-called *titipan* or *brandon* system. But under no circumstances was the resale of regie opium permitted. Despite this, a lively patungan trade existed beneath the regie, as it had beneath the farms. This trade consisted of the peddling of regie tubes (individuals could purchase up to 1 tahil daily, that is, 200 half-mata tubes), the repackaging of regie candu, and the use of regie candu to manufacture homemade tiké.[52] Villagers and travelers could find opium in food stalls and inns, and in 1907 regie inspectors revealed that the hawking of regie opium in the villages and "secret" opium dens was a general phenomenon. In Madiun, for example, the resident reported that opium hawkers could be found in nearly every village.[53] The regie chemist in Batavia confirmed the existence of an active subregie opium trade; of the samples of confiscated opium examined in the laboratory, more than two-thirds each month proved to be the regie product, or at least to contain it.

In other respects the regie sometimes resembled the farm system more than its designers had intended. Sales mantri received a salary that was independent of the quantity of their sales. Regie designers, Groeneveldt among them, felt that this was an essential aspect of the

---

51. Gavit, *Opium*, pp. 24, 255–66 (Appendix A).

52. And in at least one case morphine pills. VR, VS November 1910 in V 19/9/1911/36.

53. Resident Semarang to HIOR, June 29, 1907, no. 12695/49, and Resident Madiun to HIOR, July 11, 1907, no. 84/17, both in V 18/6/1908/1; and Circulaire HIOR, October 26, 1908, no. 3700/R in V 11/1/1911/30.

new system, so that sales mantri would have no personal stake in promoting opium smoking.[54] But because managing a regie shop created opportunities for auxiliary enterprises, many sales mantri did just that. Some of them promoted their goods outright by sponsoring gamelan concerts and by supplying patungan traders and illicit opium den holders. Others attracted a clientele by running local vice centers: selling awar-awar leaves and other opium accessories on the side, and running gaming rooms, bordellos, and pawnshops.[55] From the Ethical point of view these activities were embarrassing. The juxtaposition of regie shop and pawnhouse was especially undesirable because it implied that regie opium, like farm opium of old, was being sold on credit. Despite regie regulations to the contrary, as officials admitted in 1908, this was nearly universally the case.[56]

Aside from the incentives generated by their own enterprises, sales mantri appear to have felt that enlarging sales would enhance their reputations among the local Colonial Service, and not without cause. Some Dutch officials pressured regie personnel outright to sell more and blamed falling opium sales in their districts on the lax performance of local sales mantri. Even when the pressure was less direct, it is clear that in the regie's early years the government failed to convince its native opium officials that it earnestly desired to suppress opium consumption.

One reason for this was that no consensus yet existed among the rank and file of Dutch officials that such a goal was desirable. For the most part, attitudes about opium among members of the Colonial Service had undergone no basic change.[57] Opium smoking remained, in their view, a tolerable vice particularly suited to "eastern indolence" and was far preferable to native drunkenness.[58] One

54. This repaired, in Groeneveldt's view, a major flaw in not only the farm system but the French regie in Cochin China, in which retailers worked on a modified commission basis.

55. See VR October 1901 in V 26/3/1902/27; VR September 1908 in V 28/9/1909/7.

56. Circulaire HIOR, October 26, 1908, no. 3700/R in V 11/1/1911/30.

57. In fact, the findings of the Royal Commission appointed to study the opium problem in British India had confirmed the conventional wisdom of the colonial Dutch. See *Report of the Royal Commission on Opium* (London, 1895); and the comments of A. A. de Jongh to American interviewers in 1904, in *Report of the Philippine Commission*, p. 125.

58. Others feared the appeal of illicitly traded harder drugs such as morphine powders and pills, and European concoctions such as laudanum. See Advies van het lid van den Raad van Nederlandsch Indie, C. J. de Jaager, overgelegd by dat van den Raad, October 11, 1907, no. 16 in V 18/6/1908/1.

resident expressed concern that, denied opium, natives would turn not only to alcohol but to other non-revenue-producing stimulants such as tobacco or bottled soft drinks![59] In 1902 regie chief de Jongh declared the regie neutral regarding opium use. Whereas the regie did not encourage opium consumption, he said, its primary objective was not to suppress it but rather to correct the abuses of the farm system.[60] De Jongh pointed out that many features of the Opium Regie were designed to affect opium sales indirectly: high prices, strict policing, and removing the profit incentive from individual sellers. Once the regie was firmly established, he said, these and other features of the system would bring about a decline in consumption as a matter of course.

In fact, however, regie officials measured their success in terms of the regie's ability to match or surpass farm revenues. Reading the monthly reports of the new bureau leaves the unmistakable impression that the VOC spirit had survived the Ethical gale. When sales declined or failed to equal those of the preceding farm, officials went to great lengths to justify the falling revenues. When sales increased, reports became jubilant. It occurred to no one to apologize for the boom or to consider measures to reverse the trend.

Fortunately for those who may have been embarrassed to explain regie profit-consciousness in terms of Dutch greed, there was an Ethical rationale. If the regie sold less than the farm had done, the black market must be expanding. Any growth in regie sales, on the other hand, could be explained in terms of bringing a once clandestinely fed market into the orbit of the Opium Regie. All of this was good, and Ethical, because it helped snuff out the illegal trade in cheap—and, as the Dutch hastened to insist, inferior—opium. Only when the regie commanded the market could the vice-tax principles on which it and the farm were based have any effect. Only then would the high cost of regie opium become an effective deterrent to opium smoking.

The regie approach to the Forbidden Areas is enlightening in this respect. The Forbidden Areas had been a hallowed part of the opium farm system to which the Dutch had pointed for years as evidence of their good intentions vis-à-vis opium. Much to the consternation of those who viewed the Opium Regie as an Ethical vehicle for the gradual elimination of opium smoking, regie officials

59. Resident Makasar to HIOR, July 19, 1907, no. 95/R in V 18/6/1908/1.
60. HIOR to DF, April 2, 1902, no. 923/A in Exh 19/6/1902/40.

dismantled several of Java's Forbidden Areas. In their view, the Opium Regie made Forbidden Areas anachronistic. Since the regie did not promote opium, but only supplied the natural market where it already existed, no one need fear that the presence of its opium shops would encourage new smokers. Furthermore, for those few individuals who "required" opium but who by chance resided in a Forbidden Area, the opium ban was an unjust imposition on their individual liberty. Finally, most of these opium-free districts were really nothing of the kind; nearly all hosted a thriving black market that police measures had never satisfactorily suppressed, which was true. Why then shouldn't the state enjoy the profits flowing hitherto to opium smugglers and black marketeers?[61]

The most hallowed Forbidden Area was the Priangan, officially closed since 1824. Opium held no charms for the Sundanese, the Priangan indigenes; but by the late nineteenth century the Priangan also hosted thousands of Chinese and large garrisons of Javanese soldiers and their families. The demand for opium among these groups had for years supported a thriving clandestine trade, fed for the most part by the Ceribon opium farm.[62] Administrative and police measures designed to squelch the trade had been of little avail. In 1900 Priangan resident C. W. Kist estimated that there were at least 3,000 Chinese opium smokers in the region, including 350 addicts, and a smaller but still substantial number of opium-smoking Javanese. He argued that short of physically removing the Chinese and Javanese there was no inhibiting the inward flow of opium. The ban, he went on, was particularly vexatious for the Javanese, who had been stationed there arbitrarily and who suffered legal jeopardy should they try to pursue opium habits learned earlier in farm or regie districts. Far better for the Opium Regie to acknowledge and meet the existing demand.[63] Batavia agreed, and in 1902 opium—regie opium—became legal in the Priangan, as it did in other smaller Forbidden Areas as well.[64] By 1904, the first

61. Regie chief E. F. Jochim summarized these arguments in HIOR to DF, August 24, 1907, no. 2794/R in V 18/6/1908/1.

62. Many observers, such as Scheltema ("The Opium Trade," p. 109), dated the Priangan black market to 1886, when the Ceribon opium farmer won the government coffee transport contract in the region, the first Chinese to do so.

63. Resident Preanger-Regentschappen to GG, April 23, 1900, no. 4213/28 in V 23/1/1904/21.

64. SvNI 1902, no. 266. Officially, regie opium was legally available to Chinese and to native soldiers. Some Forbidden Areas remained, however, and the Dutch made much of them in describing the regie to outsiders. See Shanghai Memorandum, p. 1. KVvNI 1906. Appendix DD, III, note a, contains a list of Forbidden Areas as of that year.

year in which all Java was serviced by the Opium Regie, opium was legally available in more places than it had ever been under the opium farms.

What is more, business was booming. In that year Java recovered from a slump in native agriculture which had prevailed in many parts of the island in 1902 and 1903. With 1904 came steadily rising opium sales in most residencies, peaking at the summer harvest, and this trend continued into the following year. In 1905 Opium Regie sales in almost all residencies equaled or surpassed those of the immediately preceding opium farms; in that year income from the regie topped f20 million and accounted for 15.87 percent of all colonial revenues.[65] The Opium Regie appeared to be the true heir of the farm.

This was precisely what bothered its critics. Many of the abuses of the farm system seemed miraculously to have been resurrected in new garb under the regie. Only now the state took its profits directly rather than through its Chinese collaborators. These perceptions prompted a new outcry against Holland's opium policy. Once again humanitarian critics quoted *Baboe Dalima* on the floor of Parliament, and reform-minded publicists in the tradition of Pieter Brooshooft took up the cause.

Representative of these was J. F. Scheltema, an Indies journalist since the 1880s and former editor of *De Locomotief*. Scheltema launched his attack on the Opium Regie in September 1902 in the *Bataviaasch Nieuwsblad*. His articles were inspired by the recent decision to open the Priangan and Bantam to Opium Regie stores. They contained a stinging indictment of the government for its "two-faced" policy: in violating the Forbidden Areas, especially the Priangan, the government was both "hypocritical" and "immoral." The article so rankled Governor General Willem Rooseboom that he indicted Scheltema for "inciting hate and contempt against the government." The Council of Justice in Batavia sentenced him to detention for three months.[66] But Scheltema took up the attack again a few years later when, as a visiting scholar at Yale University, he wrote a two-part article for the *American Journal of Sociology*. Address-

65. "Graphisch Overzicht van den loop van het dagdebiet van opium gedurende de jaren 1902 tot en met 1905," in KVvNI 1906, Appendix DD; and Shanghai Memorandum, p. 315. The 1905 figure is f20.25 million.
66. The sentence was dropped to one month by the supreme court. See J. F. Scheltema, *De Opiumpolitiek der regeering en de vrijheid der drukpers in Nederlandsch Indie* (The Hague, 1903), which includes the offending articles, the case, appeals, and verdicts.

ing himself to the United States as a new colonial power, he painted Holland's opium policy in the Indies as a "shameful instance" of "the West encroaching upon the East." The Opium Regie, he lamented, had, like all good intentions and humanitarian impulses in the Indies, succumbed to the pressure for profit. "The few who conscientiously, in action as in words, wanted to make this opium service a clean service, a working base for the final abolishment of the opium habit, have striven in vain."[67]

In Parliament others echoed Scheltema's indictment. In the deliberations over the colonial budget in late 1906, for example, several members spoke out against government profiteering in opium and attacked the opium habit in the harshest terms. Said one member in a speech before the lower house which displayed the condescension and broad hopes that informed the Ethical spirit: "Our Indies peoples belong to the East. Wonderful things are happening in the East nowadays. These people are experiencing a regeneration. They are rising from a century-long death sleep and reviving themselves." Holland must not contribute to stifling that regeneration by providing a body- and soul-deadening drug that was synonymous with the decay of the past.[68]

Such indictments of the regie rankled regie officials and other defenders of the status quo who, like Indies councilman C. J. de Jaager, found the objecting members of Parliament woefully ill informed about Indies affairs. The oft-cited *Baboe Dalima*, said de Jaager, was an "untruthful" book, no better than the "pornographic booklets" containing "so-called revelations of secret goings-on in the cloister."[69] Regie chief E. F. Jochim, who was called on to respond to the outcry in Parliament, thought no better of his critics. Members of Parliament, he wrote, knew little of opium—having edified themselves on the subject by reading De Quincey, Perelaer, and missionary Zegers. They knew even less of the regie. It was not surprising,

67. Scheltema, "The Opium Trade," pp. 250, 248. Scheltema's writing particularly irritated the Dutch when it began circulating internationally; it was published in Japan, for instance, and most European countries, even penetrating, as one horrified observer discovered, "deep into the Italian press." O. van Beresteyn to MvK, October 14, 1907, in V 12/12/1907/Z24. See Note: Department van Kolonien, "Bestryding preventief en repressief van onjuiste oordeelvellingen in de buitenlandse pers over Nederland en zyne kolonien"; and "Verslag der werkzaamheden van het Perskantor van het Algemeen Nederlandsch Verbond," October 10, 1907 (Zeer Vertrouwelyk), both in VKG 12/12/1907/Z24.
68. Extract: Voorlooping verslag, IIᵉ kamer. Begrooting 1907.
69. Advies van het lid van den RvNI, October 11, 1907, no. 16 in V 18/6/1908/1.

he added, that the recommendations they made were either totally unrealistic (a complete ban) or a repetition of the old failed remedies of farm days.[70]

Jochim agreed with the majority of his Colonial Service colleagues that the evils of opium smoking were greatly exaggerated; and he took great pride in the first-rate candu manufactured in the regie's modern factory. He vigorously opposed any policy that attempted artificially to separate opium from its natural market among the Indies population or to deny that market its full requirements. Such attempts would be inordinately troublesome to enforce, and expensive to boot; not only would Holland lose the millions it now collected from opium revenues, it would also be forced to pay out vast sums to squelch the smuggling that would be the inevitable consequence of such a policy. But Jochim was not without his Ethical impulses. He viewed the Opium Regie as part of a broad Dutch-initiated process of intellectual and economic development in which Indonesians, freed from the tyranny of subsistence agriculture and exposed to positive Western ideas, would gradually come to view opium smoking as "mistaken."[71]

Although it was not novel at the time, the role that education might play in changing social mores was now mentioned far more frequently than before. In response to a referendum in 1907, several residents—when asked to comment on ways the state might suppress the opium habit—replied that the only effective measure was to bring Indonesians, by education and example, to a higher stage of moral and intellectual development in which they themselves would spurn opium as undesirable. Enlightenment would succeed where coercion and regulation had failed.[72]

Within the Colonial Service this was a popular view. It was basically an Ethical variation on the older laissez-faire attitude that prevailed under the farm. But some members of the Colonial Service were not content to rely so passively on the outcome of what all agreed would be a prolonged process. One measure they frequently put forward was the registration of opium smokers; this would

70. HIOR to DF, August 24, 1907, no. 2794/R in V 18/6/1908/1.
71. Ibid.; Circulaire HIOR, October 26, 1908, no. 3700/R in V 11/1/1911/30.
72. GG to Residents, October 18, 1907, no. 2863a in V 18/6/1908/1. This circular, prepared at the request of the Indies Council, asked residents to comment on: (a) the extent of the opium habit in their residencies; and (b) the possibility and desirability of combating it. See also HIOR to DF, August 24, 1907, no. 2794/R in V 18/6/1908/1.

permit the regie to deny opium to the young. But Chief Inspector Jochim was pessimistic about this measure. The elementary state of regie organization and bookkeeping, especially in local shops, he observed, was not adequate for a workable system of registration. Attempting such a program would lead inevitably to abuses. Relenting to pressure from Holland, however, Jochim finally submitted a draft proposal for a simple registration program in 1909, which was only very gradually adopted in years to come.[73]

Another measure frequently proposed was finding an effective antidote to opium. Several such antidotes were circulating in Asia during the decade, and conscientious humanitarians urged the state to test remedies and, if found effective, distribute them to opium smokers at state expense. Regie chemists did devote some attention to examining opium cures. Most antiopium products then on the market, they discovered, were in fact morphine preparations. The most popular were the so-called antiopium pills, mostly of Chinese manufacture, which began flooding central Java at mid-decade. These were swiftly declared contraband, along with all other non-regie products.[74] Other preparations, indigenous surrogates and European pharmaceutical compounds designed to relieve the symptoms of withdrawal were all examined and found wanting.[75] None was judged sufficiently effective to warrant government expense in manufacturing and distributing it.[76] Dutch initiatives to treat opium addiction as a curable disease lay two decades in the future.

Meanwhile profits streamed in. (Visiting Buleleng, Bali, H. H. van Kol, a member of Holland's upper house of Parliament, discovered that in 1910 the Opium Regie there yielded f240,000 to the state— 137 percent more than the opium farm had done ten years before.[77]

---

73. Circulaire HIOR, October 26, 1908, no. 3700/R; and Circulaire HIOR, March 1, 1909, no. 700/R, both in V 11/1/1911/30.

74. VR March and November 1906 in V 5/4/1907/19; and VR November 1910 in V 19/9/1911/36.

75. Primarily *combretum sundaicum*, known by the Chinese as *tiong hing soe*. Resident Pekalongan to HIOR, June 21, 1907, no. 5281/41 and Director van Landbouw (Agriculture) to Assistant Resident Central Celebes, August 26, 1907, no. 4494, both in V 18/6/1908/1.

76. Assistant Resident Central Celebes to Resident Menado, August 26, 1907, no. 4494 in V 18/6/1908/1. Assistant Resident A.J.N. Engelberg personally wrote Dr. F. G. van Marle, who was reputed to have had good results with an antiopium medicine in Yogyakarta and referred his formula to the regie. See also Resident Pekalongan to HIOR, June 21, 1907, no. 5281/41 in V 18/6/1908/1.

77. H. H. van Kol, *Driemaal dwars door Sumatra en zwerfttochten door Bali* (Rotterdam, 1914), p. 420.

The regie's best year, 1914, lay just ahead.)[78] Studying the regie monthly reports for 1910, an anonymous official in The Hague expressed his frustration with all this in a note he penciled at the top of one page. It read: "Reading this report makes one despair for the working of the Regie—there is no indication whatsoever that any-one strives to reduce the use of opium."[79]

78. See *Verslag Opiumfabriek*, 1914, and graphs in succeeding yearly reports. Opium sales and revenues soared even higher in the early 1920s. See Verslag betreffende de Opium- en Zoutregie en de Zoutwinning over het jaar 1938, Bijlage 1.

79. Atop VR, VS December 1910 in V 19/9/1911/36.

12

Epilogue:
Waning Kings and Customs

The Ethical years brought revolutionary changes for Java's Chinese community. Because the opium farm had played such an important role in structuring the Chinese economy and social order, its loss was traumatic—all the more so coming in the wake of catastrophic financial losses among the community's patrons. But the changes now facing the Chinese were more comprehensive than this. Coming of age as the century turned, the new generation of peranakans had to fend for themselves amid a rapidly changing social and political milieu, one in which modernity had many faces and in which being Chinese became both more important and more complicated. The anti-Chinese sentiment that surfaced as part of the movement against opium farms now swelled among Dutch and Javanese alike. And this in turn was inevitably exacerbated by the assertive responses many Chinese made to their altered circumstances.[1]

The demise of the farms meant not only that the Chinese were kept from the legal opium trade and its vast profits but also that the former opium-farm Chinese lost their organizations as a force in the countryside and, as a result, their controlled access to Java's rural markets. This was especially so because the Dutch now tightened up

1. See "Geen Rassenhaat," *IG*, 18, 1 (1886), 768; and the anti-Chinese statements of the director of the Colonial Service two decades later in Overzicht van de beschouwingen welke ten grondslag liggen aan de voorstellen van den Hoofdinspecteur De Jongh en den DBB, in VKG 15/10/1909/R20.

the pass (1897) and residential (1900) regulations from which opium farmers' men had been routinely deferred. Now all Chinese traders needed a special travel pass for the simplest trip, and violators of the zoning rules were subject to fines and forced resettlement in officially designated Chinese neighborhoods.[2] As the regie gradually replaced the opium farm throughout Java, Batavia prevailed on local officials to impose these rules strictly. Indeed, regie profits were thought to depend on it.[3]

One tangible consequence of the rigidity with which travel and residency rules were applied was a wave of failures among Chinese businesses that depended on rural markets. Stricter rules meant that Chinese traders sold fewer goods; they also interfered with the collection of outstanding debts from village clients, debts that were customarily settled in rice or other agricultural commodities. As a result, in the immediate postfarm period, many Chinese petty traders defaulted with their wholesale patrons; and they, in turn, defaulted with European import-export houses from whom they had received advances. A Surabaya newspaper reported that bankruptcies among Chinese middlemen in the wake of the establishment of the Opium Regie in Madura, Pasuruan, and Besuki had cost European companies in Surabaya nearly f14 million in 1896.[4]

These bankruptcies reflected the breakdown of the Chinese commercial networks that had been so closely affiliated with the opium farms. Other changes simultaneous to the disbanding of the farms also hastened this deterioration. Chief among them was the rapid growth of the Chinese community in Java. It had increased by approximately eighty-seven thousand people between the early 1870s and 1900.[5] This population increase was made up in part by an influx of new immigrants in numbers far greater than had come to Java at any time in the past. Moreover, most of these immigrants were of Hakka and Cantonese origin, not Hokkiens like most earlier arrivals. As we have seen, singkehs like these traditionally found

2. Lea Williams, *Overseas Chinese Nationalism: The Genesis of the Pan-Chinese Movement in Indonesia, 1900–1916* (Glencoe, Ill., 1960), pp. 28–29, 32; P. H. Fromberg, "De Chineesche Beweging op Java" (1911) in *Verspreide Geschriften*, p. 427.

3. See the comments of the residents of Madiun and Semarang in HIOR to GG, September 18, 1903, no. 2554/R in V 13/1/1904/34.

4. Fromberg, "De Chineesche Beweging en het *Koloniaal Tijdschrift*," in his *Verspreide Geschriften*, pp. 475–90; the Madura, Pasuruan, and Besuki opium farms were closed in 1894 (Madura) and 1895. SvNI 1894, nos. 161–63; and SvNI 1895, nos. 241–43.

5. From 190,603 in 1873 to 277,265 in 1900. KVvNI 1902. Bijlage A.

patrons in the nether levels of the peranakan networks and worked their way to material sufficiency as part of them. But the economic crisis of the 1880s had strained these constellations severely. They did not survive the loss of the opium farm and its monopolistic structure. As a result, newcomers now had to shift for themselves. Since the old economic incentives for assimilating to peranakan culture were now missing, they rejected peranakan ways and leaders and formed a new, separate community of unassimilated (*totok*) Chinese.[6]

As need-driven totoks competed fiercely with one another, and with peranakan, Arab, and Javanese merchants, their aggressive practices and alien presence set off new fears about "the Chinese." This in turn prompted one of the first acts of modern organized self-assertion among the Javanese. In 1909 Tirtoadisurjo founded *Sarekat Dagang Islam* precisely to help indigenous traders ward off Chinese competition. And as the new organization blossomed into a popular mass movement called Sarekat Islam, sinophobia took root alongside other powerful feelings in the germination of modern Indonesian nationalism.[7]

The Chinese Officer System was another casualty of the passing of the opium farms. Though the institution itself survived until 1931, it was sapped of its vitality when the opium farm was abolished. This was because Chinese officers were no longer economically important to the colony. Having decided to harvest the profits of opium directly, the colonial state no longer had a stake in the integrity of the peranakan patronage constellations. And without these patronage constellations, Chinese officers were no longer effective brokers on behalf of their own community. What is more, to the growing totok group peranakan officers were unsuitable leaders because, as Malay-speaking mixed-bloods, they were not authentically Chinese.

Nevertheless, something of the old days lingered. In many areas, senior Chinese officers remained figures of honor among the peranakans and continued to play out the role of patriarch and patron. Their deaths were marked by extravagant public rites, as Liem

6. G. William Skinner, "The Chinese of Java," p. 3; G. William Skinner, "The Chinese Minority," in *Indonesia*, ed. Ruth T. McVey, 105 (New Haven, Conn., 1963).

7. Ricklefs, *History of Modern Indonesia*, pp. 158–59. Anti-Chinese violence involving Sarekat Islam branches erupted in 1913 and 1914.

Thian Joe records of Major Be Biauw Tjoan's passing in 1904.[8] A few, like Oei Tiong Ham of Semarang, carried on in the grand style well through the 1910s. But for the most part, the officers came to play an increasingly administrative role. Instead of being kings among their own, they became factotums in the Dutch administration. Enticed to serve by special privileges and obliged to don European-style military uniforms as their official garb, little by little they became, as one observer sensitive to the changing colonial order predicted, "superfluous pieces of furniture."[9]

The loss of the opium farms, the deterioration of the farm-based patronage constellations, and the subsequent weakening of the Chinese Officer System occurred in tandem with—and to a degree precipitated—new shifts in the cultural and political orientation of the Chinese of Java. Ever sensitive to the winds of opportunity, some peranakan families of means had begun, in the 1880s, to educate their sons (and a few of their daughters) in Dutch. Children of Chinese officers were permitted to attend the schools set up for Europeans. Others learned Malay and Dutch, as well as physics, arithmetic, writing, and drawing at missionary schools and from private tutors.[10] Doing so was not merely practical. Even young people schooled only in Malay or who attended old-style Hokkien-dialect schools could not wholly escape the seductive pulls of Westernization, which was then becoming synonymous with modernity and power. (Sometime around 1900 the first crude moving pictures were shown on the Semarang alun-alun.)[11] Chinese youths in the cities evidently defied the statutes to don Western dress and yearned to be rid of their braids and other signs of backwardness.[12] These early tugs of Western-driven modernity coincided and in some ways clashed with other cultural forces that pulled the Javan Chinese in a wholly different direction—toward China itself.

As Phoa Keng Hek, the Dutch-educated son of a Chinese officer,

8. Liem, *Riwajat*, p. 179. See also Go Gin Ho's commemoration of Tan Tjin Kie's spectacular funeral, *Peringatan dari Wafatnja Majoor Tan Tjin Kie* (Batavia, 1919). Tan was the Chinese major of Ceribon.

9. Williams, *Overseas Chinese Nationalism*, pp. 126–28. Quote from Henri Borel, *De Chineezen in Nederlandsch-Indie* (Amsterdam, 1900), p. 33.

10. Lombard-Salmon, *Literature in Malay*, p. 18; Leo Suryadinata, *The Chinese Minority in Indonesia* (Singapore, 1978), p. 5.

11. Liem, *Riwajat*, p. 168.

12. Hoven, *In Sarong en kabaai*, p. 93.

wrote "to all Chinese" in 1900, "A large number of Chinese here do not know the wonderful teaching of Confucius."[13] In that year Phoa and twenty other peranakans joined to form the Tiong Hoa Hwe Koan (Chung-hua hui-kuan), or THHK, the first modern Chinese organization in Java. Phoa and his colleagues were part of a cultural revival among Southeast Asian Chinese which had emerged, in Java, in the 1880s. In that decade Chinese novels translated into Malay suddenly became popular, and local publishers began issuing them in volume. Alongside books such as *The Romance of the Three Kingdoms* and *The Green Peony* came moralizing works (*A Hundred Years of Filial Piety*) and Malay translations of Confucian classics. The latter proliferated from the 1890s on and were especially popular among peranakans.[14] News of K'ang Yu-wei's (Kang Youwei) failed attempts to reform "the weakness and rottenness of China"—in the words of Kwee Tek Hoay, local historian of the THHK—quickened local interest as well, and in 1903 K'ang himself visited Java.[15] In the ensuing years the Chinese thrilled to Japan's victory in the Russo-Japanese War (1904–5), and to the arrival of Chinese naval cruisers in 1907. Liem Thian Joe remarks that these were the first such vessels to visit Java in some 260 years. "Almost every one of the Chinese felt proud," he wrote.[16] In the same year, Chinese in Batavia set up a branch of Sun Yat-sen's revolutionary United League (Tung-meng hui).[17]

This swelling attention to the Chinese heritage as well as to contemporary affairs in their country of origin was important for the Javan Chinese in two ways. First, it provided them a new and positive cultural identity in the midst of racial hostility and social confusion in the colony. Second, it bore with it new patterns of leadership more suitable to Java's increasingly heterogeneous Chinese community and to the adversarial relationship it now assumed vis-à-vis the colonial government.

The THHK was originally established as a society for the promotion of Confucian thought and conduct and, implicit in this, for the reform of peranakan practices and behavior. It sought to do this by

13. Phoa is excerpted in Leo Suryadinata, *Political Thinking of the Indonesian Chinese, 1900–1977: A Sourcebook* (Singapore, 1979), p. 5. Phoa wrote in Malay.
14. Lombard-Salmon, *Literature in Malay*, pp. 22, 24, 30.
15. Kwee Tek Hoay, *The Origins of the Modern Chinese Movement in Indonesia*, trans. Lea Williams (Ithaca, 1969), p. 2; Liem, *Riwajat*, p. 174.
16. Liem, *Riwajat*, p. 191; Kwee, *Origins of the Modern Chinese Movement*, p. 19.
17. Lombard-Salmon, *Literature in Malay*, p. 33.

promoting new-style elementary schools teaching Mandarin. As Kwee records, its schools soon "spread like a tide over all Indonesia."[18] By 1908 there were fifty-four THHK schools, as well as official "inspectors" from China to supervise them. (One of the first of these, a man known as Lauw Soe Kie in Java, took up his inspection tour benobled with the rank of admiral in the Chinese navy.)[19] The THHK evolved into an important social and political organization with branches throughout Java, serving as an institutional forum for addressing Chinese grievances and agitating successfully with the Dutch for reforms. Their efforts resulted in the establishment of state-sponsored Dutch-Chinese schools modeled after the colonial schools for European children. The first was opened in 1908; by 1914 there were twenty-seven of them.[20] At mid-decade (1906–7) Java's Chinese merchants, building on models prevalent in Singapore, Hong Kong, and Shanghai—and at the urging of the Chinese government—began founding Chambers of Commerce as well. The new Chambers performed various intermediary functions among Chinese individuals and groups on the one hand, and between them and the colonial government on the other—just as the Chinese officers had once done. They also served as agencies of the government of China. Until 1912, for example, the Chinese Chambers of Commerce in Java functioned as unofficial Chinese consulates.[21]

The leadership of local THHK branches was primarily in peranakan hands, and leading peranakan families such as the Bes, Tans, Oeis, and Liems were prominently represented on its all-Java coordinating board, set up in 1910.[22] Peranakans dominated the leadership of the Chambers of Commerce too, though in these organizations totoks often played an equally important and sometimes a dominating role. While some Chinese officers backed and participated in these organizations, leadership positions were for the most part filled by a new post-opium-farm generation of Javan Chinese. Working among the more heterogeneous Chinese community of the twentieth century, they exercised influence of a far

18. Kwee, *Origins of the Modern Chinese Movement*, p. 62.
19. Ibid., p. 20; Liem, *Riwajat*, p. 191; Suryadinata, *Chinese Minority*, pp. 7–8.
20. Liem, *Riwajat*, p. 222; Suryadinata, *Chinese Minority*, p. 8.
21. See Williams, *Overseas Chinese Nationalism*, chap. 3; and Kwee, *Origins of the Modern Chinese Movement*.
22. Liem, *Riwajat*, p. 198.

more circumscribed nature than had leaders of their fathers' and grandfathers' time. Moreover, in their efforts to reform Dutch-Chinese policy, they stood in an adversarial rather than a collaborationist relationship with the Dutch.[23] By 1910 they had not only succeeded in the school issue but had also won a liberalization of the repressive pass system. In 1919 the Dutch abolished the residential zoning system as well.[24]

The Cabang Atas never recovered its dominant economic position. Some of the peranakan elite, like the once powerful financier of the Kediri kongsi, Tan Boen In, died in poverty and disgrace.[25] Generally, however, they remained well-off families of prominence and good name. Their sons, Dutch-educated when possible, moved increasingly into white-collar occupations and Western professions; their daughters contracted good marriages.[26] Many of them carried on family businesses with varying degrees of success and, more shrewdly than they could possibly have known, invested in urban real estate. But few amassed fortunes of the old kind. One who did, however, was Oei Tiong Ham.[27] Oei was the last of Java's nineteenth-century Chinese "kings" and among the first of Java's twentieth-century corporate businessmen and modern community leaders. He was an opium farmer and Chinese officer who also became a strong supporter of the new Chinese organizations.

Oei Tiong Ham's Fukien-born father, Oei Tjie Sien, arrived in Semarang in 1858 at the age of twenty-three, having fled China for Java during the Taiping rebellion. He married into a locally established family and with exceptional enterprise followed the traditional path to economic success as part of the peranakan-dominated

23. Williams, *Overseas Chinese Nationalism*, pp. 105, 133–34.

24. Fromberg, "De Chineesche Beweging," p. 427; SvNI 1919, no. 50.

25. Tan died, impoverished, in 1897 following his release from prison. KVvNI 1897, p. 179; 1898, Bijlage HH.

26. Suryadinata, *Chinese Minority*, p. 9, says that peranakan children went to THHK schools only when they failed to qualify for Dutch-medium schools.

27. The account of Oei Tiong Ham's life which follows was compiled from the following sources: Liem, *Riwajat*, pp. 122, 151, 153, 154, 182, 187, 218, 232; Williams, *Overseas Chinese Nationalism*, pp. 102–3; Michael Richard Godley, *The Mandarin-Capitalists from Nanyang: Overseas Chinese Enterprise in the Modernization of China, 1893–1911* (Cambridge, 1981), pp. 18–19; RAvNI, 1886–1908; *The Oei Tiong Ham Concern: A Short Survey of Its Development and Progress* (Semarang[?], 1934), unpaged; Madame Wellington Koo [Oei Hui-lan], *No Feast Lasts Forever* (New York, 1975), chaps. 2–4; Tjoa Soe Tjong, "O.T.H.C. [Oei Tiong Ham Concern]—100 jaar: Een stukje economische geschiedenis van Indonesia," *Economisch-statistische Berichten*, 1, 2394 (June 26, 1963), and 2, 2396 (July 17, 1963); and Liem Tjwan Ling, *Raja Gula: Oei Tiong Ham*.

economy. In 1863 Oei Tjie Sien founded a small business in Semarang buying and selling colonial produce and specializing in
sugar. He named it the Kian Gwan kongsi. Oei expanded his enterprises during the economic boom following the Agrarian Law of
1870. By the mid-1880s he was well positioned to take advantage of
the economic crisis that was then ruining Java's opium farmers. In
1886 his son Oei Tiong Ham, about twenty years old at the time, was
named Chinese lieutenant of Semarang, a sure sign that the Oei
family had arrived. The Oeis moved into opium farming in 1890–
91 at a time when many former farmers were declaring bankruptcy.
They acquired opium farms in Semarang, Surakarta, Yogyakarta,
and Surabaya.

Oei Tjie Sien was a frugal man and a traditionalist who followed
the old ways of Amoy as he remembered them. He insisted on a
Chinese education for his sons, and Oei Tiong Ham was therefore
sent to an old-style (pre-THHK) Chinese school. But he also provided him lessons in Malay, the peranakan lingua franca. During
Oei Tiong Ham's entire lifetime he evidently communicated in
Hokkien dialect and Malay, using interpreters when necessary. He
never learned Dutch. But unlike his father, the younger Oei was
inclined to Western ways in other respects. He is still remembered as
the first Javan Chinese successfully to petition Batavia, in 1889, to
wear coat, tie, and trousers in public. When his father died in 1900,
he promptly cut off his Manchu braid, an example he encouraged
his employees to follow. Having taken over the family enterprises in
1893, Oei Tiong Ham proceeded to dominate the central and east
Java opium market until the final dismantling of the farms themselves.

The opium farms, however, were only a part of Oei's growing
commercial empire. In 1893 Oei incorporated the Kian Gwan
kongsi to form the Handel Maatschappij Kian Gwan. Having cor-
nered the Java sugar market and the central Java opium market,
he expanded his company apparatus by establishing branches
throughout Java. The Kian Gwan soon traded in virtually every
important export crop of the Indies. Next Oei added shipping
facilities to his empire by gaining a controlling interest in both the
Semarang Steamship Navigation Company and the Heap Eng Moh
Steamship Company (known as the "Red Funnel" line) of Singapore, a city that became his secondary base of operations.

Kian Gwan became a true capitalist conglomerate integrating

plantations, mills, shipping lines, and banks with complementary enterprises. (Kian Gwan manufactured gunny sacks and fertilizer for the company plantations, for instance.)[28] This differed dramatically from earlier opium-farm-based commercial empires, just as it also differed from the majority of the more traditionally conceived Chinese companies of the early twentieth century.[29] Oei's true competitors were not his fellow Chinese merchants, but large European trading firms with branches in Semarang, such firms as the Nederlandsche Handelmaatschappij and the Internationale en Handelsvereeniging Rotterdam. Although Oei insisted that ownership of his company remain with the family, otherwise he broke with tradition. He groomed his sons carefully, selecting only a few for important responsibilities and eventually disinheriting all but nine of them. (This involved moving to Singapore in 1921, since the laws of the Netherlands Indies forbade disinheriting sons. Altogether Oei had thirteen sons, as well as thirteen daughters.) More important, he employed many nonfamily members in key positions, including great numbers of European managers and engineers. Abandoning Chinese bookkeeping practices as well, he hired teams of Western-trained accountants and placed a Dutch accountant over them.[30]

By the first decade of the twentieth century Oei was a figure in world trade. He had agents in London and throughout Asia, and carefully cultivated useful connections everywhere. He was particularly instrumental in establishing commercial ties between the Indies and Japan and claimed an acquaintance with the Meiji leader Hirobumi Ito. The Dutch consul in Kobe Japan informed Batavia—for Oei was important enough to spy on—that he was received with honors by the Chinese who traded in Japan, all of whom were under his influence and supported by his capital.[31] He thought of himself

28. See Tjoa, "O.T.H.C.," 1:606.

29. Hendrick Sneevliet, the Dutch socialist later known as the Comintern agent "Maring" in China, and for several years a resident of Semarang, deplored the mentality of the Chinese there, who, he said, failed to adopt modern business practices. His comments are excerpted in Liem, *Riwajat*, p. 228, from a report Sneevliet wrote on the occasion of the Koloniale Tentoonstelling of 1914. See also Lea Williams's article discussing the failure of most Indonesian Chinese businesses in passing from a limited kongsi structure to a more expansive capitalist one: "Chinese Entrepreneurs in Indonesia," *Explorations in Entrepreneurial History*, 5, 1 (October 15, 1952), pp. 34–60. For a specific discussion of kongsis and corporations, see pp. 51–53.

30. See Tjoa, "O.T.H.C.," 2:607, 1:606.

31. See Extract uit een particuliere nota den Consul der Nederlanden te Kobe betreffende verschillende onderwerpen (no date) in VKG 30/4/1907/H9; and the documents in VKG 30/7/1907/Z14.

as an internationalist. For his children in Semarang Oei provided
not a Dutch but an English tutor, a Miss Jones from Australia.[32] And
although all his eight wives (or concubines) were Javan Chinese—
including daughters of such Cabang Atas families as the Tans and
the Hos—he married one of his daughters to a U.S. consular official,
Caulfield Stokes, another to the U.S.-educated Chinese diplomat
Wellington (Vi Kyuin) Koo.[33]

Despite his international orientation and travels, Semarang remained Oei's base of operations. He had a grand villa there, located
in the European quarter, with extensive gardens and a zoo. Here he
entertained guests lavishly, including King Chulalongkorn of Thailand, all of whose consorts were accommodated comfortably. This,
at least, according to Oei's daughter, who also recalls that at her
father's house "after dinner the guests would be offered opium
pipes, as casually as cigars."[34]

Oei supported the emerging pan-Chinese organizations of the
new Indies, contributing generously to the THHK schools, including a Chinese-English middle school for THHK graduates. And he
was the primary backer of the Semarang Chinese Chamber of Commerce. His support for these organizations was not particularly
ideological, however. Rather, it seems to comport with the role he
played as a man of means and influence in the local Chinese community. It was also good for business. But Oei carefully avoided an
adversarial role vis-à-vis the Dutch. Indeed, he did his best to curry
favor with officials. As opium farmers and Chinese officers had
done before, he presented them with gifts and entertained them. He
was the consummate good citizen. At the ascension of Queen Wilhelmina in 1898, it was the Oeis—Oei Tiong Ham's brother and
partner actually, Captain Oei Tiong Bhing—who organized the
parade in Semarang. And when Dutch officials made preparations
to establish the Opium Regie in his farm territories, Oei smoothed
the way by permitting regie employees to study his farm operations
beforehand.[35] Later he cooperated scrupulously when police sus-

32. Koo, *No Feast Lasts*, p. 62.
33. Godley, *Mandarin Capitalists*, p. 49; Madame Wellington Koo (Oei Hui-lan) is
his second daughter by his first wife, Goei Bing Nio. See Koo, *No Feast Lasts*, p. 54 and
chap. 10.
34. Koo, *No Feast Lasts*, pp. 42–43. E. Stark, an artist who visited Java and was
entertained by Oei, wrote that Oei had changed his estimation of his "yellow
brothers." Stark described Oei's Semarang villa as "enchanting." E. Stark, *Uit Indie,
Egypte en Het Heilige Land* (Amersfoort, 1913), p. 30.
35. VR September 1897 in V 26/3/1902/12. Oei also agreed not to dump his
surplus opium on the market at the end of his term.

pected Kian Gwan ships of carrying smuggled opium.[36] Oei also provided the land for the Colonial Exhibition (Koloniale Tentoonstelling) of 1914 in commemoration of the liberation of the Netherlands, along with a loan of f200,000.

Oei Tiong Ham was Chinese captain of Semarang until 1902, when he stepped down because of the demands of his business. His brother became the official major the following year. In 1908, however, the Dutch named Oei Tiong Ham honorary major. So identified with the position was he, however, and so prominent, that in Semarang and beyond he was known simply as "Major" even before he was officially appointed.[37] Oei died in Singapore in 1924. His body was returned to Semarang. Liem Thian Joe, who probably attended the funeral rites, tells us that Oei's mourners wore European-style white suits and hats.[38]

Oei Tiong Ham's self-conscious modernity was mirrored everywhere among Java's peranakans. By 1910 they already preferred Western clothing for weddings, and Liem commented later, nostalgically, that all the old customs died "after THHK raised its banner."[39] Replacing them in many cases were new ways adapted not from China but from the Dutch. Young peranakans of means now joined sports clubs to play soccer and learned to comport themselves in a style appropriate to the Western professionals they emulated. (Few at the time could gain the international experience of Oei Tiong Ham, but his transnational perspective, as well as the dispersal of his family around the world, prefigured a later trend among descendants of the Cabang Atas.)

The new winds from the West and from China brought new attitudes about opium as well. For self-Westernizers, opium played no part in the preferred, modern life-style. For most of Java's Chinese, however, including totoks, a more important force for change came from reformists in China, for whom opium symbolized the national "weakness and rottenness." Ong Hong Siong, for example, was sent by the government of China to inspect the THHK schools in 1907; he and other emissaries urged civic-minded Chinese in Java

36. VR, VS May 1908 in V 28/9/1909/7; VR November 1907 in V 17/6/1908/10.
37. See "Extract uit een particuliere nota van den Consul de Nederlanden te Kobe betreffende verschillende onderwerpen" in VKG 30/4/1907/H9, in which a Dutch consul in Japan refers to Oei as major a year before his appointment.
38. Liem, *Riwajat*, p. 264.
39. Ibid., pp. 114, 215.

to make an issue of opium use.[40] Taking note of such activities around Buitenzorg, the assistant resident predicted that the local Chinese would take "the lead from these strangers from China" and that there would be a "quick rise in the number of Chinese who feel ashamed to smoke [opium]."[41]

Branches of the THHK and the Chinese Chambers of Commerce were the first organizations in Java to engage actively in antiopium propaganda and to sponsor programs designed to discourage opium use in their community. In 1907, to cite one example, Chinese civic leaders in Surabaya distributed an antiopium drug, free, to seven hundred people.[42] Changing attitudes about opium are also reflected in peranakan literature. *Lo Fen Koei*, a Malay-language novel of 1903 by Gouw Peng Liang, depicts an "opium farmer"— from the context, actually a local farm manager or subfarmer—as a very nasty man.[43]

Thus did Holland's subjects begin to grasp the initiative that the Dutch were so reluctant to take. Awareness also rose among the Javanese. The young noblewoman Kartini—a regent's daughter who was later to wed Regent Djojoadiningrat of Rembang—raised the issue in a letter to a Dutch woman, Stella Zeehandelaar, in 1899, calling opium the "curse of the people."[44] Javanese groups that emerged during the ensuing decade alongside their Chinese counterparts—and partly inspired by them—took a similar stand. By 1910 leaders of the pryayi reform association Budi Utomo approached the colonial government about cooperating in an antiopium education campaign.[45]

The direct initiatives taken by indigenous reform organizations, and later by openly nationalist ones, mirrored a quiet and gradual transformation in customs and manners among pryayi, similar to that occurring among peranakans. At the heart of this change was a

40. Ibid., p. 191.

41. Assistant Resident Buitenzorg to Resident Batavia, May 10, 1907, no. 4792/44 in V 18/6/1908/1.

42. See Resident Bantam to HIOR, May 25, 1907, no. 127/9, and Resident Surabaya to HIOR, April 15, 1907, no. 1370/R, both in V 18/6/1908/1.

43. See Nio Joe Lan, *Sastra Indonesia-Tionghua* (Jakarta, 1957), pp. 46–47.

44. Raden Adjeng Kartini, *Letters of a Javanese Princess* (Kuala Lumpur, 1976), p. 8.

45. MvK to GG, January 13, 1910, no. 40/82 in V 13/1/1910/40/82. Akira Nagazumi writes that Chinese group initiatives such as the THHK helped to move "the educated Javanese to make some attempt to unite themselves." Akira Nagazumi, *The Dawn of Indonesian Nationalism: The Early Years of the Budi Utomo, 1908–1918* (Tokyo, 1972), p. 28.

shift toward a more Western social style, a "modern" style appropriate for one who aspired to a career in the colonial bureaucracy of the twentieth century or who, like Oei Tiong Ham, desired to participate in the increasingly cosmopolitan life of urban Asia and Southeast Asia. For the Javanese, as Heather Sutherland remarks, an interest in horse racing and playing tennis replaced hunting and other social skills of the older pryayi world.[46] Opium smoking, like polygamy and betel chewing, became a mark of being backward, or simply old-fashioned. These changes in customs and manners occurred first among the elite, and they eventually were echoed by many in the population at large.

In one case in the early twentieth century, hundreds of opium-smoking Balinese consulted native priests who were running an eight-day opium-addiction clinic in Buleleng, offering a cure involving ritual foods, oath taking, medicines, and controlled abstinence.[47]

The colonial regime declined to work with Budi Utomo in 1910. But a few years later the combined clamor of Indonesian organizations and Dutch Ethicists finally forced the regime's hand. So did the growing international movement against the narcotics trade, now being recognized, as the American Hamilton Wright put it, "as an evil . . . [that] threatens the social fabric of many Western nations."[48] By the 1920s programs had been initiated which were designed to harness the apparatus of the state to curtail and, eventually, put an end to the opium habit. Opium smokers became subject to strict licensing requirements; schoolchildren were admonished to avoid the opium vice; and antiopium societies actively propagandized with the support of subsidies from the colonial government.[49]

These combined forces succeeded. Regie records reveal that sales of the smallest denominations of opium—small tubes of candu and hermetically sealed packets of tiké—dropped off first as the casual

46. Sutherland, *Making of a Bureaucratic Elite*, p. 43.
47. Resident Bali and Lombok to HIOR, July 10, 1907, no. 2456/35 in V 18/6/1908/1.
48. Quoted in van Otterloo, *De Opiumschuiver*, p. 13.
49. "Verslag betreffende de Opium-en Zoutregie en de Zoutwinning over het jaar 1935," pp. 41–45. Three antiopium societies receiving small subsidies were: Antiopium vereeniging Batavia; N.I. Groot Loge der Internationale orde Goed Tempelieren Bandoeng; and N.I. Anti-opium vereeniging. These societies, as well as the government's literature bureau, the Volkslectuur, or Balai Pustaka, also distributed antiopium morality tales such as *Korbannja tjandoe atawa drama di loro-ireng* [Victims of candu, or the tragedy in Loro-ireng] (Batavia, 1934).

smokers and mildly addicted discontinued their habit. (Meanwhile, a smaller number of individuals in the cities moved from opium smoking to morphine injecting.) Addiction clinics were established in several hospitals for the more difficult cases, invariably totok Chinese.[50] Improving public health facilities and conditions combined with other social, administrative, and political forces to limit further the demand for opium among the Javanese, and the crushing rural depression of the 1930s forced many hangers-on out of the market.

Charles TeMechelen estimated that in the 1880s one Javanese in twenty used opium; by 1928, according to Opium Regie statistics, one in six hundred did so.[51] By the late 1930s the Dutch Opium Regie was still in business, but among the Javanese it was serving only the diehards, mostly old men and a few others who clung to opium's addicting relief and pleasures against the tide of social change.

A few years later, Japanese conquerors having come and gone, money-strapped Indonesian patriots seeking independence from Holland sold off what remained of the regie's opium stocks to help pay for their revolution.[52]

50. Van Otterloo, *De Opiumschuiver*, pp. 8, 42. For declining sales of the small tubes and tiké, see "Verslagen Opiumfabriek," for the 1910s and 1920s.

51. TM: Rapport 1888; van Otterloo, *De Opiumschuiver*, p. 4.

52. See Robert B. Cribb, "Opium and the Indonesian Revolution," *Modern Asian Studies*, 22, 4 (1988), 701–22.

Glossary

adat	customary law, honored custom
afdeling	district of a Dutch assistant resident, often coterminous with the domain of a bupati/regent
alun-alun	central square of a Javanese town
awar-awar	*ficus septica*, a tree indigenous to Java and the Sunda islands, the ground leaves of which were used to mix with opium for smoking
bandar	port official (shahbandar); manager of local opium store; also tollkeeper
bupati	regent, highest-ranking territorial official in the native administrative corps
Cabang Atas	peranakan Chinese elite in nineteenth-century Java, literally "the upper branch"
cakat	candu made for the mass market
cako	candu made for the upper-class market
candu	opium that has been refined for smoking
cemplon	large native freight-bearing sailing vessel common to north-central Java, frequently used in opium smuggling
desa	village
duit	copper penny (on the average 120 to the Dutch guilder), common means of cash exchange in rural Java throughout the nineteenth century; from 1854 circulated alongside the cent (100 to the guilder)
dukun	native healer, herbalist
gamelan	Javanese orchestra
geleng	a wad or ball of tiké, ordinarily weighing around 100 milligrams; in farm days wrapped in Chinese paper; smallest purchasable quantity of opium

257

258
Glossary and Opium Weights

jagabaya	rural crime specialist
jaksa	native judicial official
jicing	opium dross, scraped from the bowls of used opium pipes
jukung	light canoelike sailing craft used for coastal fishing and riverine traffic
Kabupaten	bupati/regent's residence, seat of a regency; or the regency itself
kampung	village or neighborhood
kapetengan	village policeman appointed to keep bandits, arsonists, and other bad elements at bay
kemandah	commander of small contingent of sea police in antismuggling task force
ketrangan	investigative report prepared by native officials offering clear, unambiguous accounts of crimes and other disturbances and often used to prosecute suspects
Kongkoan	the local Chinese Council, collective Chinese officers in town or city
kongsi	a syndicate or partnership formed to capitalize and/or manage a given enterprise, such as an opium farm; loosely, a Chinese company
kuasa pacht	manager of an opium farm at local, regional, or residency level
lurah	village headman
madat	opium; sometimes used to mean candu, but more generally means opium in any form
magang	youth in training for a career in Pangreh Praja, usually as an unpaid aide in a pryayi official's establishment
mantri	low ranking native functionary serving under pryayi official or (later) colonial department
mata-mata	spies, agents of the opium farm who policed the farm monopoly; the kepala mata-mata was the chief spy or agent
Pangreh Praja	collectively, the indigenous administrative corps, bupati and their subordinates
patih	a bupati's chief administrative officer
patungan	a peddler of opium; an unofficial (that is, illegal) opium den; a pattern of petty trade in opium beneath the official opium farm structure
peranakan	locally born Chinese or Chinese mestizo; and the Chinese-Indonesian culture that predominated among the Javan Chinese in the nineteenth century
piagem	a Javanese document of employment; contract
pryayi	Javanese elite and their culture; native official
rust en orde	peace and order, Dutch watchwords for good colonial administration
santri	student of a traditional religious teacher; in Java, generally a devout, "orthodox" Muslim

singkeh   a new Chinese immigrant, and someone unassimilated to peranakan culture

sumbangan   customary gifts offered in exchange for favors

tanda   a token of respect (sumbangan)
  hormat

tiké   an opium preparation made by blending candu with awar-awar leaves and other ingredients

totok   singkeh; generally used to differentiate between assimilated (peranakan) and unassimilated (totok) Chinese communities in Java

warung   small roadside stall or shop

wayang   Javanese puppet theater

wedana   native official directly subordinate to the bupati; an assistant wedana was lowest-ranking territorial official in the native administrative corps

Weights Used in Java Opium Trade

1 mata	= .38 grams	= approx. 380 milligrams (also timbang, hoen)
100 mata	= 1 tahil	= approx. 38 grams
16 tahil	= 1 kati	= approx. 618 grams
100 kati	= 1 picul	= approx. 61.8 kilograms

Bibliography

Archives

Netherlands Ministry of Colonies

The archives of the former Netherlands Ministry of Colonies for the years prior to 1900 are housed in the Algemeen Rijksarchief (General State Archives), The Hague. For the years 1900 and after, the ministry's archives are under the jurisdiction of the Internal Affairs Department (Binnenlandse Zaken) in The Hague.

A prominent part of these archives, and that which I consulted most extensively, consists of reports from the governor general to the minister. These reports often included extensive related correspondence and appendices, and they were sent to The Hague in bundles called Mailrapporten (MR). As the problems they addressed were taken up by the minister, his staff separated some of the individual reports from the Mailrapporten and refiled them as Verbaal (V), Verbaal Kabinets Geheim (VKG, secret verbaal), and Exhibitum (Exh). Each of these deals with a specific topic and is identified by a filing date and number. Locating a specific document in the archives (a Memorie van Overgave, MvO, or transfer memorandum, for example) entails identifying the Verbaal, Exhibitum, or Mailrapport in which it was permanently filed. In the documentation for this study, a typical citation from these archives—for example, DF to GG, October 19, 1867, no. 16849/B in VKG 27/1/1869/17c—means that the letter from the director of finance to the governor general of October 19, 1867, no. 16849/B, can be found in the secret verbaal (VKG) dated January 27, 1869, and numbered 17c. (See the List of Abbreviations.)

The Ministry of Internal Affairs archives in The Hague also contains stamboeken, or the collected service records of members of the Colonial

Service. An individual service record, or Staat van Dienst (SvD), is cited by the name of the official, followed by a letter and number that locate the volume and folio of the stamboek in which the record may be found.

Koninklijk Instituut voor Taal- Land- en Volkenkunde, Leiden

a. The Charles TeMechelen Papers (TMC), in several bundles marked H422a, b, c, d, e, and H423.

b. G. T. Rouffaer, "Indische Aanteekeningen gedurende mijne 1ᵉ reis (Nov. 1885–Febr. 1890)." Rouffaer's travel notebook, H721.

c. R.D.M. Verbeek Collection, containing several letters from A. A. de Jongh, chief inspector of the Opium Regie, H588.

Government Publications

Netherlands and Netherlands India (Dutch East Indies)

Administratieve voorschriften voor de opiumregie. Batavia, 1907.
Bijblad op het Staatsblad van Nederlandsch-Indie. Batavia, annual.
Department van Gouvernements bedrijven in Nederlandsch-Indie. Opiumfabriek: Jaarverslagen. Batavia, annual from 1908.
Extract: Voorlopig verslag. Tweede Kamer, Begrooting, 1907.
Naam- en Ranglijst der Officieren bij den Land en Zeemagt in Nederlandsch-Indie. Batavia, 1882.
Onderzoek naar de Mindere Welvaart der Inlandsche bevolking op Java en Madoera. 10 vols. Batavia, 1905–14.
Opiumregie. *Resi Tjandoe*. Batavia, 1920.
Opiumregie. *Verslag betreffende den Dienst der Opiumregie*. Batavia, 1915–33.
Regeerings-Almanak. Batavia, annual.
Staatsblad van Nederlandsch-Indie. Batavia, annual.
Verslag betreffende de Opium- en Zoutregie en de Zoutwinning. Batavia: Opium- en Zoutregie, 1935, 1938.
Wettelijke bepalingen voor de Opiumregie. Batavia, 1907.

Other

Great Britain. *Royal Commission on Opium, Final Report*. London: Printed for Her Majesty's Stationery Office, 1895.
International Opium Commission. *Report of the International Opium Commission*. Shanghai: North-China Daily News and Herald Ltd., 1909.
Straits Settlements and Federated Malay States. *Proceedings of the Commission Appointed to Inquire into Matters Relating to the Use of Opium in the Straits Settlements and the Federated Malay States*. Singapore: Government Printing Office, 1908.
United States. Bureau of Insular Affairs. *Report of the Committee Appointed by*

the Philippine Commission to Investigate the Use of Opium and the Traffic Therein. Washington, D.C.: War Department, 1905.

Contemporary Periodicals

Indisch Weekblad van het Recht. Batavia, 1863–1910.
De Locomotief. Semarang, 1864–1910.
Semarangsch Advertentieblad. Semarang, 1844–50; 1854–62.

Books and Theses

Abendanon, J. H. *De Nederlandsch-Indisch Rechtspraak en Rechtsliteratuur van 1849 tot 1907.* Leiden: S. C. van Doesburgh, 1908.
Akkeren, Ph. van. *Een Gedrocht en toch de volmaakte mens; Suluk Gatolotjo.* The Hague: Academisch Proefschrift, Utrecht, 1951.
Albrecht, J. E. *Soerat Ketrangan dari pada hal kaadaan Bangsa Tjina di Negri Hindia Olanda.* Batavia: Albrecht en Rusche, 1890.
Anderson, Benedict O'Gorman. *Java in a Time of Revolution.* Ithaca: Cornell University Press, 1972.
Bastin, John. *Essays on Indonesian and Malayan History.* Singapore: Eastern Universities Press, 1961.
———. *The Native Policies of Sir Stamford Raffles in Java and Sumatra.* Oxford: Oxford University Press, 1957.
Becker, Alton L., ed. *Writing on the Tongue.* Ann Arbor: Center for South and Southeast Asian Studies, University of Michigan, 1989.
Be Ik Sam. *Vijftien millioen vermeerdering der staatsinkomsten zonder belasting verhooging; Open Brief aan Z. M. den Koning der Nederlanden.* Yogyakarta: H. Buning, 1886.
Bemmelen, J. F. van, et al. *Nederlandsch-Indie onder het regentschap van Koningin Emma, 1890–1898.* Batavia, G. Kolff, 1898.
Berg, L.W.C. van den. *De Inlandsche Rangen en Titels op Java en Madoera.* Batavia: Landsdrukkerij, 1887.
Berg, N. P. van den. *Munt- Crediet- en Bankwezen, Handel en Scheepvaart in Nederlandsch-Indie.* The Hague: Martinus Nijhoff, 1907.
Blokland, Njonja van. *Doekoen Djawa oetawa kitab dan roepa-roepa obat njang terpake di Tanah Djawa.* Batavia: Albrecht, 1899.
Boeke, J. H. *Inleiding tot de economie der Inheemsche Samenleving in Nederlandsch-Indie.* Batavia: Albrecht, 1931.
Boekoe Peringatan 1907–1937. Semarang: Tiong Hwa Siang Hwee, 1937.
Booth, Anne, W. J. O'Malley, and Anna Weidemann. *Indonesian Economic History in the Dutch Colonial Era.* New Haven, Conn.: Yale Center for International and Area Studies, Southeast Asia Monograph Series, no. 35, 1990.

Borel, Henri. *De Chineezen in Nederlandsch-Indie*. Amsterdam: L. J. Veen, 1900.

Brooshooft, Pieter. *De ethische koers in de koloniale politiek*. Amsterdam: J. H. de Bussy, 1901.

——. *Memorie over den toestand in Indie*. Semarang, 1888.

Burger, Dionijs Huibert. *De Ontsluiting van Java's Binnenland voor het Wereldverkeer*. Wageningen: H. Veenmen en Zonen, 1939.

Catalogus van de Boeken en Kaarten uitmakende de Bibliotheek van het Department van Kolonien. The Hague, 1898.

Colenbrander, H. T., and J. E. Stokvis, eds. *Leven en Arbeid van Mr. C. Th. van Deventer*. Amsterdam: P. N. van Kampen en Zoon, 1916.

Coolhaas, W. Ph. *A Critical Survey of Studies on Dutch Colonial History*. The Hague: Martinus Nijhoff, 1960.

——, ed. *Generale Missiven der V.O.C.* 2 vols. The Hague: Martinus Nijhoff, 1964.

Couperus, Louis. *The Hidden Force* [1900]. Trans. Alexander Teixeira de Mattos. Rev. and ed. E. M. Beekman. Amherst: University of Massachusetts Press, 1985.

——. *De Stille Kracht* [1900]. Bussum: Van Holkeman en Warendorf, 1973.

Day, Clive. *The Policy and Administration of the Dutch in Java*. New York: Macmillan, 1904.

Delden, A.J.W. van. *Blik op het Indisch Staatsbestuur*. Batavia: W. Bruining, 1875.

De Quincey, Thomas. *Confessions of an English Opium Eater*. London: Taylor and Hessey, 1823.

Deventer, C. Th. van. *Strafzaak Ho Tjiauw Ing; Pleidooi van den Verdediger*. Semarang, 1891.

Djoko Suryo. "Social and Economic Life in Rural Semarang under Colonial Rule in the Later 19th Century." Ph.D. diss., Monash University, 1982.

Donker Curtius, H. H. *Relaas van het den Regent van Magettan (Residentie Madioen), ten laste gelegd opium sluiken, en het daarnaar ingesteld onderzoek*. Surabaya: Gebr. Donker en Co., 1892.

Elout van Soeterwoude, W. *De Opium-vloek op Java*. The Hague, 1890.

——, ed. *De Opium-Vloek*. 4 vols. The Hague, 1891, 1893, 1895, 1899.

Elson, R. E. *Javanese Peasants and the Colonial Sugar Industry: Impact and Change in an East Java Residency, 1830–1940*. Asian Studies Association of Australia, Southeast Asia Publications Series, no. 9. Oxford: Oxford University Press, 1984.

Encyclopaedie van Nederlandsch-Indie. 4 vols. The Hague: Martinus Nijhoff, 1905.

Encyclopaedie van Nederlandsch-Indie. 4 vols., 2d ed. rev. The Hague: Martinus Nijhoff, 1917–21, with 5 supplements, 1927–40.

Fromberg, P. H. *Verspreide Geschriften*. Leiden: Leidsche Uitgeversmaatschappij, 1926.

Furnivall, John S. *Netherlands India: A Study of a Plural Economy.* New York: Macmillan, 1944.

Gavit, John Palmer. *Opium.* London: George Routledge and Sons, 1925.

Geertz, Clifford. *The Religion of Java.* Glencoe, Ill.: Free Press, 1960.

——. *The Social History of an Indonesian Town.* Cambridge, Mass.: MIT Press, 1965.

Gericke, J.F.C., and Taco Roorda. *Javaansch-Nederlandsch Handwoordenboek.* Leiden: E. J. Brill, 1901.

Gerritsen, Will, "De Chinese Opium-entrepreneurs in Java: James Robert Rush' *histoire intégrale* van de prive exploitatie van een negentiende eeuws koloniaal gouvernementsmonopolie." Doctoraalscriptie, Vakgroep Culturiele Antropologie, Instituut voor Culturiele en Sociale Antropologie, Katholieke Universiteit Nijmegen, 1982.

Gilman, Alfred Goodman, Louis S. Goodman, and Alfred Gilman, eds. *The Pharmacological Basis of Therapeutics.* New York: Macmillan, 1980.

Godley, Michael Richard. *Mandarin-Capitalists from Nanyang: Overseas Chinese Enterprise in the Modernization of China, 1893–1911.* Cambridge: Cambridge University Press, 1981.

Gonggrijp, G. L. *Brieven van Opheffer aan de redactie van het Bataviaasch Handelsblad.* Maastrict, 1913.

Gonggrijp, George. *Schets eener economische geschiedenis van Nederlandsch-Indie.* Haarlem: De Erven F. Bohn, 1928.

Groeneveldt, W. P. *Rapport over het opium monopolie in Cochin-China.* Batavia: Landsdrukkerij, 1890.

Groneman, Isaac. *Een Ketjoegeschiedenis, Vorstenlandsche Toestanden II.* Dordrecht: J. P. Revers, 1887.

——. *Kitab Pendjagaan diri dan obatnja waktoe ada penjakit Cholera.* Yogyakarta: H. Buning, 1901.

——. *Tegen 't Cholera Gevaar.* Semarang: H. A. Benjamins, 1909.

——. *Uit en over Midden Java, Onuitgegeven en uitgegeven brieven over opiumpacht, Chineezenwoeker, en andere Javaansche belangen.* Zutphen: W. J. Thieme en Cie., 1891.

Haak, J. *Opiumregie met normaal tjandoe.* Semarang, 1889.

Hasselman, B.R.P. *Mijne Ervaring als Fabricant in de Binnenlanden van Java.* The Hague: Martinus Nijhoff, 1862.

Hasselman, C. J. *Algemeen Overzigt van de uitkomsten van het Welvaart Onderzoek gehouden op Java en Madoera in 1904–1905.* The Hague: Martinus Nijhoff, 1914.

Heeres, J. E., ed. *Corpus Diplomaticum Neerlando-Indicum.* Vol. 3. The Hague, 1907–38.

Heyne, K. *De nuttige planten van Nederlandsch-Indie.* 3 vols. Buitenzorg: Department van Landbouw, Nijverheid en Handel, 1927.

Hogendorp, Dirk van. *Berigt van den tegenwoordigen toestand der Bataafsche Bezittingen in Oost-Indien enz.* Delft: Privately printed, 1799.

266
Bibliography

Horne, Elinor Clark. *Javanese-English Dictionary*. New Haven, Conn.: Yale University Press, 1974.
Hoven, Therese. *In sarong en kabaai*. Amsterdam: L. J. Veen, 1892.
Idema, H. A. *Parlementaire Geschiedenis van Nederlandsch-Indie 1891–1918*. The Hague: M. Nijhoff, 1924.
International Order of Good Templars, Dutch East Indies Grand Lodge. *Indie en het Opium*. Batavia: Kolff, 1931.
Jacobs, Julius. *Eenigen Tijd onder De Baliers: Eene reisbeschrijving met aanteekeningen betreffende hygiene, Land- en Volkenkunde van de eilanden Bali en Lombok*. Batavia: G. Kolff, 1883.
Jonge, J.K.J. de, ed. *De opkomst van het Nederlandsch gezag op Java; Verzameling van onuitgegeven stukken uit het oud-koloniaal archief*. Vol. 4. The Hague, 1873.
Kartini, Raden Adjeng. *Letters of a Javanese Princess* [1911]. Kuala Lumpur: Oxford University Press, 1976.
Klerck, E. S. de. *History of the Netherlands Indies*. 2 vols. Rotterdam: W. L. en J. Brusse, 1938.
Kloppenburg-Versteegh, Mevrouw J. *Indische planten en haar geneeskracht*. Semarang: Masman en Stroink, 1907.
Kol, H. H. van. *Driemaal Dwars door Sumatra en zwerftochten door Bali*. Rotterdam: W. L. & J. Brusse's Uitgeversmaatschappij, 1914.
———. *Nederlandsch-Indie in de Staten Generaal van 1879 tot 1909*. The Hague: Martinus Nijhoff, 1911.
Koo, Madame Wellington [Oei Hui-lan], with Isabella Taves. *No Feast Lasts Forever*. New York: Quadrangle, 1975.
Kraan, Alfons van der. *Lombok: Conquest, Colonization and Underdevelopment, 1870–1940*. Asian Studies Association of Australia, Southeast Asia Publications Series, no. 5. Singapore: Heinemann Educational Books, 1980.
Kwee Tek Hoay. *The Origins of the Modern Chinese Movement in Indonesia*. Trans. and intro. Lea Williams. Ithaca: Cornell Modern Indonesia Project Translation Series, 1969.
Lauts. *Het Eiland Balie en de Balienezen*. Amsterdam: G.J.A. Beijerninck, 1848.
Liem Thian Joe. *Riwajat Semarang (Dari Djamannja Sam Poo Sampe Terhapoesnja Kongkoan]*. Semarang: Boekhandel Ho Kim Yoe, 1933.
Liem Tjwan Ling. *Raja Gula: Oei Tiong Ham*. Surabaya: Liem Tjwan Ling, 1979.
Lindenborn, M. *Jan Lambrecht Zegers; Zendeling van Indramajoe 1870–1890*. Netherlands: Nederland Zending Vennootschap, n.d. [1919].
Lindesmith, Alfred R. *Opiate Addiction*. Bloomington, Ind.: Principia Press, 1947.
Lombard-Salmon, Claudine. *Literature in Malay by the Chinese of Indonesia: A Provisional Annotated Bibliography*. Paris: Editions de la Maison des Sciences de l'Homme, 1981.

Machielse, A. *Opheldering in de zaak der Chateau Lafitte*. Surakarta: Vogel vd Heiple, 1901.

Money, William B. *Java: or, How to Manage a Colony*. London: Hurst & Blackett, 1861.

Nagazumi, Akira. *The Dawn of Indonesian Nationalism: The Early Years of the Budi Utomo, 1908–1918*. Tokyo: Institute of Developing Economies, 1972.

Nederburgh, S.C.H. *Opium-smokkelhandel*. The Hague: Martinus Nijhoff, 1899.

Nieuwenhuys, Rob. *Oost-Indische Spiegel*. Amsterdam: EM. Querido, 1972.

—— [E. Breton de Nijs]. *Tempo Doeloe; Fotografische documenten uit het oude Indie*. Amsterdam: EM. Querido, 1973.

Nieuw Nederlandsch biografisch woordenboek. Vols. 1–10. Leiden: A. W. Sijtoff, 1911–37.

Nio Joe Lan. *Sastra Indonesia-Tionghoa*. Jakarta: Gunung Agung, 1957.

Nunn, G. Raymond. *Indonesian Newspapers: An International Union List*. Distributed by the Chinese Materials and Research Aids Service Center, 1971.

The Oei Tiong Ham Concern: A Short Survey of Its Development and Progress. Semarang [?]: N. V. Handelmaatschappij Kian Gwan, 1934.

Ong Eng Die. *Chinezen in Nederlandsch-Indie; Sociografie van een Indonesische bevolkings groep*. Assen: Van Gorcum, 1939.

Onghokham, "The Residency of Madiun: Pryayi and Peasant in the Nineteenth Century." Ph.D. diss., Yale University, 1975.

Otterloo, Antonie de Mol van. *De Opiumschuiver in het Hospitaal*. Utrecht: Kemink, 1933.

Oudgast. *Onze Oost*. Amsterdam: J. A. Sleeswijk, 1897.

Perelaer, M.T.H. *Baboe Dalima*. 2 vols. Rotterdam: Uitgevers Maatschappij "Elsevier," 1886.

——. *Baboe Dalima* [English ed.]. Trans. E. J. Venning. London: Vizetelly and Company, 1888.

——. *Het oordeel de Nederlandsch pers over "De Spoliatie."* Rotterdam, 1885.

——. *De spoliatie gepleegd door de Nederlandsch-Indische Regeering ten opzichte van het particulier landbezit op Java*. Rotterdam, 1884.

Piepers, M. C. *Macht tegen Recht; De vervolging der Justitie in Nederlandsch-Indie*. Batavia: H. M. van Dorp, 1884.

——. *De Politierol*. Batavia: Ogilvie, 1868.

Pigeaud, Th. *Javaanse Volksvertoningen*. Batavia: Volkslectuur, 1938.

Rengers, W. J. van Welderen Baron. *Schets eener Parlementaire geschiedenis van Nederland van 1849 tot 1901*. The Hague: Martinus Nijhoff, 1948.

Ricklefs, M. C. *A History of Modern Indonesia*. London: Macmillan, 1981.

Roo, D.L.W.G. de. *De invoering van de opiumregie*. Netherlands, 1897.

——. *De verkoop van opium op Java*. Nijmegen, 1892.

Roorda, Taco. *Javaansche Brieven, Berigten, Verslagen, Verzoekschriften, enz.* Leiden: E. J. Brill, 1875.

Scheltema, J. F. *De opiumpolitiek der regeering en de vrijheid der drukpers in Nederlandsch-Indie.* The Hague: W. P. van Stockum, 1903.

Schrieke, B. *Indonesian Sociological Studies.* Vol. 1. Bandung: Sumur Bandung, 1960.

Skinner, G. William. *Chinese Society in Thailand: An Analytical History.* Ithaca: Cornell University Press, 1957.

Stark, E. *Uit Indie Egypte en Het Heilige Land.* Amersfort: P. Dz. Veen, 1913.

Steinmetz, H. E. [Eckart]. *Indische brieven aan een Staatsraad.* Haarlem, 1888.

Struick, N. J. *Opiumpacht of opiumregie.* The Hague: Cremer, 1889.

Suryadinata, Leo. *The Chinese Minority in Indonesia.* Singapore: Chopmen Enterprises, 1978.

——. *Political Thinking of the Indonesian Chinese, 1900–1977: A Sourcebook.* Singapore: Singapore University Press, 1979.

——. *The Pre–World War II Peranakan Chinese Press of Java: A Preliminary Survey.* Athens, Ohio: Ohio University Center for International Studies, Southeast Asia Program, 1971.

——. *Prominent Indonesian Chinese in the Twentieth Century: A Preliminary Survey.* Athens, Ohio: Ohio University Center for International Studies, 1972.

Sutherland, Heather Amanda. *The Making of a Bureaucratic Elite.* Asian Studies Association of Australia, Southeast Asia Publications Series, no. 2. Singapore: Heinemann Educational Books, 1979.

——. "Pangreh Pradja: Java's Indigenous Administrative Corps and Its Role in the Last Decades of Dutch Colonial Rule." Ph.D. diss., Yale University, 1973.

Tan Gin Ho. *Peringatan dari wafatnja Majoor Tan Tjin Kie.* Batavia: G. Kolff, 1919.

Thomas, Theodoor. *Eenige opmerking naar aanleiding van het pacht-stelsel op Java.* Leiden: E. J. Brill, 1893.

Tien Ju-k'ang. *The Chinese of Sarawak: A Study of Social Structure.* London: London School of Economics and Political Science, Monographs on Social Anthropology, 1953.

Tjoa Tjoe Koan. *Hari Raja Orang Tjina.* Batavia: Albrecht, 1887.

Vandenbosch, Amry. *The Dutch East Indies.* Berkeley: University of California Press, 1944.

Velden, B. N. van der. *De Opiumregie in Nederlandsch-Indie.* Batavia, 1937.

Vlekke, Bernard H. M. *Nusantara: A History of Indonesia.* The Hague: W. van Hoeve, 1965.

Waal, E. de. *Aanteekeningen over koloniale onderwerpen.* The Hague: Martinus Nijhoff, 1865.

Wallace, Alfred Russel. *The Malay Archipelago* [1869]. Singapore: Graham Brash, 1983.

Wertheim, W. F. *Indonesian Society in Transition: A Study of Social Change*. The Hague: W. van Hoeve, 1956.
Wetboek van koophandel; Kitab perniaga'an. Trans. F. Wiggers. Batavia: Taman Sari, 1911.
Wetboek van koophandel voor Nederlandsch-Indie. Amsterdam: Johannes Muller, 1846.
Willmott, Donald E. *The Chinese of Semarang: A Changing Minority Community in Indonesia*. Ithaca: Cornell University Press, 1960.
Wiselius, J.A.B. *De opium in Nederlandsch- en Britisch Indie*. The Hague, 1886.
Zegers, Jan Lambrecht. *Het opium-vraagstuk in Nederlandsch Oost Indie*. Nijmegen, 1890.

Articles and Scholarly Papers

"Een Afzonderlijke Opiumpolitie." *Bataviaasch Nieuwsblad*, no. 85 (March 12, 1903).
"Akals van pandhuispachters." *Insulinde*, no. 11 (1898).
Anderson, Benedict O'Gorman, trans. "Suluk Gatoloco." *Indonesia*, no. 32 (1981), 109–50; no. 33 (1982), 31–88.
Baks, C. "Chinese Communities in Eastern Java: A Few Remarks." *Asian Studies*, 8 (August 1970), 248–59.
——. "De Chinezen in Oostelijk Java, een demografisch onderzoek naar de penetratie over de periode 1815–1930." Typescript, 1962.
Baud, J. C. "Proeve van eene geschiedenis van den handel en het verbruik van opium in Nederlandsch-Indie." *BKI*, 1 (1853), 79–220.
"Bespreking van de opiumpacht op Java, ingeleid door den Heer Castens." *VIG* (1872), 49–112.
"Bespreking van de opium-quaestie en de invoering van het licentie-stelsel door de Blitarsche Landbouwvereeniging." *Tijdschrift voor Nijverheid en Landbouw in Nederlandsch-Indie*, 36 (1888), 50–53.
Bool, H. J. "De opiumpacht op Java." *Vragen des Tijds*, 15 (1888–89), 75.
Boomgaard, Peter. "Buitenzorg in 1805: The Role of Money and Credit in a Colonial Frontier Society." *Modern Asian Studies*, 20 (1986), 33–58.
Boorsma, W. G. "Een opiumsurrogaat?" *Teysmannia*, 5 (1894).
Boxer, C. R. "Notes on Chinese Abroad in the Late Ming and Early Manchu Period Compiled from Contemporary European Sources (1500–1750)." *T'ien Hsia Monthly* (December 1939), 447–68.
Carey, Peter. "Changing Javanese Perceptions of the Chinese Communities in Central Java, 1755–1825." *Indonesia*, 37 (April 1984), 1–47.
——. "Waiting for the 'Just King': The Agrarian World of South-Central Java from Giyanti (1755) to the Java War (1825–30)." *Modern Asian Studies*, 20 (1986), 59–137.

Carlier, C.J.P. "Beschrijving van de vogelsnestklippen te Karang Bollong." *Tijdschrift voor de Indische Taal-, Land- en Volkenkunde* (1853), 304.

Castens, C. "De opiumpacht op Java." *VIG* (March 26 and April 9, 1872), 49–112.

Cheng U Wen. "Opium in the Straits Settlements." *Journal of Southeast Asian History*, 2 (March 1961), 52–74.

"Het Chineesche Gouvernement en de Chineezen op Java." *TNI*, 20 (1858), 50.

"Een Chineesche parvenu op Java." *TNI*, 15 (1853), 357.

"De Chineezen als geldschieters der Javanen beschouwd." *TNI*, 21 (1859), 58–61.

Cramer, G. J. Putnam. "Het opiumgebruik en de sluikhandel in opium op Java en Madoera." *IT*, no. 11 (December 10, 1889).

Creutzberg, P. "Geldwezen in Indonesie in de 19ᵉ en begin 20ᵉEeuw." Typescript. n.d.

Cribb, Robert B. "Opium and the Indonesian Revolution." *Modern Asian Studies*, 22 (1988), 701–22.

Davelaar, W.A.J. van. "Middenpersonen tusschen de districts beambten en dessa-hoofden op Java." *TBB*, 6 (1892), 77–84.

Dedem, W. K. baron van. "Eene bijdrage tot de studie der opium-quaestie op Java; de Officieele Litteratuur." *IG*, no. 1 (March–June 1881), 403–38, 1071–90; no. 2 (August 1881), 289–321.

——. "Nota over de opium-kwestie op Java, met naschrift en debat." *VIG* (November 3, 1876), 103–222.

Deventer, C. Th. van. "Korte opmerkingen naar aanleiding van art 23 van het opiumpacht reglement." *IWR*, no. 1071, 1884.

Diehl, F. W. "The Opium-tax Farms in Java, 1813–1914: The Quest for Maximisation of Government Revenue and Chinese Tax Farmers' Profits." Paper presented at the Conference on Indonesian Economic History in the Dutch Colonial Period, Australia National University. Typescript, 1983.

Dijkstra, J. F. "Opium, Koffie en nog wat." *TNI* (1897) 951.

DIXI. "Kritiek van M.T.H. Perelaer's opium-roman 'Baboe Dalima.'" *IG*, no. 2 (1886), 1085–92.

Elout van Soeterwoude, W. "De opiumpacht in Nederlandsch-Indie." *VIG* (1889), 139–226.

Elson, R. E. "Sugar Factory Workers and the Emergence of 'Free Labor' in Nineteenth-Century Java." *Modern Asian Studies*, 20 (1986), 139–74.

Fokkens, F. "Afschaffing van pachten op Java en Madoera en in verband daarmede verscherping van het toezicht op de beweging van der Vreemde Oosterlingen." *VIG* (1897), 1–36.

"Het getal opiumkitten op Java." *IG*, no. 2 (1888), 1927.

Go Gien Tjwan. "The Changing Trade Position of Chinese in Southeast Asia." *International Social Science Journal*, 23 (1971).

Groneman, Isaac. "Opium-feilen." *IG*, no. 2 (1890), 1332–36.

————. "De opium-quaestie." *IG*, no. 1 (1887), 386–97.

H. B. "De Chineezen op Java." *De Indische Mail*, 1 (1886), 195–98.

H.E.E. "Nederzettingen van Chineezen in de Binnenlanden. *De Indische Mail*, 1 (1886), 880–83.

"Historische Nota over de dessabesturen op Java." KVvNI 1877, Bijlage N.

Hoetink, B. "Chineesch officieren te Batavia Onder de Compagnie." *BKI*, 78 (1922), 1–138.

Holtzappel, C.J.G. "The Indigenous Basis of the Revenue Farming System in Java." Paper presented at the Conference on Revenue Farming, Research School of Pacific Studies, Australia National University, Typescript, 1988.

Huizer, H.D.P. "De opium-regie in Nederlandsch-Indie." *IG*, no. 1 (1907), 36.

"Iets over de toeneming der Chineesche bevolking op Java. Statistieke opgaven van 1815–1861." *TNI* (1864), 373–74.

Een Indisch Journalist. "Een bijdrage over de opium-quaestie." *Eigen Haard* (1888), 553–56.

Kielstra, E. B. "Java's grootste ramp." *De Gids*, 4 (October 1888), 32.

Koesoemodikdo. "Soewatoe Timbangan jang Tiada Diminta." *TBB*, 30 (1906), 34–40.

Koorders, S. H. "Kleine Schetsen van Merkwaardige Javaansche Planten." *Teysmannia*, 11 (1900), 558–77.

Kramer, John C. "Speculations on the Nature and Pattern of Opium Smoking." *Journal of Drug Issues* (Spring 1979), 247–55.

Laps, Mr. "Eenige losse opmerkingen over Amfioen overtredingzaken." *IWR*, no. 514, 1873.

Locher-Scholten, E. B. "Mr. P. Brooshooft, Een Biografische Schets in Koloniaal-Ethisch Perspectief." *BKI*, 123 (1976), 306–49.

Lombard-Salmon, Claudine. "The Contribution of the Chinese to the Development of Southeast Asia: A New Appraisal." *Journal of Southeast Asia Studies*, 12 (1981), 260–75.

"Het loon van de koffieplantende bevolking op Java in verband met art. 56 van het Regeeringsreglement." *IG*, no. 2 (1888), 1818–33.

Lubbers, P. "De invloed der economische depressie op het opiumgebruik in Nederlandsch-Indie." *Koloniaal Studien*, 19 (1935), 118–26.

Meeter, P. "Opiumverpachting en Chineesche officieren." *IT*, nos. 2–3 (October 8 and 15, 1889).

"Nadeelen door de Chineezen in de desa's op Java veroorzaakt." *TNI*, no. 2 (1850), 216.

"De Nota van de Kamer van Koophandel en Nijverheid te Batavia over de toelating der Chineezen." *De Locomotief*, no. 95 (November 27, 1865).

"De opiumregie in Cochin-China." *IG*, no. 1 (1889), 836–39.

"Opium Snippers." *Weekblad van Neerlandsch-Indie*, no. 32 (June 7, 1891), 1704–7.

"Een pactergeschiedenis." *IT*, nos. 2–3 (December 3, 1889).

Paku Buwana IV. "Teachings on Right Conduct, or *Wulang Reh*." Trans. Martin Hatch and Suranto Atmosoputro. Typescript, n.d.

Partowidjojo. "Nota soesoelan boewat troesken tjaritaan sedikit menerangken jang tersebut di nota tertjitak dalam tijdschrift voor Binnenlandsch-Bestuur di-katja 228 Di No. 111 Hal Pacht Amfioen." *TBB*, 5 (1891), 360–66.

"De 'prembe' en de opiumpacht." *IG*, no. 1 (1893), 236–39.

"Resident contra Hoofd-inspecteur III." *Weekblad van Neerlandsch-Indie*, no. 32 (June 7, 1891), 1692–94.

Roo, L.W.G. de. "Nota en voordracht over de opiumkwestie met debat, en brief van kolonel van Zuijlen over de opium-regie in Fransch Cochin-China." *VIG* (1889), 227–39; (1890), 2–64.

Rouffaer, G. P. "Charles TeMechelen, In Memoriam." *Nederlandsch-Indie Oud en Nieuw*, no. 9 (1918), 305–12.

Scheltema, J. F. "The Opium Trade in the Dutch East Indies." *American Journal of Sociology*, 13 (July–September 1907), 79–112, 224–51.

Schuurmans, N. D. "De opiumschuiver. Fragment van een onuitgegeven leerdicht van Pakoe Boewono II (A.D. 1749). Vertaald en toegelicht." *TBB*, 9 (1894), 575.

Skinner, G. William. "Change and Persistence in Chinese Culture Overseas: A Comparison of Thailand and Java." *Nan Yang Hsueh Pao*, 16 (1960), 86–100.

——. "The Chinese Minority." In *Indonesia*, ed. Ruth T. McVey, 97–117. New Haven, Conn.: Human Relations Area Files Press, 1963.

——. "Java's Chinese Minority: Continuity and Change." *Journal of Asian Studies*, 20 (May 1961), 353–62.

Soeropringgo. "Panjelidikan dari djalannja pentjoeri dan gogol-gogol." *TBB*, 30 (1906), 353–58.

Sollewijn Gelpke, J.H.F. "Dessa bestuur op Java." *IG*, no. 2 (1879), 136–44.

"Staat aantoonende de opbrengst der amfioen verpachting in de geheele res. Kedirie, in 1831 tot en met 1844." *TNI*, no. 2 (1849), 57.

Steiner, William Glenn. "Drug Problems." *Encyclopedia Britannica*, 5:1048–60. 1974 ed.

Struick, N. J. "Een paar opmerking naar aanleiding der bespreking in de *IG*, met eenige cijfers betr. de opiumregie in Fransch-Indie." *IG*, no. 2 (1889), 1986.

Sutherland, Heather Amanda. "Notes on Java's Regent Families: Part I." *Indonesia*, no. 16 (1973), 112–47.

TeMechelen, Charles. "Eenige dagen het desaleven meegeleefd." *Tijdschrift voor de Inlandsche Taal-, Land- en Volkenkunde*, 25 (1879), 165–95, 256–318.

Tjoa Soe Tjong. "O.T.H.C. [Oei Tiong Ham Concern]—100 jaar: Een economische geschiedenis van Indonesia." *Economisch-statistische Berichten*, no. 2394 (June 26, 1963), 604–7; no. 2396 (July 17, 1963), 650–53.

"De toestand der residentie Rio in 1849." *TNI*, 15 (1853), 410–30.

Van Niel, Robert. "Government Policy and the Civil Administration in Java during the Early Years of the Cultivation System." *Proceedings*, Conference on Modern Indonesian History, July 18–19, 1975 (Madison, Wis., 1975), pp. 61–79.

Vermeulen, Johannes T. "The Chinese in Batavia and the Troubles of 1740." *Journal of the South Seas Society*, 9 (1953), 1–68.

Verwijk, J. J. "De Volkskoffiecultuur in Pasoeroean." *TBB*, 4 (1892), 1–11.

"Verzameling qualificatien van vergrijpen ter policierol gestraft." *IWR*, no. 176, 1866.

"Waarom produceert Nederlandsch-Indie geen opium?" *IG*, no. 2 (1890), 1738.

Williams, Lea E. "The Ethical Program and the Chinese of Indonesia." *Journal of Southeast Asian History*, 2 (July 1961), 35–42.

Winter, Carel Frederick. "Verbod tegen het gebruik van amfioen, Soerakarta 1840. Oorzaak van dit verbod door Pakoe Boewon II." *TNI*, 3 (1840), 588.

"De zaak contra TeMechelen." *Weekblad van Neerlandsch-Indie*, no. 32 (June 7, 1891), 1683–84.

"Zullen nu de Chineezen van de opiumpacht worden uitgesloten? Over hunne vermoedelijke uitsluiting met het oog op de Chinesophobie van den Min. van Kol. P. Mijer." *TNI*, 19 (1857), 60.

Index

275

Library of Congress Cataloging-in-Publication Data

Rush, James R. (James Robert), 1944–
  Opium to Java / James R. Rush.
  (Asia East by South)
  p. cm.
  Includes bibliographical references.
  ISBN 0-8014-2218-3 (alk. paper)
  1. Opium trade—Indonesia—Java—History—19th century.
I. Title. II. Series.
HV5816.R87 1990
363.4′5′095982—dc20   89-45974